Yale Studies in English: Benjamin Christie Nangle, Editor

Volume 153

Attribution in Restoration Poetry

A STUDY OF ROCHESTER'S *POEMS* OF 1680

by David M. Vieth

NEW HAVEN & LONDON: YALE UNIVERSITY PRESS, 1963

To Rose

and to her Mother and Father

as a Modest Memorial

to their Selflessness

This Book is Affectionately Dedicated

Preface

Recent years have witnessed a steady growth of interest in Rochester's life and works. When the preliminary research for the present volume commenced a little more than a decade ago, Rochester was all but unknown to many professors of English literature. Today, an acquaintance with his poetry is occasionally found even among undergraduates at American universities, and the time may not be far off when his name is a commonplace among educated readers. Since 1950 alone, Rochester has been the subject of two scholarly editions, a paperback volume of selected poems, a popularized biography, and a novelized account of his life, not to mention numerous articles in learned journals. As this study goes to press, a pamphlet edition of Alexander Bendo's bill has just appeared, and one of the pioneer biographies will soon be available in a revised edition.

In retrospect, serious scholarly concern with Rochester, which began with the second quarter of the twentieth century, seems to divide into two traditions whose superficial kinship conceals a fundamental divergence in premises and purposes. The older tradition, dominantly British and continental in its origins, is typified by the contributions of John Hayward, Johannes Prinz,

Vivian de Sola Pinto, and John Harold Wilson. This tradition has tended to stress Rochester's biography rather than his poetry, which it has generally treated in terms of critical assumptions inherited from the nineteenth century. If the work of some of its practitioners has been characterized by casual scholarship and a penchant for popular publication, they are nevertheless responsible for most of what we now know about Rochester's life.

The other, more recent tradition, which has thus far been almost exclusively American, began in 1950 with a book by James Thorpe and continued in the work of the bibliographer William B. Todd as well as in several of my own articles published in preparation for the present study. Underlying this newer tradition is the premise that Rochester's importance resides primarily in his poetry, so that the principal goal of scholarship ought to be a satisfactory edition of his works—a goal unfortunately still some distance from realization. Appropriately, therefore, this tradition has emphasized bibliographical and textual investigation, and it has insisted upon more rigorous standards of scholarship. Its critical sympathies, to the extent that it has revealed any, appear to favor more modern trends in literary interpretation; in the future, one hopes, this critical approach will yield a better appraisal of the nature and value of Rochester's poetry, thereby according him his proper place in the current revival of interest in the English Augustan Age. Among the services it performed, Thorpe's book provided the most significant breakthrough in Rochester scholarship to date: a recognition that the earliest printed collection of his works, the *Poems on Several Occasions* of 1680, is absolutely crucial to an understanding of the many problems of the Rochester text and canon.

The present study is firmly linked to the scholarly tradition initiated by Thorpe, while at the same time it seeks to enlarge the rather narrow limits within which this tradition has hitherto operated. Besides exploring more deeply the intricate character of the collection represented by the *Poems* of 1680, it places this collection in a series of larger contexts. At one extreme, for example, it clarifies the relationships between the *Poems* of 1680 and the many later editions of Rochester's works; at the opposite extreme, it views this collection in relation to contemporary manuscripts. More than any previous book on Rochester, the present volume systematically confronts the difficult problems of authenticity posed by the poems that have been attributed to him. More than any earlier study of a Restoration poet, it attempts to tap the rich reservoir of poetical manuscripts that have come down to us from the late seventeenth century. In the process, it develops new techniques of textual criticism which should be applicable to other poets and other literary periods. Also, it focuses attention more sharply on various aspects of the poems themselves: on their dates of composition, the persons they satirize, the biographical and historical backgrounds that gave them birth, and their meaning and value as literary artifacts. In this last connection, it is hoped that critical analysis such as that in Chapter 4 may point the way toward future treatments of the poetry of Rochester and his contemporaries. Finally, the present study recognizes that an extended discussion of Rochester's *Poems* of 1680 must necessarily concern itself with other important members of the tightly knit Court circle which determined the destiny of English literature as it moved toward the climax of the Augustan Age.

A book of this kind, especially one which has been so long in preparation, has inevitably profited from the assistance of many persons on both sides of the Atlantic. Three debts are paramount. First, to Maynard Mack, of Yale University, I am indebted for originally stimulating my interest in Augustan

literature in a graduate seminar, for suggesting Rochester as a
topic for a doctoral dissertation, and for subsequently directing
the dissertation on which the present study is based. In the final
version, Chapters 4 and 11 have specially benefited from his
criticisms.

Second, to James M. Osborn I am grateful for favors which
are embarrassing in both their extent and their variety. As friend,
counselor, and the best teacher of English composition I have
ever encountered (though he has never formally taught such
a course), he has encouraged my work on Rochester from its
very beginnings, schooling a neophyte in the ways of scholarship
and allowing me full use of his incomparable collection of seventeenth-century manuscripts. During the writing of the present
volume, every chapter of which he read, criticized, and reread, his
patience with the book was exceeded only by his patience with
its author. Hardly a page is without some trace of his influence.

Third, to the participants in the Yale edition of Restoration
political verse, especially George Lord, its director, and Elias
Mengel, of Georgetown University, its textual editor, I am indebted for informing me of a number of important poetical manuscripts which would otherwise have escaped my notice. Several
of the conclusions ventured in succeeding pages took shape during
informal conversations with this group of scholars.

Among a multitude of other kindnesses, the following stand
out particularly. John Harold Wilson, of Ohio State University,
and James Thorpe, of Princeton University, aided and encouraged my interest in Rochester, especially in its initial stages when
it most needed encouragement. Arthur Mizener, of Cornell
University, and Richard C. Boys, of the University of Michigan,
repeatedly supplied me with information from their first-line
index to poems in miscellanies. During the preparation of my
doctoral dissertation, Joan Thirsk helped to locate a large number of previously unrecorded manuscript texts of Rochester

poems in the British Museum and the Bodleian Library. Edwin Wolf II, then of the Rosenbach Company, directed my attention to two important Restoration manuscripts, including the one now designated the Yale MS. G. Blakemore Evans, of the University of Illinois, apprised me of some manuscripts of Rochester poems in the Cambridge University Library. John Hayward replied to my queries and generously permitted me to film two early Rochester editions in his private collection. The late C. H. Wilkinson assisted in locating and filming a rare Restoration book. Fredson Bowers, of the University of Virginia, and William B. Todd, now of the University of Texas, inadvertently helped me to formulate the textual theory which is presented in Chapter 2.

At various points in my investigation of Rochester, Slava Klima, of McGill University, assisted with information and ideas; several chapters in the present volume have profited from his suggestions. Helpful comments on Chapter 2 were provided by Talbot Donaldson, of Yale University; on Chapter 4 by Aubrey Williams, of the University of Florida; and on Chapters 9 and 10 by Walter N. King, of Montana State University. Eugene Waith, of Yale University, read the entire manuscript for the Yale Studies in English and offered many valuable criticisms.

After the book was already complete in manuscript, David Foxon, of the British Museum, called my attention to copies of two rare eighteenth-century editions of Rochester's works. About the same time, George H. Jones, of Kansas State University, supplied me with significant new biographical information on Rochester from manuscript sources in the Public Record Office, the British Museum, and the Bodleian Library; though I have taken account of some of this material in Chapter 6, I have not wished to make more direct use of it without examining it personally.

Robert H. Taylor has kindly allowed me to publish information from three early manuscripts in his possession. For help in locating manuscript material in their collections, and (where necessary) for permission to publish portions of this material, I am indebted to the following: Sterling Library, Yale University; Harvard University Library; Princeton University Library; Folger Shakespeare Library; Ohio State University Library; University of Illinois Library; Humanities Research Center, University of Texas; Henry E. Huntington Library, San Marino, California; British Museum; Bodleian Library; the Librarian, All Souls College, Oxford; Cambridge University Library; the Director and Secretary, Victoria and Albert Museum; the Archbishop of Canterbury and the Trustees of Lambeth Palace Library; Edinburgh University Library; the Trustees of the National Library of Scotland; and the Österreichische Nationalbibliothek, Vienna.

In its original form as a doctoral dissertation at Yale University, this study was supported by Selden and Sterling Fellowships. Subsequent progress was greatly facilitated by grants-in-aid from Montana State University and from the American Philosophical Society. Besides allowing me the year's leave of absence from my teaching duties during which the book was completed, the University of Kansas provided funds to prepare the manuscript and to help defray printing costs; I am particularly grateful to John H. Nelson, Dean of the Graduate School, and George R. Waggoner, Dean of the College of Liberal Arts and Sciences. Benjamin Nangle, editor of the Yale Studies in English, assisted at all stages in the process of publication.

D. M. V.

Lawrence, Kansas
December 1961

While this book was in press, evidence came to my attention which probably requires a revision of the dating of Rochester's "scepter" lampoon on King Charles ("I' th' isle of Britain, long since famous grown"). Rochester's poem, whose composition I had assigned on circumstantial grounds to late summer of 1675 (see below, pp. 177–78, 187), seems to be mentioned in a letter dated 20 January 1673/4 (K. H. D. Haley, *William of Orange and the English Opposition 1672–4*, Oxford, Clarendon Press, 1953, pp. 60–61, 172).

Fresh information on Rochester's life and works will doubtless continue to appear in substantial quantity; indeed, one purpose of the present study is to provide a frame of reference for evaluating such discoveries, which in their turn may call for modification of some of my conclusions. No changes of this kind are suggested by the new edition of Pinto's biography (*Enthusiast in Wit: A Portrait of John Wilmot Earl of Rochester*, Lincoln, Univ. of Nebraska Press, 1962).

D. M. V.

New Haven
August 1962

Contents

Works Cited by Cue Titles

Athenae Oxonienses and *Fasti Oxonienses*	Anthony à Wood, *Athenae Oxonienses. . . . To Which Are Added The Fasti,* ed. Philip Bliss, London, F. C. and J. Rivington, 1813–20.
Case	Arthur E. Case, *A Bibliography of English Poetical Miscellanies 1521–1750,* Oxford, The Bibliographical Society, 1935.
Catalogue of Royal and Noble Authors	Horace Walpole, *A Catalogue of the Royal and Noble Authors of England,* Strawberry Hill, 1758.
Collected Works	*Collected Works of John Wilmot, Earl of Rochester,* ed. John Hayward, London, Nonesuch Press, 1926.
Court Wits	John Harold Wilson, *The Court Wits of the Restoration,* Princeton Univ. Press, 1948.
CSPD	*Calendar of State Papers, Domestic Series.*
CTB	*Calendar of Treasury Books.*
Day and Murrie	Cyrus Lawrence Day and Eleanore Boswell Murrie, *English Song-Books 1651–1702,* Oxford, The Bibliographical Society, 1940.
Dorset	Brice Harris, *Charles Sackville, Sixth Earl of Dorset,* Urbana, Univ. of Illinois Press, 1940.
Dryden Bibliography	Hugh Macdonald, *John Dryden: A Bibliography of Early Editions and of Drydeniana,* Oxford, Clarendon Press, 1939.

HMC	Reports of the Royal Commission on Historical Manuscripts.
Sixth Report	*Sixth Report.*
Seventh Report	*Seventh Report.*
Bath	*Manuscripts of the Marquis of Bath.*
Buccleuch and Queensberry	*Manuscripts of the Duke of Buccleuch and Queensberry.*
Dartmouth	*Manuscripts of the Earl of Dartmouth.*
Kenyon	*Manuscripts of Lord Kenyon.*
Laing	*Laing Manuscripts Preserved in the University of Edinburgh.*
Le Fleming	*Manuscripts of S. H. Le Fleming, Esq., of Rydal Hall.*
Montagu	*Manuscripts of Lord Montagu of Beaulieu.*
Ormonde	*Manuscripts of the Marquess of Ormonde.*
Rutland	*Manuscripts of His Grace the Duke of Rutland.*
Stopford-Sackville	*Manuscripts of Mrs. Stopford-Sackville, of Drayton House, Northamptonshire.*

Lives of the Poets	Theophilus Cibber, *The Lives of the Poets of Great Britain and Ireland,* London, R. Griffiths, 1753.
"Oldham Bibliography"	Harold F. Brooks, "A Bibliography of John Oldham," *Oxford Bibliographical Society Proceedings and Papers,* 5 (1940), 1–38.
Pepys	*The Diary of Samuel Pepys,* ed. Henry B. Wheatley, London, George Bell and Sons, 1893–99.
Poems	*Poems by John Wilmot, Earl of Rochester,* ed. Vivian de Sola Pinto, London, Routledge and Kegan Paul, 1953.

Poetical Register   Giles Jacob, *The Poetical Register: or, the Lives and Characters of the English Dramatick Poets*, London, E. Curll, 1719–20.

Poetical Works   *The Poetical Works of John Wilmot, Earl of Rochester*, ed. Quilter Johns, Halifax, Eng., Haworth Press, 1933.

Restoration Drama   Allardyce Nicoll, *A History of English Drama 1660–1900:* vol. *1, Restoration Drama*, 4th ed., Cambridge Univ. Press, 1955.

Pinto, *Rochester*   Vivian de Sola Pinto, *Rochester: Portrait of a Restoration Poet*, London, John Lane the Bodley Head, 1935.

Prinz, *Rochester*   Johannes Prinz, *John Wilmot, Earl of Rochester: His Life and Writings*, Leipzig, Mayer and Müller, 1927.

Rochester-Savile Letters   *The Rochester-Savile Letters*, ed. John Harold Wilson, Columbus, Ohio State Univ. Press, 1941.

Rochester's Poems   *Rochester's Poems on Several Occasions*, ed. James Thorpe, Princeton Univ. Press, 1950.

Stationers' Register   *A Transcript of the Registers of the Worshipful Company of Stationers; from 1640–1708*, London, privately printed, 1913–14.

Term Catalogues   *The Term Catalogues, 1668–1709*, ed. Edward Arber, London, privately printed, 1903–06.

"Text of Rochester"   David M. Vieth, "The Text of Rochester and the Editions of 1680," *Papers of the Bibliographical Society of America*, *50* (1956), 243–63.

Works of Etheredge   *The Works of Sir George Etheredge,*
ed. A. Wilson Verity, London, J. C.
Nimmo, 1888.

Works of Sedley   *The Poetical and Dramatic Works of
Sir Charles Sedley,* ed. V. de Sola Pinto,
London, Constable, 1928.

PART I

The Collection of 1680

I.

Perspectives

I

In late summer or early autumn of 1680, at the height of the hysteria generated by the Popish Plot, Londoners with a taste for racy literature were buying a book purporting to be the *Poems on Several Occasions* of John Wilmot, Earl of Rochester—the wild, witty young courtier whose dramatic repentance and death had occurred just a few weeks before. Despite the obvious interest of this volume, its external features could not have inspired much confidence in its reliability. It was a surreptitious publication— as even its title page implied by omitting any printer's or publisher's name, by describing the volume falsely as "Printed at Antwerp," and by identifying its author only as "the Right Honourable, the E. of R – – –." Thumbing through its leaves, a prospective purchaser would have found little to suggest that this book possessed any serious significance. It was a slim octavo volume of 152 pages, badly printed on cheap paper. Many of its sixty-one poems were blatantly pornographic, and some of them plainly were not even written by Rochester. Appearances were deceiving, however, for this unimpressive volume—with which the following study is largely concerned—ranks among the most important books published in England during the late seventeenth century.

To begin with, Rochester's *Poems* of 1680 was one of the most popular and influential publications of the Restoration period. Again appearances are deceiving, for this "first edition" of Rochester is not a single printed book. It is a whole series of closely similar editions, all issued during a relatively short interval to meet what must have been an overwhelming public demand. Ten separate editions of 1680 have been recorded, and at least two or three more were probably published. Most of the known editions survive in only one or two copies, while others apparently were read into extinction—mute testimony to their popularity. The later editions of 1680 all descend from the earliest, which has been designated the Huntington edition because one of two extant copies is preserved in the Henry E. Huntington Library at San Marino, California. Only the Huntington edition can properly be called the first edition of Rochester.

If Rochester's *Poems* of 1680 is a series of a dozen or more separate editions rather than a single publication, the book is also deceiving in that the collection of poems it represents is not in essence a printed collection at all. As we shall see, the Huntington edition was printed with few alterations from a manuscript miscellany which had probably been assembled earlier in the same year. Hence the printed volume is valuable to literary scholars mainly insofar as it preserves features of its manuscript source. Indeed, in dealing with the Rochester editions of 1680, we are really dealing with this earlier collection. Contrary to what one might expect, the manuscript miscellany, compiled by a conscientious scribe, contrasted sharply with the unreliable appearance of the book that was printed from it. The poems in this manuscript collection were meticulously selected and arranged, it was transcribed with care, its text was relatively free of corruption, and its ascriptions—that is, statements regarding authorship—were mostly correct. By a fortunate accident, this manuscript miscellany survives in another copy, designated the Yale MS., which will figure prominently in the present study.

Furthermore, the *Poems* of 1680 is misleading even in its claim to be an edition of Rochester, for its manuscript source was evidently assembled along rather different lines. This manuscript miscellany seems to have been a kind of anthology of Restoration poetry, with the emphasis almost exclusively upon writers having some connection with the Court of Charles II. Included in the collection were poems by Buckhurst, Sedley, Etherege, Buckingham, Mulgrave, Dryden, Oldham, D'Urfey, Aphra Behn, Alexander Radcliffe, and Sir Carr Scroope. Among these fashionable versifiers, Rochester was merely the poet whose work was represented most fully. Because of its miscellaneous character, the collection is valuable not only for the study of Rochester but for other key authors of the period. It preserves important texts of their poems, and its ascriptions assist in establishing the canons of their works; moreover, the complicated interconnections underlying the arrangement of the collection help to solve problems of various sorts. For these reasons, the scope of the present study is by no means limited to Rochester: subsequent chapters will require extensive excursions into other significant areas of Restoration literature.

Nevertheless, even though its manuscript copy-text was not primarily a collection of Rochester's poetry, paradoxically the Huntington volume of 1680 retains its status as the first edition of his works. Indeed, despite its remarkable shortcomings, it is the most important edition of Rochester published prior to the twentieth century. In addition to its spurious matter, the Huntington edition provides the first printing of the heart of the Rochester canon. Also, it is the earliest extant source of numerous texts and ascriptions—including many false ascriptions—in nearly all of the fifty or more reprintings of Rochester's poetry that occurred during the century following his death. Hence the Huntington edition is significant not only for its texts of genuine poems but because it originated so many problems of authenticity which were then transmitted to later Rochester editions. Examination of these problems is a necessary first step in any systematic effort to establish the Rochester canon, which has hitherto remained one of the most puzzling areas of inquiry in English literary scholarship. Failure to establish the canon has, in turn, frustrated previous attempts to produce a satisfactory edition of Rochester's works.

Problems of authenticity are only one concern of the present study, but they are scarcely separable from any thorough investigation of the poems in the 1680 editions. As a necessary minimum, therefore, the following pages assemble and analyze all available data on the authorship of these sixty-one poems together with several dozen others which are in some way connected with the poems in the 1680 editions. Though the poems to be discussed total slightly under a hundred of the approximately 250 which have been attributed to Rochester, they include a substantial majority of those which are probably authentic. The remaining genuine poems are limited to a few appearing in Jacob Tonson's edition of 1691 and a few more scattered in other printed volumes and in manuscripts. As recently as 1950, James Thorpe, the latest scholar to deal extensively with these problems of authorship, doubted "that the Rochester canon can ever be established with any degree of certainty." [1] Though Thorpe did not greatly overestimate the difficulties, his statement now appears too pessimistic. The present study offers conclusions regarding the authenticity of nearly all the poems it considers, while the methods of investigation it develops should solve most similar problems posed by the remaining 150 poems. The discussions of text and canonicity in subsequent chapters may be regarded as prolegomena to a future critical edition of Rochester's works.

Apart from their relevance to Rochester and other Restoration poets, the 1680 editions have acquired special interest for bibliographers and textual critics by raising some basic questions of methodology. Though the resulting debate, conducted intermittently over the past decade, has sometimes produced opinions which were controversial or even incorrect, it has led to fruitful reappraisals of traditional techniques. In particular, because the interrelationships of the 1680 editions resemble those of a manuscript stemma, and because manuscripts must be consulted to define the relationships precisely, these editions tacitly challenge some claims of the scholarly discipline that has come to be known as analytical bibliography. The present study continues the dialogue on methodology by introducing (in Chapter 2) a new principle of textual criticism which was evolved largely as a means for dealing with poems in the 1680 editions.

Since the Rochester editions of 1680 present many deceiving appearances, an understanding of their significance requires that a number of false perspectives be dispelled. At the same time, false perspectives must be replaced by true ones, so that the 1680 editions may be seen in their mutually meaningful relationships

---

1. *Rochester's Poems,* p. xxix. A number of works frequently cited on following pages will be designated by cue titles, a full list of which is given following the Contents page; see pp. xvii–xx above.

with other areas of scholarly concern. Accordingly, the next few pages of this chapter place the 1680 editions in the context of later editions of Rochester's works, while the remainder of the chapter suggests the new perspective which results when these printed texts are viewed in relation to contemporary manuscripts. Chapter 2 outlines some general methods for dealing with problems of authenticity like those encountered in the 1680 editions, and Chapter 3 explores the intricate relationship of the Huntington edition to the manuscript miscellany from which it was printed. The eleven chapters in Part II develop a variety of perspectives on individual poems or groups of poems in the 1680 editions, and Part III provides, for each of these sixty-one poems, a comprehensive list of other early texts and ascriptions.

II

The most obvious obstacle to understanding the Rochester text and canon has hitherto been the multiplicity of problems posed by the many editions of his works that had been published by the end of the eighteenth century. Difficulties are caused by the sheer number of these editions. Also, some editions, evidently read to pieces, either are not known to be extant or survive in only one or two copies found in widely scattered locations. Because the early editions of Rochester are relatively inaccessible, few students of his poetry have even *seen* most of them, and detailed analysis would scarcely have been feasible before the era of microfilm. Further confusion results from the fact that many of these editions bear similar, undistinctive titles—usually either *Poems on Several Occasions by* or *The Works of* Rochester. Thus, when editions were published in two or more different series in the same year—as happened in 1714, 1718, and 1731—their titles alone do not afford clear identifications. The confusion is compounded because the only bibliography, that of Johannes Prinz, lists the editions in simple chronological order instead of grouping them by series (*Rochester*, pp. 348–85). Since these editions will be mentioned frequently in following pages, a brief survey is needed to give the reader a proper perspective on their relationships to the editions of 1680. Editions published later than those of 1680 have not, of course, been fully investigated, so that statements regarding them must be considered to some extent tentative.

Because the titles of Rochester editions are inadequate for precise identification, some form of bibliographical notation is essential. The following scheme, which has proved practicable in informal use, will be cited when necessary in subsequent chapters. All early editions of Rochester belong either to one of three major series, which began publication in 1680, 1691, and 1707, or to a single minor series beginning in 1718. These four series will be designated A, B, C, and D respectively. Within each series, individual editions are ordinarily designated by the dates of their imprints. Except for the 1680 editions, which are more complicated, different editions appearing in the same series in the same year are designated a, b, c in order of their publication. If an edition is in more than one volume, a volume number may be indicated by an arabic numeral. Thus the first volume of the second of two editions published in the C series in 1721 becomes C-1721-b-1. Piracies are designated by the letter P. Unlike systems based upon a consecutive numbering, this scheme will usually allow newly discovered editions to be integrated smoothly into their proper series. Also, it is compatible with Thorpe's set of symbols for the 1680 editions. Thus the Huntington edition becomes A-1680-HU, while the two known copies of this edition become A-1680-HU-HU and A-1680-HU-PE. The symbols introduced in the present study are fully identified in the checklist of early Rochester editions in the third section of Appendix B.

In the A series, the 1680 editions were followed by at least four later editions, all titled *Poems on Several Occasions*. The earliest of the four was published in 1685 by Andrew Thorncome (A-1685). A-1685 was printed from the Harvard edition of 1680 (A-1680-HA) but omits nine of its poems which Thorncome may have considered blasphemous or obscene. Evidently Thorncome feared prosecution, for he also bowdlerized some of the texts he included, and his title page identifies Rochester only as "a late Person of Honour." To the poems he took from A-1680-HA, Thorncome added five more which had not previously appeared under Rochester's name. Two of these five poems were written by Thomas Randolph before Rochester was born, while the other three offer little evidence that they are authentic.

The next edition in the A series was published in 1701 by "A. T.," who may have been Thorncome (A-1701). In this and the two succeeding editions in the same series, Rochester is identified on the title page as "the R. H. the E. of R." Though printed largely from Thorncome's earlier edition, A-1701 omits four poems, including one of those introduced in 1685, and adds two others—the first probably printed from an edition in the B series, the second certainly spurious. A-1701 was followed by an edition published in 1713 by an unidentified "A. B." (A-1713).[2] A-1713 reprints the entire contents of A-1701, together with three more poems restored from one of the 1680 editions and a group of eight poems probably taken from C-1709. The last edition in the A series, also published by "A. B.," did not appear until 1731

2. The date of this edition is sometimes given as 1712. In the imprint of the only known copy, preserved in the Victoria and Albert Museum, the last figure of the date, though smudged, appears to be "3" rather than "2." I am grateful to the officials of the Victoria and Albert Museum for verifying this conclusion.

(A-1731). This hitherto unrecorded edition is preserved in a copy in the Folger Shakespeare Library. A-1731 is merely a reprint, not page for page, of the entire contents of A-1713. Still another edition, announced by the bookseller Francis Saunders but apparently never published, seems to belong to the A series. Though this edition was entered in the *Stationers' Register* in 1690 and advertised in a booklist two years later, no copy has been discovered.[3]

The earliest edition in the B series was published by Jacob Tonson in 1691 as Rochester's *Poems, &c. on Several Occasions* (B-1691). Boasting a preface by Thomas Rymer and a pastoral elegy on Rochester by John Oldham (both first ascribed to their authors in B-1714), this edition assigns to Rochester thirty-nine poems together with Alexander Bendo's bill and a text of *Valentinian* printed from the quarto of 1685. Because B-1691 is an honest publication carefully assembled by the most reputable bookseller of the day, most students of Rochester formerly considered it the best early edition of his works. In two major respects, however, B-1691 is inferior to A-1680-HU. Unlike the text of A-1680-HU, that of B-1691 is expurgated, sometimes by alteration of readings but usually by omission of offensive lines and stanzas.[4] Also, whereas A-1680-HU was printed entirely from manuscript sources, about three-quarters of the poems in B-1691 derive wholly or partially from earlier printed texts, chiefly from one of the 1680 editions. As a result of false ascriptions in its printed sources, five of the thirty-nine poems in B-1691 are probably spurious. Nevertheless, B-1691 retains considerable

3. Most of the evidence on this "lost" edition is given by Thorpe, *Rochester's Poems*, pp. xxv–xxvi, 172.
4. For conclusive evidence in support of this claim, see my note, "An Unsuspected Cancel in Tonson's 1691 'Rochester,' " *Papers of the Bibliographical Society of America*, 55 (1961), 130–33.

value because nine apparently genuine poems—eight of them printed from manuscripts—are here ascribed to Rochester for the first time.

B-1691 was followed by two editions bearing the same title and reprinting the same contents. The edition of 1696 (B-1696) was printed from B-1691, while that of 1705 (B-1705) was printed from B-1696. In 1714, the collection was reduced from octavo to duodecimo, augmented with new material, and rechristened the *Works* of Rochester (B-1714). To the contents of B-1705, B-1714 added two Rochester poems and the epilogue to a third, two other poems which merely refer to Rochester, some of Rochester's correspondence, and part of Robert Wolseley's preface to *Valentinian*. In 1732, the entire contents of B-1714 were reprinted as the "fourth edition" (B-1732). Editions in the B series were pirated at least twice. In 1710, Henry Hills reprinted the entire contents of B-1705 with Henry Savile's "Advice to a Painter" as Rochester's *Poems on Several Occasions* (B-1710-P). In 1718, an unknown publisher reprinted twenty-eight poems from B-1696 and three from an edition in the C series as Rochester's *Works* (B-1718-P).

Little reliance can be placed upon editions in the C series, the first of which was published by Benjamin Bragge in 1707 as the *Miscellaneous Works* of Rochester and Roscommon (C-1707-a). Bragge's volume comprises three parts: a section of Rochester's works numbering thirty-five poems and preceded by the memoir of the Earl attributed to Saint-Évremond; a smaller section of Roscommon's works; and a group of miscellaneous poems including three that are here attributed to Rochester. Of the poems assigned to Rochester in C-1707-a, not more than one-quarter are probably genuine. Many of the Rochester ascriptions were taken from unreliable printed sources—among them the miscellanies usually known as *Poems on Affairs of State*, the second volume of Buckingham's *Miscellaneous Works,* 1705, and one of the 1680 editions. C-1707-a is not entirely without integrity, for Bragge made some effort to secure better texts than those he found in the sources of his ascriptions. Nevertheless, he would have had difficulty locating authentic material to fill out his section of Rochester, for he apparently felt obliged to omit all poems previously printed by Tonson. C-1707-a does not include *any* of the thirty-nine poems that had appeared in B-1691, B-1696, and B-1705. Perhaps Tonson possessed a copyright on this material, or Bragge thought that he did. In one instance, Bragge's scruples (or fears) reached a curious extreme: since Tonson had printed the main part of "A Satyr against Mankind" without the epilogue, Bragge printed the epilogue without the poem proper.

Later in 1707, the C series passed into the hands of Edmund Curll, who reissued the sheets of C-1707-a as the "second edition" of the *Works* of Rochester and Roscommon (C-1707-b). Besides a new title page, Curll added a preface and a complete text of "A Satyr against Mankind." [5] In 1709, he reprinted the contents of C-1707-b as a two-part "third edition" of the *Works* (C-1709). Part 1 of C-1709, the section allotted to Rochester, augments the preliminaries with a text of Alexander Bendo's bill, reprints in a different order all thirty-eight of the poems attributed to Rochester in C-1707-b, and introduces six more poems. Curll divided the collection into two separate volumes in 1714, enlarging its contents and calling it the "fourth edition" of the *Works* of Rochester, Roscommon, Dorset, etc. (C-1714-1 and C-1714-2). In C-1714-1, which corresponds to Part 1 of C-1709, the preliminary matter is greatly expanded, all but one of the forty-four poems in C-1709 are reprinted in a changed order, and no fewer than thirty poems are added from various other sources, mainly

5. For the relationship of C-1707-b to C-1707-a, see Thorpe, *Rochester's Poems,* p. xxxiii.

one of the 1680 editions. Curll's editions, like Tonson's, were pirated at least twice. C-1709 was the copy-text for a spurious "third edition" of 1709 (C-1709-P), which in turn was the copy-text for a piracy by J. Bradford in 1711 which reprints only the first few pages of C-1709-P (C-1711-P).

Whether Curll published any other editions in the C series remains uncertain. The next few editions in this series carry no printers' or publishers' names, but Horace Walpole believed that the edition of 1718 (C-1718-1 and C-1718-2), which immediately follows C-1714, was "printed by Curl." [6] C-1718-1, the volume of Rochester's works, represents a reduction in the size of the collection: the preliminary matter is slightly smaller, ten poems printed as Rochester's in C-1714-1 have been omitted (though three of these reappear in C-1718-2), and only one brief poem is added. After C-1718 came two editions in 1721 (C-1721-a-1 and C-1721-a-2, C-1721-b-1 and C-1721-b-2). C-1721-a-1 gives exactly the same contents as C-1718-1, with the section of Rochester's poems reprinted page for page. C-1721-a and C-1721-b, two closely similar but entirely separate editions, are superficially distinguishable because the title page of C-1721-a-2 is dated 1720 rather than 1721. Another two-volume edition appeared in 1731 (C-1731-1 and C-1731-2), while a one-volume edition was brought out by T. Goodourl in 1735 (C-1735). In 1739 there were three different two-volume editions which cannot be assigned symbols until their relationships have been more fully investigated. Though editions in the C series continued to appear at frequent intervals until the last quarter of the eighteenth century, these later reprintings hold little significance for the present study.

6. *Catalogue of Royal and Noble Authors*, 2, 41. Also, in the preliminary matter of C-1718-2 (p. viii), two adjacent footnotes refer to books "printed for *E. Curll*" and "printed for *B. Lintot*"; neither note appears in C-1714-2.

Ascriptions in the two editions in the D series are virtually worthless. Interestingly, these seem to be the only early editions of Rochester that do not derive in some measure from A-1680-HU. The first edition in the D series, printed for Thomas Dryar and sold by T. Harbin and W. Chetwood, was published in 1718 as Rochester's *Remains* (D-1718). Of the twenty-four poems included in D-1718, two are probably authentic. A preliminary investigation suggests that D-1718 derives, not from earlier printed sources, but from a seventeenth-century manuscript miscellany made up of poems by many different authors. The other edition in the D series, issued without publisher's name in 1761 as Rochester's *Poetical Works* (D-1761), reprints nineteen poems from D-1718 together with a large quantity of verse and prose apparently written some time after Rochester's death. D-1761 surely ranks among the most preposterous frauds in the history of publishing: its 253 pages of closely spaced text include only one poem that is probably genuine.

III

Paradoxically, though understanding of the Rochester text and canon has been hindered by inadequate knowledge of the early editions of his works, it has also suffered from a tendency to overemphasize their importance. Besides placing the editions in a distorted perspective—a case of the forest not seen clearly because of the trees—this too-exclusive preoccupation has diverted attention from other important evidence. Much of this evidence, notably early manuscript versions of poems attributed to Rochester, not only possesses value in its own right but bears significantly on the problems posed by the editions. Nevertheless, a review of the many books and articles published on Rochester during the past thirty-five years will reveal a steady, if usually slow, evolution toward the views advocated in the present study, which therefore preserves a continuity with its predecessors.

Until a decade ago, students of Rochester were unanimous in regarding editions later than those of 1680, especially the editions published by Jacob Tonson, as the best early collections of the Earl's works. Though the editions of 1680 were acknowledged to be sources for some of these later volumes, they were usually ignored because of the questionable circumstances of their publication, their numerous wrong ascriptions, the obscenity of their contents, and the assumption that corruption had been introduced into their texts by editorial tampering. Preferences for later editions were indicated by John Hayward, Johannes Prinz, Quilter Johns, John Harold Wilson, Vivian de Sola Pinto, Harry Levin, and Ronald Duncan. These preferences are reflected even in the editions of Rochester published by Pinto in 1953 and by Duncan in 1959.[7]

7. Hayward termed B-1691 "the most satisfactory edition" of Rochester's works, adding that "the predominant texts" in his collection of 1926 were "those of the editions of 1685, 1691 and 1707" (*Collected Works*, pp. xi, xii). Prinz remarked that B-1691 "is considered to be the best collection of Rochester's authentic lyrics" (*Rochester*, p. 351). Johns listed his copy-texts as A-1685, B-1696, and two editions in the C series dated 1739 and 1757; the editions of 1685 and 1696, he observed, "would undoubtedly seem the most reliable" (*Poetical Works*, pp. 233, 234). Wilson called B-1691 "the only reliable edition of Rochester's work" ("Two Poems Ascribed to Rochester," *Modern Language Notes, 54* [1939], 458–60). Pinto's edition was based primarily upon the "authority" of Tonson's editions (*Poems*, pp. xl–xli, xliv, xlviii). Levin's selections from Rochester's poetry were printed from B-1714 (*A Satire against Mankind and Other Poems by John Wilmot, Earl of Rochester*, Norfolk [Conn.], New Directions, 1942, p. [31]). Duncan, in his "Note on the Text," seems to indicate that the "early editions . . . chiefly used" for his collection of 1948 were A-1713, B-1714, C-1718, and C-1735 (*Selected Lyrics and Satires of John Wilmot, 2nd Earl of Rochester*, London, Forge Press, 1948, p. 30). Duncan's later paperback volume of selections from Rochester seems to be based primarily upon one of Tonson's editions (*Rochester*, London, Edward Hulton, 1959). The editions of Levin and Duncan will not ordinarily be cited in the present study.

In 1950, however, James Thorpe took an important step. He recognized that the editions of 1680, despite their obvious faults, constitute the best early printed collection of Rochester's poetry and are therefore a prime point of departure for investigation of the text and canon. As sometimes happens with new insights into familiar material, Thorpe's general conclusions were so sensible that the misconceptions previously prevalent concerning the editions of 1680 now seem scarcely credible. In conjunction with his principal insight, Thorpe was the first to observe that later editions such as A-1685 and B-1691, not the 1680 editions, contain texts corrupted by editorial alteration. As a further corollary of his new perspective on the 1680 editions, Thorpe's notes on the authorship of the sixty-one poems marked a significant advance in the study of the Rochester canon. These notes on the poems include extensive lists of other texts and ascriptions in early printed sources.

Thorpe performed a valuable service by shifting attention from later to earlier printed texts. Nevertheless, he declined to take the next logical step: the assembling of contemporary manuscript versions of the poems in the 1680 editions. Though such versions have survived in considerable numbers, only one manuscript, Harvard MS. Eng. 636F, figured prominently in Thorpe's investigation. Also—a circumstance related to his slight concern with manuscripts—Thorpe made little attempt to examine the variants in his other early printed texts of poems in the 1680 editions; thus he could not establish their lines of descent as a means of assessing the origins and value of the ascriptions they contain.

In the interval since Thorpe's book, a tendency to give greater weight to manuscripts has been evident even in places where one might not expect it. Pinto's edition of 1953, though otherwise a casual embodiment of outdated principles, nevertheless makes

a perfunctory effort to list early manuscript versions of the poems
it includes. In an article also published in 1953, the bibliographer
William B. Todd stressed the importance of independently descended texts, especially manuscripts, in dealing with the problems of the 1680 editions.[8] This same emphasis was continued
and intensified in two of my own articles published in preparation for the present study.[9]

The present study begins, as it must, where Thorpe left off.
It takes the necessary next step by systematically investigating
early poetical manuscripts related to those which lie behind the
1680 editions and similar unauthorized publications of the Restoration period. Presumably this is also the last step: where no
authorized version of a poem has survived, the independently
descended manuscripts, together with any printed texts representing independent descent, will afford the closest possible approach to what Rochester wrote. Since Thorpe's volume is the
starting point for the present study, and since it provides texts
for most of the poems to be discussed, the reader may wish to
keep a copy of his book at hand for convenient reference.

Unfortunately, few scholars—indeed, few specialists in Restoration literature—are acquainted with the wealth of manuscript material available in this period. The common types and
even the physical appearance of these manuscripts are generally
unfamiliar. Thus there is little understanding of the nature and
value of their texts or of the ascriptions which frequently accom-

8. "The 1680 Editions of Rochester's *Poems:* With Notes on Earlier
Texts," *Papers of the Bibliographical Society of America*, 47 (1953), 43–
58. See also G. Blakemore Evans's appeal, in the same year, for more extensive use of manuscript materials in the Restoration period ("The Text
of Dryden's *Mac Flecknoe*," *Harvard Library Bulletin*, 7 [1953], 32–
54).
9. "Text of Rochester"; "Order of Contents as Evidence of Authorship: Rochester's *Poems* of 1680," *Papers of the Bibliographical Society of
America*, 53 (1959), 293–308.

pany these texts. The heading of a poem may include a note identifying its author, or the author's name may be inscribed ("signed") at the end of the poem; numerous examples of such ascriptions in manuscripts are reproduced in Part III. More broadly, few scholars have been conscious of the significant role of literary manuscripts during the Restoration period, the large numbers of manuscripts which have been preserved, and their resultant usefulness for study of the texts and canons of Restoration authors. Scholarly attitudes have usually been conditioned by the twentieth-century notion that a writer wishing to reach an audience would naturally seek to have his works printed. In the Restoration period, however, as in earlier periods of English literature, the normal means of "publication" for many authors was circulation in manuscript. Often the works of such authors—Rochester is a prime example—came to be printed only by sheer accident.

Because few scholars are familiar with manuscripts of the Restoration period, their proper use requires what may strike many readers as an unaccustomed perspective, even a novel mode of perception. Much previous study of the Rochester text and canon has been conducted from a curiously myopic point of view. This distorted perspective—prevalent among bibliographical specialists, but also among less sophisticated editors—is the unacknowledged assumption that printed books are somehow intrinsically more significant than manuscripts. Like other prejudices, it is seldom supported by arguments, and it is sometimes denied most emphatically by those who are most guilty of it. The fallacy of this assumption is evident from the fact that unauthorized printed texts such as the Rochester editions of 1680 *derive* from manuscripts like those which have survived. At best, therefore, these printed texts are no more reliable than the kinds of manuscripts that served as their sources.

Furthermore, manuscripts of the Restoration period—except, of course, those few which were copied from printed books—possess special value in three other major respects:

(1) Ascriptions in such manuscripts are usually more trustworthy than those in unauthorized printed texts. The probable explanation is that printers and publishers were strongly influenced by the profit motive. A poet like Rochester must have offered severe temptations, for the sale of a book could be stimulated by falsely attributing some of its contents to a popular author. Thus, as the preceding section of this chapter has already suggested, most wrong ascriptions to Rochester seem to have originated in early editions of his works. Copyists of Restoration manuscripts, on the other hand, had less incentive to misrepresent the authorship of the texts they transcribed. Even manuscript miscellanies, which may have stemmed from some sort of commercial enterprise, were evidently produced for discriminating purchasers under conditions that minimized the likelihood of false ascriptions.

In their treatment of ascriptions in manuscripts, students of Restoration literature have frequently favored the questionable assumption that the testimony of manuscripts has less value than that of printed books. To cite a relatively moderate example, Thorpe maintained without giving evidence that "attributions in commonplace books are usually based on nothing more substantial than common report or the sensibilities of the compiler" (*Rochester's Poems*, p. xxviii). Such a conclusion is barely a half-truth, while in any event these ascriptions are at least as reliable as those found in unauthorized printed texts.

(2) Contemporary printed texts frequently descend from sources which are still extant, so that they provide no information not available in their sources. With manuscript texts, on the other hand, the sources have generally vanished. Consequently,

a manuscript often preserves important evidence, such as textual readings or an ascription, which is not otherwise available. The apparent reason for this circumstance is that printed texts tend to be transmitted in patterns of direct descent, with each text extant in at least one copy. That is, surviving printed texts are usually related to one another as ancestor and descendant. Manuscript texts, by contrast, tend to be transmitted in patterns of independent descent, so that surviving versions are related to one another in a collateral fashion. Thus the texts and ascriptions in most extant manuscripts are likely to possess independent value.

Because of this circumstance, situations encountered in practice are occasionally very deceptive. If a poem carries ascriptions in several dozen printed texts but in only two or three of the manuscript versions, the printed texts and their ascriptions may all descend from one unreliable source whereas each manuscript text and its ascription preserves independent testimony. Failure to understand this kind of situation can approach an extreme form of the premise that printed texts are inherently more significant than manuscripts. Students of Rochester have sometimes tended to assume falsely that when the same ascription is repeated in successive reprintings of an unauthorized text, each such ascription possesses independent standing.

(3) Manuscript versions of a work are useful and often indispensable in determining the derivation of printed texts and of any ascriptions contained in these texts. In many instances, the source (or sources) of a printed text cannot be fully ascertained without reference to a group of independently descended versions of the same work. Such a group—as the next chapter will explain—may be difficult to identify unless it includes at least two manuscripts. For example, the mere fact that a printed text $P2$ exhibits variants against another printed text $P1$ will not demonstrate that $P2$ does not derive from $P1$; this can be shown only if the variants of $P2$ agree with readings in other texts which

are known to descend independently of P1. Thus, lacking a substantial number of manuscripts, Thorpe could not analyze the derivation of printed texts and ascriptions outside of those in the 1680 editions. Indeed, without recourse to manuscript texts and their ascriptions, the problems of the Rochester canon could scarcely be solved.

IV

A few further remarks are in order concerning some little-known phenomena of the kinds of manuscripts which will be frequently cited in subsequent chapters. Three matters call for comment: the common forms in which these manuscripts occur, the phenomenon which I have elsewhere termed "linked groups" of poems, and the dates which often appear in poetical texts. Since all of these features still require extensive investigation, the following remarks should be regarded as guides to future research rather than established conclusions.

(1) Apart from special categories such as holograph drafts, poetical manuscripts of the Restoration period tend to approximate one of three general types. The most basic type, which seems to be a major source of the other two, consists of the loose sheets in which poems originally circulated either singly or in small groups. These sheets, which survive in surprising numbers, may be preserved in their original separate form, in unbound bundles of many such manuscripts, or as the contents of bound volumes probably assembled long after the poems had ceased to circulate. Sheets formerly in circulation almost always retain creases showing where the paper was folded when it was passed from hand to hand. The outside of the folded sheet may bear the title of the contents or the name and address of some person to whom the sheet was sent. In addition to these distin-

guishing marks, bound volumes of formerly loose sheets are usually recognizable because they contain leaves of heterogeneous sizes and shapes, inscribed in many different hands.

Most other poetical manuscripts of the period belong to the variety which has in the past been designated vaguely as "commonplace books." In reality, these manuscripts, almost all of them bound volumes, divide into two distinct types that differ materially in character and usefulness. Besides commonplace books in the strict sense, they include other volumes, often of greater value, which can be described accurately as "manuscript miscellanies," a term that has recently been gaining wider currency. Though some surviving examples necessarily fall between these two extreme categories, the twin concepts of the commonplace book and the manuscript miscellany are indispensable in defining the precise character of many individual volumes.

The general nature of commonplace books is well known. Since the average collection of this kind was compiled by its owner for personal use, it typically exists in a single copy transcribed in a comparatively amateurish hand. Most commonplace books seem to have been assembled over periods of several years, as may be suggested by variations in their handwriting or in the color of the ink. The contents of these volumes, reflecting the whims of the compiler, tend to be heterogeneous, ranging from poetry to miscellaneous items like maxims of conduct, historical narratives, political records, household accounts, and recipes. The sources of a commonplace book may be as various as its contents, with verses copied from printed texts occurring rather frequently. Such verses are often fragments instead of complete texts.

The external appearance of a manuscript miscellany will usually suggest that it was copied off in a relatively short time, possibly no more than a few days. Often a manuscript miscellany exists in several copies, all transcribed by the same professional hand, with different copies giving roughly the same contents in the same order. These contents, consisting typically of a homogeneous collection of poems with perhaps some related prose pieces, are likely to reflect careful selection and arrangement. Since most volumes of this type derived their material from good manuscript sources, they are generally more valuable to the scholar than commonplace books.

Manuscript miscellanies raise several puzzling questions which probably cannot be answered without much further investigation. Their occasional survival in multiple copies from the same professional hand argues that they were prepared, not for the scribes' own use, but for some commercial purpose. Exactly what sort of enterprise the scribes conducted remains uncertain, however. As yet there is no substantial evidence to link their activities with "Captain" Robert Julian, the disreputable "secretary to the muses" who sold manuscript copies of lampoons. Nor has any other clue to their identity been discovered. In any event, since a few days would be required to transcribe even a single copy of a manuscript miscellany, and since the scribes evidently took pains to secure good manuscript sources, these volumes were scarcely produced for clients with small incomes. Possibly they were purchased by persons of rank and wealth who considered them superior to printed books.

More important to the textual scholar, it is not easy to ascertain what kind of archetype or original was used for manuscript miscellanies which survive in multiple texts. Perhaps there was a single master copy from which the others were taken, or the archetype may have been merely a pile of loose sheets formerly in circulation. If there is a clear answer to this question, the resulting evidence of scribal practices during the Restoration period could prove valuable in solving textual problems posed by individual poems.

In the absence of more certain data concerning manuscript miscellanies, an example may help to clarify their general character. Less carefully assembled than some similar collections, this example nevertheless seems typical in other respects. At least three copies are known to exist: Bodl. MS. Firth C. 15, Taylor MS. 2, and a volume at Ohio State University which will be designated the Ohio MS. All three manuscripts are in the same professional hand, all are bound folio volumes, all give a table of contents preceding the text, and all include title pages bearing similar inscriptions: "A Collection of Choyce Poems. Lampoons, and Satyrs from 1673 to 1689. Never Extant in Print" (Taylor), "A Choice Collection of Poems, Lampoons, Satyr's &cᵃ:" (Bodleian), and "A Choyce Collection of Poems. &c." (Ohio). Apparently compiled shortly before 1700, this collection consists of poems and a few prose pieces, mostly satirical, arranged in roughly chronological order from the early 1670s through the early 1690s.

The Ohio manuscript totals seventy-three items,[1] the Bodleian manuscript seventy-seven items, and the Taylor manuscript seventy-eight items. Of the seventy-nine poems and four prose pieces occurring in at least one of these manuscripts, no fewer than seventy-one items appear in all three. Among the remaining twelve items, two appear in both the Taylor and Ohio texts, one appears in both the Taylor and Bodleian texts, five appear only in the Bodleian text, and four only in the Taylor text.

To judge from some other manuscript miscellanies surviving in multiple texts, these three volumes differ more than usual in

---

1. This figure includes only the first hand in the Ohio MS. A second hand has added three more poems dating from the late eighteenth century.

the order of their contents. Hence their archetype may have been a pile of heterogeneous loose sheets rather than a single master copy. Nevertheless, a comparison of the three manuscripts reveals some close resemblances in their arrangement. If the items in the collection are arbitrarily numbered 1 to 73 in the order of the Ohio manuscript, with the letters A through J representing additional items in the Bodleian or Taylor manuscripts or both, the order of the Bodleian text is 1, 2, 3, 6, 4, 5, 7, A, B, C, D, 8, 9, 10, 11, 12, 13, 14, 15, 30, 17, 16, 18, 19, 20, 21, 22, 23, E, 26, 28, 24, 25, 27, 29, 31, 32, 33, 34, 35, 36, 37, 38, 39, 40, 41, 42, 43, 44, 45, 46, 47, 56, 49, 50, 61, 57, 52, 54, F, 53, 55, 58, 59, 60, 72, 62, 63, 65, 70, 67, 69, 66, 68, 71, 48, 73, while the order of the Taylor text is 1, 2, 6, 3, 7, 8, 9, 10, 11, 12, 13, 4, 5, 14, 15, 30, 31, 17, 18, 19, 20, 16, 21, 22, 23, 25, 24, 26, 27, 29, 32, 34, 35, 28, 36, 37, 39, 40, 38, 52, 53, 54, 41, 42, 43, 44, 45, 46, 47, 58, 56, 59, 60, G, 49, 50, F, 55, 48, 61, 51, H, 62, 63, 64, 65, 66, 67, 68, 69, 70, 72, I, 71, J, 73, 33, 57.

Like most manuscript miscellanies, this collection provides some ascriptions, including a few that are merely general (e.g. "By a Lady"). Twelve items carry the same ascription in all three volumes, while a thirteenth, lacking ascription in the Ohio text, is assigned to the same author in both the Bodleian and Taylor manuscripts. Four poems appearing in all three volumes carry ascriptions only in the Taylor text, and three more poems carrying ascriptions in the Bodleian text are omitted from the other two manuscripts. Significantly, in no instance do ascriptions in the three manuscripts *contradict* one another.

(2) Besides being passed about singly in manuscript sheets, Restoration poems seem to have circulated in groups containing anywhere from two to five items. Groups consisting of more than five poems may have existed, though I have not encountered any. From texts circulating in loose sheets or manuscript pamphlets,

"linked groups" were sometimes copied without alteration into manuscript miscellanies and commonplace books. Thus the existence of a linked group can be suspected if several poems appear together in the same order in two or more manuscript volumes or printed collections—especially if this same group forms the sole contents of a loose sheet that was passed from hand to hand. Usually the poems in such groups were brought together because of some similarity in their contents: the poems may have been composed by the same author, they may satirize the same person, they may represent a verse correspondence or the documents in a quarrel, or they may be a poem together with an answer to it.

If the phenomenon of linked groups is to serve any useful purpose, it should be conceived in purely bibliographical terms. That is, the existence of a linked group can be suspected only if the group survives in two or more texts that almost certainly descend independently from one archetype. The mere circumstance that several related poems appear together in a single text will not make them a linked group, nor will the presence of such a group be firmly established if it might have been brought together in the same form by more than one scribe. Paradoxically, therefore, the existence of a linked group would be most certain if there were *no* apparent linkage of the contents of the poems.

Linked groups are usually valuable as a means to some other end. For instance, since the reliability of ascriptions may vary from one linked group to another, the identification of such groups can assist in evaluating evidence of authorship. Also, an understanding of the linking principle of a group may clarify the character of its individual poems, as when the identity of persons being satirized is in doubt. A further application of the linked groups, together with some examples, will be found in Chapter 3.

(3) The dates which often appear in manuscripts of Restoration poems, and occasionally in printed texts, have in the past

been interpreted with inadequate knowledge of their significance and reliability. Future investigation should include, among other things, a tabulation of all available instances where these dates can be compared with known dates of composition. In the absence of such full information, however, some conclusions can be suggested. Almost all dates of this kind belong to one of two categories: dates specifying an exact day and dates giving only the year. Aside from exceptional cases like the poems of John Oldham, who meticulously dated many of his own works, dates specifying an exact day usually seem to indicate when some transcript of the poem was made. Dates giving only the year, which are far more numerous, seem to be guesses at the date when a poem was composed. Their testimony should not be accepted uncritically—as has happened, for example, with the date in Oldham's transcript of *Mac Flecknoe*. Frequently they vary from the true date of composition by a year in either direction, and sometimes by as much as two years, though rarely by a longer interval.

2.

Methods of Attribution in Restoration Poetical Texts

I

Since problems of authorship are an important aspect of the poems to be considered in succeeding chapters of this study, a survey of available methods of attribution is a necessary preliminary. Such a survey will also help to clarify the treatment of the approximately 150 additional poems, largely spurious, which at one time or another have been assigned to Rochester; a few of these poems have already been the subjects of separate articles, while the rest will be discussed in future publications. Most of the procedures to be used, being simple, obvious, and relatively well-known, need only be mentioned in passing. One major method has hitherto been little understood, however, and must therefore be explained in much greater detail.

Among the types of evidence traditionally invoked to decide

questions of authenticity, probably the most desirable is testimony which is authoritative in the strictest sense—that is, it can be readily traced to the purported author of a work. This type of evidence may consist of a direct statement by the author, a text of the work published with his permission and perhaps under his personal supervision, or a manuscript draft of the work in his own handwriting. In evaluating a direct statement by an author, especially a statement denying his authorship, the possibility of bad faith should at least be recognized, since authors have on occasion been known to disown their genuine productions. Elkanah Settle, for example, may have been less than candid in claiming that he did not write "A Session of the Poets" (see Chapter 12). The question of the author's honesty may likewise be raised by authorized publications. Furthermore, such publications should be examined to verify that they really are authoritative, that the author intended all of their contents as his own, and that his supervision was close enough to prevent the publisher or printer from foisting spurious material into a volume merely to fill it out to a prescribed number of gatherings.

Two holograph manuscripts figure prominently in the present study: the poetical notebook of John Oldham (Bodl. MS. Rawl. Poet. 123), and a volume at the University of Nottingham containing poems in the hands of Rochester and his wife (see Chapter 7). Holograph manuscripts may pose either of two problems: the handwriting may be difficult to identify positively, or the author may have transcribed works composed by other persons. Oldham's notebook, for instance, contains transcripts of several poems by other writers, notably *Mac Flecknoe* and "A Satyr against Mankind"—a circumstance which led one scholar to conclude that Oldham himself composed these two pieces.[1] Reason-

---

1. Percy L. Babington, "Dryden not the Author of 'MacFlecknoe,'" *Modern Language Review, 13* (1918), 25–34.

able assurance that a holograph manuscript comprises an author's genuine work will be obtained if its contents are plainly in process of revision or are ascribed to him in other contemporary sources.

Authoritative evidence is sometimes surprisingly complex, for it can assume negative as well as positive forms. An author may deny that he wrote a work, or another author may claim it. Though Rochester is not known to have made any direct statements regarding the authorship of his genuine poems, several pieces wrongly ascribed to him were printed in authorized collections of their works by such writers as Oldham, Aphra Behn, Thomas D'Urfey, and Alexander Radcliffe. Occasionally the situation is more intricate. In one interesting instance, a scrap of verse attributed to Rochester was ascribed to Cowley by Rochester himself.[2]

The kinds of data thus far described might be designated primary authoritative evidence. Secondary authoritative evidence— hearsay evidence, if one prefers—would then consist of testimony apparently traceable to the purported author but only by a longer and more circuitous route. Ordinarily it has been passed on by the author's friends or relatives or by other persons presumed to have intimate knowledge of his activities. The commoner forms of secondary authoritative evidence, which are analogous to those of the primary type, include statements by such persons in letters, diaries, and similar sources, printed texts of the author's work published under their supervision, or manuscript copies of his work in their handwriting. For example, the authenticity of Rochester's famous translation from Seneca ("After Death, nothing is, and Nothing, Death") is established in a letter addressed to him by an acquaintance. The best evidence for Mulgrave's

2. See my communication, "Rochester and Cowley," *London Times Literary Supplement,* 12 October 1951, p. 645.

authorship of "On the Enjoyment of his Mʳˢ" ("Since now my Silvia, is as kind as faire") is its appearance under his name in a printed miscellany edited by his friend Alexander Pope. The poems surviving in Lady Rochester's handwriting at least suggest the possibility that her husband may have composed them.

Secondary authoritative evidence necessarily poses problems similar to those inherent in the corresponding forms of the primary type. Added uncertainty results because persons presumed to have a close connection with the author will at best be less knowledgeable than the author himself. Like primary authoritative evidence, the secondary type may either affirm or deny that a work was composed by its purported author.

A third type of evidence is more troublesome. Evidence in this miscellaneous category consists of ascriptions (that is, statements regarding authorship) which are not demonstrably authoritative, and which often fail even to provide a means of identifying their immediate sources: either they give little, if any, text of the work to which they refer, or they patently followed a route of transmission different from that of the text which they accompany. Ascriptions of this kind may take many forms. Besides handwritten notations of authorship in early printed texts, they include numerous ascriptions in letters, diaries, memoirs, biographical accounts, prefaces, dedications, plays, poems, or compendia of literary history like those of William Winstanley, Thomas Pope Blount, Giles Jacob, and Theophilus Cibber.

The difficulty with these ascriptions is that with no warrant of authority, and in the absence of enough text to suggest the nature of their sources, their reliability may be almost impossible to assess. Often there is no guarantee that they were not merely copied from untrustworthy printed sources. Many ascriptions of this kind can be dated, however, and their dates afford a rough criterion for their use. If such an ascription is not antedated by any printed source assigning the work to the same author, it almost certainly represents independent testimony and may, indeed, provide valuable evidence. Thus the best evidence for Rochester's authorship of "A Ramble in St. James's Park" is an ascription in a letter dated seven years before the poem was assigned to him in print. On the other hand, if this type of ascription cannot be shown to antedate the earliest printed ascription to the same author, and if there is no other indication that it possesses independent standing, it may well derive from a printed source and should probably be disregarded.

In some special cases, the date of a work may provide conclusive proof that an ascription is incorrect. The purported author cannot have written a work if it refers to events that occurred after his death, or if it was certainly in existence before his birth. Though few cases of this kind are encountered in the present study, they are surprisingly numerous among the approximately 150 other poems which have been attributed to Rochester. Several poems included in Rochester's *Remains* of 1718 (D-1718) were certainly written after his death, while two poems in the edition of 1685 (A-1685) had already been printed in Thomas Randolph's *Poems* some nine years before Rochester was born. This latter kind of situation is best demonstrated by printed texts of a work, since they not only identify it positively but can almost always be dated more accurately than manuscript versions. In less extreme cases, the date of a work may render an ascription implausible. The purported author is not likely to have written the work if it was already in existence when he was still a child, or if its date falls within a period of his mature life when he would scarcely have composed such a work. Thus Rochester probably did not write the brief obscene poem entitled "The Wish" ("O that i could by some Chymick Art"), which was apparently in print when he was only fourteen years old.

The attitudes expressed in a work may offer strong evidence against its authenticity if they are contrary to opinions known to have been held by the purported author at the time the work was written. In the most general kind of situation, a work might reflect religious or political convictions at variance with the known beliefs of the purported author. For example, Rochester's apparent tolerance toward Roman Catholicism casts doubt on his authorship of the anti-Catholic sentiments of "On Rome's Pardons" (see Chapter 14). In more limited instances, a work might satirize friends of the purported author or even the author himself. Evidence of this kind suggests that Rochester did not write the lines beginning "To make my self for this Employment fit," which lampoon some of his cronies.[3] Care must be exercised, however, when dealing with satires of the Restoration and early eighteenth century: one must be certain that possible ironies in the work have been interpreted properly, that the satire of the purported author's friends is not mere comradely joshing, and that the purported author would not have satirized himself— as Rochester apparently did in his verses "To the Post Boy" (see Chapter 6). Significantly, when internal evidence is applied in this fashion to problems of authorship, it must, aside from exceptional cases, be used only as a negative argument. Thus, though a work is probably spurious if it contradicts its purported author's known attitudes, the circumstance that it agrees with his attitudes would ordinarily be a weak argument for its authenticity.

The literary style of a work is frequently the least reliable criterion of its canonicity, for judgments concerning style are inevitably subjective, nor is this subjectivity much reduced by such expedients as "verse tests." Moreover, to analyze the qualities of an author's style, a substantial corpus of his unquestion-

---

3. See my communication, "Rochester and 'A Young Gentleman,' " *London Times Literary Supplement*, 23 September 1955, p. 557.

ably genuine work is needed, and this corpus has not hitherto existed for Rochester—a deficiency which the present study is partly designed to remedy. Nevertheless, despite its shortcomings, the criterion of style may be admissible if it tends to corroborate other evidence of authorship, or if a work is written in a distinctive manner. Also, it may have to be employed if other evidence is inadequate or totally lacking. In the absence of strong external evidence, considerations of style must be used to support Rochester's authorship of the lines "To the Post Boy," the satire usually called "Timon" (see Chapter 11), "A very Heroical Epistle in Answer to Ephelia" (see Chapter 13), and the lyric beginning "Tell mee noe more of Constancy." [4]

For works attributed to Restoration poets of Rochester's social prominence and personal habits, one further type of evidence—to which the rest of this chapter is devoted—furnishes the most important, most extensive, and least understood source of information on authorship. This class of evidence consists of the great bulk of those ascriptions which often appear in early texts of a work (excluding, of course, texts that are strictly authoritative). Texts containing such ascriptions are found in large numbers in manuscripts formerly in circulation, in commonplace books and manuscript miscellanies, and in printed volumes derived from manuscripts similar to those which have been preserved.

Since these ascriptions, like the texts in which they occur, are not demonstrably authoritative, the problem is to assess their relative degrees of reliability. This, in turn, is essentially a question of the kinds of sources from which the ascriptions derive—especially whether they derive from extant sources. By far the best means of evaluation is provided by the accompanying texts,

4. See my article, "A New Song by Rochester," *London Times Literary Supplement*, 6 November 1953, p. 716.

whose relationships to one another can be analyzed according to the principles of textual criticism so as to suggest the probable origins of both the texts and their ascriptions. It is generally true that an ascription tends to follow the same route of transmission as its companion text and can therefore, under normal conditions, be considered part of that text. Admittedly, of course, an ascription (like a title) is more easily detachable from the text than a reading which is integral to the work; it is more susceptible to inadvertent omission during successive copyings, and a scribe might occasionally insert an ascription from some source other than the exemplar of his text. As often happens in textual study, however, the proposition can be given the necessary precision by putting it into negative form: *If an ascription appears in a text which probably derives from another extant text containing the same ascription, and if there is no evidence that this ascription does not derive from the source of the text, then it cannot be assumed to represent independent testimony and should not be allowed any weight.* After such questionable ascriptions have been ruled out, those which remain can be used in determining the author of the work.

Approached in this manner, the task of evaluating ascriptions in early texts requires, as a preliminary step, that we investigate the sources of the texts themselves. Specifically, we must identify and eliminate from consideration all texts, together with their ascriptions, which probably derive from other extant texts and their ascriptions. For reasons explained in the preceding chapter, special attention must be given to printed texts and to manuscript versions which may have been copied from them. False ascriptions originated more frequently in printed texts than in manuscripts. Also, these false ascriptions are often widely disseminated because printed texts, unlike manuscripts, tend to be transmitted in patterns of direct descent with each text extant in at least one copy.

Unfortunately, the traditional principles of textual criticism do not provide any convenient method of identifying texts which derive from other extant texts. The remainder of this chapter therefore introduces what amounts to a new principle—the principle of "probability"—as the basis for an easier, more rigorous procedure. Though it is relatively true, as the late Sir Walter Greg observed, that "the elimination of derivatives is perhaps not generally a very difficult task," [5] the following pages necessarily require some rather technical discussion. Readers to whom textual concerns are uncongenial will find it possible to skip over the rest of this chapter and proceed immediately to Chapter 3.

II

A method of identifying texts which derive from other extant texts can assist in solving several kinds of scholarly problems. For example, when the true text of a work can be recovered only by reconstructing the archetype of surviving versions, the procedure can be simplified by eliminating in advance all versions derived from extant sources. Also, such a method may help to establish priority among different editions of a printed book when the techniques of analytical bibliography prove insufficient. Thus, if two editions were printed one from the other but their order remains uncertain, the edition containing the derivative text must

5. W. W. Greg, *The Calculus of Variants* (Oxford, Clarendon Press, 1927), Note A, pp. 55–56. Greg anticipates very little of the following discussion, and most of what he says could be formulated more clearly in terms of Quentin's principle of "intermediaries." The brevity of his remarks, which occupy only a page and a half, is a measure of the scant attention which textual critics have hitherto bestowed upon the type of problem discussed in this chapter.

obviously be the later of the two. A similar though much more complicated problem, summarized in the next chapter, is posed by the 1680 editions of Rochester's poems. In the present study, of course, the need to identify texts derived from other extant texts arises primarily as part of the task of evaluating any ascriptions they may contain.

Like some previous innovations in textual theory (e.g. Quentin's principle of "intermediaries"), the new principle of "probability" is a fundamentally simple concept which represents an extension of older methods rather than a replacement for them. Though the concept of probability does not contradict any received principles, it has never, to my knowledge, been granted a theoretical statement. Indeed, in the latest book on textual criticism it not only escapes attention but is unconsciously violated.[6] Other textual scholars, perhaps more conversant with the types of problems posed by manuscripts, have seemed implicitly aware of the phenomenon which the principle of probability serves to explain: namely, if two or more manuscript versions of a work share variants against a printed text—that is, if they preserve common readings which do not appear in this printed text —they usually do not derive from it. Some such conclusion is likely to emerge empirically from any extensive experience with manuscripts. Apparently the theory behind this conclusion has not been examined, however, nor have the limits and potentialities of the resulting method been defined.

Heretofore, the method of reconstructing archetypes has been the most thoroughgoing, and sometimes the only, means of detecting texts derived from other extant texts in stemmas (genealogical trees) which include some manuscripts. Compared with

6. Vinton A. Dearing, *A Manual of Textual Analysis* (Berkeley and Los Angeles, Univ. of California Press, 1959). See my review in *Journal of English and Germanic Philology*, 59 (1960), 553–59, especially the discussion of the epilogue to the *Man of Mode* on p. 558.

this traditional procedure, the method based on the principle of probability offers two signal advantages. (1) It is more convenient to use. The method of reconstructing archetypes entails the intricate exercise of working out the *entire* stemma of the surviving texts. By contrast, the method based on the principle of probability requires detailed definition only of that portion of the stemma which involves printed texts and manuscripts derived from them. This is the easiest portion to establish, since all (or nearly all) printed texts of a work will survive in at least one copy, whereas many of the formerly existing manuscripts will have been lost. (2) It will usually achieve greater certainty than the method of reconstructing archetypes, which is less rigorous than is sometimes assumed. Because the portion of a stemma involving printed texts will be more completely extant than the portion consisting of independently descended manuscripts, it can be established with more confidence. Also, the new method, unlike the method of reconstructing archetypes, minimizes the need for subjective judgments concerning *direction* of textual change.

The method based on the principle of probability was developed originally to deal with a special class of Restoration poetical texts. Hence any attempt to apply it to other categories of Restoration literature, or to the literatures of other periods and other countries, should take account of differing conditions which might require modifications of the method. This special class consists of poems for which no authoritative version is known to exist, which circulated in manuscript for a time after their composition, and which were finally printed from manuscripts in circulation. Relevant too are cases like *Mac Flecknoe*, where part of the stemma of a poem answers the foregoing description. Despite the limiting conditions attached to this class of Restoration poems, it is by no means a small category. It numbers, in all, several thousand items, among them most works attributed to Rochester. It includes many poems by Restoration noblemen and gentlemen, for whom it was socially unacceptable to publish their own work. Also included are numerous political lampoons whose publication might have rendered their authors liable to prosecution.

Characteristically, such poems enjoyed a wide circulation during a comparatively short interval. As a result, they survive in numerous manuscript versions whose relative dates are almost impossible to determine. The dates of these manuscripts therefore offer little aid in establishing their textual relationships to one another and to any printed versions. Fortunately, the principle of probability does not depend upon the dating of the manuscripts—though in rare instances where precise dates are available, they may serve as corroborating evidence. In earlier literary periods, where manuscript circulation of a work often extended over a much longer time, even approximate dates for surviving manuscripts might occasionally be valuable.

The usefulness of the principle of probability is greatly increased because some possible types of texts derived from other extant texts are seldom encountered in practice. Obviously, a work which is not preserved solely by oral tradition must survive in either manuscripts or printed versions or in both. Hence, aside from conflated forms—that is, instances where a text combines readings from two or more different sources—four types of texts derived from extant texts represent the maximum theoretically possible: (1) a manuscript derived from an extant manuscript, (2) a printed text derived from an extant manuscript, (3) a manuscript derived from a printed text, and (4) a printed text derived from a printed text.

Largely because manuscript texts tend to be transmitted in patterns of independent descent—that is, surviving manuscripts are usually related to one another in a collateral fashion—the first two of these four types are rare.[7] When they do occur, their presence is often revealed by special circumstances, as in an example to be discussed later (Chapter 7). Even if instances of these first two forms went undetected, little harm would ordinarily result. Moreover, if evaluation of the ascriptions in early texts is the primary concern (as it generally is in the present study), the third and fourth types are chiefly significant, since false ascriptions originated more frequently in printed texts than in manuscripts. Thus two types of texts derived from extant texts—a manuscript or printed version derived from a printed source—represent the only two forms of much importance for our purposes. These happen to be exactly the two types to which the principle of probability can be directly or indirectly applied.

To exploit its potential to the full, the principle of probability must be employed in combination with some traditional methods of textual criticism. The most useful of these methods is Dom Henri Quentin's principle of "intermediaries," which should therefore be briefly explained.[8] Given three variant texts A, B, and C of the same work (the symbols are interchangeable), Quentin held that if the readings of two of these texts never agree against the readings of the third, the third occupies an intermediate position on the line of transmission connecting the other two. Thus if A and B agree against C, and B and C against A,

7. The second type differs from the first only in involving a translation to a different medium of transmission (from manuscript to print). In other respects, a text printed from a manuscript will bear the same relationship to the existing manuscripts (exclusive of those derived from printed sources) that they bear to each other.

8. For a more detailed explanation of Quentin's principle, see J. Burke Severs, "Quentin's Theory of Textual Criticism," *English Institute Annual 1941* (New York, Columbia Univ. Press, 1942), pp. 65–93.

but never A and C against B, B would be intermediary between A and C. This relationship can be illustrated in a nondirectional diagram:

$$A \text{——} B \text{——} C$$

As a more recent critic has observed, Quentin's principle is universally valid only when stated in negative form—the principle of "exclusion" (Dearing, p. viii). Thus, in the example, B could *not* be intermediary between A and C if they agree against it.

By itself, we should note, the principle of intermediaries affords no evidence of the *direction* of textual change. If B is intermediary between A and C, and if we rule out the possibility of conflation, a directional diagram might take any one of five forms:

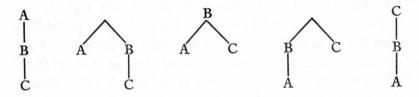

III

The new method of detecting texts derived from other extant texts can conveniently be divided into two consecutive steps. The first step, which depends directly upon the principle of probability, consists of isolating a group of two or more manuscripts which do not derive from any given printed text of the same work. The second step, which will be deferred to the next section of this chapter, concerns the use of this group of independent manuscripts to determine the derivation of all the remaining texts. Though the two steps are not entirely distinguishable from one another in theory, an arbitrary separation helps to clarify the principles involved, and it may be desirable in some practical applications.

We may begin with a hypothetical textual situation which is designed primarily to illustrate the principle of probability though it also corresponds to some actual situations and frequently represents part of a much larger group of texts. Let us assume that we have two or more manuscripts M_1, M_2, . . . M_n (where n is the total number of manuscripts) and a single printed text P_1. Our problem is to ascertain whether any of the manuscripts derives from P_1. Let us assume in addition that the manuscripts all share variants against P_1, and that these variants are unquestionably significant. For our purposes, the distribution of variants among the manuscripts need not be specified in more detail, since we are not concerned with the relationships of the manuscripts among themselves. It will matter very little if one of the manuscripts is an ancestor of another, or even of P_1—nor would such relationships occur very often in practice. For the sake of clarity, let us assume for the present that our texts give no evidence of conflation or of separate descent from different author's drafts. To render the example more concrete, the reader may wish to visualize a specific situation consisting of three manuscripts M_1, M_2, and M_3, together with the printed text P_1.

We can now formulate an important preliminary conclusion concerning our hypothetical group of texts. Given the conditions we have indicated, it follows that if *any* of the manuscripts derives from P_1, *all* are so derived, whereas if *any* of them descends independently of P_1, *all* are independent of this printed text. (Hence, as a limited case, if any of the manuscripts can be dated earlier than P_1, all are independent of it.) The truth of this proposition can best be demonstrated by adopting a negative approach; that is, we can show that the contrary conclusion would be untenable. Accordingly, in terms of our special example of three manuscripts M1, M2, and M3, a situation where one or more of these manuscripts derived from P1 while the rest did not would take forms like those illustrated in the following diagrams. (Many similar arrangements are, of course, conceivable.)

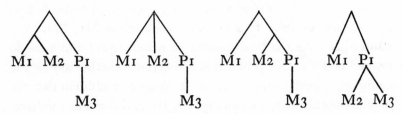

Under the conditions we have stipulated, however, these stemmas, as well as comparable ones which could be devised, would be impossible because they violate Quentin's principle of intermediaries. In all such relationships, the printed text P1 would have to be intermediary between at least two of the manuscripts, whereas we have specified that the manuscripts share variants against P1; in a Quentin triad, the two extreme texts cannot agree against their intermediary. Thus the correctness of our preliminary conclusion is established.

This preliminary conclusion enables us to proceed to the next stage of the argument. From this conclusion it follows that one of two opposite statements must be true: either (1) *all* of the manuscripts derive from the printed text P1, or (2) *none* of the manuscripts derives from P1. Again the situation can best be approached in a negative fashion. Since there is no third possibility, the probable truth of the second statement—that none of the manuscripts derives from P1—can be demonstrated by showing that the first statement is indefensible. For the sake of argument, then, let us assume that all the manuscripts descend from P1. Let us also assume that no hypothetical intermediaries are needed to explain the interrelationships of the manuscripts;

as we shall see shortly, the presence of such intermediaries would merely strengthen our case. In terms of our special example of three manuscripts M1, M2, and M3, the condition that they share variants against P1 will therefore limit the stemma to one of the following two forms, in which the symbols for the manuscripts are interchangeable:

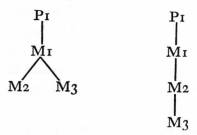

For our purposes, of course, the exact form of the interrelationships among the manuscripts is immaterial.

At this point our new principle enters the picture, for we must consider the *probability* that a situation like the ones depicted in these diagrams would ever occur. We must remember that printed texts (unlike manuscripts, which are usually unique) normally existed in several hundred to several thousand copies which were virtually identical. Even such phenomena as stop-press variants or cancels will rarely alter this basic circumstance —though, if they are present, they should be taken into consideration. Thus, when two or more manuscripts derive from the same printed text, they almost always derive from different copies and therefore do not share variants against the printed text. Conversely, in our example, the shared variants among the manuscripts mean that M1, M2, and M3 must all descend from *one* copy of P1.

The chance that such a situation would ever occur poses an elementary problem in mathematical probability. To keep our arithmetic simple, let us assume that the printed text P1 existed in 1000 copies, a figure which may well approximate the average size of a single issue of a moderately popular Restoration book. Initially, no significance attaches to the probability (it is one in 1000) that the manuscript closest to P1, say M1, would derive from some particular copy of this printed text; for our purposes, any copy could serve as the source. Given the derivation of M1 from P1, however, the probability that a second manuscript, say M2, would derive from M1 rather than any of the 1000 printed copies is only one in 1001. In turn, if M2 thus derives from M1, and M1 from P1, the odds that a third manuscript M3 would derive from M1 or M2 rather than a printed copy are two in 1002, and the combined probability that all three manuscripts would derive from the same printed copy is the *product* of this figure with the figure for two manuscripts—that is, two in 1002 multiplied by one in 1001, or one in 501,501.

Continuing the process, if three manuscripts derive in the above-mentioned fashion from a single printed copy, the odds that a fourth manuscript M4 would derive from M1, M2, or M3 rather than P1 are three in 1003, so that the chance of all four manuscripts deriving from a single copy of P1 is three in 1003 multiplied by one in 501,501, or one in 167,668,501. For five manuscripts, the probability of derivation from the same printed copy is one in 42,084,793,751, while for six manuscripts it is one in 8,459,043,543,951. For seven manuscripts or more, the figures are, of course, sufficiently astronomical. Thus it is highly unlikely that our manuscripts derive from P1, and their descent must therefore, in all probability, be independent of this printed text.

The foregoing calculations should provide adequate support for the conclusion we set out to establish, other considerations being equal. To be sure, other considerations will seldom be entirely equal, especially because manuscripts were copied by human scribes. It is conceivable, for instance, that two or more manuscripts might descend from a single printed copy if they were the work of one scribe or of several friendly scribes who made a practice of loaning each other their transcripts. In the absence of evidence suggesting such circumstances, however, and under the proper limiting conditions, the principle of probability will yield the following general conclusion: *When two or more manuscript versions of a work agree in some of their readings against a printed text, they almost certainly do not derive from it.*

A strict limitation on the principle of probability is that there must always be at least *two* manuscripts sharing variants against the printed text P1; with only a single manuscript the principle affords no usable conclusions. Indeed, two manuscripts are needed before there can *be* any agreement against a printed text.

Likewise, the principle is inapplicable if in place of two manuscripts M1 and M2, we have one manuscript M1 and one printed text, say P2, which share variants against P1. In this situation, the shared variants fail to yield any probability that M1 and P2 do not derive from P1. The difference is that P2, which we have substituted for M2, would have existed in many copies rather than only one. To demonstrate the point, let us assume, as we did when dealing with two or more manuscripts, that M1 and P2 derive from P1, and also that their variants do not require us to postulate a hypothetical intermediary. Two stemmas will then be theoretically possible:

The situation illustrated in the first diagram has little bearing on the point under discussion, for it would occur only under special circumstances. The relationship depicted in the second diagram occurs quite commonly in practice, however, because the principle of probability does not operate as it would if P2 were a manuscript. Given the derivation of P2 from P1, the probability that M1 would then derive from P2 rather than P1 is roughly one chance in two, since the two printed texts would have existed in approximately the same number of copies. Such odds have no value as evidence, nor are they altered if in place of one manuscript and one printed text, we have two printed texts P2 and P3 sharing variants against P1.

A more complex situation results if we have two manuscripts M1 and M2 and a printed text P2, the question being whether any of these three texts derives from P1. The principle of probability assures that if M1 and M2 share variants against P1 and P2, they almost certainly do not derive from either of these printed texts. The relationship of P2 to P1, however, entails other complications which can be better handled by the methods outlined in the next section of this chapter. Generally, these supplementary methods must be used whenever the relationships among several printed texts are being investigated.

A further limitation on the principle of probability has thus far remained implicit. Our theoretical discussion of the principle assumed that no printed text besides P1 was either actually or potentially present. In practice, however, the basic group of two or more manuscripts and one printed text is often only part of a larger group including additional printed texts. When this is the case, care must be taken that the variants shared by some of the manuscripts against P1 do not derive from another printed text. It is even possible that such variants might be corruptions originating in a later printed text P2 which itself descends from

P1. If the manuscripts were copied from P2, they would, as we have seen, almost always descend radially from this printed text and would not share variants against it:

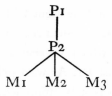

Consequently, before the principle of probability can be applied, all early printed texts of a work must be located, and the common readings of the manuscripts must be tested against each of the printed texts in turn. This task is less onerous than it sounds, for it can usually be performed from a single collation of the variants in all surviving versions.

IV

After a group of texts which do not derive from the known printed versions has been isolated by the principle of probability or some other reliable procedure, it furnishes the means of identifying any remaining texts which *are* derived from such sources. Unlike the first step of the method, this second step relies almost entirely upon traditional principles of textual criticism.

To illustrate the method of determining whether a given text derives from some specific printed source, let us consider a typical example. Assume that we have a text T1 whose derivation we wish to establish, a printed text P1 which represents the suspected source, and a group of texts which we already know do not derive from P1. T1 may be either a manuscript or a printed text. For simplicity's sake, let us assume that the readings of T_1 give no evidence of conflation; the techniques for dealing with conflation will be discussed separately.

In this example, the readings of T_1 will present one of two situations: either (1) they include some readings which also appear in the group of independent texts but do not appear in P_1, or (2) they fail to include such readings. Let us first examine the former situation, in which T_1 shares some variants with the independent texts against P_1. As with prior stages of the argument, this situation can best be approached in negative fashion by assuming for the moment that T_1 derives from P_1. To keep the example concrete, the reader may again wish to visualize the group of independent texts as three manuscripts M_1, M_2, and M_3. The assumption that T_1 derives from P_1 would then yield the following type of stemma diagrams, in which M_1, M_2, and M_3 are depicted in several of their possible interrelationships:

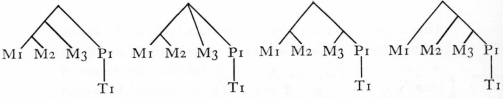

Such stemmas are not feasible, however, because they violate Quentin's principle by making P_1 intermediary between texts which agree against it. Hence, if some readings of T_1 agree with those of the independent texts against the readings of P_1, T_1 cannot derive from P_1. Its relationship to P_1 must therefore be either collateral or ancestral.

If T_1 is a manuscript version, we shall scarcely need to inquire whether its relationship to P_1 is ancestral or collateral. For reasons already discussed, the relationship will almost always be collateral. Even if it were ancestral, little harm would ordinarily result. On the other hand, when T1 is a printed text, the question of collateral or ancestral relationship to P1 assumes much greater importance. If T1 and P1 are both dated, and if T1 is later than P1, the relationship cannot be ancestral and must therefore be collateral. If dates are lacking for either T1 or P1 or for both, or if these two printed texts carry the same date, the situation can best be handled by interchanging the symbols so that P1 becomes the text whose derivation is in question and T1 its suspected source.

Let us now consider the alternative situation where the readings of T1 exhibit *no* significant agreement with the group of independent texts against P1. If such is the case, and if T1 cannot be dated earlier than P1, P1 may well be intermediary between T1 and the independent texts. This would necessarily mean that T1 derives from P1. Moreover, there will be a strong probability that T1 derives from P1 because P1, being a printed text, would formerly have existed in several hundred to several thousand copies. Thus there is little chance of a line of textual transmission leading to T1 which would bypass P1 without preserving some of the readings that appear in the group of independent texts but not in P1. (Interestingly, the element of probability makes this a special case where, for practical purposes, Quentin's principle of intermediaries applies not only in its negative form as the principle of exclusion but in the positive sense which Quentin originally gave it.) The presumption that T1 was copied from P1 will perhaps be further strengthened if the readings of T1 exhibit little or no variation from those of P1.

To secure maximum validity, the resulting conclusion should be stated in negative form: if the readings of T1 exhibit no significant agreement with the group of independent texts against P1, and if there is no other evidence that T1 descends independently of P1, then we cannot assume that T1 does not derive from P1. This conclusion requires that there be no other printed text identical with P1 from which T1 and P1 might descend independently.

In the foregoing account of the two steps to be followed in identifying texts derived from other extant texts, our discussion has been purposely limited to ideal cases so as to clarify the principles involved. Unhappily, many situations encountered in practice are less than ideal. The texts being analyzed may fail to include two manuscripts which are independently descended, or their variants may be inadequate either in number or in character to support clear-cut conclusions. The latter difficulty is specially acute in short poems such as songs, though it may arise occasionally in the analysis of longer texts. If the basic method thus proves insufficient, attention must be given to other considerations having a possible bearing on the derivation of texts. This procedure is desirable in any event, since additional data will be valuable as corroborating evidence.

Most obviously, the dates of the texts, if any of these can be established precisely, may serve to exclude some forms of derivation. Thus, if two texts can be assigned to different dates, the earlier cannot derive from the later. Reliable dates are usually available for printed texts, while in rare instances even an approximate date for a manuscript may afford evidence relevant to its derivation.

Probabilities concerning the derivation of a text may sometimes be strengthened by the general character of the collection in which it appears. Thus, if a manuscript miscellany or printed book characteristically derives its material from manuscript sources, any individual text in this collection may well derive from a similar source unless there is evidence to the contrary. Conversely, if a text is suspected of derivation from a particular printed source, and if other texts in the same collection were demonstrably taken from this source, the text in question is probably so derived.

Also, though the principle of probability is advantageous because it minimizes subjective judgments as to which variants are correct or corrupt, such judgments may be desirable as corroborating evidence after the basic method has been applied. If text T_1—the text being evaluated—incorporates variants which are otherwise peculiar to the printed text P_1 and its descendants, and especially if these variants appear to be corruptions possibly originating in P_1, the case for the derivation of T_1 from P_1 will be strengthened. Conversely, the case for independent descent will be strengthened if the variants which T_1 shares with the group of independent texts appear to be correct where P_1 is corrupt. In one special situation, a virtually airtight case can be obtained because the element of subjectivity is reduced to a minimum. Suppose that we have a series of editions $P_1, P_2, \ldots P_n$ where each edition was printed from the one preceding it, with the text deteriorating progressively in successive editions. T_1 will almost certainly derive from one of these editions if it exhibits corrupt variants which originated in editions later than the first.

A final point concerns the procedure for detecting conflation in instances where at least one source of the conflated text is still extant. Many Restoration scholars, supposing that most poetry of this period was viewed by contemporaries as mere ephemera, have not realized how frequently texts were constructed by combining readings from two different sources. The danger with conflation is that if its presence goes unnoticed, conclusions based on the methods previously outlined may be seriously distorted or totally wrong. For example, if text T_1 combines readings from a lost manuscript and a printed text P_1, it will probably share variants with the group of independent texts against P1 even though P1 is one of its sources.

Fortunately, the problem is simplified because some possible types of conflation involving one or more extant sources seldom occur in practice—or, if they did occur, would ordinarily cause little harm. Here, as earlier, we are concerned with texts transmitted in either manuscript or printed form or in both. Hence, if we limit our attention to instances of conflation where there are only two sources, six types of conflated texts represent the maximum theoretically possible: (1) a manuscript conflated from two manuscripts, (2) a printed text conflated from two manuscripts, (3) a manuscript conflated from a manuscript and a printed text, (4) a printed text conflated from a manuscript and a printed text, (5) a manuscript conflated from two printed texts, and (6) a printed text conflated from two printed texts.

Because surviving manuscripts of a work are generally related to one another in a collateral fashion, conflated texts in the first two categories with either source extant are almost never encountered. For the same reason, the manuscript source would not usually be extant in the third and fourth types. Moreover, for reasons which are not entirely clear, derivation of the third and fifth types seems to be virtually nonexistent in Restoration texts—though if it did occur, it could be detected.[9] Texts conflated from three or more sources, extant or not, are so rare that they scarcely require discussion.

Thus, if our sole purpose is to identify texts which derive wholly or partially from extant sources, we need normally consider only the fourth and sixth categories, consisting of printed texts conflated either from two printed texts or from one printed

9. Because conflated texts of the third type almost never occur in practice, the problem of conflation did not need to be considered in the earlier discussion of the principle of probability.

text and a manuscript which would rarely have survived. The former situation is the easier of the two to recognize, since both sources will almost always be extant. A printed text T1 is probably conflated from two earlier printed texts P1 and P2 (or possibly their descendants) if it shares variants with P1 against P2, and with P2 against P1, but not with the group of independent texts against *both* P1 and P2. The case for such derivation will be strengthened if T1 incorporates variants which are otherwise peculiar to P1 or P2 and their descendants. On the other hand, T1 is probably conflated from a lost manuscript and an earlier printed text P1 (or one of its descendants) if it shares variants with the group of independent texts against P1 but also incorporates variants which are otherwise peculiar to P1 and its descendants. If they ever occur, cases where T1 is a manuscript conflated from two printed texts, or from one printed text and a lost manuscript, could be detected by exactly the same means.

When, as in the present study, the early texts of a work are being investigated primarily to assess the value of the ascriptions they may contain, instances where conflated texts have at least one source extant will require an extended rule of procedure. If such a text gives the same ascription as any of its extant sources, and if there is no evidence that this ascription was taken from some other source, then it cannot be assumed to represent independent testimony and should not be allowed any weight. Conversely, if this ascription differs from those in the extant sources of the text, it may well constitute admissible evidence of the authorship of the work.

3.

The Yale Manuscript and the Editions of 1680

I

The collection of 1680, the most important early collection of Rochester's poems, survives in two independently descended texts, a manuscript and a printed book. The manuscript is a large Restoration manuscript miscellany now in the Yale University Library. Since it has no convenient shelfmark, it has been designated simply the Yale MS. The printed book, preserved in two slightly variant copies, is the Huntington edition of 1680 (A-1680-HU). Besides being the almost exclusive ancestor of the other editions of 1680, this volume, as we noted in Chapter 1, is the earliest extant source of numerous texts and ascriptions in nearly all the forty or more later reprintings of Rochester's works during the century following his death.

Because of the central importance of the Yale MS. and the

Huntington edition, any extensive investigation of Rochester's poetry, such as the special studies which will be found in Part II, requires an understanding of the complex problems posed by these two texts. Chief among the problems are the textual relationships among the various editions of 1680, the textual relationship of the Yale MS. to the Huntington edition, the value of the ascriptions in the Yale MS. and the 1680 editions, and the meaning of the arrangement of their contents. Some of the points covered in this chapter have been established in detail in prior publications and need only be summarized; other information is here presented fully for the first time.

For readers who are unfamiliar with the subject, the external data concerning the publication of the 1680 editions should be reviewed; nearly all of this information was brought together in 1950 by James Thorpe, whose facts and conclusions either have not been further investigated or have not required substantial revision as a result of such investigation.[1] The Huntington edition bears the title *Poems on Several Occasions By the Right Honourable, the E. of R – – –* and the imprint "Printed at Antwerp, 1680." It consists of 152 pages with the signatures running A-I⁸K⁴. Its contents total sixty-one poems, all assigned to Rochester even though many are patently not his compositions. Including the Huntington edition, ten separate editions bearing verbally identical titles can be certainly distinguished, with a strong probability that at least two or three others formerly

---

1. *Rochester's Poems*, pp. ix–xxxviii. Thorpe's volume provides bibliographical descriptions of the extant editions of 1680 (pp. 153–59). Previous articles on these editions included John Hayward, "Rochester on Charles II," *London Times Literary Supplement*, 25 October 1934, p. 735; Philip Gray, "Rochester's *Poems on Several Occasions*: New Light on the Dated and Undated Editions, 1680," *The Library*, 4th ser., *19* (1938–39), 185–97; V. de S. Pinto and Donald Dale, "The 1680 'Antwerp' Edition of Rochester's Poems," *The Library*, 4th ser., *20* (1939–40), 105–06; James Thorpe, "The Earliest Edition of Rochester's Poems," *Princeton University Library Chronicle*, 8 (1946–47), 172–76.

existed. Of the ten editions, three besides the Huntington contain 152 pages and give the imprint "Printed at Antwerp, 1680," four more also consist of 152 pages but have the imprint "Printed at Antwerpen" with no date, while the remaining two carry this dateless imprint but contain only 136 pages. Even a superficial examination shows that the ten editions are closely interrelated, for they assign the same sixty-one poems to Rochester in the same order. None of the editions gives any printer's or publisher's name; all are obviously surreptitious.

Evidently the earliest of the 1680 editions, the Huntington edition, was published after Rochester's death on 26 July 1680 and before the following November. The date of its imprint would be enough to suggest that it might have been undertaken shortly after 26 July to capitalize on the sensational circumstances of the Earl's deathbed repentance. This inference is confirmed by Anthony Wood's testimony (*Athenae Oxonienses, 3,* 1230) that

> no sooner was his breath out of his body, but some person, or persons, who had made a collection of his poetry in manuscript, did, meerly for lucre sake (as 'twas conceiv'd) publish them under this title, *Poems on several Occasions.* Antwerp (alias Lond.) 1680.

The Huntington edition was certainly in existence by 2 November 1680, for on that date Samuel Pepys mentioned it in a passage which also reflects Rochester's high reputation as a poet at the time of his death. Referring to the desk drawer where he normally kept his paper, blank paper-books, flute, and music books, Pepys continued:

> There is also in the same drawer a collection of my Lord of Rochester's poems, written before his penitence, in a

style I thought unfit to mix with my other books. However pray let it remain there; for as he is past writing any more so bad in one sense, so I despair of any man surviving him to write so good in another.[2]

The volume Pepys mentions is now in the Pepysian Library at Magdalene College, Cambridge, and it is one of only two known copies of the Huntington edition (A-1680-HU-PE); the other copy, reproduced in facsimile by Thorpe, is in the Henry E. Huntington Library (A-1680-HU-HU).[3] Since Pepys had already perused the book and was, indeed, away from London on 2 November, the Huntington edition must have been published several days or even weeks earlier. As Thorpe concluded, "it seems probable that the first edition appeared in August or September of 1680" (*Rochester's Poems*, p. xxvii).

Dates of publication are more difficult to establish for the other 1680 editions. Presumably the four dated editions appeared before the end of the year Old Style (24 March 1680/1). Among the undated editions, the Harvard edition (A-1680-HA) was certainly in existence by 1685, when it served as the major source of Andrew Thorncome's edition of Rochester (A-1685). As Thorpe observed, "there is no proof" that the last of the undated editions, the Bodleian edition (A-1680-BOD), "did not come

2. *Letters and The Second Diary of Samuel Pepys*, ed. R. G. Howarth, 2d impression (London and Toronto, J. M. Dent and Sons; New York, E. P. Dutton, 1933), p. 105.

3. The HU and PE copies represent variant states of A-1680-HU, for leaves A7 and A8 are cancels in both copies, and these cancels, though exhibiting no important textual differences, were printed from entirely separate settings of type. The reason for the cancellation is not apparent and could not, perhaps, be ascertained without a copy of A-1680-HU in its original state. The presence of the cancels affords some slight additional evidence that A-1680-HU is the earliest of the 1680 editions, since cancels are more likely in a first edition than in later reprints. I am indebted to William B. Todd for first noticing these cancels, and to the staffs of the Pepysian and Huntington Libraries for verifying their existence.

out as late as 1690" (p. xxvii). On the other hand, it seems likely that these editions were produced to satisfy an immediate demand and were therefore all published during the early 1680s. Despite the probability that some of the editions appeared after 1680, they will for convenience be designated collectively as "the editions of 1680" or, less gracefully but more concisely, as "the 1680 editions."

Soon after the first publication of the 1680 editions, an effort was made to locate the printer, probably with a view to prosecution. The *London Gazette* for 22–25 November 1680 carried this advertisement:

> Whereas there is a Libel of lewd scandalous Poems, lately Printed, under the name of the Earl of *Rochesters*, Whoever shall discover the Printer to Mr. *Thom L Cary*, at the Sign of the *Blew Bore* in *Cheap-side*, *London*, or to Mr. *Will Richards* at his house in *Bow-strete Covent-Garden*, shall have 5 *l*. reward.

Philip Gray conjectured that Will Richards was a certain publisher named W. Richard, that Thomas L. Cary was a relative of the John Cary whom Rochester appointed one of his executors, and that both were acting as agents for Rochester's family. Gray's identification of Cary is possibly correct, but Will Richards seems to have been a servant of Buckhurst (Dorset) and friend to Etherege and other Court Wits who is mentioned occasionally in contemporary lampoons.[4] The attempt to trace the printer of

---

4. Harris, *Dorset*, pp. 75–76. *The Letterbook of Sir George Etherege*, ed. Sybil Rosenfeld (London, Oxford Univ. Press, 1928), pp. 211–13, 304, 313, 324–25, 338. Lampoons referring to Richards include "To Will: Richards. 1689" ("We two have plotted twenty years & more"), in B. M. Harl. MS. 7317, fol. 97ᵛ, and Osborn MS. Chest II, Number 9, p. 531; "An Epistle From Mʳˢ Mathews to Will: Richards" ("Dear Sweet Richards William"), in B. M. Harl. MS. 7319, fol. 262ʳ, and Vienna MS. 14090, fol. 370ᵛ; and an imitation of Rochester's "A Ramble in St. James's

Rochester's poems apparently failed, for nothing more is heard of it.

There is little doubt that the 1680 editions were printed in London; both Wood and the *London Gazette* advertisement assume that the Antwerp imprint is merely a blind. The printers and publishers remain unknown to this day. Thorpe's investigation of types and type ornaments did not produce even tentative identifications, though he ventured some shrewd guesses as to how many printers were involved and which editions came from the same printing houses (pp. xxi–xxvi). Such questions are, however, interesting mainly to the bibliographical specialist, since their answers could scarcely shed much new light on the Rochester text and canon.

The most notable of Thorpe's contributions to our knowledge of the 1680 editions was probably his analysis of their relationships to one another. He succeeded in locating seventeen copies representing ten separate editions, each printed from an entirely different setting of type.[5] Basing his procedure primarily upon his collation of the substantive variants in the editions (pp. 160–68), Thorpe began, as was proper, by limiting himself as much as possible to the distributional evidence afforded by this collation. He found that the simplest and most nearly nondirectional stemma required him to postulate the former existence of two more editions and a single copy consisting of a mixture of the sheets of two extant editions. Next, working on the prin-

---

Park" entitled "The Rose Tavern Clubb. 1687" ("Much wine had pass'd with much discourse"), which appears in Bodl. MS. Firth C. 15, p. 260, Victoria and Albert Museum MS. Dyce 43, p. 766, Vienna MS. 14090, fol. 406^r, the Ohio MS., p. 236, and Taylor MS. 2, p. 188.

5. Since 1953, there have been persistent rumors that an edition unrecorded and unsuspected by Thorpe exists in a single imperfect copy lacking the title leaf. This edition is said to be a descendant of the postulated mixed copy A-1680-Z and an ancestor of A-1680-BMb. Applications to the reputed owner of the book have proved ineffectual.

ciple that "the text tended to deteriorate in successive editions"
(p. xiii), Thorpe concluded that the variants in his collation
indicated the Huntington edition to be the first. This result
yielded a fully directional stemma in which the primary relationships among the editions were exactly as they appear in the
diagram on page 71 below.

Viewed from the perspective of later investigations, however,
some of Thorpe's conclusions regarding editions other than the
Huntington now seem provocative. Of the Pforzheimer edition
(A-1680-PF), he remarked that it "had some editorial supervision; it supplied, for example, the full names of some of the
persons and things that had previously been represented by
initials" (p. xvi). Similarly, Thorpe noted that the Sterling
edition (A-1680-S) exhibits some "accidental reversions to the
readings in earlier editions" and that it "either had editorial
supervision or an enterprising compositor—in any event, it freely
regularizes the text wherever the sense was (or seemed to be)
obscure" (pp. xvii–xviii). He further considered it "quite likely"
that the printer of this edition also produced the editions
designated as Princeton B (A-1680-PRb), British Museum A
(A-1680-BMa), and British Museum B (A-1680-BMb), as well
as possibly the Pforzheimer edition (p. xxiv).

Thorpe offered some perceptive conjectures concerning the
relationship of the Huntington edition to the lost manuscript
which served as its copy-text:

> It seems altogether probable that this book was printed from
> a manuscript "Collection of Rochester's Poems" which had
> been gotten together according to the pattern I have men-
> tioned. The collector first assembled a considerable number
> of pieces, most of which were by Rochester; he did this
> work (apparently) with intelligence and skill, and he uti-

lized good manuscript sources. Then he filled out his collection with miscellaneous poems of doubtful authorship, poems which were about Rochester or had some connection with him or were casually attributed to him or had some special interest for the compiler. The bookseller snapped up this manuscript collection of poems and, without editorial supervision, had them hastily set up into type in the same order that they had occupied in the manuscript collection.

Thorpe modestly termed these remarks "a brief speculation . . . on a subject about which there can never be certainty" (pp. xxxi–xxxii). Soon after his book was published, however, the discovery of the Yale MS., which came to light in 1951 although it was not described in print until 1956, proved that his conjectures were remarkably close to the truth.

In 1953, Thorpe's choice of the Huntington edition as the first was disputed in an article by William B. Todd.[6] Todd's procedure, which was not followed to any extent by Thorpe, was in essence identical with some of the textual methods outlined in the preceding chapter. Thorpe's conclusions concerning priority among the 1680 editions had been based almost entirely upon the *internal* evidence afforded by their textual differences. Todd, by contrast, also invoked the *external* criterion of other early texts of the same poems, chiefly manuscript versions, which he believed were not descended from the 1680 editions; thus they could be expected to preserve readings anterior to many of the readings in the editions. Wherever the 1680 editions exhibited variants among themselves, the editions which agreed with these "separate texts," as Todd called them, would presumably represent earlier and more correct states of the text.

6. William B. Todd, "The 1680 Editions of Rochester's *Poems:* With Notes on Earlier Texts," *Papers of the Bibliographical Society of America,* 47 (1953), 43–58.

Todd tended, however, to assume that his separate texts must themselves be earlier than the first of the 1680 editions and even that they were ancestors of the first edition. Either of these assumptions, applied to Todd's particular group of separate texts, would be irrelevant and often dubious. Indeed, some of the texts he used were almost certainly descendants of the editions. The minimum condition is simply that the separate texts should stand in a *collateral* (or ancestral) relationship to the editions, since they would then normally preserve some anterior readings. Thus texts dated later than the 1680 editions would be admissible so long as they represented a line of textual transmission that bypassed the editions. Despite these shortcomings in his theory, Todd succeeded in emphasizing some features of the 1680 editions about which Thorpe had not been fully explicit.

Assembling and collating a group of separate texts in the British Museum and Bodleian Libraries, Todd found that for a selected set of significant variants, the Pforzheimer edition followed the readings of his separate texts more closely than did the other 1680 editions. This selective study led him to conclude that the Pforzheimer edition rather than the Huntington was the first. Hence he rearranged Thorpe's stemma so as to reverse the direction of textual change between these two editions. The weakness in Todd's reasoning, which he apparently did not suspect and which Thorpe had not adequately pointed out, is that *more than one* of the 1680 editions derived readings from manuscript sources. Moreover, Todd's separate texts were not sufficiently numerous to reveal this situation clearly. As subsequent investigation has shown, the Huntington edition was printed entirely from manuscript sources whereas the Pforzheimer edition merely consulted them for a few readings. Besides the service he performed in calling attention to the special character of the Pforzheimer text, Todd noted evidence that the Sterling, the Princeton B, and possibly the British Museum A editions derived some corrected readings from the Pforzheimer edition.

The conflicting conclusions of Todd and Thorpe were reconciled in a paper which I delivered before the Modern Language Association at its meeting in 1954 and published as an article in 1956 ("Text of Rochester"). This paper attempted to repair the theoretical deficiencies of Todd's article, and it utilized nearly four times as many independently descended separate texts; the nonderivative status of these texts was determined partly by the principle of probability discussed in the preceding chapter. Among the new separate texts, the most crucial were those in the recently discovered Yale MS.

The Yale MS. was acquired from the Rosenbach Company in 1951 and donated to the Yale University Library by Mr. James M. Osborn. It is an unusually clear and fine example of a Restoration manuscript miscellany: its poems are selected and arranged with great care, it is transcribed in a professional hand, and its general appearance suggests that it was copied off during a brief interval of time. These characteristics imply that the Yale MS., like surviving families of manuscript miscellanies, formerly existed in several more copies in the same handwriting—one of them the copy-text from which the first of the 1680 editions was printed. The collection of poems in the Yale MS. must have been assembled about spring of 1680. Several of the poems probably were not in existence before late 1679 or early 1680, and most of the collection was printed in late summer or early autumn of that year as the first of the Rochester editions. Although the Yale MS. itself could conceivably be a transcript made at some subsequent period, there is no evidence that its date is substantially different from that of the original copy of the collection.

The Yale MS. is a bound quarto volume of 406 numbered

pages bearing the title "Songs & Verses Upon severall occasions."
Most of the manuscript, extending through page 391 and including all or part of fifty-nine poems, is in a single late seventeenth-century hand. A less professional hand has added, at a
slightly later date, eight more poems which seem to have no
integral connection with those in the first hand and will not be
discussed in this chapter; they are listed in Appendix A. Unfortunately, the manuscript is marred by seven gaps where leaves
have been cut out (pp. 35–44, 63–66, 77–86, 115–32, 153–58,
161–84, 195–212). No list of contents is included which might
supply information about the missing material—though, as we
shall see, other evidence enables us to identify many of the poems
which formerly occupied these gaps. The only clue to the original
ownership of the volume is the name "Hansen" written beneath
the title; the name may be in the second of the two hands.

The table at the end of this chapter (see below, p. 91) lists,
in order, all fifty-nine poems still extant in the first hand of the
Yale MS. Even a glance at the second and third columns of the
table will reveal that this portion of the manuscript is unmistakably related to the 1680 editions in some fashion. Aside from
the gaps, the Yale MS. gives roughly the same poems in almost
exactly the same order. The differences in contents and arrangement are remarkably minor. The last poem in the 1680 editions,
"On Rome's Pardons" (number 72), does not appear in the
Yale MS., which in turn includes eleven poems lacking in the
editions (numbers 3, 47, 53, 55, 58, 61, 62, 67, 69, 70, and 71).
The manuscript exhibits three small differences in arrangement:
one poem occurs slightly earlier than in the 1680 editions (number 34), one occurs slightly later (number 54), and the order
of two others is reversed (numbers 45 and 46).

Several circumstances, taken together, demonstrate that the

Yale MS. is not descended from any of the 1680 editions. Its external characteristics as a manuscript miscellany would suggest that like most surviving collections of this type, it derives exclusively from manuscript sources. Also, it is difficult to believe that the scribe of the Yale MS. would have taken the trouble to copy an entire printed book amounting to 149 pages of text in the earlier editions, meanwhile interspersing his text with at least eleven more poems. The strongest evidence, however, consists of the readings of the Yale MS.: in numerous significant instances scattered throughout the portions of text which it shares with the 1680 editions, the manuscript differs from all the editions and agrees with other separate texts ("Text of Rochester," pp. 248–49). Two further arguments are afforded by the ascriptions in the Yale MS. and by its differences from the editions in contents and arrangement ("Text of Rochester," pp. 249–51). This additional evidence will be discussed later in another connection.

Since the Yale MS. must therefore bear a collateral or ancestral relationship to the 1680 editions, its text constitutes the best available criterion for determining which edition is the first. Wherever the 1680 editions exhibit variants among themselves, the editions agreeing with the Yale MS. will preserve earlier states of the text—except, of course, for instances of conflation and correction of obvious misprints by later compositors. A tabulation of these variants demonstrates that the direction of textual change is consistently away from the Huntington edition and toward the other editions. The results are particularly striking in the editions related most closely to the Huntington: for the editions designated as Folger (A-1680-F), Harvard (A-1680-HA), and Princeton A (A-1680-PRa), as well as the postulated edition X (A-1680-X), the figures support the priority of the

Huntington edition almost unanimously ("Text of Rochester,"
pp. 256–57). A more specialized test, too intricate to summarize
here, utilizes the Yale MS. and the other separate texts in combination with the Princeton A edition, which stems from an intermediate position between the Huntington and Pforzheimer editions even though it is not in the direct line of textual transmission. This test establishes that the direction of change is from
the Huntington to the Princeton A and Pforzheimer editions,
not from Pforzheimer to Princeton A and Huntington ("Text
of Rochester," pp. 257–58). The presence of conflation in the
Pforzheimer text is indicated by variants between the Pforzheimer and Huntington editions in which *both* readings agree
with readings in the Yale MS. and other separate texts ("Text of
Rochester," pp. 252–53, 254–55, 258).

With the Huntington edition firmly established as the first,
the evidence shows that the Yale MS. is not an ancestor of the
1680 editions. It can scarcely have been the copy-text for the
Huntington edition, since it exhibits no marks of use by a printer.
More important, in numerous significant readings scattered
throughout the portions of text which it shares with the Yale
MS., the Huntington edition differs from the manuscript and
agrees with other separate texts. Thus the Yale MS. and the
Huntington edition must be related in a collateral fashion, both
descending independently from a lost manuscript archetype
("Text of Rochester," pp. 259, 262). This relationship involves
a complication, however, for a number of variants between the
Yale MS. and the Huntington edition represent cases in which
both agree with the separate texts. Such variants indicate that
the portions of text shared by the Yale MS. and the edition do
not derive entirely from their archetype ("Text of Rochester,"
pp. 262–63). The exact nature of this conflation is a question
which could probably be answered only if additional manuscript

copies of the collection are discovered. Fortunately, the phenomenon is not sufficiently extensive to affect the conclusions previously formulated.

Several other questions must also remain without satisfactory answers. Was the archetype the copy-text for the Huntington edition? Probably not, if the text underwent conflation during its passage from the archetype to the edition; such contamination would be more likely to occur in an intervening manuscript. Was the archetype a single manuscript copied by one scribe, or was it a pile of heterogeneous loose sheets which had circulated from hand to hand? Probably it was a single manuscript, since otherwise the Yale MS. and the editions might not exhibit such close correspondence in their order and contents. If the archetype was a single homogeneous text, was it produced by the scribe of the Yale MS.? Probably it was, if we can trust the analogy of surviving families of Restoration manuscript miscellanies: normally all members of such a family are in the same handwriting. Was the archetype the original copy of the collection? Probably we shall never know.

Regardless of the answers to these questions, the Yale MS. and the editions of 1680 can be arranged in the stemma from my earlier article ("Text of Rochester," p. 261) which is reproduced on page 71 below. The primary relationships among the editions remain as in Thorpe's stemma, with the Huntington edition and the Yale MS. independently descended from the archetype, here designated Manuscript Q. A broken line indicates the consultation of manuscript sources by the Pforzheimer edition, while three more broken lines show the possible consultation of the Pforzheimer text by the Sterling, Princeton B, and British Museum A editions. The diagram omits the source or sources other than Manuscript Q from which some additional readings passed into the Huntington edition or the Yale MS. or both.

Also omitted is the source of the last poem in the 1680 editions, "On Rome's Pardons" (number 72), which the evidence suggests was not derived from Manuscript Q ("Text of Rochester," p. 251).

These earlier studies of the 1680 editions have established some basic conclusions. Their concentration on questions of priority has, however, resulted in a disproportionate emphasis on this one phase of the subject, thereby diverting attention from more pressing concerns. To be sure, future investigation must include substantial work along previous lines, especially a more rigorous analysis of certain textual and bibliographical aspects of the 1680 editions. For example, comparison with the editions themselves shows that Thorpe's collation, though adequate for earlier studies and for the present volume, omits some variants essential to any thorough investigation of the many later Rochester editions which derived part of their text from the editions of 1680. A full collation of the accidentals in the 1680 editions may eventually be called for, and a closer examination of purely mechanical features could possibly yield evidence of more than merely academic interest. Identification of the printers and publishers, while not necessary, would be desirable.

In the meantime, the most neglected question raised by the 1680 editions is the authenticity of the sixty-one poems printed there. Though Thorpe contributed much new information on the authorship of these poems (pp. xxviii–xxxii, 169–91), his notes were admittedly "not exhaustive," for his primary purpose was to place the editions in their right order. Nor did the question of canonicity figure prominently in the two subsequent articles by Todd and myself. The problems of authorship posed by the sixty-one poems are important partly because the 1680 editions, in addition to their spurious matter, contain the heart of the Rochester canon. They are more important because so many false attributions passed from the 1680 editions into numerous later editions of Rochester's works.

Any discussion of these problems of authenticity must cover several related areas. The differing ascriptions given by the Yale MS. and the Huntington edition must be evaluated. The arrangement of contents in the edition and the manuscript must

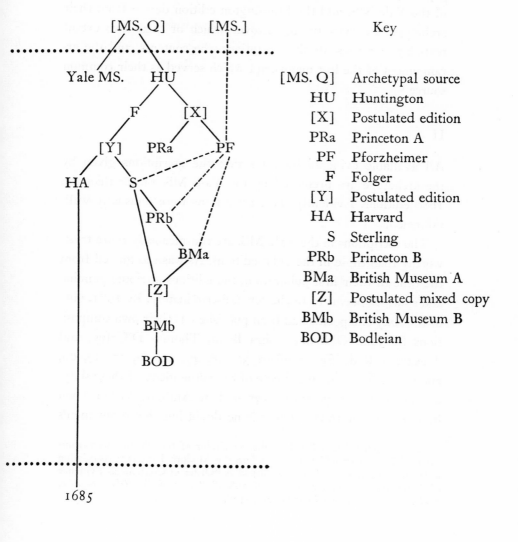

[MS. Q]	Archetypal source
HU	Huntington
[X]	Postulated edition
PRa	Princeton A
PF	Pforzheimer
F	Folger
[Y]	Postulated edition
HA	Harvard
S	Sterling
PRb	Princeton B
BMa	British Museum A
[Z]	Postulated mixed copy
BMb	British Museum B
BOD	Bodleian

be examined, for this arrangement, we shall find, is an indispensable key to the authorship of the poems. Because order of contents is so crucial, and because the order and contents of the manuscript and the edition are not identical, it is necessary to ascertain as nearly as possible what poems formerly occupied the gaps in the Yale MS. Above all, since the most significant features of the Yale MS. and the Huntington edition derive from their archetype, we must try to discover which of these two extant texts better represents the ascriptions, the contents, and the arrangement of the lost manuscript which served as their common source.[7]

II

All available evidence indicates that the ascriptions given by the archetype are preserved by the Yale MS. rather than the 1680 editions. Evidently these ascriptions were unusually well-informed.

The ascriptions in the Yale MS. are conspicuously more trustworthy than those in the 1680 editions. As was recognized from the time of their first publication, the editions attribute genuine and spurious poems to Rochester indiscriminately. By 1684, nine of the sixty-one poems had been published as their own compositions by John Oldham, Aphra Behn, Thomas D'Urfey, and Alexander Radcliffe (numbers 36, 48, 49, 50, 56, 57, 59, 60, and 68). The common estimate of the authenticity of these sixty-one poems was apparently expressed by Anthony Wood when he remarked in 1692, "There is no doubt but that other men's

7. The conclusions offered in the remainder of this chapter were summarized in a paper which I read before the Modern Language Association at its meeting in 1959. It was published as "Order of Contents as Evidence of Authorship: Rochester's *Poems* of 1680," *Papers of the Bibliographical Society of America*, 53 (1959), 293–308.

poems are mixed among them" (*Athenae Oxonienses, 3,* 1230).

By contrast, the Yale MS. is more reliable in its ascriptions than most Restoration manuscript miscellanies—which, in turn, are generally superior in this respect to unauthorized printed texts. None of the seven poems which the Yale MS. assigns explicitly to Rochester is among the many false attributions of the 1680 editions. Out of the total of twenty-three ascriptions in the Yale MS. (all of them listed in the table on p. 91 below), only two are probably incorrect, and one of these two was seemingly distrusted by the scribe himself. The satire usually known as "Timon" (number 51), which the manuscript assigns to Sedley, was probably written by Rochester (see Chapter 11). "Upon a late fall'n Poet" (number 62), a hitherto unknown lampoon on Dryden composed in late March 1678, was evidently rumored about London to be Shadwell's answer to *Mac Flecknoe,* which immediately precedes it in the Yale MS. with an ascription to Dryden (number 61). "Upon a late fall'n Poet" does not, however, contain any reference to *Mac Flecknoe,* and internal evidence renders Shadwell's authorship doubtful. The scribe of the Yale MS. registered his skepticism by noting that this lampoon was merely "Suppos'd to be Written by Mr Shadwell." Thus the ascriptions in the Yale MS., unlike those in the 1680 editions, seem to possess some standing.

Apparently these ascriptions are a fairly accurate record of those given by the archetype. Of the twenty-three ascriptions in the Yale MS., all but two (for poems number 45 and 62) are supported by other contemporary evidence, chiefly ascriptions in numerous independently descended separate texts of the same poems. This means that the ascriptions in the Yale MS. were almost certainly transmitted through the archetype along with the text, since otherwise their presence in the Yale MS. would be difficult to explain. It is unlikely that the archetype provided no marks of authorship, or gave a unique set of ascriptions, or assigned all its poems to Rochester like the 1680 editions, and that the scribe of the Yale MS. then inserted a very nearly correct set of ascriptions from a variety of other sources. Probably the ascriptions in the archetype were very similar to those in the Yale MS., if not virtually identical.

A further circumstance suggests that these ascriptions are similar not only to those of the archetype but to those of the lost copy-text for the Huntington edition—assuming, of course, that this copy-text was not itself the archetype. As we have argued, the Yale MS., the archetype, and the copy-text for the edition were probably transcripts of the same manuscript miscellany in the same handwriting. In surviving examples of such families of manuscript miscellanies, the ascriptions, like the contents and the text, differ relatively little from one member of the family to another. Thus it would be strange if the ascriptions in the archetype or in the copy-text for the Huntington edition had varied appreciably from those of the Yale MS. The differences in ascriptions between the Yale MS. and the edition must have resulted primarily from the printer's attempt to pass off the entire contents of his volume as authentic Rochester.

In the absence of evidence to the contrary, these arguments yield the first of several working assumptions for dealing with the authorship of poems in the 1680 editions: *If the Yale MS. ascribes a poem to some author other than Rochester, then an attribution to Rochester in the 1680 editions, or in sources descended from the 1680 editions, constitutes no evidence whatever that Rochester wrote the poem.*

In accordance with this rule, the ascriptions in the Yale MS. serve to disqualify the last remaining evidence supporting the authenticity of nine poems in the 1680 editions which students of Rochester have already viewed as spurious or doubtful. "Captain [Radcliffe's] Ramble" (number 68), one of two poems in the 1680 editions by Alexander Radcliffe, is correctly assigned in the manuscript. So are "On a Giniper Tree now cut down to make Busks" and "On the Death of Mr. Greenhill The Famous Painter" (numbers 49 and 50), which are two of a group of three poems by Aphra Behn. "Satyr" (number 56), "An Apology to the fore-going Satyr by way of Epilogue" (number 57), and "Upon the Author of a Play call'd Sodom" (number 59) are a group of three poems in the 1680 editions by John Oldham; in the Yale MS., this group is correctly ascribed to Oldham along with a fourth poem, "Upon a certaine Woman who by her falshood & scorne was ye Death of my Friend" (number 58). Three poems comprising a group of lampoons on Edward Howard are all attributed in the Yale MS. to authors other than Rochester. The first (number 44) is correctly ascribed to Buckhurst. The second (number 45), a satire of uncertain authorship assigned in other contemporary sources to Buckhurst or Wycherley, is here attributed to Henry Savile. Though the third lampoon (number 46) has been accepted as genuine by some students of Rochester (e.g. Thorpe, p. 184), the Yale MS. is probably correct in assigning it to Edmund Ashton (see Chapter 10).

Three further ascriptions in the Yale MS. are more interesting. "A Session of the Poets" (number 52), which recent studies of Rochester have unanimously classified as authentic, carries the ascription "Suppos'd to be written by Elk: Settle." Tentative though it is, this ascription disqualifies all external evidence that Rochester composed the poem (see Chapter 12). "Timon" (number 51) has hitherto been assigned to Rochester on the basis of attributions in printed sources. Since the Yale MS. ascribes "Timon" to Sedley, these printed ascriptions, which all apparently descend from the 1680 editions, are invalid. Thus the case for Rochester's authorship must rest solely on other evidence (see Chapter 11). A still more striking situation is presented by the well-known "Song" beginning "I cannot change as others do" (number 37), which has been universally attributed to Rochester and has, indeed, been praised as one of his finest lyrics. The evidence supporting Rochester's authorship is limited, however, to the 1680 editions and sources descended from them, whereas the Yale MS. ascribes the poem to one of Rochester's archenemies, Sir Carr Scroope. Apparently this song is by Scroope, while the immediately following poem, "The Mock Song" (number 38), is Rochester's obscene burlesque of Scroope's lyric (see Chapter 8).

III

In places where the Yale MS. and the Huntington edition differ in their contents or arrangement, all available evidence suggests that again, as in its ascriptions, the Yale MS. preserves the features of the archetype. Evidence in support of this conclusion is afforded by the "linked groups" of poems discussed in Chapter 1. As the reader will recall, these are groups of two to five poems which circulated together in manuscript pamphlets or loose sheets before being copied into manuscript miscellanies and commonplace books, where they often appear linked in the same order in two or more large volumes. Several such linked groups evidently passed unaltered through the archetype into both the Yale MS. and the Huntington edition, as is shown by the occurrence of the same groups in other independently descended texts. Examples include "An Allusion to Horace" and the three succeeding poems, which represent a quarrel between Rochester and Scroope (numbers 10 through 13), the four Buckhurst-Etherege epistles (numbers 40 through 43), and the three lyrics beginning "Give me leave to rail at you," "Nothing adds to your fond Fire," and "Phillis, be gentler I advice" (numbers 24 through 26).[8]

In four instances, however (shown by double vertical lines in the table appended to this chapter), linked groups occur at places where the Yale MS. and the Huntington edition exhibit differences in contents or arrangement. In all four instances the Yale MS. apparently preserves the group in its original form, which would therefore have been its form in the archetype:

(1) A two-poem group consisting of Rochester's "A Satyr against Mankind" followed by the "Answer" which begins "Were I to choose what sort of Shape I'd weare" (numbers 2 and 3). Though the Huntington edition omits the "Answer," the Yale MS. gives both poems together and in order, as do Harvard MS. Eng. 623F, Harvard MS. Eng. 636F, Cambridge MS. Add. 6339, and Edinburgh MS. DC.1.3. This group might, however, have been formed independently by two or more copyists, since the second poem is rather obviously a reply to the first. Evidence that this happened is found in the Cambridge manuscript, which differs from other examples of the group in omitting the epilogue to Rochester's satire and in giving the main part of the poem in a fragmentary state.

(2) A group comprising the four Rochester songs beginning "How blest was the Created State," "While on those lovely looks I gaze," "Against the Charmes our Ballocks have," and "By all Loves soft, yet mighty Pow'rs" (numbers 32 through 35), which occur in that order in Harvard MS. Eng. 636F. The Yale MS. gives the first two poems and part of the third in order, with the remainder of the group removed by the fifth gap. The Huntington edition, by contrast, prints the third and fourth poems

---

8. The Rochester-Scroope satires and the Buckhurst-Etherege epistles are discussed in Chapters 5 and 9, respectively. The group of three lyrics appears in Folger MS. M. b. 12 and Victoria and Albert Museum MS. Dyce 43; these two manuscripts are probably in the same handwriting.

in reverse order and inserts between them the song beginning "Room, room, for a Blade of the Town" (number 36).

(3) A group consisting of the three satires on Edward Howard beginning "Come on ye Critticks! find one fault who dare," "Thou damn'd Antipodes to common sense," and "As when a Bully, draws his Sword" (numbers 44 through 46; see Chapter 10). The three poems appear in this order in the Yale MS. and in *The Annual Miscellany: For The Year 1694,* 1694, where they were printed from a manuscript. Also, the latter part of the first poem and all of the second occur together and in order in Edinburgh MS. DC.1.3. The Huntington edition, however, prints the second and third poems of the group in reverse order.

(4) A group of five satires on Mulgrave and Scroope including "Ephelia to Bajazet," "A very Heroical Epistle in Answer to Ephelia," "On Poet Ninny," "My Lord All-Pride," and "A Familiar Epistle to Mr Julian Secretary of the Muses" (numbers 63 through 67; see Chapter 13). The Huntington edition prints only the first four poems, but all five occur together and in order in the Yale MS. and in Osborn MS. Chest 11, Number 14, as well as in British Museum Egerton MS. 2623, where they constitute the entire contents of a manuscript pamphlet bearing marks of circulation from hand to hand. Moreover, a transcript of the group may have been the copy-text for the broadside *A Very Heroical Epistle from My Lord All-Pride to Dol-Common,* 1679, which gives the second and fourth poems in order and includes an allusion to the first poem. Other texts of the group offer a complication, however, for the first four poems appear without the fifth in Huntington MSS. 8736–38 and Edinburgh MS. DC.1.3. Thus a smaller linked group may have existed in a form identical with the four poems printed in the Huntington edition. The full five-poem group must nevertheless have appeared in the archetype of the Huntington edition and the Yale

MS., since otherwise the presence of the fifth poem in the Yale MS. would be difficult to account for. The alternative explanation, that the archetype gave only the first four poems and that the scribe of the Yale MS. (or of an intermediary) then happened to insert the fifth poem in its proper position, is highly improbable.

The consistent results produced by these four linked groups imply that in the remaining cases where differences occur between the Yale MS. and the Huntington edition, the order and contents of the archetype, and perhaps also of the lost copy-text for the edition, are represented by the Yale MS. For example, the last poem in the 1680 editions, "On Rome's Pardons" (number 72), fails to appear either in corresponding position or anywhere else in the extant portion of the Yale MS. Since further arguments suggest that "On Rome's Pardons" was not among the poems removed by the seven gaps (see Chapter 14), it probably did not appear in the archetype or in the copy-text for the Huntington edition. The printer may have taken this brief anti-Catholic satire from some other source to fill a blank space on the recto of K4, the last leaf of the Huntington volume. More important, the probability that the Yale MS. preserves the order and contents of the archetype means that subsequent conclusions based on the arrangement of the collection should follow the order and contents of the Yale MS. rather than those of the 1680 editions.

Arguments stemming from the four linked groups should not, however, be viewed as more conclusive than they really are. The existence of a linked group is difficult to prove, nor is the evidence concerning these four groups as extensive or unequivocal as one could desire. In surviving families of manuscript miscellanies, the various members are often not identical in contents or arrangement; hence the archetype or the copy-text for the

Huntington edition may have differed from the Yale MS. in ways which the available evidence cannot reveal. On the other hand, the differences between the Huntington edition and the Yale MS. are most likely to have arisen during the process of printing, since this constituted a shift from one medium of transmission to another. Significantly, almost all of the eleven additional poems in the Yale MS. occur near the end of the collection, where the printer might have omitted some material in order to limit his book to a prescribed number of gatherings. Until new evidence comes to light, we should assume that the order and contents of the archetype and of the copy-text for the Huntington edition were those of the Yale MS.

IV

This conclusion lends special importance to the question of what poems formerly occupied the seven gaps in the Yale MS., for the same poems may have appeared in the same order in the archetype. Since the Yale MS. and the Huntington edition are much alike in their contents and arrangement, it is tempting to suppose that the poems removed by the gaps were those which presently occupy the corresponding portions of the edition—except, of course, for the fifth gap, which involves a difference in order between the edition and the Yale MS., and also the seventh gap, which included part of a poem not printed in the edition (number 47). Aside from these variations, the corresponding poems in the Huntington edition supply approximately the right amount of text, and in all seven cases one or more of these poems is unusually obscene, which would explain the motive for their excision from the manuscript.

Such an assumption could remain only tentative, however, were it not for a peculiarity of the first hand in the Yale MS.

The scribe, whose hand is very neat and regular, ordinarily wrote exactly sixteen lines on a page, or the equivalent of sixteen lines where provision had to be made for titles, spaces between stanzas, or similar interruptions of the text. Thus a simple process of counting lines can determine whether the gaps in the Yale MS. will accommodate the corresponding portions of text in the editions.

A few statistics will illustrate the degree of accuracy attainable by this test. Of the original 391 pages in the first hand, ninety fall within gaps, while twenty-eight others give fewer than sixteen lines of text because they contain the conclusion of one poem without space to begin the next. Normally the scribe began a new poem on the same page if the preceding poem required no more than five lines; the sole exception to this practice is a page containing three lines with the rest left blank (p. 226). Of the remaining 273 pages, 231—approximately eighty-five per cent— include exactly sixteen lines or the equivalent. No page, aside from those at the end of a poem, numbers fewer than fifteen lines or more than eighteen: twenty-two pages have fifteen lines or the equivalent, eighteen have seventeen lines, and two have eighteen lines. These departures from the standard sixteen-line measure are almost all explicable as attempts to conclude a poem at the bottom of a page, to avoid splitting a couplet between two pages, or to space stanzas attractively. The number of leaves removed by the gaps is indicated most reliably by the scribe's pagination, which exhibits no errors in the extant portion of the manuscript. Unfortunately, because the missing leaves were cut very close to the spine of the volume with a sharp instrument, the stubs are virtually impossible to count.

This test suggests that for five of the seven gaps, the contents of the Yale MS. were as conjectured. Indeed, the first three gaps almost certainly did not remove any poem in its entirety. The

first gap would be filled exactly by the latter part of Rochester's
"A Ramble in St. James's Park" (number 4), the second by the
latter part of his "The Imperfect Enjoyment" (number 6), and
the third by the missing portions of "The Argument" and
Rochester's "An Allusion to Horace" (numbers 9 and 10). Likewise, the seventh gap probably removed only the missing parts
of Mulgrave's "On the Enjoyment of his M^{rs}" and Aphra Behn's
"The Disappointment" (numbers 47 and 48), though it is barely
possible that a single short poem intervened between these two;
the slight uncertainty regarding this gap results because Mulgrave's verses were not printed in the Huntington edition, while
other early texts of the poem fail to yield a consistent line-count.
The sixth gap would be filled exactly by the latter part of "The
Mock Song," all of "Actus Primus Scena Prima," and all of the
Buckhurst-Etherege epistles except the concluding lines of the
fourth, which are still extant after the gap (numbers 38 through
43). The probability that these poems occupied the sixth gap is
increased because the four Buckhurst-Etherege epistles constitute a linked group.

It is apparent, however, that the contents of the fourth and
fifth gaps were not identical with the corresponding portions of
the Huntington edition, for in both cases the gaps are too large.
An explanation of this discrepancy is suggested by the fact that
elsewhere in its text, the Yale MS. gives eleven poems which
were not printed in the edition. Thus the fourth and fifth gaps
may have contained the corresponding poems in the edition together with several additional poems which the printer omitted
for some undetermined reason, perhaps because they were obviously not Rochester's. If this explanation is correct, the fourth
gap would have included the songs beginning "In the Fields of
Lincolns Inn," "Vulcan contrive me such a Cup," "As Cloris full
of harmless thoughts," "Quoth the Dutchess of Cl——, to Mrs.

Kn——," "I Rise at Eleven, I Dine about Two," and "Love a Woman! y'are an Ass" (numbers 17 through 22), together with about seven more pages of text. The fifth gap is complicated by a difference in arrangement between the Yale MS. and the Huntington edition, but the presence of a linked group at this point (numbers 32 through 35) indicates the probable order of both the Yale MS. and the archetype. The fifth gap, then, would seem to have included the latter part of the song beginning "Against the Charmes our Ballocks have," all of the songs beginning "By all Loves soft, yet mighty Pow'rs" and "Room, room, for a Blade of the Town" (numbers 34 through 36), and all of one additional short poem.

On the basis of the foregoing conclusions, the first column in the table at the end of this chapter lists the poems in the order they presumably occupied in the archetype. (See below, p. 91.)

V

It is a paradox that although their attributions are unreliable, the 1680 editions descend from an archetype whose poems were arranged in a careful, intricate order determined largely by their authorship. The only Rochester scholar who has sensed the significance of this order is Thorpe. In addition to his speculation (quoted earlier) regarding the manuscript copy-text for the Huntington edition, Thorpe arbitrarily divided the contents of the 1680 editions into two groups, a section of thirty-three poems which are mostly by Rochester, followed by a section of twenty-eight poems which are mostly by other authors. Thorpe also noted that two spurious poems in his first group "are answers to Rochester poems and follow the poems that they answer," but he did not pursue this tantalizing insight (pp. xxx–xxxi).

The principles on which the archetype was organized can be

further clarified. Briefly, the first of the two major sections of the collection consists entirely of poems which the scribe evidently thought were written by Rochester or concerned Rochester in some way—that is, satires on him, poems which he answered, or poems written in answer to his. The second major section consists entirely of poems which the scribe evidently thought were written by miscellaneous authors other than Rochester. This scheme accounts for all of the seventy-one poems which the evidence suggests were included in the archetype.

The two-part division of the archetype, which is not readily discernible in the 1680 editions, is emphasized by the distribution of ascriptions in the Yale MS. The extant portion of the manuscript assigns seven of its first eight poems to Rochester, with no further marks of authorship appearing until Scroope's "Song" (number 37). After this poem, however, the fifteen remaining ascriptions *all* designate authors other than Rochester. The complete absence of ascriptions between "The Maim'd Debauchee" (number 8) and Scroope's lyric is puzzling, but since most poems in the first half of the collection seem to be Rochester's, the scribe possibly intended that an attribution to Rochester should be understood unless some explicit sign was given to the contrary, or unless the text of a poem indicated plainly that it was not his.

Before the two major sections of the collection can be examined in detail, it is important to determine the point of division between them, which Thorpe may have located several poems too early. One method for establishing this point is provided by the circumstance that the section of poems by or concerning Rochester is further divided into two subsections. The first subsection, comprising what might loosely be termed satires and translations, ends with Rochester's "Upon Nothing" (number 15). The second subsection, consisting entirely of songs, ends with "The Mock Song" (number 38). The next few poems are clearly not songs; for example, "Actus Primus Scena Prima" (number 39) is a burlesque in pentameter couplets of the manner of the heroic drama. It is reasonable to suppose that the end of the subsection of songs is also the end of the section of poems by or concerning Rochester, which would place the point of division between "The Mock Song" and "Actus Primus Scena Prima."

This conclusion is supported by evidence of authorship supplied in other contemporary sources for the poems surrounding the point of division. The song beginning "By all Loves soft, yet mighty Pow'rs" (number 35), which Thorpe chose as the end of the first section, is the last of a linked group of four songs; this group appears in Harvard MS. Eng. 636F with all four poems ascribed to Rochester, and there is no reason to doubt the authenticity of any one of them. The song beginning "Room, room, for a Blade of the Town" (number 36) is almost certainly a satire on Rochester by Thomas D'Urfey (see Chapter 6). Though the fifth gap in the Yale MS. causes difficulties, Scroope's lyric and the mock answer to it, which immediately follow the gap, would fit logically into the first section as a song which Rochester burlesqued, together with the burlesque itself (numbers 37 and 38). At this point we enter quite different territory, for none of the next dozen poems seems to concern Rochester in any way, and various contemporary sources including the Yale MS. assign all of these poems to other authors: in order, they are ascribed to Buckhurst, Buckhurst, Etherege, Buckhurst, Etherege, and Buckhurst (numbers 39 through 44); Buckhurst, Wycherley, or Savile (number 45); Ashton, Mulgrave (numbers 46 and 47), and Aphra Behn (numbers 48 through 50). Indeed, the first eight of these dozen poems may have been located together because of their connection with Buckhurst.

A second working assumption for dealing with the authorship

of poems in the 1680 editions can now be formulated: *If, in the section of poems by or concerning Rochester, a poem appears to be a satire on him, a poem which he answered, or a poem written in answer to one of his, then an attribution to Rochester in the 1680 editions, or in sources descended from the 1680 editions, constitutes no evidence whatever that he wrote it. Conversely, the presence of any other poem in this section constitutes strong evidence of Rochester's authorship.*

Simple though this rule may seem, it is not always easy to apply. Internal or external evidence suggests, however, that nine poems in the first section of the collection are probably not authentic because they are satires on Rochester, poems which he answered, or poems written in answer to his. The songs by Scroope and D'Urfey have already been mentioned (numbers 36 and 37). "The Answer" (number 3), which is omitted from the 1680 editions, is a reply to Rochester's "A Satyr against Mankind" (number 2). "The Argument" (number 9) is a satire on Rochester by an unknown author (see Chapter 6). "An Allusion to Horace" and the three following poems (numbers 10 through 13) preserve a literary feud between Rochester and Scroope; the first and third poems are by Rochester, while the second and fourth are Scroope's rejoinders (see Chapter 5). The song beginning "Nothing adds to your fond Fire" (number 25), which is an answer to the preceding poem, may have been written by Rochester's wife, since a manuscript draft in the process of revision survives in her handwriting (see Chapter 7). The Yale MS. unfortunately gives no ascription for this lyric.

Two other songs may be light-hearted lampoons on Rochester written by his cronies (see Chapter 6). The song beginning "I Rise at Eleven, I Dine about Two" (number 21), which is not extant in the Yale MS., depicts a typical day in the life of a Restoration rake such as Rochester. A contemporary anecdote, found in a letter dated from London early in 1673, describes how these verses were composed as a satire on Rochester by his friend Buckhurst. The song beginning "In the Fields of Lincolns Inn" (number 17), also not extant in the Yale MS., satirizes the sexual prowess of a person named Strephon, which was a pastoral pseudonym commonly applied to Rochester. Though one early manuscript assigns this song to Rochester, another ascribes it more plausibly to Sedley.

There is no real reason to question Rochester's authorship of the other twenty-nine poems in the first half of the collection. Evidently the scribe of the archetype thought they were Rochester's, and this conclusion clarifies and strengthens the case for their authenticity. Such additional evidence, to be sure, is scarcely required to prove that Rochester wrote "A Satyr against Mankind" (number 2), "A Letter fancy'd from Artemisa in the Town, to Cloe in the Country" (number 4), "The Maim'd Debauchee" (number 8), "An Allusion to Horace" (number 10), or "Upon Nothing" (number 15). Nevertheless, some of the twenty-nine poems, especially the songs, have hitherto been assigned to Rochester on very flimsy evidence, and doubts have recently been indicated concerning his authorship of "The Mock Song" as well as the songs beginning "Quoth the Dutchess of Cl——, to Mrs. Kn——" (number 20), "Against the Charmes our Ballocks have" (number 34), and "By all Loves soft, yet mighty Pow'rs" (number 35). The organization of the collection furnishes a much-needed warrant that these poems are probably genuine.

In the second half of the collection—the section of poems by miscellaneous authors—a question is raised by the presence of five satires which may have been written by Rochester: "Timon" (number 51), "Tunbridge Wells" (number 55), "A very Heroical Epistle in Answer to Ephelia" (number 64), "On Poet

Ninny" (number 65), and "My Lord All-Pride" (number 66).
The probable explanation for this anomaly is that the scribe of
the archetype *did not know* the five satires might be Rochester's.
Four of the five poems appear in the Yale MS. without ascription, while the fifth, "Timon," is there ascribed to Sedley. Moreover, four of the poems—all but "Tunbridge Wells"—continue
to pose problems of authorship even today, so that the scribe's
ignorance is understandable. Evidently the scribe did not intend
to attribute to Rochester any poems in the second half of his
collection. This conclusion allows the formulation of a third
working assumption for dealing with the authorship of poems in
the 1680 editions: *If a poem appears in the section of poems by
miscellaneous authors, then an attribution to Rochester in the
1680 editions, or in sources descended from the 1680 editions,
constitutes no evidence whatever that Rochester wrote it.* Thus,
of the five satires, those four which are printed in the editions
—the same four whose authenticity is less than certain—can be
assigned to Rochester only on the basis of other evidence (see
Chapters 11 and 13).

This rule also disqualifies all remaining support for Rochester's
authorship of eight more poems which have been considered
spurious or questionable. "Actus Primus Scena Prima" (number
39) is ascribed in another early manuscript to Buckhurst. The
Buckhurst-Etherege epistles (numbers 40 through 43) were almost certainly composed by those two authors, as is shown by
ascriptions in other manuscripts for all four poems (see Chapter
9). There is no longer any reason to suppose, as Thorpe did
(p. 185), that Rochester wrote "To all curious Criticks and Admirers of Meeter" (number 54). "A Call to the Guard by a
Drum" (number 60) is by Alexander Radcliffe, and "Ephelia to
Bajazet" (number 63) is probably by Etherege (see Chapter
13). Similarly discredited is most of the evidence for Rochester's

authorship of "The Disappointment" (number 48), which is the first of three poems by Aphra Behn; apparently the only ascription to Rochester that does not descend from the 1680 editions occurs in a late, unreliable printed text (D-1718).

VI

The meticulous arrangement of the archetype arouses curiosity concerning the scribe's basic purpose in assembling his manuscript miscellany. Since he selected a remarkable number of well-known poems by authors who were in vogue during the years immediately preceding 1680, he may have designed his collection as an anthology of what he considered to be the best nondramatic verse produced during these years, especially by members of the influential Court circle. As the most significant poet of the time, the scribe apparently chose Rochester, who is represented much more fully than any other writer, and whose work is accorded first place in the collection. Such a choice should not surprise anyone capable of appreciating the contemporary opinion of Rochester which is expressed in the earlier quotation from Pepys. Dryden's principal achievements between 1666 and 1680 were, after all, in the drama, though he is appropriately represented in the collection by his single outstanding poem of the 1670s, *Mac Flecknoe*. The scribe's special regard for Rochester is reflected in two further circumstances. The section of Rochester poems, which contains no demonstrably mistaken attributions, was evidently put together with slightly more care than the second half of the collection. Also, this section emphasizes Rochester's importance by augmenting his genuine compositions with at least nine more poems that merely concern him in some way.

As his second-ranking poet—also no surprise—the scribe apparently selected Buckhurst, who is represented by six poems and possibly a seventh, most of them concentrated in a group immediately following the section of poems by or concerning Rochester. Like the Rochester section, this group includes not only Buckhurst's own poems but several more which are in some way connected with his (numbers 39 through 46). After Buckhurst, the writers most favored are Oldham with four poems, Aphra Behn, Etherege, and Sir Carr Scroope with three each, and Alexander Radcliffe with two. Buckingham is represented by one poem and possibly a second, Sedley by one lyric and one ascription which is probably incorrect. Mulgrave, D'Urfey, and Edmund Ashton receive one poem apiece, while Shadwell, Settle, and Henry Savile are at least credited with single ascriptions. In some instances, of course, the scribe evidently did not know the authorship of the poems he included.

If the scribe designed an anthology along the lines suggested, he nevertheless made two significant omissions: his section of poems by miscellaneous authors, unlike his section of Rochester poems, contains no love lyrics, and political satires appear only among the last few poems of the collection. The reason for this latter omission may be given by another manuscript miscellany, Taylor MS. 1, which is almost certainly in the same hand as the Yale MS. and consists *entirely* of political pieces. Probably the Yale and Taylor manuscripts were intended as mutually exclusive collections, for they have only two poems in common, and both poems appear at the end of the Yale MS. where the scribe may have added them after his other material gave out (numbers 69 and 70).[9] Possibly he also compiled a collection of songs which is not known to be extant.

9. Like the Yale MS., Taylor MS. 1 is in two late seventeenth-century hands. The first hand, which is almost certainly the same as the first hand of the Yale MS., occupies pp. 1–188. The second hand merely added one poem on pp. 189–92.

Whatever the scribe's plan may have been, the Yale MS., even in its mutilated state, is among the finest Restoration manuscript miscellanies that have come down to us. More than any of his contemporaries, this unidentified scribe was responsible for transmitting the text of Rochester's poetry to future generations. Twentieth-century readers have cause to be grateful for his painstaking efforts.

Table

The following table compares the contents, arrangement, and ascriptions of the Yale MS. and the 1680 editions. In the farthest left column, all poems appearing in the editions or in the first hand of the manuscript are indicated by their initial lines in normalized form. The poems are listed and numbered in the presumptive order of the archetype.

The next column lists, in the order they occupy there, the poems in the 1680 editions. The presence of a poem in the editions is signified by its number in appropriate position. Since the editions assign all of their sixty-one poems to Rochester, individual attributions have not been recorded.

The third column lists, in the order they occupy there, the poems in the first hand of the Yale MS. Poems included in the manuscript are signified by a note of the ascription which is given, or of the absence of any explicit sign of authorship, or of the portion of the poem still extant. The seven gaps where leaves have been cut out are indicated to the left of this column. Poems marked "text not extant" are not actually present in the manuscript but presumably appeared on the excised pages. Ascriptions in the Yale MS. occur at the beginning of a poem.

The fourth column records the conclusions concerning the authorship of the poems which are formulated elsewhere in this study.

To the left of the first column, double vertical lines indicate the four linked groups of poems which occur in places where the Yale MS. and the 1680 editions differ in their contents or arrangement. Also shown are the principal points of division in the archetype: (1) between the section of poems by or concerning Rochester and the section of poems by miscellaneous authors, and (2) between the subsection of satires and translations and the subsection of songs.

First Lines	1680 Editions	Yale MS.	Author
1 Dear friend I hear this town does so abound	1	Rochester	Rochester
2 Were I who to my cost already am	2	Rochester	Rochester
3 Were I to choose what sort of shape I'd wear	Not included	No ascription	Griffith or Pococke (answer to 2)
4 Much wine had pass'd with grave discourse	4	Rochester (title and first 13 lines extant)	Rochester
5 Cloe by your command in verse I write	5	Rochester	Rochester
		1st Gap	
6 Naked she lay clasp'd in my longing arms	6	Rochester (title and first 12 lines extant)	Rochester
7 O love how cold and slow to take my part	7	Rochester	Rochester
		2d Gap	
8 As some brave admiral in former war	8	Rochester	Rochester
9 Say heav'n-born muse for only thou canst tell	9	No ascription (title and first 12 lines extant)	Unknown (satire on Rochester)
10 Well sir 'tis granted I said Dryden's rhymes	10	All extant except title and first 4 lines	Rochester
		3d Gap	

Linked Group

First Lines	1680 Editions	Yale MS.	Author
11 When Shakespeare Jonson Fletcher rul'd the stage	11	No ascription	Sir Carr Scroope (answer to 10)
12 To rack and torture thy unmeaning brain	12	No ascription	Rochester
13 Rail on poor feeble scribbler speak of me	13	No ascription	Sir Carr Scroope (answer to 12)
14 After death nothing is and nothing death	14	No ascription	Rochester
15 Nothing thou elder brother ev'n to shade	15	No ascription	Rochester
16 'Tis not that I am weary grown	16	No ascription	Probably Rochester
17 In the fields of Lincoln's Inn	17	Text not extant	Probably Sedley (satire on Rochester)
18 Vulcan contrive me such a cup	18	Text not extant	Probably Rochester
19 As Chloris full of harmless thoughts	19	Text not extant	Probably Rochester
20 Quoth the Duchess of Cleveland to Mrs. Knight	20	Text not extant	Probably Rochester

4th Gap

Subsection of satires and translations ← | → Subsection of songs

First Lines	1680 Editions	Yale MS.	Author
21 I rise at eleven I dine about two	21	Text not extant	Probably Buckhurst (satire on Rochester)
22 Love a woman you're an ass	22	Text not extant	Probably Rochester
		[Probably several more songs were removed by this gap.]	
		4th Gap	
23 Fair Chloris in a pigsty lay	23	No ascription	Probably Rochester
24 Give me leave to rail at you	24	No ascription	Probably Rochester
25 Nothing adds to your fond fire	25	No ascription	Probably Rochester's wife (answer to 24)
26 Phyllis be gentler I advise	26	No ascription	Rochester
27 What cruel pains Corinna takes	27	No ascription	Probably Rochester
28 Love bade me hope and I obey'd	28	No ascription	Probably Rochester
29 To this moment a rebel I throw down my arms	29	No ascription	Probably Rochester

First Lines	1680 Editions	Yale MS.	Author
30 How happy Chloris were they free	30	No ascription	Rochester
31 All my past life is mine no more	31	No ascription	Rochester
32 How blest was the created state	32	No ascription	Probably Rochester
33 While on those lovely looks I gaze	33	No ascription	Probably Rochester
34 Against the charms our ballocks have	See below	No ascription (title and first 4 lines extant)	Probably Rochester
35 By all love's soft yet mighty pow'rs	35	Text not extant	Probably Rochester
36 Room room for a blade of the town	36	Text not extant	Thomas D'Urfey (satire on Rochester)
	34	[Probably one more song was removed by this gap.] 5th Gap	
37 I cannot change as others do	37	Sir Carr Scroope	Probably Sir Carr Scroope (burlesqued in 38)
38 I swive as well as others do	38	No ascription (title and first 4 lines extant) 6th Gap	Probably Rochester

Linked Group

Section of poems by or concerning Rochester and subsection of songs

First Lines	1680 Editions	Yale MS.	Author
39 For standing tarses we kind nature thank	39	Text not extant	Probably Buckhurst
40 Dreaming last night on Mrs. Farley	40	Text not extant	Buckhurst
41 As crafty harlots use to shrink	41	Text not extant	Etherege
42 If I can guess the devil choke me	42	Text not extant	Buckhurst
43 So soft and am'rously you write	43	Last 6 lines extant	Etherege
44 Come on ye critics find one fault who dare	44	Buckhurst	Buckhurst
45 Thou damn'd antipodes to common sense	See below	Henry Savile	Possibly Henry Savile, Buckhurst, or Wycherley
46 As when a bully draws his sword	46	Edmund Ashton	Edmund Ashton
47 Since now my Sylvia is as kind as fair	45 Not included	Mulgrave (title and first 12 lines extant)	Mulgrave
48 One day the am'rous Lysander	48	Last 10 lines extant	Aphra Behn

6th Gap

7th Gap

Section of poems by authors other than Rochester

Linked Group

	First Lines	*1680 Editions*	*Yale MS.*	*Author*
49	Whilst happy I triumphant stood	49	Aphra Behn	Aphra Behn
50	What doleful cries are these that fright my sense	50	Aphra Behn	Aphra Behn
51	What Timon does old age begin t' approach	54 / 51	Sedley	Probably Rochester
52	Since the sons of the muses grew num'rous and loud	52	"Suppos'd to be written by Elk: Settle"	Possibly Settle
53	Under this stone does lie	Not included	No ascription	Buckingham
54	Have you seen the raging stormy main	See above	No ascription	Unknown
55	At five this morn when Phoebus rais'd his head	Not included	No ascription	Rochester
56	Now curses on ye all ye virtuous fools	56	Oldham	Oldham
57	My part is done and you'll I hope excuse	57	Oldham	Oldham
58	No she shall ne'er escape if gods there be	Not included	Oldham	Oldham

First Lines	1680 Editions	Yale MS.	Author
59 Tell me abandon'd miscreant prithee tell	59	Oldham	Oldham
60 Rat too rat too rat too rat tat too rat tat too	60	No ascription	Alexander Radcliffe
61 All human things are subject to decay	Not included	Dryden	Dryden
62 A sad mischance I sing alas	Not included	"Suppos'd to be Written by Mr Shadwell"	Unknown
63 How far are they deceiv'd who hope in vain	63	No ascription	Probably Etherege
64 If you're deceiv'd it is not by my cheat	64	No ascription	Probably Rochester
65 Crush'd by that just contempt his follies bring	65	No ascription	Probably Rochester
66 Bursting with pride the loath'd impostume swells	66	No ascription	Probably Rochester
67 Thou common shore of this poetic town	Not included	No ascription	Possibly Buckingham
68 Whilst duns were knocking at my door	68	Alexander Radcliffe	Alexander Radcliffe

Linked Group

First Lines	1680 Editions	Yale MS.	Author
69 I sing the praise of a worthy wight	Not included	No ascription	Unknown
70 From a proud sensual atheistical life	Not included	No ascription	Unknown
71 As Colin drove his sheep along	Not included	No ascription	Probably Buckhurst
72 If Rome can pardon sins as Romans hold	72	Not included	Possibly Rochester

Section of poems by authors other than Rochester ← | → Probably not in archetype

PART II

Special Studies

4.

Rochester's "Epistolary Essay": A Crux for Critics and Scholars

I

The most broadly significant literary controversy of the mid-twentieth century has unquestionably been the collision of the New Criticism with the group of older disciplines popularly designated as historical scholarship. In their zeal to analyze a poem as a rhetorical construct, New Critics have been accused of indulging in unwarranted subtleties of interpretation while neglecting aspects of the poem's "background"—biographical, historical, and linguistic matters—that bear importantly on its meaning. Historical scholars, in turn, have been charged with inability to read a poem, or even with unjustified use of works of literature as mere excuses for specialized research projects leading ultimately to irrelevance and futility.

Surely it is a truism that these two methods of literary study, rightly applied, are complementary rather than contradictory, and that the many disputes between their respective adherents are conflicts, not of issues, but of personalities. It may be less obvious that lack of coordination between the disciplines of the New Criticism and those of historical scholarship can cause serious difficulties when dealing with specific problems requiring both kinds of skills for satisfactory solution. A case in point is the first poem in the Rochester editions of 1680, the satire cryptically entitled "An Epistolary Essay from M. G. to O. B. upon their Mutual Poems" ("Dear Friend. I Hear this Town does so abound"). Though critics and scholars must share responsibility for the disappointing treatment hitherto accorded the "Epistolary Essay," the New Critics are guilty at worst only of ignoring the poem, thereby depriving the scholar of their special insights. On the other hand, failure to read the poem properly has betrayed historical scholars into mistakes even in the types of investigation at which they claim to be peculiarly proficient.

Misunderstanding of the satirical structure of the "Epistolary Essay" has led to at least four errors within the provinces of biography and literary history. First, the composition of the poem has been dated as much as ten years too early, resulting, among other things, in misrepresentation of Rochester's development as a poet. Second, the poem has been adduced as false witness for a distorted interpretation of Rochester's character as a man and as a literary artist; in reality, the attitudes reflected in this satire are just opposite to those it is alleged to express. Third, evidence concerning Rochester's relations with two contemporary poets has remained concealed.

Fourth and most far-reaching, the status of the "Epistolary Essay" as a document illustrating the growth of a distinctive

Augustan poetical technique has gone unrecognized. It may be presumptuous, in an age which excelled at various forms of oblique attack, to single out one kind of ironical satire as more typically Augustan than another. Nevertheless, the spiritual temper of the times perhaps appears most profoundly in satires utilizing structures like that of Pope's *Dunciad,* which many readers have considered the greatest of Augustan poems and which could scarcely have been written in any earlier or later period of English literature.

Essentially the *Dunciad* structure functions through ironic approval of a spectrum of disvalues that are diametrically opposed to the traditional Christian-classical standards shared by most of the contemporary audience. Whether the speaker of the poem is a *persona* who is himself satirized—a favorite device with Rochester—or remains anonymously omniscient, the satire operates by ironically replacing traditional norms with their direct contraries: the poet seems to praise what he censures and to disparage what he really praises. This technique is basically simpler than those which (as in some of Swift's prose works) employ less than a 180 degree reversal of point of view, but its very simplicity allows the satirist to project a wider and richer range of norms than is feasible with a more complex approach. At its most elaborate, as in the *Dunciad,* the technique approximates a total transvaluation of values, so that the world of the poem resembles a full inversion of the imputed normative scheme of the actual world.

The poetical ferment of the decade 1670–80 produced several satires which notably anticipate the *Dunciad.* Of these, *Mac Flecknoe* is easily the best as well as the best known. Dryden's satire should, however, be viewed not as an isolated achievement but as a culmination of a tradition whose form had already

been partly delineated in other poems. Indeed, it is worth speculating whether *Mac Flecknoe* would have been cast in its present
mold if prior examples had not shown Dryden the way.

Among the more important poems belonging clearly to the
Dunciad type, the earliest seems to be Buckhurst's lampoon on
Edward Howard beginning "Come on ye Critticks! find one fault
who dare," which was actually written some months before the
decade began (summer of 1669) and enjoyed wide circulation
(see Chapter 10). About the middle of the decade, the inverted
world of Augustan satire received its most nearly archetypal
expression in Rochester's "Upon Nothing," an ironic eulogy of
an Uncreation opposite to God's original act. (Significantly, as a
youth Pope composed imitations of these two poems, and he
later incorporated several lines from his imitation of Buckhurst
into the *Dunciad*.)[1] Rochester also contributed "A very Heroical Epistle in Answer to Ephelia" and the "Epistolary Essay,"
both discussed in detail in this chapter. With less success, John
Oldham attempted a similar ironic technique in *A Satyr against
Vertue*, composed in July 1676. Other poems like Rochester's
mock-heroic "The Maim'd Debauchee," written about 1675,
share to a smaller extent in the development of the tradition.
(In passing, it is noteworthy that all seven of these poems were
included in the collection represented by the Yale MS. and the
Rochester editions of 1680.)

Fortunately, though students of Rochester have misunderstood the ironical satire of his "Epistolary Essay," the closely
analogous technique of "A very Heroical Epistle in Answer to

1. Pope's poems are "To the Author of a Poem, intitled, Successio,"
an imitation of Buckhurst's satire, and "On Silence," an imitation of
"Upon Nothing." See Arthur E. Case, "The Model for Pope's Verses *To
the Author of a Poem Intitled 'Successio,'* " *Modern Language Notes,* 43
(1928), 321–22; and *The Poems of Alexander Pope,* Twickenham edition, 6 (*Minor Poems*), ed. Norman Ault and John Butt (London, Me-
thuen; New Haven, Yale Univ. Press, 1954), 15–19, 463–64.

Ephelia" has been rightly interpreted. Before proceeding to the "Epistolary Essay," therefore, it may be helpful to examine the "Heroical Epistle" in some detail.

II

"A very Heroical Epistle in Answer to Ephelia" ("If your deceiv'd, it is not by my Cheat") is the second of a pair of verse epistles purportedly exchanged by a man and woman bearing the pseudonyms Bajazet and Ephelia; both poems belong to the tradition of fictitious verse letters stemming from Ovid's *Heroides*. In the first epistle, headed "Ephelia to Bajazet" and probably composed by Etherege, Ephelia reproaches Bajazet for his inconstancy in their love affair. Rochester's poem, as its title implies, is Bajazet's arrogant rebuttal. Bajazet is a *persona* (that is, a dramatic speaker who is not strictly the same person as the author) representing John Sheffield, Earl of Mulgrave, whose conceit and self-sufficiency are satirized in both poems but especially in the second. The "Heroical Epistle" concludes with allusions to Mulgrave's affair with Mall Kirke, which was in progress in 1674–75 and ended in a duel between Mulgrave and Mall's brother Percy on 4 July 1675; probably the two poems were written later the same summer. The case for the dating and authorship of the Bajazet-Ephelia epistles is presented elsewhere (Chapter 13); though the external evidence that Rochester wrote the "Heroical Epistle" is less than conclusive, the resemblance of its ironic technique to that of the "Epistolary Essay," which is almost certainly Rochester's, provides additional warrant for its authenticity. Etherege's poem will not be discussed in this chapter, since the "Heroical Epistle" is self-contained and can therefore be understood without reference to Ephelia's complaint.

Missing the ironic use of the *persona* in the "Heroical Epistle," students of Rochester's poetry initially jumped to the mistaken conclusion that it represented an intimate revelation by Rochester speaking in his own person. Johannes Prinz, supposing the poem to have "the value of a self-confession," cited it as evidence that "Rochester proved himself a real worldling, living without any high purpose and not fulfilling any definite range of duties for the benefit of the commonweal. His conception of life was ego-centric" (*Rochester*, p. 212). Vivian de Sola Pinto claimed that in the "Heroical Epistle," Rochester's "complete egoism . . . is stated frankly and with a boldness that must have shocked many who practised it in their lives, but who never had the courage to admit such principles openly." In the latter part of the poem, moreover, Pinto discerned Rochester's hedonistic "dream of Oriental luxury," his conception of "the life of the senses under perfect conditions" (*Rochester*, pp. 170, 171). The true character of the "Heroical Epistle" as a satire on Mulgrave was first pointed out by John Harold Wilson, whose insight evidently came through a combination of scholarship with criticism, since he was also the first to discover the allusions at the end of the poem to Mulgrave's affair with Mall Kirke. Wilson did not, however, deal with the poem in detail. His interpretation was subsequently adopted by James Thorpe and, apparently, by Pinto.[2]

Regrettably, any attempt to analyze the technique of the "Heroical Epistle," which is one of the deftest satires in Restoration literature, will seem to damage its delicate comic texture. For the most part, the traditional norms used in the poem hover in suspension and are all the more effective for not being made

2. See Part III for fuller documentation of the previous commentary on the "Heroical Epistle."

explicit. Without analysis, however, the poem's complex, allusive structure cannot be fully appreciated.

The satire of the "Heroical Epistle" works through Bajazet's unconscious violation of implicit norms, the poem's thematic center being an ironic inversion of that aggregate of traditional ideas well known to literary scholars under the term "degree." Though these ideas are usually associated with the Renaissance period, the notion of degree persisted in the thinking of most Englishmen until well into the eighteenth century. To cite a few obvious examples, this concept is explicit in Pope's *Essay on Man* and implicit in the *Dunciad,* while in the Restoration it is sufficiently evident in *Absalom and Achitophel.* Thus it was readily available to Rochester for poetic exploitation.

According to the notion of degree, the entire universe, from God down through angels, man, animals, plants, and inanimate objects to nothing or chaos, was one vast unbroken hierarchy, the "great chain of being." Analogous to this primary scale of existence were many sub-hierarchies: as God controlled the universe, so in society the king ruled his subjects, in human psychology reason governed the appetitive impulses, among the planets the sun took pre-eminence, and so on through the familiar list. Each member of the hierarchy was endowed with exactly those faculties needed to fill his appointed place and function, so that his own happiness, as well as the order and harmony of the whole, required that he neither sink below his assigned level nor aspire above it. He possessed specific rights and obligations in relation to his superiors, inferiors, and equals in the hierarchy, and proper observance of these relationships was both productive of, and supported by, the traditional values of individual character and social conduct.

After pompously ranking himself among "the Great" and as-

suring Ephelia that there should be nothing surprising about his
inconstancy, Bajazet formulates his "principles" in a passage
which comprises the thematic core of the poem:

> In my dear self, I center ev'ry thing,
> My *Servants, Friends,* my *Mrs.* and my *King,*
> Nay Heav'n, and *Earth,* to that one poynt I bring.
> We'll manner'd, honest, generous, and stout,
> Names by dull *Fools,* to plague Mankind found out;
> Shou'd I regard I must my self constrain;
> And 'tis my *Maxim,* to avoid all pain.[3]

A rich spectrum of traditional values suffuses this passage,
which is best understood as a series of variations on the theme
of subversion of degree. The first line is a broad statement of the
theme: by selfishly claiming complete autonomy for his "dear
self," Bajazet implicitly denies the system of rights and depend-
encies which was essential to the traditional ideal of social and
universal corporateness. Subsequent lines develop variations of
the theme by exploring it in specific hierarchies. In the second
line, Bajazet attempts to cancel the traditional conception of a
stratified society by asserting his absolute supremacy over his
servants (inferiors), his friends (equals), his mistress (Ephelia),
and even his king (superior). In the climactic third line, he sub-
verts the whole universal order ("Heav'n, and *Earth*") by cen-
tering it all upon the "one poynt" of his individual ego, thereby
usurping God's place in the chain of being.

3. The text used for the "Heroical Epistle" is that of A-1680-HU, p.
140, with four minor emendations (enclosed in pointed brackets) based on
the following independently descended versions of the poem: Yale MS.;
Osborn MS. Chest ɪɪ, Number 14; Huntington MS. Ellesmere 8736;
B. M. Egerton MS. 2623; Bodl. MS. Don. b. 8; Edinburgh MS. DC.1.3;
A Very Heroical Epistle, 1679. This text was established by reconstructing
the archetype, but discussion of my procedure must await a critical edition
of Rochester's works.

These three lines function reflexively to charge the opening lines of the poem with a significance they would not otherwise possess:

> Madam,
> If your deceiv'd, it is not by my Cheat,
> For all disguises, are below the Great.
> What *Man,* or *Woman,* upon *Earth* can say,
> I ever us'd 'em well above a *Day?*
> How is it then, that I inconstant am?
> He changes not, who always is the same.

The notion that perpetual inconstancy constitutes a kind of constancy is a weary cliché of seventeenth-century love poetry. In the context of Rochester's satire, however, the cliché is revitalized, for the alleged absence of any consistency in Bajazet's behavior suggests the absolute Chaos antithetical to the divine Logos. Bajazet's life is, by implication, a succession of small acts of Uncreation.

The next several lines of the later passage develop a corollary of Bajazet's previous proposition. Asserting his self-sufficiency in opposition to the concept of degree, Bajazet dismisses as "Names by dull *Fools,* to plague Mankind found out" those values of individual and social conduct—courtesy, honesty, generosity, courage, and the like—which were traditionally thought necessary to bind together the corporate structure of society. Violation of social order then shades almost imperceptibly into a related violation of the accepted hierarchy of individual human psychology. Instead of subordinating passion and appetite to the control of reason, Bajazet rejects any idea of self-discipline (as well as external restraint) and claims a right to unlimited self-indulgence. The last two lines of the passage hint at a secondary theme which we shall encounter later in the poem: Bajazet's

attitude approaches a self-centered materialism in which good
and evil are merely physical pleasure and pain.

Bajazet continues:

> You fondly look, for what none e're cou'd find,
> Deceive your self, and then call me unkind,
> And by false Reasons, wou'd my falshood prove,
> For 'tis as natural to change, as love:
> You may as justly at the *Sun*, repine,
> Because alike it does not always shine:
> No glorious thing, was ever made to stay,
> My blazing *Star*, but visits and away.
> As fatal too it shines, as those 'ith' *Skyes*,
> 'Tis never seen, but some great *Lady* dyes.

The initial portion of this passage culminates in the fourth
line, where Bajazet's argument is ironically qualified by the
ambiguous key word "natural." Few readers of Shakespeare will
need to be reminded of the double signification of the concept of
"nature" in the seventeenth century. "Love" was "natural" in
terms of a supra-sensual nature, belonging exclusively to humans
and their superiors in the great chain, which endowed its pos-
sessors with the faculties of speech and reason and enabled them
to recognize moral obligations and enter into warm social relationships. "Change," on the other hand, would be "natural" in
terms of a lower, amoral, animal nature—a sort of "law of the
jungle." Bajazet's "nature" descends, somewhat attenuated, from
Edmund's "nature" in *King Lear*. In this context, the word
"change," implying an amorphous subhuman carnality, correlates
with earlier suggestions that Bajazet's behavior represents a self-
centered materialism and, ultimately, a sort of anti-Logos.

The fifth line introduces a complex image pattern (drawn,
appropriately, from the physical world) which extends through

the remainder of the passage. In comparing himself to the sun, Bajazet intends to illustrate his previous argument, but his metaphor recoils upon him ironically in several ways. First, since the sun was accorded a high rank both in the general hierarchy of physical nature and in the special hierarchy of the planets, the comparison inflates Bajazet's arrogance to ridiculously cosmic proportions. Second, since it was commonplace to cite the sun's pre-eminence among the planets as analogous to the monarch's position in the state, the image recalls Bajazet's egotistical desire to subordinate the whole social order, including the king, to himself. Third, the sun as generous sustainer of the forces of life contrasts with Bajazet's selfish, niggardly treatment of other people. Fourth, the sun as a traditional symbol of stability (opposed, for example, to the moon, a symbol of changeableness) conflicts with Bajazet's boasted inconstancy. Bajazet concedes this last discrepancy by remarking, "No glorious thing"—e.g. Bajazet himself!—"was ever made to stay."

With the sun image thus disqualified, Bajazet substitutes the image of a comet ("blazing *Star*"), which, unlike the sun, can function as a vehicle for the idea of transience: it merely "visits and away." Like the sun comparison, however, the comet metaphor carries connotations which are scarcely flattering to Bajazet. Since it too is a cosmic image, it continues the previous emphasis on Bajazet's enormous conceit. This hyperbole is now reinforced by the notion of the deterministic influence which the stars were supposed to exert upon human fate, a despotic control like that which Bajazet wishes to impose upon his fellowmen. The poem itself specifies a still more ominous significance: a comet was believed to portend some major disaster in human affairs, especially the death of an important person ("fatal . . . some great *Lady* dyes"). Not even the heroic overtones of such a catastrophe are granted to Bajazet, since the ironic framework of the poem constantly insists that he is too silly to achieve the realm of heroic action and grand passions except in daydreams. The "blazing *Star*" has a further relevance, for the phrase alludes to Mulgrave's Star of the Garter—a fitting emblem of the exalted role which Mulgrave, in real life, apparently felt was his peculiar destiny.[4] A final deflation of Bajazet's heroic pretensions is accomplished by the sexual pun in the last word of the passage, "dyes"; by implication, Bajazet imagines himself so irresistible that no "great *Lady*"—apparently the only kind of lady he considers worth mentioning—can encounter him without experiencing an orgasm.

The next passage in the "Heroical Epistle" provides its principal development of the idea that Bajazet's position is amorally materialistic. (In this connection, it is worth remembering that many Augustan satirists, including Pope in the *Dunciad*, accused their contemporary society of placing cash values above all else.)

> The boasted favor, you so precious hold,
> To me's no more than changing of my Gold;
> What e're you gave, I paid you back in Bliss,
> Then where's the Obligation pray of this?
> If heretofore you found grace in my *Eyes*,
> Be thankful for it, and let that suffice.
> But *Women*, *Beggar-like*, still haunt the Door,
> Where they've receiv'd a *Charity* before.

4. The *London Gazette* for 16–20 September 1675 carried the following advertisement: "Lost or stolen on Monday the 13 of *Sept.* instant, out of the house of the Right Honourable the Earl of *Mulgrave* at *Charing-cross*, an Order of the Garter, or George, being a Certonix Stone, set round with 10 Rose Diamonds, of the value of 40 *l.* apiece, with a George engraven on the one side of the Onix. and a George enameled on the other side. If any one can give notice of it to Mr. *Hinde* a Goldsmith at the *Old Exchange*, shall have twenty Guinea's Reward." Was the theft possibly a prank by Rochester or some of his cronies?

Bajazet is satirized in these lines for trying to reduce human values, symbolized by his love affair with Ephelia, to the level of a commercial transaction. The relationship was no different, Bajazet argues, from "changing of my Gold," and since "I paid you back in Bliss," any "Obligation" or business contract has been fulfilled. Even in these monetary terms, however, Bajazet has apparently perpetrated a swindle. The "Bliss" he gave Ephelia in return for her chastity cost him nothing, and the exchange doubtless netted him some pleasure, since otherwise he would scarcely have bothered with her. Moreover, there are hints that Bajazet feels too grand to be required to pay any bills. Ephelia is advised to be thankful for anything she got from him, while in the concluding couplet, Bajazet compares his dealings with women to the action of a wealthy man instructing his servants to toss a few pennies to a crowd of beggars at the door of his magnificent mansion. (Mulgrave's residence was to become part of the present Buckingham Palace.) A further dimension is added by the ironic use of the words "grace" and *"Charity,"* implying a perversion, not just of general human values, but of Christian values as well.

The climactic passage of the poem, in which Bajazet depicts the life of a Turkish sultan as his ideal of existence, is a devastating symbolic summary of his attitudes:

> Oh happy *Sultan*! whom we barb'rous call,
> How much refin'd art thou above us all:
> Who envys not the joys of thy *Serail?*
> Thee like some *God*! the trembling Crowd adore,
> Each *Man's* thy *Slave*, and *Woman kind*, thy *Whore.*
> Methinks I see thee underneath the Shade,
> Of Golden ⟨canopies⟩, supinely laid,
> Thy ⟨crouching⟩ *Slaves*, all silent as the Night,

But at thy nod, all active, as the light!
Secure in solid Sloth, thou there dost reign,
And feel'st the joys of Love, without the pain.
Each *Female*, courts thee with a wishing Eye,
While thou with awfull pride, walk'st careless by;
Till thy kind Pledge, at last, marks out the *Dame*,
Thou fancy'st most, to quench thy present flame.
Then from thy Bed, submissive she retires,
And thankful for the grace, no more requires.
No loud reproach, nor fond unwelcome sound,
Of *Womens* Tongues, thy sacred Ear ⟨dares⟩ wound;
If any do, a nimble *Mute*, strait tyes
The *True*-⟨love⟩-*knot*, and stops her foolish cryes.

Though the absurdity of Bajazet's egocentric daydream is
evident without exegesis, the passage achieves much of its satiric
force by combining and objectifying motifs already introduced
in the poem. The theme of monarchy is developed most obviously. Earlier, Bajazet wished to center all of society, including
the king, upon the "one poynt" of his colossal ego; now, in his
reverie, he *is* the king. Nor is he just a limited monarch, like
Charles II; he is an Oriental despot with powers of life and
death over any subject who ventures a "loud reproach" against
his absolute will. Gone altogether is the traditional concept of
a creative interdependency linking together king, nobles, and
commoners. Bajazet's imaginary reign as sultan is a one-way
arrangement: his subjects, "trembling" and "crouching," have no
purpose except to be "submissive," obey his smallest whim, court
him "with a wishing Eye," and "adore" his "awfull pride"—
whereas the sultan himself has no responsibilities. The name
"Bajazet" is specially appropriate to this passage, since it is the

name of the haughty Turkish emperor in Marlowe's *Tambur-laine.*[5]

Bajazet's dream of despotism embraces a second theme, the extinction of human values. The system of individual rights inherent in the structure of a limited monarchy is, of course, "re-fin'd" away completely. The spiritual poverty of Bajazet's attitude toward other people is emphatic: he sees no value in his fellowman except as a *"Slave,"* nor any in woman except as a *"Whore."* Other people exist merely to be *used.* As for the human values of love, the *"True-love-knot"* is a strangler's noose.

Human values are submerged in a pervasive materialism, for Bajazet imagines a sensual paradise for himself—the physical "joys" of existence "without the pain." Other human beings are barely permitted the status of domestic animals, while the relationship of woman to man, with its traditional spirituality, is reduced to the carnal and monetary level of prostitution. The "joys of Love" end in seeking to "quench" a "present flame." This metaphor of the four elements is intricate: though "flame" as the highest element suggests the traditional nobility and permanence of love, its use in implied combination with the baser element of water ("quench") emphasizes that Bajazet's passion is physical as well as brief and unfixed ("present flame") and that it represents descent from a higher level (fire) to a lower (water). Even Bajazet's prosaically mercenary "changing of my Gold" reappears in this passage as the resplendent "Golden canopies" under whose "Shade" he can vegetate "supinely" in "solid Sloth."

If Bajazet covets royal privileges, the passage contains repeated hints that his program likewise impinges, Satan-like, upon

5. Apparently there is no allusion to Racine's *Bajazet,* though Rochester may well have known the play.

divine prerogative. These hints continue the previous ironic use of "grace" and *"Charity"* in addition to the notion of Bajazet as a kind of anti-Logos. The sultan is adored "like some *God,"* he has a "sacred Ear," his command is a "nod" (the Latin *numen*), and he bestows "grace" on his harem by sleeping with them. The religious terminology is supported by a light-darkness metaphor, initiated by the sun and comet images, which re-emerges in the description of the sultan's *"Slaves,* all silent as the Night" who, at his "nod," become "active, as the light." Carrying the traditional symbolic import of light and darkness, this image pattern implies a perversion of the divine fiat of Creation, "Let there be light." Similarly, the phrase "Secure in solid Sloth" suggests a mock-Aristotelian Unmoved Mover or perhaps the Lucretian gods, lazily at ease and indifferent to human sufferings.[6] This phrase also anticipates the "Force inertly strong" of Pope's goddess of Dulness.

At the conclusion of the "Heroical Epistle," Bajazet's romantic reverie dissolves into a pained recognition of the actual world in which he must live—a world where Mulgrave, unlike the sultan, could be ignominiously waylaid while leaving his mistress's bedchamber or defeated by her indignant brother in a duel:

> Thou fear'st no injur'd *Kinsmans* threatning Blade,
> Nor Mid-night Ambushes, by *Rivals* laid;
> While here with aking Hearts, our joys we tast,
> Disturb'd by Swords, like *Democles* his Feast.

In this world of "aking Hearts" (suggestive of Keats's "heart high-sorrowful and cloyed"), Bajazet still views life as a purely sensual "Feast" whose "joys" he longs to "tast." Always hang-

6. Rochester translated one of the relevant passages from *De Rerum Natura* (1.44–49) in his lines beginning "The Gods, by right of Nature, must possess" (B-1691, p. 109).

ing over him, however, is the sword symbolic of human limitations (in Mulgrave's case, the real sword of Percy Kirke) which no mortal, certainly not Bajazet, can hope to elude.

III

The form of "An Epistolary Essay from M. G. to O. B. upon their Mutual Poems" resembles that of the "Heroical Epistle" even in superficial features. Both poems are satiric verse epistles. In each, the speaker is a *persona,* and he is depicted writing to an acquaintance who is also characterized, though less fully: as Bajazet addresses Ephelia, so M. G. addresses his fellow-versifier O. B., whose literary accomplishments he considers superior to his own. In both poems, the satire operates ironically through the speaker's violation of traditional norms which remain largely implicit. In each case, the *persona* is satirized for his self-sufficiency, though with different thematic emphases: whereas the "Heroical Epistle" explores the general issue of individual freedom in conflict with social and universal corporateness, the "Epistolary Essay" focuses more narrowly upon the individual poet in relation to his public and to a body of inherited literary tradition.

The remarks of earlier commentators on the "Epistolary Essay" are enough to suggest a similarity to the "Heroical Epistle." Some of these comments are almost identical with those made concerning the "Heroical Epistle" before Wilson perceived that the latter poem did not represent Rochester speaking in his own person. Prinz, viewing the "Epistolary Essay" as "an intimate personal confession" and a "confession of self-sufficiency" on Rochester's part, praised the Earl's "unceremonious open-heartedness, modesty, and self-confidence" in having thus "openly declared himself an outlaw of literature" (*Roch-*

ester, pp. 118, 176, 211). Pinto interpreted the "Epistolary Essay" as a proclamation of Rochester's "naked self-worship" resulting inevitably from his "hedonism." Pinto also stated that the attitude of self-indulgence allegedly expressed by Rochester in this poem

> was the principle governing the lives of most of the men of Rochester's class in the reign of Charles II, but he was the only one who had the courage to proclaim it openly. . . . Like Shaw's Andrew Undershaft, he not only did wrong things, "he said them and thought them: that was what was so dreadful." The Rochester who wrote these lines was the perfect "wild gallant" of the period. . . . He was the embodiment of the type which Mr. W. H. Auden has called the Aesthetic Hero, the man who lives entirely for pleasure only and whose life bears no relation to truth.[7]

Basically this same interpretation was put forth more briefly by John Hayward, Wilson, and Thorpe. Like Pinto, Wilson saw in the "Epistolary Essay" a general reflection of the "independent spirits and highly developed egos" of Rochester's circle of fashionable wits (*Court Wits*, p. 174).

The "Epistolary Essay" even begins in somewhat the same fashion as the "Heroical Epistle." After remarking on the adverse public response to a poem (or poems) which he and O. B.

---

7. Vivian de Sola Pinto, "John Wilmot, Earl of Rochester, and the Right Veine of Satire," *Essays and Studies*, 6 (1953), 56–70; see Part III for fuller documentation of the previous commentary on the "Epistolary Essay." Several months after the present study was completed, my interpretation of the "Epistolary Essay" was anticipated in a brief article by Marvin Delmar Palmer, "The Identity of 'M. G.' and 'O. B.' in Rochester's 'An Epistolary Essay from M. G. to O. B. Upon Their Mutual Poems,' " *Modern Language Notes*, 75 (1960), 644–47. Since Palmer's remarks add nothing to my discussion, and especially since he accepts the traditional identification of M. G. and O. B. as Martin Clifford and the Duke of Buckingham, I have allowed the text of Chapter 4 to stand as originally written.

have recently written, M. G. states his general "principles" of poetic composition:

> I'm none of those who think themselves inspir'd,
> Nor write with the vain ⟨hopes⟩ to be admir'd;
> But from a *Rule* I have (upon long tryal)
> T' avoid with care all sort of self denyal.
> Which way so'ere desire, and fancy lead,
> (Contemning *Fame*) that *Path* I boldly tread;
> And if exposing what I take for wit,
> To my dear self a pleasure I beget,
> No matter tho the cens'ring ⟨critic⟩ fret.
> ⟨Those⟩ whom my *Muse* displeases, are at strife,
> With equal spleen against my course of life,
> The least delight of which, ⟨I'd⟩ not forgo,
> For all the flatt'ring praise, *Man* can bestow.
> If I design'd to please, the way were then,
> To mend my Manners, rather than my *Pen*:
> The first's unnatural, therefore unfit,
> And for the second, I despair of it,
> Since Grace is not so hard to get as Wit.[8]

M. G.'s procedure as a poet, outlined in the first half of this passage, is inseparable from social conduct which parallels that advocated by Bajazet in the corresponding lines of the "Heroical Epistle": both speakers propound a doctrine of unlimited self-indulgence in opposition to self-discipline or external restraint. It is almost as if Rochester were echoing the "Heroical Epistle."

---

8. The text used for the "Epistolary Essay" is that of A-1680-HU, p. 3, with emendations (enclosed in pointed brackets) based on the following independently descended versions of the poem: Yale MS.; Osborn MS. Chest II, Number 28; Harvard MS. Eng. 623F; Harvard MS. Eng. 636F. As with the "Heroical Epistle," this text was established by reconstructing the archetype.

As Bajazet's *"Maxim"* of behavior in the face of social obligations was "to avoid all pain" to himself, so M. G.'s *"Rule"* of
writing is "T' avoid with care all sort of self denyal." Bajazet
tried to center the whole social order in his "dear self"; M. G.
similarly ignores the sensibilities of other people if "To my dear
self a pleasure I beget." The latter half of the passage expands
M. G.'s denial of the ideal of social corporateness: neither praise
nor blame will persuade him to relinquish the "least delight"
of his self-centered "course of life." Also, as Bajazet claimed
that "change" was "natural," so M. G., in a corresponding statement, feels that any mending of his "Manners" would be "un-
natural."

The first half of the passage satirizes M. G.'s methods of
writing by presenting them as ironic inversions of traditional
standards which almost any Augustan would have considered essential to good poetry. Instead of submitting his verses to the collective good taste and judgment of educated readers, as an Augustan poet was expected to do, M. G. disavows any ambition "to be
admir'd," despises *"Fame,"* and cares nothing for the "cens'ring
critic." He rejects the notion that poetry is better written by
those few geniuses who are "inspir'd" with "Wit"—here appropriately equated with God-given "Grace." In contrast to the
Augustan belief that good writing required long study and painstaking revision based on a knowledge of "nature," the practice of
classical authors, and the rules derived from nature and the
ancients, M. G. lets his undisciplined pen ramble wherever "desire, and fancy lead." Whether ideas like M. G.'s were actually
entertained by any Restoration poet is scarcely relevant, for the
attempt to express them would have exposed him to public
ridicule.

M. G.'s succeeding remarks preserve the close connection between poetic composition and social conduct. His materialistic

distortion of poetic values offers a parallel to the passage in the
"Heroical Epistle" where Bajazet compares the human values
of his affair with Ephelia to "changing of my Gold":

> Perhaps ill *Verses*, ought to be confin'd
> In meer good breeding like unsav'ry Wind:
> Were reading forc'd, I shou'd be apt to think,
> Men might no more write scurvily than stink:
> But 'tis your choice, whether you'll read, or no,
> If likewise of your smelling it were so.
> I'd Fart just as I write for my own ease,
> Nor shou'd you be concern'd unless you please.
> I'll own, that you write better than I do,
> But I have as much need to write as you.
> What though the ⟨excrement⟩ of my dull *Brain*,
> ⟨Runs⟩ in a ⟨costive and⟩ insipid strain;
> Whilst your rich head, eases it self of Wit,
> Must none but *Civit Cats* have leave to shit?

It is difficult to understand why the irony of this passage has gone
undetected, since M. G.'s comparison of his poetry to excrement
should appear ridiculous even to readers who lack a knowledge
of Augustan literary criteria. Previous commentators were perhaps misled by the Romantic theory of literature as self-expres-
sion, which is not unlike M. G.'s statement that his motive for
composing verses is a "need to write" for his "own ease." Whatever the cause of the misinterpretation, M. G.'s notion of poetry
as mere physical excretion contrasts ironically with the traditional
belief that poetry was a product of those higher faculties, such
as speech, reason, and a moral sense, which differentiated man
from the beasts. So exalted was this conception that the poetic
process was sometimes likened to God's act of imposing Logos
upon Chaos. The traditional view is reflected in Dryden's well-
known description of a heroic poem as "undoubtedly the greatest

Work which the Soul of Man is capable to perform." [9] Dryden's choice of the word "Soul" is specially significant.

Moreover, the ironic equation of bad writing with excrement is a familiar device of Augustan satire, serving, for example, as the basic metaphor of Book II of the *Dunciad*. Rochester's use of this device in the "Epistolary Essay" closely resembles a prose passage in Pope's *Peri Bathous* whose irony is beyond question. Pope's *persona* offers

> what seems to me an undoubted Physical Maxim, That Poetry is a *natural* or *morbid Secretion from the Brain*. As I would not suddenly stop a Cold in the Head, or dry up my Neighbour's Issue, I would as little hinder him from necessary Writing. It may be affirm'd with great truth, that there is hardly any human Creature past Childhood, but at one time or other has had some Poetical Evacuation, and no question was much the better for it in his Health . . . I have known a Man thoughtful, melancholy, and raving for divers days, but forthwith grow wonderfully easy, lightsome and cheerful, upon a Discharge of the peccant Humour, in exceeding purulent Metre. Nor can I question, but abundance of untimely Deaths are occasion'd by want of this laudable Vent of unruly Passions; yea, perhaps, in poor Wretches, (which is very lamentable) for meer Want of Pen, Ink, and Paper! [1]

M. G. continues:

> In all I write, shou'd Sense, and Wit, and Rhyme,
> Fail me at once, yet something so sublime,

9. *The Poems of John Dryden*, ed. James Kinsley (Oxford, Clarendon Press, 1958), *3*, [1003].
1. *The Art of Sinking in Poetry*, ed. Edna Leake Steeves (New York, King's Crown Press, 1952), pp. 12–13.

> Shall stamp my *Poem,* that the *World* may see,
> It cou'd have been produc'd by none but me;
> And that's my end, for *Man* can wish no more,
> Than so to write, as none e're writ before.

These lines are double-edged, and the ironic structure of the "Epistolary Essay" emphasizes the pejorative implication that M. G.'s verses are unique only in their silliness. Here again, previous commentators were probably confused by nineteenth-century assumptions: M. G.'s idiosyncrasy bears a striking likeness to Romantic worship of untrammeled individualism. In any literary period, however, M. G. would surely have appeared foolish in his eagerness to write poetry "as none e're writ before" so that "the *World* may see, / It cou'd have been produc'd by none but me." In the Augustan age especially, with its insistence that a poet conform to corporate norms such as "Sense, and Wit, and Rhyme," M. G.'s erratic way of achieving a Longinian "sublime" would have seemed an absurd violation of traditional canons of literary excellence.

The succeeding passage serves to enlarge the poem's range of values:

> ⟨But⟩ why am I no *Poet* of the times?
> I have *Allusions, Similies* and *Rhymes,*
> And *Wit,* or else 'tis hard that I alone,
> Of the whole Race of *Mankind* shou'd have none.
> Unequally the partial hand of *Heav'n,*
> Has all but this One only blessing giv'n.
> The *World* appears like a ⟨large⟩ Family,
> Whose *Lord* opprest with *Pride* and *Poverty.*
> (That to a few great ⟨plenty⟩ he may show)
> Is fain to starve the num'rous Train below.
> Just so seems *Providence,* as poor, and vain,

Keeping more Creatures than it can maintain.
Here 'tis profuse, and there it meanly saves,
And for One *Prince*, it makes Ten thousand *Slaves*.
In Wit, alone 't has been ⟨munificent⟩,
Of which so just a share to each is sent,
That the most Avaricious ⟨is⟩ content.
⟨Who ever⟩ thought (the due divisions such)
His own too little, or his *Friends* too much.
Yet most *Men* shew, or find great want of Wit
Writing themselves, or judging what is writ.

Apparently these lines are to be construed in terms of the great chain of being. The comparison of God's ordering of the universe to the duties of a paterfamilias was a commonplace, and these two hierarchies, in turn, suggest the scale of literary values which M. G. seeks to pervert, thereby relating this passage to the thematic context of the rest of the poem. In the traditional view of the chain of being, God had abundantly created all varieties of life which could conceivably exist, and each form was blessed with every ability needed to perform its allotted function (the principle of "plenitude"). But in M. G.'s dissatisfied vision of his place in the hierarchy (as in Bajazet's), Providence seems arbitrary and miserly in its gifts. M. G. could have arranged things so much better! M. G. even accuses his Creator of the *"Pride"* which he himself exhibits. It is incidentally noteworthy that Rochester's quip about the equal distribution of wit is borrowed from Descartes's *Discourse on Method*.[2]

2. In the *Discourse on Method*, the first sentence of Part I reads: "Good sense is, of all things among men, the most equally distributed; for every one thinks himself so abundantly provided with it, that those even who are the most difficult to satisfy in everything else, do not usually desire a larger measure of this quality than they already possess" (trans. John Veitch, London, J. M. Dent and Sons; New York, E. P. Dutton, 1934, p. 3). Beside the line "In Wit, alone 't has been ⟨munificent⟩," Alexander Pope wrote in his copy of B-1696, "The Thought is Taken from yᵉ first

Admitting an "Arrogance" similar to Bajazet's, M. G. next makes his most elaborate assertion of autonomy against the "musty Customes" of traditional poetic theory which society tries to impose upon him:

> But I, who am of sprightly vigour full,
> Look on *Mankind,* as envious and dull.
> Born to my self, my self I like alone,
> And must conclude my judgment good, or none.
> For ⟨should⟩ my sense be naught, how ⟨could⟩ I know,
> Whether another *Mans* ⟨be⟩ good or no?
> Thus I resolve of my own *Poetry,*
> That 'tis the best, and ⟨that's⟩ a Fame for me.
> If then I'm happy, what does it advance,
> Whither to merit due, or Arrogance?
> Oh! but the *World* will take offence ⟨thereby⟩,
> Why then the *World* ⟨will⟩ suffer for't, not I.
> Did e're this sawcy *World,* and I agree
> To let it have its beastly Will ⟨of⟩ me?
> Why shou'd my prostituted sense be drawn,
> To ev'ry Rule their musty Customes spawn?
> But *Men,* will censure you, 'tis ⟨ten⟩ to One,
> When e're they censure, they'll be in the wrong.

In the last couplet of the "Epistolary Essay," where M. G. reveals the practical consequence of his misanthropic conception of poetry, his stance dwindles to a Gulliver-like anticlimax:

> These things consider'd, make me (in despight
> Of idle Rumour) keep at home and write.

---

lines of desCartes's Method." For permission to reproduce this note by Pope and the one cited later on in the chapter, I am grateful to the Henry W. and Albert A. Berg Collection of The New York Public Library.

Though the point is not essential to the main thesis of this chapter, one of the subtler effects attained in some Augustan satires of the *Dunciad* type is that their ironic inversion of traditional values undergoes a full 360 degree rotation, so that passages taken out of context may seem to read quite straightforwardly. This phenomenon is discernible in the "Epistolary Essay" and the "Heroical Epistle." In a sense it is true, as M. G. maintains, that a poet must write "as none e're writ before," since otherwise he would lack originality. Similarly, despite the ironic qualification of Bajazet's statement that "No glorious thing, was ever made to stay," there is a residue of truth which Robert Frost formulated in almost the same words as "Nothing gold can stay." Though Bajazet is satirized in terms of traditional values, the complex of attitudes which he embodies owes a debt to the equally venerable tradition of *le libertinage,* whose roots went back some two thousand years in Western history. Moreover, both Bajazet and M. G. pose the eternal problem of individual freedom in conflict with social and universal law, to which Bajazet superadds the problem (hence a further relevance of *Tamburlaine*) of a dream of human perfection in conflict with human limitations. It would be a rare reader who had not, like Bajazet, imagined a sultanic utopia free of physical hardships and the frictions incident to one's daily dealings with other people. In much the same manner, M. G.'s concluding complaint about the injustice of public opinion has a pathetic validity:

> There's not a thing on Earth, that I can name,
> So foolish, and so false, as common Fame.
> It calls the *Courtier Knave,* the plain *Man* rude,
> Haughty the grave, and the delightful lew'd.
> Impertinent the brisk, Moross the sad,
> Mean the familiar, the reserv'd one mad.

> Poor helpless *Woman,* is not favour'd more,
> She's a sly *Hypocrite,* or publick *Whore.*
> Then who the Devil, wou'd give this—to be free
> From th' innocent reproach of infamy.

At least two of Rochester's contemporaries were so impressed with the cogency of this passage that they transcribed it out of context into their commonplace books.

IV

Once the critic's concern with the "Epistolary Essay" has received minimal attention, the scholar's task is vastly simplified. The similar satiric accusations in the "Epistolary Essay" and the "Heroical Epistle" should lead even a casual reader to suspect that M. G., like Bajazet, represents Mulgrave. To the specialist in Restoration literature, internal evidence alone—though there is some corroborating external evidence—should be enough to confirm this identification. M. G., we have seen, is satirized primarily for his arrogant self-sufficiency and for his bad poetry. Likewise, beginning about 1675, Mulgrave was attacked in numerous lampoons for his overweening conceit, especially regarding his abilities as lover and soldier, with the emphasis later shifting to include his pretensions as a poet. These lampoons are too well known to require enumeration; sufficient illustration is afforded by the "Heroical Epistle" and by another satire, "My Lord All-Pride," which is discussed elsewhere (Chapter 13). By the late 1670s, such lampoons had made Mulgrave's name virtually a synonym for pride. A Restoration reader who understood the irony of the "Epistolary Essay" could scarcely have mistaken M. G. for anyone else.

The external evidence for this identification includes the cryptic heading "An Epistolary Essay from M. G. to O. B. upon their Mutual Poems," which is found in the first edition of 1680 and appears also as part of the title in Harvard MS. Eng. 636F. The two pairs of initials have not hitherto been satisfactorily explained. Alexander Pope, in his copy of Tonson's 1696 edition of Rochester, altered them to "M. C." and "D. B." and glossed them as "Mat Clifford" and "Duke of Buckingham." As Thorpe objected, however, Pope's opinion is unreasonable. There is no other evidence that Rochester ever quarreled with Martin Clifford, who was his friend Buckingham's secretary. Thorpe conjectured instead that the initials "may have been chosen haphazardly to mystify the other wits, or they may stand for classical names as a parody on the current epistolary vogue (such as Mercurius Grammaticus to Ovidius Britannicus)" (*Rochester's Poems*, pp. 172–73). Pinto, alleging that a "pencil note" similar to Pope's inscription appears in the Bodleian copy of Tonson's edition of 1691, nevertheless adopted much the same conclusion as Thorpe (*Poems*, p. 191). Happily, Thorpe's conjectures are rendered unnecessary by the identification of Mulgrave as the poem's *persona*. One pair of initials, at any rate, is easily explained as the first letters of the two syllables of his name: *Mul-Grave.*

Other titles in early texts of the poem may afford further external evidence that M. G. is Mulgrave. Unfortunately, the exact significance of these titles, all of which suggest that the "Epistolary Essay" was addressed by Rochester to Mulgrave, remains in doubt. Examples include "To My Lord Mulgrave, from Rochester" (Harvard MS. Eng. 636F); "A Letter To My Lord Mulgrave," with the poem signed "Rochester" (Harvard MS. Eng. 623F); "A Letter from My Lord Rochester to the Earl of Mi——" (Osborn MS. Chest 11, Number 28); "An

Epistolary Essay very delightfull and solid from yᵉ Lᵈ: R: to
yᵉ Lᵈ: M: upon their mutuall Poems" (Yale MS.); "An Epistolari essay from E. R. to E. M." (Saunders's "lost" edition);
and "From E. R. to E. M." ("Portland Miscellany").[3] In light
of the foregoing discussion of the "Epistolary Essay," the apparent implication of these titles, that M. G. represents Rochester
while O. B. represents Mulgrave, can scarcely be correct. Moreover, M. G. praises O. B. as a better poet than himself, an attitude which Rochester is not likely to have adopted toward Mulgrave at any time during their relationship. Strikingly, however,
these titles all agree that the poem is directed at Mulgrave in
some way. As the only explanation which seems to make sense,
they may preserve a confused knowledge that the poem was
written by Rochester as a satire on Mulgrave.

With M. G. identified as Mulgrave, the identity of O. B. is
rather easily ascertained. Much of the necessary information is
provided by the opening lines of the "Epistolary Essay," which
have not yet been quoted:

> *Dear Friend.*
>
>   I Hear this *Town* does so abound
> With sawcy *Censurers,* that faults are found
> ⟨With⟩ what of late we (in *Poetique* rage)
> Bestowing, threw away on the dull Age;
> But (howsoe're *Envy,* their ⟨spleen⟩ may raise,
> To Rob my ⟨brow⟩ of the deserved *Bays)*
> Their thanks at least I merit, since through me,

---

3. The "Portland Miscellany" (which is a manuscript volume) should
be distinguished from the Portland MS., the collection of holographs of
Rochester and his wife which is discussed in Chapter 7. These misleading designations were introduced by Pinto (*Poems,* p. 163); I have avoided
altering them for fear of causing further confusion.

They are partakers of your *Poetry:*
And this is all I'le say in my defence,
T' obtain one Line of your well-worded sense,
I'd be content t' have writ the *Brittish Prince.*

From these and later lines of the poem, two general circumstances emerge concerning O. B. First, O. B. is a poet whom
Mulgrave would have considered better than himself, and Mulgrave's inflated estimate of his own talents, at least as charged
by Rochester and other satirists, helps to limit the number of
candidates. M. G. admits to O. B. that "you write better than
I do" and that "T' obtain one Line of your well-worded sense, /
I'd be content t' have writ the *Brittish Prince,*" i.e. Edward
Howard's *The Brittish Princes,* a byword in the Restoration for
bad poetry. M. G. also ranks his correspondent among the *"Civit
Cats"* of verse, envying the way "your rich head, eases it self
of Wit." Furthermore, though the technique of indirection used
in the "Epistolary Essay" may render its precise nuances of
tone a bit uncertain, O. B. seems to be a poet whose merits
Rochester himself would have conceded. If M. G. had lavished
extravagant encomiums on his friend, the effect would have been
derogatory, but his actual attitude of rather grudging praise does
not undergo much ironic qualification.

A second circumstance is that Mulgrave and O. B. have been
closely associated in the composition of one or more poems which
the "sawcy *Censurers*" of the town have criticized adversely.
Despite the plural word "Poems" in the title of the "Epistolary
Essay," the concentrated public fault-finding described in its
text suggests a single poem rather than several. Though the exact
nature of the collaboration between M. G. and O. B. is not quite
clear, some details can be gathered. O. B. certainly composed part

of their "Mutual" poem, for its readers are termed "partakers of your *Poetry*," and the collaboration gave M. G. at least "one Line of your well-worded sense." Apparently M. G. also contributed a share, since it was "we" whose "*Poetique* rage" resulted in "Bestowing" this poem on the public. But the public —perhaps skeptical of M. G.'s ability, though he claims the cause was "*Envy*"—determined to "Rob my brow of the deserved *Bays*," evidently by giving its meager "thanks" solely to O. B. and denying that M. G. wrote any portion of the poem. M. G.'s remark that "through me, / They are partakers of your *Poetry*" might conceivably mean that M. G. had tried to pass off the entire poem as his own composition, or even that M. G. was O. B.'s patron. Possibly both meanings should be inferred.

The information given concerning O. B. could scarcely apply to anyone other than John Dryden. To Dryden, if to no one else, Mulgrave would have accorded the status of being a better poet than himself. Dryden's superiority as a writer was also recognized by Rochester; in "An Allusion to Horace," for instance, Rochester allows the laureate approximately the same measured praise expressed in the "Epistolary Essay." About 1675, shortly before Dryden dedicated *Aureng-Zebe* to him, Mulgrave became Dryden's patron, or so the public believed. During subsequent years—certainly until Rochester's death in 1680—it was widely assumed that Dryden and Mulgrave were working as close confederates in literary matters. The initials O. B. are still not definitely explained, but an obvious guess is that they stand for "Old Bays." Bays, of course, was the common nickname for Dryden derived from *The Rehearsal*, and during his "retirement" from the stage in 1676 and 1677, if not at other times, Dryden's age seems to have been a popular joke (he was sixteen years older than Rochester). One lampoon dubbed him "That Antient grave *Wit*" and "This Reverend *Author*," while another derided his "Bed-rid Age." [4]

If M. G. and O. B. are Mulgrave and Dryden, the date at which Rochester composed the "Epistolary Essay" can be determined with some degree of confidence. Wilson, unaware of the poem's irony, concluded that Rochester addressed it to Mulgrave after May 1669, the approximate date when *The Brittish Princes* was published, and before the near-duel the following November which began the lifelong enmity between the two Earls (*Court Wits*, p. 239). Wilson's date was accepted by Pinto (*Poems*, pp. 191–92).

In view of the true purpose of the "Epistolary Essay," however, the poem was surely not in existence before 1675, when Dryden and Mulgrave seem to have formed their alliance. Moreover, it was probably not written before other references to Mulgrave's literary activities begin to crop up in contemporary lampoons several years later. Though the occasion of the "Epistolary Essay" could doubtless be established more firmly if more were known about Mulgrave's career, the circumstances specified concerning the "Mutual" poem correspond closely to those surrounding "An Essay upon Satyr," which was circulating in manuscript in November 1679. Students of Dryden now believe that "An Essay upon Satyr" was largely Mulgrave's work and that Dryden's assistance was minor, but the "*Town*" conspired to "Rob" Mulgrave of the "deserved *Bays*" by crediting most or all of this lampoon to the laureate. The description of the "Mutual" poem is not incompatible with Rochester's known

4. The two lampoons are "A Session of the Poets" ("Since the Sons of the Muses, grew num'rous, and loud"), quoted from A-1680-HU, p. 111, and "A Familiar Epistle to Mr Julian Secretary of the Muses" ("Thou Comon Shore of this Poetique Towne"), quoted from the Yale MS., p. 352.

opinion on the authorship of "An Essay upon Satyr"; on 21 November 1679, he informed his friend Henry Savile that "I have sent you herewith a Libel, in which my own share is not the least; the King having perus'd it, is no ways disatisfy'd with his: the Author is apparently Mr. [Dryden]; his Patron my [Lord Mulgrave] having a Panegerick in the midst." The *"Town"* certainly found fault with "An Essay upon Satyr," as M. G. complains it did with the "Mutual" poem, expressing its displeasure most forcibly by having Dryden cudgeled. "An Essay upon Satyr" also sparked a quarrel between Mulgrave and Lady Sophia Bulkeley. Since Rochester had a manuscript copy of Mulgrave's lampoon by 21 November, he probably composed the "Epistolary Essay" in late November or early December 1679.[5]

This conclusion supports two further inferences of differing sorts. Restoration scholars have generally assumed that Rochester retorted in some fashion to the attack on him in "An Essay upon Satyr." Though his revenge was long believed to be the beating of Dryden in Rose Alley on the night of 18 December 1679, Wilson has demonstrated the weakness of the evidence traditionally cited in favor of this theory. Instead, Wilson maintained, Rochester's answer was the counterblast at Mulgrave in "My Lord All-Pride"; but the dating of this lampoon involves difficulties suggesting that it may have been written somewhat earlier (see Chapter 13). Rochester's answer, or part of it, seems to be the "Epistolary Essay." As Wilson observed, Rochester's letter to Henry Savile (quoted in the preceding paragraph) reflects a "very mild reaction" to "An Essay upon Satyr," hardly the tone of a man who would hire a crew of ruffians to cudgel Dryden.[6] The same is true of the cool irony of the "Epistolary

5. Wilson, *Rochester-Savile Letters*, p. 73. HMC, *Ormonde*, 5, 242.
6. Wilson, "Rochester, Dryden, and the Rose-Street Affair," *Review*

Essay," which thus affords a new argument against Rochester's complicity in the Rose-Alley outrage.

In another direction, the "Epistolary Essay," as probably the last long poem we possess from Rochester's pen, helps to register the state of his poetic development near the end of his brief career. Comparison with the "Heroical Epistle" leaves the impression that the "Epistolary Essay," though written more than four years later, is the poorer of the two poems. It misses the light touch and the mock-heroic manner which are so effective in the "Heroical Epistle"; Bajazet is exquisitely ridiculous because his conceit is invincible, whereas M. G., by admitting some of his failings, is too often merely pathetic. Though almost twice the length of the "Heroical Epistle," the "Epistolary Essay" never achieves the same rich range and interconnection of themes. It offers nothing equal to the symbolic complexity of the sun and comet images or to Bajazet's brilliantly comic vision of himself as the sultan. Even its use of an interlocutor is slightly clumsy.

Irritated by the attack in "An Essay upon Satyr," Rochester apparently attempted, with less than full success, to repeat the previous triumph of the "Heroical Epistle." His partial failure suggests that by the closing phase of his life, his poetic powers may have fallen into decline or disuse. Even if he had lived longer, he might never have surpassed the literary feats of his younger years.

---

of *English Studies*, *15* (1939), 294–301; *Court Wits*, p. 118; *Rochester-Savile Letters*, p. 115.

5.

Rochester, Scroope, and Horace: A Literary Feud

I

Among the literary disputes of the Restoration to which Rochester contributed, those in which his role is best documented are his quarrels with John Sheffield, Earl of Mulgrave, and Sir Carr Scroope. Rochester's relations with Mulgrave were a major concern of the preceding chapter; the present chapter explores some central aspects of his vendetta against Scroope.

Like other quarrels in which men have spent their energies, the enmity between Scroope and Rochester had inconspicuous beginnings. So far as is known, the two men remained on moderately good terms until the winter of 1675–76. For instance, in the song he wrote for Etherege's *The Man of Mode* (acted 11 March 1675/6), Scroope gave an attractive portrayal of "the charming *Strephon*," who, like Dorimant, the hero of the play, is modeled upon Rochester.¹ About this time, however, Scroope apparently ventured some indiscreet criticisms of Rochester's poetry, to which the Earl retorted by penning three unflattering lines on the baronet. Thereafter the dispute waxed steadily in bitterness, lasting possibly until Rochester's death on 26 July 1680 (Scroope died several months later). Besides the four satires discussed in this chapter, documents relating directly to the quarrel include "The Mock Song," probably written by Rochester during the winter of 1676–77 as a burlesque of one of Scroope's lyrics; a four-line squib dated 1677 in which, as in "The Mock Song," Rochester may satirize Cary Frazier, a Court beauty whom Scroope hoped to marry; a reference to Scroope in a letter addressed by Rochester to his friend Henry Savile in October 1677; and "On Poet Ninny," an angry lampoon on Scroope possibly composed by Rochester early in 1678.² Rochester's example was followed by numerous other satirists, mostly unidentified, who poured forth their own libels on Scroope. In its most distant ramifications, the Scroope-Rochester feud, like that between Rochester and Mulgrave, is inseparable from the division of literary London during the middle 1670s into two broad factions, one led by Rochester and the other by Dryden. Scroope inevitably gravitated into Dryden's orbit.

The heart of the Rochester-Scroope dispute is a series of four satires, written between late 1675 and early 1677, which were gathered into a "linked group" in the order of their composition. After circulating widely in manuscript, this group finally reached print in 1680 in the first edition of Rochester's poems, the Hun-

1. *The Dramatic Works of Sir George Etherege,* ed. H. F. B. Brett-Smith (Oxford, Basil Blackwell, 1927), 2, 276, 323. In this chapter, all dates of dramatic performances and publication of plays are taken from Nicoll, *Restoration Drama.*

2. "The Mock Song" and the four-line squib are discussed in Chapter 8. Rochester's letter is printed in Wilson, *Rochester-Savile Letters,* p. 46. "On Poet Ninny" is discussed in Chapter 13.

tington edition (A-1680-HU).[3] Rochester began the quarrel with
(1) "An Allusion to Horace. The 10th Satyr of the 1st. Book"
("Well Sir, 'tis granted, I said D—— Rhimes"), which is aimed
primarily at Dryden but contains the Earl's initial three lines
on Scroope. Scroope answered with a somewhat longer passage
on Rochester in (2) "In defence of Satyr" ("When Shakes.
Johns. Fletcher, rul'd the Stage"), also an imitation of Horace.
Rochester retaliated with (3) "On the suppos'd Authour of a
late Poem in defence of Satyr" ("To rack, and torture thy unmeaning Brain"), a withering personal attack on Scroope. In
(4) "The Answer" ("Raile on poore feeble Scribler, speak of
me"), Scroope blandly dismissed his tormentor and implied that
he would take no further part in the controversy. Apparently
he was as good as his word, for he is not known to have written
any other satires on Rochester.

Students of Restoration literature have generally agreed that
the first and third satires of the linked group are by Rochester
and the second and fourth by Scroope, even though some early
sources assign "In defence of Satyr" and "The Answer" to
Rochester, while others ascribe "In defence of Satyr" to Buckingham or to Buckingham and Rochester in collaboration. The
traditional ascriptions were adopted by J. Woodfall Ebsworth,
John Hayward, Johannes Prinz, Quilter Johns, John Harold
Wilson, and James Thorpe.[4] Several of these scholars were quite
positive in their opinions, especially regarding the first and second
poems. Thorpe said of "In defence of Satyr" that "there seems
to be no real question about Scroope's authorship" (*Rochester's
Poems*, p. 175). Earlier, Prinz denied that Buckingham had
"anything to do with this satire" and asserted further that "no

---

3. The titles and texts used in this chapter for the four-poem linked
group are those in Thorpe, *Rochester's Poems*, pp. 40–50.
4. See Part III for documentation of the previous scholarship on the
four poems belonging to the linked group.

greater blunder could, in fact, be made than believing [Rochester] to be part author" of the poem. "The supposition of Rochester's collaboration," he added, is "preposterous" (*Rochester*, pp. 97–98).

Preposterous or not, such conclusions are advocated by Rochester's most recent editor, Vivian de Sola Pinto. Though he does not question Rochester's authorship of "An Allusion to Horace," Pinto doubts that Scroope wrote any of the four satires, considers the authorship of the last three uncertain, and favors the view that "In defence of Satyr" was a collaboration by Buckingham and Rochester. Whether other students of the Restoration will accept Pinto's contentions remains to be seen. At the very least, however, this challenge to the traditional interpretation suggests that earlier scholars, by not investigating the matter thoroughly, left themselves needlessly vulnerable to Pinto's line of argument. The evidence in the case should therefore be examined to determine whether Pinto's unique position is defensible against the majority opinion.

II

Remarking disarmingly that the second, third, and fourth poems (which he terms a "flyting") present "difficult problems to the editor," Pinto argues his case in a single paragraph more than two pages long (*Poems*, pp. 223–25). For convenience in discussion, the evidence, arguments, and conclusions offered in this paragraph may be rearranged under nine heads. Pinto makes the following claims:

(1) Though a passage in "In defence of Satyr" is traditionally thought to refer to Rochester's part in a fatal brawl at Epsom in June 1676, there were many other street fights during the

reign of Charles II, and the poem may allude to one of these instead.

(2) Since the Epsom affair was often cited to Rochester's disadvantage by his enemies, "some collector of Rochesteriana like the editor of 1680," jumping to the conclusion that "In defence of Satyr" referred to this episode, may then have ascribed the poem to Scroope because Scroope had been attacked in "An Allusion to Horace" and might be expected to reply.

(3) It would be "strange" for Scroope to answer the attack in "An Allusion to Horace" with a "defence of satire" (rather than, presumably, a defence of Scroope).

(4) In a manuscript copy of "In defence of Satyr" in the Folger Library, the name "Rochester" is written in the margin beside line 46, "obviously in the belief that the poem is Rochester's." A similar marginal notation identifies the person satirized in line 25 (a mistake for line 35) as "Scroop."

(5) There was a "tradition" that Rochester wrote "In defence of Satyr," as witness the Folger manuscript and attributions to Rochester by Thomas Pope Blount and Giles Jacob.

(6) "In defence of Satyr" is "very much in Rochester's manner and contains a number of phrases used by him in his authentic poems." In lines 22–27 especially, the "thought and movement of the verse" strike Pinto as "characteristic of Rochester."

(7) Since "In defence of Satyr" is ascribed to Buckingham in his *Works* of 1715 (a mistake for 1704 or 1707), the poem may be "an anonymous lampoon written by Rochester possibly in collaboration with Buckingham."

(8) The "collector of Rochesteriana like the editor of 1680" who attributed "In defence of Satyr" to Scroope may then have gone on to compose both "On the suppos'd Authour" and "The Answer," which Pinto thinks are "two pieces of doggerel."

(9) Rochester, "with his love of impersonations and disguises," may have written all of the poems himself.

Since much of Pinto's case hinges upon the passage in "In defence of Satyr" which is usually thought to satirize Rochester, we may begin by examining these lines carefully. They read in full:

> But why am I this *Bug bear* to ye all?
> My *Pen* is dipt in no such bitter Gall.
> He that can rail at one he calls his *Friend,*
> Or hear him absent wrong'd, and not defend;
> Who for the sake of some ill natur'd Jeast,
> Tells what he shou'd conceal, Invents the rest;
> To fatal *Mid-night* ⟨frolics⟩,[5] can betray,
> His brave *Companion,* and then run away;
> Leaving him to be murder'd in the *Street,*
> Then put it off, with some *Buffoone* Conceit;
> This, this is he, you shou'd beware of all,
> Yet him a pleasant, witty *Man,* you call
> To whet your dull Debauches up, and down,
> You seek him as top *Fidler* of the *Town.*

The seventh through the tenth lines of this passage are traditionally supposed to refer to an incident which occurred at Epsom on the night of Saturday, 17 June 1676, or very early the following morning. As nearly as the story can be reconstructed from contemporary accounts,[6] a crew of gentlemen-rakes, in-

---

5. "Frolics" is the reading of all early texts except the Yale MS., A-1680-HU, and texts descended from A-1680-HU. The Yale MS. and A-1680-HU read "quarrels."

6. HMC, *Seventh Report,* p. 467. *Correspondence of the Family of Hatton,* ed. Edward Maunde Thompson (Westminster, Camden Society, 1878), *1,* 133–34. *Selections from the Correspondence of Arthur Capel Earl of Essex,* ed. Clement Edwards Pike (London, Royal Historical Society, 1913), pp. 59, 61.

cluding Rochester, Etherege, George Bridges, a certain Captain
Downs, and possibly William Jephson, were amusing themselves
by tossing in a blanket some fiddlers who refused to play for
them.[7] A barber, hearing the noise, came to investigate, whereupon the revellers seized him instead. To escape a blanketting,
he cannily offered to show them the house of the handsomest
woman in town—which, unknown to them, was actually the
house of the constable. Learning that the rakes wanted a whore,
the constable understandably declined to admit them. They broke
down the doors and proceeded to beat him severely, but he
escaped at last and returned in short order with the watch.

Probably outnumbered by now, the rioters sobered up tem-
porarily and Etherege made a speech promising an end to the
disturbance. The watch had begun to disperse when Rochester,
prompted by some mysterious impulse, suddenly drew his sword
upon the constable. Downs grabbed hold of Rochester to prevent
his pass, the constable shouted "Murder!" and the watch came
running back. Misinterpreting the situation, one of the watch
dashed behind Downs and gave him a crashing blow on the head.
As the other gentlemen fled, Downs vainly defended himself
with a stick until he was run through the side with a half-pike.
Nine or ten days later he died of his wounds. Amid talk of bring-
ing Rochester to trial, Rochester, Etherege, and Bridges went
into hiding, but nothing further came of the matter.

7. Dryden may allude to this part of the Epsom brawl in l. 42 of *Mac
Flecknoe*, "The like was ne'er in *Epsom* Blankets tost," which occurs in a
context describing Shadwell's lute-playing. *Mac Flecknoe* was written soon
after the Epsom affair, and Dryden had reason to keep close track of
Rochester's activities, since he had just been attacked in "An Allusion to
Horace" and was doubtless meditating the retort he afterward made in the
preface to *All for Love* (pub. March 1678).

Dryden's editors have assumed that "*Epsom* Blankets" refers to the title
of Shadwell's *Epsom-Wells* (acted 2 Dec. 1672) and to the blanket-tossing
inflicted upon Sir Samuel Hearty in *The Virtuoso* (acted 25 May 1676).
This explanation is less than satisfactory, however, for *Epsom-Wells* con-

Leaving the external evidence aside for a moment, even the internal evidence does not bear out Pinto's contention that the four lines in "In defence of Satyr" could refer to any number of Restoration street brawls. The poem is more specific. The person satirized has participated late at night in a "frolic" like the one at Epsom, not in some other type of public disturbance; in this "frolic" he was somehow responsible for the death of a "brave *Companion*," just as Rochester was indirectly responsible for Downs's death; and, as in the Epsom affair, he fled *before* the death of his companion, who was subsequently "murder'd in the *Street*." Further details in the passage as a whole point to Rochester. The *"Buffoone* Conceit" by which the subject "put off" his guilt in the "frolic" appears to be Rochester's poem "To the Post Boy," one couplet of which glances at the Epsom brawl:

> frighted at my own mischeifes I have fled
> and bravely left my lifes defender dead.[8]

The line "He that can rail at one he calls his *Friend*" may refer to Rochester's attack on Scroope in "An Allusion to Horace," prior to which there is no record of a quarrel between the two men. Also, there is abundant contemporary testimony that Rochester was considered a "pleasant, witty *Man*" and was much sought-after by King Charles's courtiers to "whet" their "Debauches"; as the wittiest of the Wits, he was certainly rated "top *Fidler* of the *Town*."

Attention may next be directed to Pinto's statement that in a manuscript copy of "In defence of Satyr" in the Folger Library (no shelfmark is specified), the name "Rochester" is written beside line 46 "obviously in the belief that the poem is Rochester's." Presumably Folger MS. 789.4 is meant. Examination

---

tains no reference to tossing in a blanket, nor is there any reason why the implements of Sir Samuel's humiliation should be called "Epsom" blankets.

8. B. M. Harl. MS. 6914, fol. 21ᵛ. "To the Post Boy" is discussed in Chapter 6.

of this manuscript does not, however, support the claim made for it. Pinto gives no reason why an ascription should appear at line 46, rather than at the beginning or end of the poem according to the usual Restoration practice. Nor does he explain why the name "Rochester" beside line 46 should constitute an ascription, whereas the name "Scroop" similarly written beside line 35 merely designates the subject of that line. Actually, "Rochester" and "Scroop" are two out of fourteen marginal glosses in the Folger text which conjecturally identify the persons satirized.[9] Line 46 (as Pinto does not directly state) is the first line of the passage previously quoted from "In defence of Satyr": the marginal notation signifies, not that Rochester composed the poem, but that he is satirized in this passage.

If Pinto doubts that the passage refers to the Epsom affair, Rochester's contemporaries seemingly felt no such reservations. In addition to the marginal gloss in the Folger manuscript, the subject of the passage is identified as "Earle of Rochester" in the text in Harvard MS. Eng. 623F, as "Ld Roch." in Harvard MS. Eng. 636F, as "L^d: Rochester" in Osborn MS. Chest ii, Number 14, and, according to Pinto himself, as "Rochester" in the so-called "Portland Miscellany" (*Poems*, p. 226). Similarly, in Anthony Wood's *Fasti Oxonienses* (4, 294), an entry added in the posthumous second edition, 1721, but derived from a manuscript specifies that "In defence of Satyr" contains reflections on Rochester. The "brave *Companion*" is identified as "Captain Downes" in Harvard MS. Eng. 623F, as "Cap^{tt}. Downes" in Harvard MS. Eng. 636F, and as "Col. *Downs*" in Jacob Tonson's edition of 1714 (B-1714), while the Osborn manuscript supplies the gloss "Capt: Downs Killd:." (Editions of the *Works* of Rochester, Roscommon, Dorset, etc. from 1718

9. The notation "Scroop" does, of course, imply that the scribe did not know Scroope might have written the poem. The Folger text carries no ascription.

on include the note "Colonel *Downes*," but it may derive from Tonson's edition.) Also, the Osborn manuscript locates the "frolic" at "Epsome." No early source suggests that "In defence of Satyr" might allude to any other street brawl. Thus the evidence indicates that the passage satirizes Rochester for his part in the Epsom affair and, as a consequence, that he can scarcely have written the poem.

For the same reason, Pinto's suggestion that the Duke of Buckingham had a hand in writing "In defence of Satyr" does not carry conviction. Buckingham and Rochester were close friends at the approximate time when the poem was composed. In 1677, when Buckingham and three other leaders of the Country party were sent to the Tower for insisting that Parliament had been automatically dissolved, Rochester and the Duke were frequently together. Rochester appears, indeed, to have been instrumental in securing Buckingham's release and restoring him to the good graces of King Charles. Andrew Marvell recorded on 7 August 1677 that when Buckingham petitioned for temporary freedom on grounds of illness, "this was by Nelly, Midlesex, Rochester, and the merry gang easily procured with presumption to make it an intire liberty. Hereupon he layd constantly in Whitehall at my L: Rochester's logings leading the usuall life." Another contemporary, writing on 2 August, reported that Buckingham and the King "were very merry one night at Lord Rochester's lodgings." In October and November, Buckingham was Rochester's guest at a convivial gathering at Woodstock. Several letters from Buckingham to Rochester, mostly written in 1677, bear further witness to the Duke's friendship.[1] Unless Buckingham's attitude toward Rochester

1. *The Poems and Letters of Andrew Marvell*, ed. H. M. Margoliouth (Oxford, Clarendon Press, 1927), 2, 329. HMC, *Seventh Report*, p. 469; *Le Fleming*, p. 141. Prinz, *Rochester*, pp. 276–81.

changed radically between the summer of 1676 and the spring of 1677—there is no evidence that it did—he can hardly have written part or all of "In defence of Satyr."

The origin of the questionable ascription to Buckingham is suggested by textual evidence which Pinto does not consider.[2] The poem was first printed under the Duke's name in his *Miscellaneous Works,* 1704 (reprinted 1707), where it is headed "A Satyr upon the Follys of the Men of the Age." Not only is this edition generally untrustworthy, but its text was apparently printed from one of the Rochester editions of 1680, where the poem is, of course, assigned to the Earl; in a statement that is true but ironical under these circumstances, the heading in 1704 describes the poem as "Ascrib'd falsly to the Earl of R." Nothing about the 1704 version indicates that it offers any reliable testimony independent of its textual source. Evidently John Nutt, the publisher of the *Miscellaneous Works,* raided the earlier Rochester edition to pad out his rather small selection of Buckingham's poems; the same source supplied him with Rochester's "Timon" and the anonymous "A Session of the Poets," which he likewise assigned wrongly to Buckingham. A single manuscript text ascribing "In defence of Satyr" to Buckingham, in Bodl. MS. Rawl. Poet. 173, was copied from the 1704 or 1707 *Miscellaneous Works* and therefore furnishes no additional evidence.

From his *Miscellaneous Works,* 1704 or 1707, "In defence of Satyr" was reprinted in Buckingham's *Works* of 1715, where it is assigned to both Buckingham and Rochester. Again there is no reason to suppose that the ascription embodies any reliable information independent of earlier printed sources. Probably the publisher of the 1715 *Works,* Samuel Briscoe, adopted the

2. See Part III for a more detailed list of the early texts and ascriptions of the four poems belonging to the linked group.

clumsy premise of joint authorship to resolve the conflicting attributions he found in earlier editions. He used the same dual ascription for "Timon" and "A Session of the Poets," also reprinted from the *Miscellaneous Works,* and even for Rochester's "Upon Nothing," though he evidently printed it from a manuscript. Later texts in Buckingham's works, which assign "In defence of Satyr" either to Buckingham and Rochester or to Buckingham alone, seem to derive from the collections of 1704, 1707, or 1715. Horace Walpole, attributing the lampoon to Buckingham and Rochester, cites the 1715 *Works* as his source. There is no further evidence that Buckingham collaborated in the writing of "In defence of Satyr."

More complex questions are raised by Pinto's theory that "some collector of Rochesteriana like the editor of 1680" not only was responsible for first ascribing "In defence of Satyr" to Scroope [3] but even composed "On the suppos'd Authour" and "The Answer" himself. It is difficult to understand how "the editor of 1680" (whoever that may be) could have done either of these things. Initially one is disposed to inquire of Pinto why, if this person believed "In defence of Satyr" was Scroope's, he should print it as Rochester's—or, since the poem is attributed to Rochester in the Huntington edition, how Pinto can know that the "editor" thought Scroope wrote it. More important, at some period antedating its publication in the Huntington edition, the entire four-poem linked group was already circulating in manuscript versions which assigned the first and third poems to Rochester and the second and fourth to Scroope. Only after this interval of circulation was the group taken into the archetype

3. As one of the reasons why this "editor" would ascribe "In defence of Satyr" to Scroope, Pinto alleges that Scroope already "was known to have written lampoons." I am not aware of any such lampoons, nor does Pinto cite any.

of the Yale MS. and the Huntington edition, after which it was finally printed in the Huntington volume with no more than rudimentary "editing."

Pinto's phrase "some collector of Rochesteriana like the editor of 1680" might, to be sure, mean merely an unknown person possessing unspecified resemblances to this unidentified "editor." The point scarcely deserves further notice until Pinto supplies details concerning his ghostly "collector of Rochesteriana."

Additional points require a recognition that the attributions in the Huntington edition, which assigns all four poems of the linked group to Rochester, are without value unless interpreted in light of the ascriptions in the Yale MS. and the arrangement of the collection as a whole (see Chapter 3). From the Huntington edition, the group was reprinted under Rochester's name in the other 1680 editions and the later editions of 1685 (A-1685), 1701 (A-1701), 1713 (A-1713), and 1731 (A-1731). Further ascriptions of "In defence of Satyr" to Rochester must be suspected of derivation from these editions, especially in view of the strong internal evidence against his authorship. The text in Bodl. MS. Add. B. 106 (not mentioned by Pinto), which carries an ascription to Rochester, was probably copied from one of the 1680 editions, as were other texts in this manuscript. The text in Bodl. MS. Rawl. Poet. 172 (also not mentioned by Pinto) gives near the end of the poem a marginal notation which seems to be "Satyre by E. Rochr"; though the text itself was not copied from a printed source, the ascription appears in another hand, or the same hand at a later date, and it may therefore derive from one of the Rochester editions.

Turning now to Pinto's "tradition" that Rochester wrote "In defence of Satyr," one of his three examples, the alleged ascription in Folger MS. 789.4, has already been disqualified, leaving

only the attributions in Thomas Pope Blount's *De Re Poetica*,
1694 and Giles Jacob's *Poetical Register*, 1720. Pinto's "tradition" might be augmented by noting that the first forty-five lines
of the poem are quoted and assigned to Rochester in William
Winstanley's *Lives Of the most Famous English Poets*, 1687.
As with other such ascriptions after 1680, however, we cannot
assume that the testimony of Winstanley and Blount is independent of printed sources. Winstanley's quotation from the
poem provides no reliable evidence of independent derivation,
while Blount's thirteen lines of text are verbally identical with
the readings of most of the Rochester editions.

Furthermore, Pinto's statement about Jacob's ascription, like
his claim concerning the Folger manuscript, does not survive
scrutiny. In Jacob's list of Rochester's poems, the eleventh item
reads as follows (*Poetical Register*, 2, 232–33):

> *A Defence of Satire.* This Poem begins,
>   *When* Shakespear, Johnson, Fletcher *rul'd the Stage,*
>   *They took so bold a Freedom with the Age,*
>   *That there was scarce a Knave or Fool in Town*
>   *Of any Note, but had his Picture shown.*

And in his Answer to the Defence of Satire, written by Sir *C. S.*
he has these Lines:

> *Satire is of Divine Authority,*
> *For God made one of Man, when he made Thee.*

Though this listing is somewhat ambiguous, Jacob never states
very directly that Rochester wrote "In defence of Satyr," while
the latter part of his note implies that Scroope was the author.
The exact interpretation is immaterial, however, since Jacob's

list, as shown by the poems he includes and by the forms of his titles,[4] almost certainly derives from the 1714 *Works* of Rochester, Roscommon, Dorset, etc. (C-1714-1). In turn, the text of "In defence of Satyr" in the 1714 *Works* (which also assigns to Rochester "An Answer to the Defence of Satire, written by Sir C. Scroop") was certainly printed from one of the Rochester editions of 1680. Later editions of the collection of 1714 (e.g. 1718, 1721, 1731, 1735, 1739) attribute "In defence of Satyr" to Scroope.

Pinto's remaining two arguments require little comment. It is scarcely "strange" for Scroope to have answered "An Allusion to Horace" with a "defence of satire," for both poems belong to that peculiarly Augustan genre known as "imitation," and both are based on satires by Horace. Rochester originally attacked Scroope in an imitation of *Satires*, 1.10. Scroope retorted in kind by attacking Rochester in an imitation based primarily on *Satires*, 1.4, but probably borrowing some hints from 2.1.

Finally, Pinto alleges that "In defence of Satyr" is "very much in Rochester's manner and contains a number of phrases used by him in his authentic poems"—phrases which Pinto does not specify. Such an argument is difficult to confirm or deny, as is Pinto's similar claim that "On the suppos'd Authour" and "The Answer" are merely "two pieces of doggerel." Even if "In defence of Satyr" did resemble Rochester's style, however, this would not necessarily mean that he wrote it, for the style of a popular poet often influences lesser talents. In 1676 John Oldham was busily learning the craft of verse from Rochester's example; Scroope might have been doing likewise.

4. Also, in the second line which Jacob quotes from "On the suppos'd Authour," the reading "of Man" (rather than "on Man") is a variant characteristic of Rochester editions in the C series.

In summary, Pinto offers little real evidence to support his opinions against the traditional interpretation or against the data to be assembled in favor of that interpretation.

III

A survey of the remaining evidence in the case leaves little doubt that the four satires discussed in this chapter circulated in manuscript as a linked group, that they were composed as part of a literary quarrel in the order they occupy in the group, and that the two antagonists in this quarrel were Rochester and Scroope.

The existence of a linked group is attested by early texts of the four satires. All four appear together and in order in Harvard MS. Eng. 623F, Harvard MS. Eng. 636F, the Yale MS., and the Huntington edition; [5] moreover, the presence of the group in these last two texts implies that it occurred in the lost archetype from which the Huntington edition and the Yale MS. are descended. In Edinburgh MS. DC.1.3, which omits the first poem of the group, the last three poems are found together and in order. In Osborn MS. Chest 11, Number 14, all four poems appear in order, but only the last two are together; thus the first three poems may not represent a bibliographical linkage in this text, even though the copyist inserted cross-references showing that he understood the relationship of their contents. Two other apparent vestiges of the linked group are probably illusory. In B. M. Add. MS 34362, the appearance of the first two poems together but in reverse order may be fortuitous. The first three poems were printed together and in order in Tonson's edition of 1714, but since their texts derive from a variety of sources,

5. The linked group may also be preserved in the "Portland Miscellany," since Pinto reports that all four poems appear there (*Poems*, pp. 192, 223). Such a conclusion must remain conjectural, however, until this manuscript is released for proper analysis.

their presence in this volume probably has no bibliographical connection with manuscript examples of the group.

Evidence of a different sort suggests that the four satires constitute a series in which each poem answers the one preceding it. Even Pinto does not deny that this is true of the last three poems. Without exception, every early source which mentions the third poem indicates that it satirizes the author of "In defence of Satyr," while in the poem itself the first few lines turn on the idea that its subject has written "in *Satyrs* praise." Also without exception, every early text of the fourth poem states that it answers the third, and internal evidence is compatible with this conclusion. As for "In defence of Satyr," the heading in Osborn MS. Chest II, Number 14 notes that "The occasion off Sʳ Car Scroops writing this ensuing poem, was upon a satyr off the Lord Rochesters against the poetts, in which he abuses him," and there follows a cross-reference to "An Allusion to Horace," where the relevant three-line passage is glossed "Sʳ Car: Scroop." Similarly, the heading in Tonson's edition of 1714 explains that "The following Verses were written by Sir Car. Scrope, on his being reflected upon at the latter End of the foregoing Copy," that is, "An Allusion to Horace." This evidence of the circumstances under which the four satires were composed is, of course, reinforced by their existence as a linked group.

All surviving examples of the linked group provide evidence that the first and third satires are by Rochester and the second and fourth are by Scroope, or at least by some author other than Rochester. Harvard MS. Eng. 623F ascribes the first and third poems to Rochester and the second and fourth to Scroope. Harvard MS. Eng. 636F explicitly assigns the first and third poems to Rochester and the fourth to Scroope, while the context implies that the author of the fourth poem wrote the second. The same situation is found in Edinburgh MS. DC.1.3 except that the first poem is lacking. Osborn MS. Chest II, Number 14 explicitly assigns the first three poems to Rochester, Scroope, and Rochester respectively, with the context indicating that the second and fourth poems were written by one person. Though the Yale MS. gives no direct ascriptions and the Huntington edition attributes all four satires to Rochester, the position of the linked group in the section of poems by or concerning Rochester, together with the evident circumstance that this group preserves a literary quarrel, implies that two poems are his and two are by another author. As the ascriptions in other early texts suggest, the scribe of the archetype must have believed that Rochester composed the first and third poems.

Detailed discussion of Rochester's authorship of "An Allusion to Horace" is unnecessary, since Pinto does not question its authenticity and the evidence listed in Part III is conclusive. On "The Answer" there is no further evidence: no texts apart from the linked group are known to exist, and the poem is not mentioned elsewhere.

Several other independently derived sources attribute "In defence of Satyr" to Scroope and "On the suppos'd Authour" to Rochester. "On the suppos'd Authour" was printed from a manuscript and ascribed to Rochester in *A Collection of Poems by Several Hands*, 1693, from which it was reprinted with the same ascription in later editions of this miscellany. It was again printed as Rochester's from a manuscript source in Benjamin Bragge's *Miscellaneous Works* of Rochester and Roscommon, 1707 (C-1707-a), from which it was reprinted in later editions in this series. Though the heading in 1707, "An Answer to the Defence of Satyr Written by Sir C. Scroop," is possibly equivocal, the omission of "In defence of Satyr" from this volume must mean that the "defence" is here attributed to Scroope, and "On the suppos'd Authour" to Rochester. This is the earliest printed source which assigns "In defence of Satyr" to Scroope.

"In defence of Satyr" was also printed as Scroope's in Tonson's edition of 1714, where its text derives partially from a manuscript even though some bowdlerized readings were introduced from the Rochester editions of 1685, 1701, or 1713. The heading in this text, quoted earlier, supplies information which had not previously appeared in print but is roughly duplicated in Osborn MS. Chest 11, Number 14. Strangely, in view of his stand on the authorship of the poem, Pinto reports that a manuscript text in the "Portland Miscellany" assigns "In defence of Satyr" to Scroope.

Independent ascriptions for both poems are provided by Anthony Wood's *Athenae Oxonienses* and *Fasti Oxonienses* in passages that were added, apparently from a manuscript source, in the posthumous second edition, 1721. *Fasti Oxonienses*, assigning "In defence of Satyr" to Scroope, cites a "MS. in Mr. *Sheldon*'s Libr." and appends a catalogue of persons satirized in the poem which resembles the marginal glosses in several surviving manuscript versions. *Athenae Oxonienses* lists, as the second of two unpublished satires by Rochester, "on the supposed Author of a late Poem in Defence of Satyr, with his (*Rochester's*) Answer." This listing is slightly ambiguous, for it could conceivably mean either that "On the suppos'd Authour" was answered by Rochester or that it constitutes his answer to "In defence of Satyr." The latter interpretation is doubtless correct, especially since the *Fasti* attributes "In defence of Satyr" to Scroope. The fact that *Athenae Oxonienses* wrongly describes "On the suppos'd Authour" as unpublished is an added guarantee that its ascription to Rochester is independent of earlier printed attributions. Since the other "unpublished" satire by Rochester is said to occur in a manuscript "in Mr. *Sheldon*'s Library"—perhaps the same one cited in the *Fasti*—the ascription for "On the suppos'd Authour" may also have come from this source.[6]

The discussion in the preceding paragraphs is reducible to a few statistics. Evidence that Rochester wrote "On the suppos'd Authour" is provided by nine independently derived sources. Evidence of Scroope's authorship, or at least of some authorship other than Rochester's, is supplied by ten such sources for "In defence of Satyr" and six for "The Answer." Moreover, these ascriptions reinforce each other and are further reinforced by the many ascriptions for "An Allusion to Horace" as well as by the internal evidence presented in the second section of this chapter. In the absence of reliable testimony to the contrary— none is now available or seems likely to appear—the traditional view of the authorship of the four satires can be accepted with confidence.

IV

Because of their central importance in the development of Restoration satire, it is important to determine exactly when each of the four poems was composed. Earlier studies have established the dates of the first two poems as precisely as the evidence warrants, but the last two have not heretofore been fully investigated.

External evidence affords little help. A note in B. M. Sloane MS. 1504 indicates that "An Allusion to Horace" was in existence on 8 October 1679, and the poem must have been written before Dryden answered it in his preface to *All for Love*, published in

6. The quotations from *Athenae Oxonienses* and *Fasti Oxonienses* are taken from the 2d ed., 1721, 2, 657, 167. In the Bliss edition they appear at 3, 1232 and 4, 294.

late March 1678. Osborn MS. Chest II, Number 14 assigns the first three poems of the group to 1677, but such manuscript dates frequently err by a year in either direction, and sometimes as much as two years. Internal evidence shows that these particular dates are only approximate.

The internal evidence is complicated by Pinto, who assumes that "An Allusion to Horace" was written in spring of 1675 because it twice refers to "Buckhurst" (*Poems,* pp. 192, 194). Charles Sackville, Lord Buckhurst, became Earl of Middlesex on 4 April 1675, after which he would normally have been called by his new title (Harris, *Dorset,* p. 62). Unfortunately, Pinto overlooks a fact which Wilson had previously pointed out: the poem also refers to Otway's plays, the first of which was not produced until the following September. Aside from the possible metrical disadvantages of "Middlesex," Rochester may have preferred "Buckhurst" because it had been his friend's title for almost twenty-three years and was long familiar to the Restoration audience.

The date of "An Allusion to Horace" was established by Wilson in an article published in 1939.[7] Basing his argument on Rochester's references to plays by Lee and Otway, Wilson located the composition of the poem during the winter of 1675–76. Lee is noticed as follows:

> When *Lee,* makes temp'rate *Scipio,* fret, and rave
> And *Hannibal,* a whining Amorous *Slave,*
> I laugh, and wish the hot-brain'd *Fustian Fool,*
> In B⟨usby's⟩ hands, to be well lasht at *School.*

This passage refers to Lee's *Sophonisba* (acted 30 April 1675), in which Scipio and Hannibal are major characters. It does not,

7. John Harold Wilson, "Rochester, Dryden, and the Rose-Street Affair," *Review of English Studies, 15* (1939), 294–301.

however, allude to his *Gloriana* (acted 29 Jan. 1675/6) or to his popular *The Rival Queens* (acted 17 March 1676/7), which Rochester might well have mentioned if he had known of their existence. The passage on Otway narrows the limiting dates still more:

> Though ev'n that *Talent,* merits in some sort,
> That can divert the *Rabble,* and the *Court.*
> Which blundring S⟨*ettle*⟩, never cou'd attain,
> And puzling O⟨*tway*⟩, labors at in vain.

These lines must refer to Otway's clumsy first play, *Alcibiades* (acted 22 Sept. 1675), not to his highly successful second effort, *Don Carlos* (acted 8 June 1676). Moreover, by the date of *Don Carlos,* Rochester had revised his previous low estimate of the dramatist's merits. According to Otway's preface, Rochester recommended this play to the King and the Duke of York before its first performance, thereby assuring its success on the stage.[8] "An Allusion to Horace" must therefore belong to the last few months of 1675 or the first few weeks of 1676.

Possibly relevant to the date of "An Allusion to Horace" is Rochester's notorious "Black Will" letter, which Wilson assigned to April 1676. Writing to Henry Savile, Rochester acknowledges a report that Dryden is angry with him:

> You write me word, That I'm out of favour with a certain Poet, whom I have ever admir'd for the disproportion of him and his Attributes: He is a Rarity which I cannot but be fond of, as one would be of a Hog that could fiddle, or a singing Owl. If he falls upon me at the Blunt, which is

---

8. *The Works of Thomas Otway,* ed. J. C. Ghosh (Oxford, Clarendon Press, 1932), *1,* 174.

his very good Weapon in Wit, I will forgive him, if you please, and leave the Repartee to Black Will, with a Cudgel.[9]

Dryden's vexation, as Wilson concluded, was probably caused by Rochester's irritatingly effective attack a short time earlier in "An Allusion to Horace." Also, Rochester in this letter seems to expect the verbal revenge which Dryden afterward administered in the preface to *All for Love*. Two parallels between the letter and the poem further suggest a connection between them. Rochester's phrasing in the letter, "If he falls upon me at the Blunt, which is his very good Weapon in Wit," resembles his description of Dryden's wit in the poem:

> D⟨*ryden*⟩, in vain try'd this nice way of wit,
> For he to be a tearing *Blade*, thought fit,
> But when he wou'd be sharp; he still was blunt,
> To frisk his frollique fancy, he'd cry C——t.

More generally, both the poem and the letter find Dryden contemptible as a person while allowing him grudging praise as a writer.

"In defence of Satyr" was certainly composed after the brawl at Epsom on 17 June 1676, and probably after the death of Downs on 27 June, since it describes the brawl as "fatal." Probably, too, it was written after Rochester had mentioned the Epsom affair in "To the Post Boy," for Scroope apparently alludes to this poem as Rochester's *"Buffoone* Conceit." A *terminus ante quem* is more difficult to establish. Restoration quarrels sometimes dragged on at a lethargic pace which is almost incomprehensible in the twentieth century; Dryden, for example,

---

9. Wilson, *Rochester-Savile Letters*, p. 41; "Rochester, Dryden, and the Rose-Street Affair." Wilson's dating of this letter is based on other evidence besides its apparent relationship to "An Allusion to Horace."

waited two years before answering "An Allusion to Horace." If Scroope delayed his reply very long, however, his reference to the Epsom affair would lose much of its point. Summer of 1676 seems the most likely date for his poem.[1]

Lack of a firm *terminus ante quem* for "In defence of Satyr" poses double difficulties in dating "On the suppos'd Authour" and "The Answer." Since neither poem would have cost much time to compose, dates later than the end of 1676 seem scarcely plausible. Also, "On the suppos'd Authour" assumes a recent awareness that Scroope had written "In defence of Satyr." Scroope might easily have dashed off his six-line "Answer" in less than an hour, and the circumstance that all known texts occur in combination with "On the suppos'd Authour" argues that he replied very quickly.

In the absence of better data, help is afforded by some apparent echoes of these two satires, and also of Scroope's "Song" beginning "I cannot change as others do," in "A Familiar Epistle to Mr Julian Secretary of the Muses" ("Thou Comon Shore of this Poetique Towne").[2] Since this poem, which is a long satire on Scroope possibly written by Buckingham, can be dated spring or summer of 1677 (see Chapter 13), it may provide a needed *terminus ante quem* for "On the suppos'd Authour" and "The Answer." Initially, of course, there is the question of direction of influence. On the face of the matter, it is more likely that the epistle to Julian would allude to the other three poems than that each of them should borrow independently from the epistle. Also, the assumption that "On the suppos'd Authour" and "The An-

1. In the text of this poem in Folger MS. 789.4, Pinto reads a marginal gloss as "Hinch" and supposes that the poem must therefore be dated before Edward Montagu, Viscount Hinchingbrooke, became Earl of Sandwich in 1672 (*Poems*, pp. 225–26). The gloss is difficult to decipher, but even if it did read as Pinto claims, his conclusion would not necessarily follow.

2. The epistle to Julian is quoted from the text in the Yale MS., p. 352.

swer" were written after the epistle to Julian would require that they be dated implausibly late.

Such conclusions are further supported by the nature of the individual parallels. Scroope's "Song" includes the refrain "Will still love on, will still love on, and dye," while the epistle to Julian refers to Scroope's failures as a lover in similar phrasing (italics mine):

> *Still he loves on,* yet still as sure to misse,
> As they who wash an Ethiops face or his.

If the verbal resemblance is not merely fortuitous, the direction of influence must surely be from Scroope's lyric to the epistle. In the latter, the italicized words are tucked into the beginning of a line where few readers would notice them specially unless they concealed an allusion. Scroope's refrain, by contrast, occurs in emphatic position at the end of a stanza where it is both conspicuous and memorable—an inviting target for a satirical thrust. That Scroope's "Song" was such a target in another instance is shown by the "Mock Song" which Rochester probably wrote. It would, of course, be odd for Scroope to have borrowed the phrasing for a love song from a passage which satirizes him. Moreover, Scroope may well have composed his lyric while he was wooing Cary Frazier during the winter of 1676–77, whereas the epistle to Julian was written after the termination of this courtship (see Chapter 8).

A second parallel involves Scroope's "Answer," which is rounded off with a reference to Rochester's alleged cowardice:

> Thou can'st ⟨blast⟩ [3] no *Mans Fame,* with thy ill word,
> Thy Pen, is full as harmless as thy Sword.

3. Since "blast" is the reading of all early manuscripts including the Yale MS., the reading of A-1680-HU, "hurt," must be a corruption.

The epistle to Julian concludes with a similar hit at Scroope, who is dubbed "Strephon" (italics mine):

> Laugh at him, justle him, yet still he writes,
> In Rhyme he Challenges, in Rhyme he fights;
> Charg'd wth ye last, & basest Infamy,
> His Bus'nesse is to thinke what Rhymes to—Lye.
> W^ch found, in fury he retorts agen,
> Strephon's a very Draggon at his Pen.
> His Brother Murder'd, & his Mother Whor'd
> His Mistresse lost, *& yet his Pen's his Sword.*

Occurring as they do in emphatic position at the ends of their respective poems, one of these passages is probably a retort to the other. The retort would be pointless, however, if Scroope's "Answer" were the later of the two poems, since Rochester, whom Scroope is attacking, did not write the epistle to Julian. Evidently one of Rochester's friends, perhaps Buckingham, picked up where Scroope left off by replying to "The Answer" and possibly glancing in the same passage at earlier stages of the quarrel.

Since Rochester's "On the suppos'd Authour" was written before Scroope's "Answer," it too probably antedates the epistle to Julian. Also, it may be separately echoed in a third passage in the epistle which depicts Scroope's personality as a combination of incompatible "halves." Rochester's passage, at the conclusion of his poem, reads:

> 'Twere labour lost, or else I wou'd advise.
> But thy half *Wit,* will ne're let thee be wise.
> Half-witty, and half-mad, and scarce half-brave,
> Half-honest (which is very much a *Knave.*)
> Made up of all these Halfs, thou can'st not pass,
> For any thing intirely, but an *Asse.*

Similarly in the epistle to Julian:

> Strephon, alike, both Witts, & Fooles detest,
> Because like Aesops Batt, half Bird, half Beast;
> For Fooles, to Poetry, have noe pretence,
> And Comon Witt, supposes Comon Sense:
> Not quite soe low as Foole, nor quite a top,
> He hangs betweene 'em both, & is a Fopp.
> His Moralls like his Witt, are Motley too,
> He keepes from Arrant Knave, wth much a doe;
> But vanity & lyeing soe prevaile,
> That one Graine more of each, wou'd turne ye Scale:
> He wou'd be more a Villain, had he tyme,
> But he's soe wholly taken up wth Rhyme,
> That he mistakes his Tallent . . .

Rochester's lines, being more concise and striking, look like the original of the two descriptions. The passage in the epistle may be a mere borrowing rather than an allusion.

Possibly the unknown author of the epistle to Julian echoed the earlier poems in order to relate his contribution to prior stages of the quarrel and show his sympathies with Rochester. In any event, his lampoon seems to be the first of the many attacks on Scroope by satirists other than Rochester. It is difficult to perceive what animus could have caused such a continuing flood of abuse. Rochester's "On the suppos'd Authour," in particular, is among the most frightening invectives in the English language. One is inclined to ask, "What did Scroope do to deserve all *this?*"

6.

Verse Satires on Rochester:
The Myth and the Man

I

An important ingredient in the biography of any prominent
Restoration figure is the way he or she was portrayed in the lampoons of the day. These lampoons cannot, of course, be relied
upon for literal accuracy; hostile by their very nature, they tend
to exaggerate unfavorable personality traits and to oversimplify
or even falsify facts. Nevertheless, if their distortions are corrected by reference to more trustworthy data, Restoration lampoons can supply an added dimension which the biographer
would be foolish to ignore. At the very least, they preserve
evanescent gossip or emphasize base motives that are not clearly
revealed in other sources. Often they afford a vivid glimpse of
a person as he was seen by large numbers of his contemporaries
—resembling, in this respect, political cartoons of the twentieth

century. At their best, they offer the biographer the sort of imaginative projection of his subject's identity which he may seek in vain in the dry records that ordinarily constitute much of his raw material.

Many influences combined to make the personal satire of the Restoration what it was: contemporary stage comedy, the technique of the prose "character," earlier English traditions of satire,[1] and, increasingly, the examples of Horace, Juvenal, and Persius, whether studied directly or absorbed through the medium of adapters like Boileau. In addition, however, the peculiar worth of Restoration lampoons to the biographer and historian probably stems from two developments, superficially opposite in tendency, which were both strong during this formative period in English literature.

Evidently one of these developments amounted to a compelling desire for concreteness in poetical expression. Such a tendency seems to be urgently present during the initial stages of a major literary movement, when poets are trying to get back to essentials. To a degree, this tendency is a reaction against the unreal "poetic diction" of a previous literary mode; the preface to the *Lyrical Ballads* and *The Love Song of J. Alfred Prufrock* come quickly to mind, and the emerging Augustan sensibility was partly a revolt against the excesses of late Metaphysical poetry. A normal aspect of the desire to be concrete is a felt need for a poetical style modeled upon the spoken language of whatever segment of society best embodies the half-realized values of the new sensibility; thus Wordsworth wished to imitate the language of peasants. In the Restoration, the model was the conversation of the fashionable rakes who surrounded Charles II,

1. For a stimulating discussion of these earlier traditions, see Alvin Kernan, *The Cankered Muse: Satire of the English Renaissance* (New Haven, Yale Univ. Press, 1959).

or even of mere aspirants to membership in this circle. To illustrate the pungently realistic idiom which resulted, no better
example could be found than Rochester's satires, especially
"Timon" and "Tunbridge Wells." [2]

Furthermore, just as Wordsworth depicted particular rocks,
trees, and flowers because he felt these objects of "nature" were
most real, so the Restoration satirist, a hypersensitive member
of a civilized community, apparently felt constrained to achieve
concreteness by attacking actual *people*. Despite the dictum that
satire should be general—that it should scourge the sin rather
than the sinner—the Restoration satirist, and even a later Augustan like Alexander Pope, must have been impelled to write personal satire by pressures in the prevailing sensibility that made
the critical doctrine very difficult to observe. The satirist's conscience may have been uneasy, but his urge to use actual persons
is a circumstance for which the biographer and historian can
be grateful.

Good poetry cannot, however, be only a "slice of life" composed of realistic colloquial idiom, specific names, and particulari-
ties of personal behavior; even a mediocre poet knows, or feels,
that he must strive for a universality transcending these incidents
of the surface. Accordingly, we also find a tendency in Restoration satire to elevate its particular personages to the status of
myth. Moreover, as befitted a socially centered age, the myths
were usually not the work of a single poet, but were communal
products. After a semi-mythic characterization had been outlined
by one satirist, other satirists frequently incorporated it into their
own lampoons and filled out its details. Though this process may

2. Some of the points raised in this paragraph are developed in other directions by T. S. Eliot in his fine essay "The Music of Poetry," in *On
Poetry and Poets* (London, Faber and Faber, 1957), pp. 26–38.

strike a twentieth-century reader as mere borrowing, it more nearly resembles creative participation in a ritual.

Restoration satirists did not often achieve full success in their myth-making, but their few triumphs are so effective that the myth is more memorable than the real person on whom it is based. One remembers the Earl of Mulgrave as the haughty ass who complacently thought himself the ideal soldier and lover; or one remembers Sir Carr Scroope as the feckless fop who, though half-blind and repulsively ugly, sent his amatory verses to countless women and was so absorbed in writing poetry that he fought in rhyme rather than with his sword. Even individual performances like Dryden's portraits of Shadwell and Buckingham owe something to the tradition of myth-making in Restoration lampoons. Evidently the tradition carried over into later practice, for the curious semi-mythic world of Restoration satire seems closely akin to the half-real, half-fictional existence which Aubrey Williams has found characteristic of the personages in Pope's *Dunciad*.[3] Thus two tendencies in Restoration lampoons, the tendency to concreteness and the countertendency to myth, probably account for much of their colorful portraiture and their resultant usefulness to the biographer.

Oddly, none of Rochester's numerous biographers has provided so much as a list of the lampoons written against him during his lifetime. Though, as we shall see, there may be good reasons for this neglect, even a casual reader could guess that Rochester sustained frequent personal attacks which offer knowledge of the way he was viewed by his less sympathetic contemporaries. He was sufficiently prominent, and his questionable manner of life made him an inviting target. Also, the satirists

3. Aubrey L. Williams, *Pope's Dunciad: A Study of its Meaning* (Baton Rouge, Louisiana State Univ. Press, 1955), pp. 5, 60–86.

had part of their myth already available, for Rochester's social position was somewhat like that of a cinema star in twentieth-century America, nor was he reluctant to perpetuate the myth through his considerable talents as a *poseur*. A survey of the surviving lampoons on Rochester seems long overdue.

This survey is further necessitated by a strange irony: of the satires written against him, about half were ultimately attributed to Rochester himself. This happened largely because some of them found their way into the first edition of 1680, the Huntington edition (A-1680-HU). In the lost archetype of the Huntington edition and the Yale MS., the scribe included several such lampoons in his section of poems by or concerning Rochester; the Huntington edition, in turn, printed almost all of these lampoons as Rochester's own compositions. A study of the collection represented by the Yale MS. and the Huntington edition must therefore attempt to separate this group of satires from the poems which can be accepted as genuine Rochester.

II

The earliest lampoons on Rochester apparently originated, as so many things did in Restoration poetry, among the gentlemen-wits at Court. During 1670–75, and probably before, the Wits seem to have amused themselves by writing jocular, bawdy poems about each other. The first datable poem of this type on Rochester is a clever satirical song headed, in some eighteenth-century editions, "The Debauchee." Its entire text is here reproduced as an example, since the next few poems to be discussed are so obscene that full quotation is not desirable. Though "The De-

bauchee" is traditionally printed as seven rhymed couplets of anapestic tetrameter, the usual arrangement has been altered to emphasize the rhyming of the half-lines (except lines 5 and 7, which
may be corrupt). "Rochester" is speaking:

I Rise at Eleven,
    I Dine about Two,
I get drunk before Seven,
    and the next thing I do;
I send for my *Whore*,
    when for fear of a *Clap*,
I Spend in her hand,
    and I Spew in her *Lap*:
⟨Then⟩ we quarrel, and scold,
    till I fall ⟨fast⟩ asleep,
When the *Bitch*, growing bold,
    to my Pocket does creep;
Then slyly she leaves me,
    and to revenge th' affront,
At once she bereaves me
    of *Money*, and *Cunt*.
If by chance then I wake,
    hot-headed, and drunk,
What a coyle do I make
    for the loss of my *Punck?*
I storm, and I roar,
    and I fall in a rage,
And missing my *Whore*,
    I bugger my *Page*:
Then crop-sick, all *Morning*,
    I rail at my *Men*,

And in Bed I lye Yawning,
till Eleven again.[4]

This song is not unfriendly to Rochester. Nevertheless, it anticipates what we shall find to have been his standard satiric character as whoremaster, toper, idler, and bully.

Most students of Rochester have supposed that "The Debauchee" is his own composition—a natural assumption, since it
is written in the first person, and Rochester was quite capable
of satirizing himself. The poem was accepted as genuine by John
Hayward, Quilter Johns, Johannes Prinz, and James Thorpe;
Vivian de Sola Pinto doubted its authenticity, however, since he
omitted it from his edition.[5] Actually, as Thorpe conceded, there
is only "slight evidence" of Rochester's authorship (*Rochester's
Poems*, p. 177). "The Debauchee" was first printed as Rochester's
in the Huntington edition, from which it was reprinted with the
same ascription in the other 1680 editions and the later editions
of 1685 (A-1685), 1701 (A-1701), 1713 (A-1713), and 1731
(A-1731). From one of the 1680 editions, apparently, it was also
printed as Rochester's in Edmund Curll's *The Works Of the
Earls of Rochester, Roscommon, Dorset, &c.*, 1714 (C-1714-1),
and succeeding editions of this collection. No text is extant in the
Yale MS., for the poem was probably among those removed by
the fourth gap. Two manuscript versions, in Bodl. MS. Rawl.
Poet. 152 and Edinburgh MS. DC.1.3, carry no ascriptions. Thus
the only evidence of Rochester's authorship is the ambiguous testimony of the Huntington edition.

4. The text is that of A-1680-HU, p. 59, with two emended readings
taken from Bodl. MS. Rawl. Poet. 152 and Edinburgh MS. DC.1.3. In
l. 9 A-1680-HU reads "There" for "Then," and in l. 10 it omits "fast."
See Part III for detailed lists of the early texts and ascriptions of most of the
poems discussed in this chapter.
5. See Part III for documentation of the previous scholarship on most
of the poems discussed in this chapter.

Since the Huntington edition prints "The Debauchee" in the section of poems by or concerning Rochester, any internal evidence that it satirizes the Earl is sufficient to question its authenticity. This evidence exists, for the poem depicts a typical day in the life of just such a rake as Rochester was popularly believed to be. Moreover, as von Römer noted years ago,[6] an experience like the one described in "The Debauchee" actually happened to Rochester. Pepys records that on 2 December 1668, he

> heard the silly discourse of the King, with his people about him, telling a story of my Lord Rochester's having of his clothes stole, while he was with a wench; and his gold all gone, but his clothes found afterwards stuffed into a feather bed by the wench that stole them.

Even if "The Debauchee" does not refer to this particular incident, it might allude to a similar occurrence at some other date.

Fortunately, a newly discovered piece of external evidence seems to indicate both the true author of "The Debauchee" and its approximate date of composition. Early in 1673, the Earl of Huntingdon applied to his cousin Godfrey Thacker, in London, for the latest gossip concerning Rochester. In Thacker's reply, dated 20 March 1672/3, a postscript offers the following story:

> My Lord Buckhurst and Lord Rochester being in company, a suddaine Malancholly possest him Rochester inquiring the reason hee answered hee was troubled at Rochesters lude way of living, and in thes verses over the leafe exprest it [7]

On the reverse side of the leaf, Thacker quotes the first eight lines of "The Debauchee." Though the anecdotal quality of Thacker's account may not inspire confidence in the accuracy of

6. L. S. A. M. v. Römer, *Rochester's Sodom Herausgegeben nach dem Hamburger Manuscript* (Paris, H. Welter, 1904), p. xx.

7. Huntington MS. HA 12525. See Lucyle Hook, "Something More About Rochester," *Modern Language Notes*, 75 (1960), 478–85.

all its details, the portion most likely to be true is his ascription of the poem to Buckhurst; conceivably the rest of the story might be a fabrication to explain this ascription. The point is scarcely important, however, for Thacker's statement is the only real evidence we possess on the authorship of "The Debauchee."

Similar to "The Debauchee" is an obscene satirical "Song" beginning "In the Fields of Lincolns Inn," which may also emanate from the Court Wits and which may have been written about the same date, though clear evidence is lacking. The "Song" even resembles "The Debauchee" in attempting a prosodic *tour de force,* since it consists of four eight-line stanzas of trochaic tetrameter rhymed *abbacdcd,* with the *a* and *d* rhymes masculine and the *b* and *c* rhymes feminine.

Though the early printed texts of the "Song" attribute it to Rochester, few students of his poetry have believed that he wrote it. His authorship was rejected by Hayward, Johns, Prinz, and Pinto. Thorpe, accepting the poem as genuine, nevertheless added that "it may very possibly have been falsely attracted into the Rochester canon; but no evidence appears to disprove his authorship" (*Rochester's Poems,* p. 176). The "Song" was first printed as Rochester's in the Huntington edition, where it is found in the section of poems by or concerning Rochester. It was reprinted with the same ascription in the other editions of 1680 but was omitted from later editions. In the Yale MS. it seems, like "The Debauchee," to have been among the poems removed by the fourth gap. Two manuscript versions furnish ascriptions: Harvard MS. Eng. 636F assigns the poem to Rochester, whereas Bodl. MS. Don. b. 8, unknown to Thorpe, ascribes it to Sir Charles Sedley.

Besides the ascription to Sedley, internal evidence casts doubt on Rochester's authorship of the "Song." Its style is not strikingly Rochesterian, and in places its author apparently had dif-

ficulty maintaining his intricate rhyme scheme, as in the opening
lines:

> In the *Fields* of *Lincolns Inn*,
>> Underneath a tatter'd *Blanket*,
>> On a *Flock-Bed*, *God* be thanked,
> Feats of Active Love were seen.[8]

"*God* be thanked," with the last word pronounced as two syllables, is a feeble way to fill out a line and supply a rhyme. One
wonders whether Rochester's talents would have been so severely
strained.

More important, the "Song" may be a genial lampoon on
Rochester, for it seems to reflect the popular image of the Earl
as a sort of archetypal whoremonger. In vaguely mock-pastoral
terms, the poem describes how two men, Corydon and Strephon,
attempt simultaneous sexual intercourse with one woman. Strephon was a pseudonym commonly used for Rochester; also, in
contrast to Corydon, a mere neophyte, Strephon possesses extraordinary qualifications:

> *Coridon*'s aspiring *Tarse*,
>> Which to *Cunt*, had ne're submitted;
>> Wet with Am'rous Kiss she fitted,
> To her less frequented Ar——
> *Strephon*'s, was a handful longer,
>> Stiffly propt with eager *Lust*;
> None for *Champion*, was more stronger,
>> This into her *Cunt* he thrust.

These arguments help to clarify the external evidence on the
authorship of the "Song." The ascription in the Huntington edi-

---

8. The text is that of A-1680-HU, p. 55, except that indention is
introduced to emphasize the rhyme scheme, and the eight four-line stanzas of the copy-text are combined into four stanzas of eight lines each.

tion is ambiguous, since the scribe of the archetype may have
included the "Song" in his section of poems by or concerning
Rochester in the belief that it satirized the Earl. The ascription
in Harvard MS. Eng. 636F is likewise suspect, for this manuscript tends to attribute too much to Rochester, as is shown by
the next poem to be discussed. Moreover, in the independently
descended texts of the "Song," the character of the variants suggests that most of them resulted from memorial transmission;
possibly someone who tried to carry the poem in his head confused its subject with its author, and the false ascription then
passed into the Harvard manuscript.

No external evidence remains except the ascription to Sedley
in Bodl. MS. Don. b. 8, a volume whose attributions are unusually
trustworthy. Though Pinto questions this ascription because
"there is no other evidence" of Sedley's authorship (*Works of
Sedley*, *1*, xxvii), there is likewise no reliable testimony that anyone else wrote the "Song." Sedley may have composed it under
circumstances similar to those which led Buckhurst to write "The
Debauchee."

Probably written more than a year after "The Debauchee" is
a long, extremely bawdy narrative satire in heroic couplets beginning "Say Heav'n-born Muse, for only thou canst tell." The
earliest texts entitle this satire "The Argument," a heading which
properly belongs only to its introductory four-line synopsis; with
better reason but no visible authority, eighteenth-century editions call the poem "Bath Intrigues." This witty, if sometimes
rough and incoherent lampoon relates how Rochester is tricked
by three lascivious women at Bath, how he resolves to break up
their friendship, and how he carries out his obscene revenge. As
in "The Debauchee" and the "Song," the portrayal of Rochester,
while not very attractive, is not perceptibly hostile. Indeed, far
from being primarily a lampoon on Rochester, "The Argument"
is more interesting for its antireligious attitudes. It also deserves

special mention as a thoroughgoing attempt to use mock-epic devices for satirical purposes, a relatively rare phenomenon at this early date.[9]

Students of Rochester have unanimously concluded that he did not write "The Argument": the poem was rejected by Hayward, Johns, Prinz, Pinto, and Thorpe. Its textual history resembles those of "The Debauchee" and the "Song." First printed as Rochester's in the Huntington edition, where it appears in the section of poems by or concerning Rochester, it was reprinted with the same ascription in the other 1680 editions but drops out of later editions in this series. From one of the 1680 editions it was again printed as Rochester's in Curll's edition of 1714 and in later editions of this collection; from the edition of 1714, in turn, Giles Jacob derived his attribution. In the Yale MS., where only the title, the four-line "argument," and the first eight lines of text are extant, "The Argument" carries no ascription— though, significantly, all preceding genuine poems are ascribed to Rochester. An ascription to Rochester occurs, however, in Harvard MS. Eng. 636F.

As Thorpe has demonstrated (*Rochester's Poems*, p. 174), the ascriptions to Rochester in the Huntington edition and the Harvard manuscript cannot be correct, for "The Argument" satirizes Rochester and also reproduces the traditional satiric image of the Earl as the legendary lecher. Though the poem's principal male character is identified merely as "*R*——" in the printed texts (A-1680-HU, p. 35), the Harvard manuscript gives his full name as "Rochester," as does a marginal note in a contemporary hand in the Sterling copy of the 1680 editions (A-1680-S-S). The poem further calls him "Peer" and "Spiney

9. Dryden is supposed to have said of *Mac Flecknoe* that it was "the first piece of ridicule written in Heroics" (Joseph Spence, *Anecdotes*, ed. Samuel Weller Singer, London, 1820, p. 60). Though not strictly accurate, Dryden's remark underscores the novelty of the mock-heroic satire in "The Argument."

Lord," alluding to Rochester's slender physique. There is even
a sarcastic reference to Rochester's "lasting *Verse*." Interestingly,
"The Argument" augments the mythic characterization of
Rochester by describing him as malicious; we are told that "his
Heart with rancour swell'd" as he cast his "evil *Eye*" upon the
three women whose lewd pleasures he vowed to destroy.

No evidence is forthcoming on the true author of "The Argument," though its religious skepticism and its familiarity with the
Court seemingly point to one of the Wits. Prinz felt that the
poem "looks like a production of Alexander Radcliffe" (*Rochester*, p. 150), an opinion which Thorpe thought "reasonable"
even if "only a guess" (*Rochester's Poems*, p. 174). Without
more facts, however, speculation is futile.

Evidently "The Argument" was not in existence before spring
of 1674. Several topical allusions occur in the poem. Unfortunately, little help is afforded by references to breaking the Triple
League and to the Duke of Luxemburg, one of Louis XIV's gen-
erals, since either might have been mentioned after the early
1670s. A likely *terminus post quem* is, however, provided by the
following passage:

> To th' Tree she leads him, from a *Bough* pulls down,
> A mighty Tool, a *Dildoe* of renown;
> A *Dildoe*, long, and large, as *Hectors Launce*,
> Inscrib'd, *Honi Soit Qui Mal y' Pence*.
> *Knight* of the *Garter*, made for's vast deserts,
> As *Modern Heroe*, was for's monstrous parts.

The last couplet probably satirizes the Earl of Mulgrave, who
became Knight of the Garter on 23 April 1674.[1] The couplet
reflects the satirists' usual charges against Mulgrave: "monstrous

1. William A. Shaw, *The Knights of England* (London, Sherratt and
Hughes, 1906), *1*, 37.

parts" apparently sneers at his boasted exploits as a lover, while "*Modern Heroe*" may allude both to his arrogance and to his ambitions as a military commander. Some support for this limiting date can be found in the poem's assertion that "*Men* of *God* to *Betty* B⟨*ewly*⟩ go"; according to Thomas Duffet's *The Empress of Morocco. A Farce,* acted about December 1673, Betty Bewly had then begun "the Trade but newly." [2] "The Argument" may have been written soon after 23 April 1674, though this cannot, of course, be certainly established.

III

The spring of 1676, when Rochester celebrated his twenty-ninth birthday, marks a subtle yet definite change in the direction of his life, as appears even in the lampoons written against him. Generally this was a season of triumph. March 1676 was the month of Rochester's apotheosis as the half-angelic, half-diabolical Dorimant of Etherege's *Man of Mode.* By this date Rochester had produced most of his best poetry, which contemporaries were acclaiming as work of enduring merit. "A Satyr against Mankind" was certainly written by March, and during this winter Rochester challenged Dryden's supremacy by skillfully satirizing the laureate in "An Allusion to Horace."

On the other hand, Rochester's career now begins a gradual downward movement. The mood of pessimistic probing which lent tragic maturity to many of Rochester's poems of 1674 and 1675 was deepening into the misanthropy which partly explains his lessening literary activity during his remaining four years of life and which led finally to his dramatic deathbed repentance. In late summer of 1675, probably because he had offended the

2. *The Empress of Morocco. A Farce,* 1674, p. 34. In this chapter, all dates of dramatic performances and publication of plays are taken from Nicoll, *Restoration Drama.*

Duchess of Portsmouth in his "scepter" lampoon on King Charles, Rochester had suffered the prolonged banishment from Court during which he masqueraded as the mountebank Alexander Bendo; this banishment was a period of disillusionment, as his letters reveal.[3] In June 1676, Rochester indirectly caused the death of a companion in the notorious riot at Epsom which his enemies never forgot. Lampoons on Rochester multiplied, and no longer were they *jeux d'esprit* by close friends. While their portrayal of the Earl preserves a continuity with earlier satires, they become increasingly serious and hostile.

Among these lampoons should be listed two of the three surviving verse answers to "A Satyr against Mankind," even though both poems, the productions of clergymen far removed from the Court scene, are somewhat tangential to the tradition. The better and more widely circulated of the two, beginning "Were I to chuse what sort of Corps I'd wear," is ascribed in independently derived texts to "P," "Dr. P——," and "Dr. P——ck"; Edward Pococke, the well-known Oxford divine and orientalist, may be intended. Anthony Wood, however, assigns the poem to "one Mr. Griffith a minister." Probably Wood's authority should be preferred, though Pococke's claim cannot be ruled out entirely.[4] The second answer, a cruder effort be-

3. For the circumstances surrounding the "scepter" lampoon, see my article, "Rochester's 'Scepter' Lampoon on Charles II," *Philological Quarterly*, 37 (1958), 424–32. See also *The Famous Pathologist or The Noble Mountebank by Thomas Alcock and John Wilmot, Earl of Rochester*, ed. Vivian de Sola Pinto, Nottingham University Miscellany No. 1 (Nottingham, Sisson and Parker, 1961).

4. The poem appears without ascription in the Yale MS., p. 22; Taylor MS. 3, p. 222; Harvard MS. Eng. 623F, p. 20; B. M. Harl. MS. 6207, fol. 66ʳ; Bodl. MS. Don. b. 8, p. 564; Edinburgh MS. DC.1.3, p. 27; and the undated folio leaflet *An Answer to the Satyr against Mankind*, which was published, according to Anthony Wood, in July 1679 (*Athenae Oxonienses*, 3, 1229).

The poem is ascribed to "a Countrey Parson" in Cambridge MS. Add. 6339, fol. 17ʳ, and to "P" in Harvard MS. Eng. 636F, p. 91. It is assigned to

ginning "Were I a Sp'rit, to chuse for my own share," was written by Thomas Lessey, a fellow of Wadham College, Oxford.[5]

Griffith and Lessey address themselves chiefly to the philo-
sophic issues raised by "A Satyr against Mankind," but both
smuggle in a good deal of *argumentum ad hominem* by insinuat-
ing that Rochester's poem was merely an attempt to rationalize
his carnal pleasures. Griffith sees Rochester primarily as a volup-
tuary. After a loaded statement (echoing one of Rochester's
lines) that he would not wish to be "Baron Dog, Lord Monkey,
or Earl Bear," Griffith decries Rochester's endeavor to "Defend
Debaucheries" and make men "drunk and pockey." He pointedly

"Dr. P——" in *Poems on Affairs of State*, 1699 (Case 211-1-d), p. [2]254,
and reprinted with this ascription in 1702 (Case 211-1-e), p. [2]254; 1703
(Case 211-1-f), p. [2]254; 1710 (Case 211-1-g), p. [2]254; 1716 (Case
211-1-h), p. [2]254; and *A New Collection of Poems Relating to State
Affairs*, 1705 (Case 237), p. 267. Evidently one of these volumes is the
source of Giles Jacob's ascription to "Dr. P——" (*Poetical Register*, 2,
236). The poem is attributed to "Dr. P——ck" in *Poems on Affairs of
State*, 1703 (Case 211-2-a), p. 432, reprinted with the same ascription
in 1703 (Case 211-2-b), p. 432, and reissued in 1716 (Case 211-2-c),
p. 432.

Wood, as noted in the text above, attributes the poem to "one Mr.
Griffith a minister" (*3*, 1229). Horace Walpole also assigns it to Griffith
but cites Wood as his source (*Catalogue of Royal and Noble Authors*, 2,
39). The poem is ascribed to "the Reverend Mr. Griffith" in Tonson's
edition of 1714 (B-1714), p. 59, and reprinted with this ascription in
1732 (B-1732), p. 59. Tonson's ascription may derive from Wood; his
text was printed from the folio leaflet of 1679 with a few readings corrected from some other source, possibly *Poems on Affairs of State*, 1699,
or a later edition of this miscellany.

My quotations from the poem in the next paragraph are taken from
Poems on Affairs of State, 1699.

5. Lessey's poem is ascribed to him in *Poetical Recreations*, 1688 (Case
186), p. [2]67; B. M. Sloane MS. 1458, fol. 43[r]; and B. M. Harl. MS.
6207, fol. 60[r]. The printed version, from which my quotation in the next
paragraph is taken, lacks two long passages preserved in the manuscripts.

The third answer to "A Satyr against Mankind," beginning "Were I a
Spirit free (which Thought's as Vain," contains no personal allusions to
Rochester. It is printed without ascription in *Corinna; or, Humane Frailty.
A Poem. With an Answer to the E. of R——'s Satyr against Man*, 1699,
p. 17.

alludes to philosophies ending "In Notions of Venereal Mysteries," to "the madder Taverns lewder stews" of London, and to Court physicians with nothing to do except "compounding Lusts." Nevertheless, Griffith backhandedly compliments Rochester's "Wit, Extravagance and Mode" and numbers him among those "acutest Wits" who "when they're defil'd / Turn most extravagant, prophane and wild."

Lessey plainly has Rochester in mind in the long, rambling, rather silly description of fashionable "Hobbists" which constitutes the second half of his poem. Fortunately, his attitude is epitomized by an earlier short passage which, in the context, must glance at Rochester. This passage, besides illustrating the continuity of the semi-mythic image found in earlier satires, shows the hostile turn which lampoons on Rochester were taking. Notable new features are the references to cowardice, blasphemy, and deceit, as well as the suggestion that Rochester was considered a devil:

> 'Tis guilt alone breeds cow'rdise and distrust,
> For all Men wou'd be Valiant if they durst;
> Those only can't, who swear, and whore, and cheat,
> And sell their *Honour* at the cheapest rate:
> Whom brawling Surfeits, Drunkenness and Claps;
> Hurry on head-long to the *Grave* perhaps:
> Such some call *Devils*, but we think the least,
> And therefore kindly head them with the be⟨a⟩st.
> Chuse they themselves whose *Case* they'll please to wear,
> The Case of Dog, the Monkey, or the Bear.

Squarely in the tradition is a satirical song entitled "The Bully" which Thomas D'Urfey wrote for his comedy *The Fool Turn'd Critick*, acted 18 November 1676. Ironically, George Sherburn, believing this song to be Rochester's own composition, recently singled it out as a striking expression of Rochester's "metrically boisterous self"; [6] Sherburn's slip perhaps demonstrates the Restoration satirist's ability to trick his readers, even in the twentieth century, into acceptance of a mythic substitute for his victim's real identity. "The Bully" repeats the traditional characterization of Rochester, depicting him as whoremaster, idler, brawler, and coward. It also criticizes the King's continued tolerance toward Rochester's escapades, and it concludes with a prediction (not borne out in the event) concerning the manner of the Earl's death. The poem is reproduced in full from the earliest known text:

> Room, room, room for a man of the Town,
>   that takes delight in roring;
> That daily rambles up and down,
>   and spends his nights in whoring:
> That for the noble name of Spark
>   does his companions rally:
> Commits an out-rage in the dark,
>   then sneaks into an Ally.
>
> To every female that he meets,
>   he swears he bears affection;
> Defies all Laws, arrests, or fears,
>   by help of kind protection.
> Then he, intending further wrongs,
>   by some resenting Cully,
> Is decently run through the Lungs,
>   and there's an end of Bully. [7]

6. *A Literary History of England,* ed. Albert C. Baugh (New York and London, Appleton-Century-Crofts, 1948), p. 743.

7. *The Last and Best Edition of New Songs,* 1677 (Case 163), sig. A2ᵛ.

The fifth through the eighth lines of this song appear to be one of several contemporary attacks on Rochester for his part in the brawl at Epsom on the night of 17 June 1676, five months before D'Urfey's song was performed. This episode was discussed in detail in the preceding chapter (pp. 142–43). D'Urfey's quatrain parallels the Epsom incident: Rochester, for whatever reason, tried to "rally" his companions by drawing his sword, this "out-rage" was committed in the dark, and Rochester immediately absconded.

Students of Rochester were slow to discover that "The Bully" was written by D'Urfey. Hayward and Johns both printed it as Rochester's, while Prinz, though he suspected that the poem alluded to the Epsom affair and might therefore satirize Rochester, did not know its true author. Norman Ault cautiously assigned the poem to "Rochester or D'Urfey." Thorpe, putting the relevant bits of evidence together for the first time, concluded that "The Bully" was "probably" by D'Urfey, and Pinto subsequently omitted it from his edition of Rochester.

D'Urfey's authorship of "The Bully" is scarcely open to question. Though the poem does not appear in the only edition of D'Urfey's comedy, published in 1678, it had previously been printed in *The Last and Best Edition of New Songs*, 1677, as a song "In the Fool turn'd Critick." Any ambiguity in this implied ascription is resolved by D'Urfey's inclusion of the poem in his authoritative *A New Collection of Songs and Poems. By Thomas D'Urfey, Gent.*, 1683, under the heading "The Bully, a Song in the Fool turned Critick." There is no admissible evidence that "The Bully" was written by anyone other than D'Urfey. The poem is unfortunately not extant in the Yale MS., since it was probably part of the material removed by the fifth gap. Its position in the Huntington edition indicates, however, that it came to be printed under Rochester's name only because the scribe of the archetype included it in his section of poems by or concerning Rochester as a satire on the Earl. From the Huntington edition, it was reprinted as Rochester's in the other 1680 editions and in the later editions of 1685 (A-1685), 1701 (A-1701), 1713 (A-1713), and 1731 (A-1731). From one of the 1680 editions, apparently, it was also printed as Rochester's in Benjamin Bragge's *Miscellaneous Works* of Rochester and Roscommon, 1707 (C-1707-a), and later editions in this series (C series). A single manuscript text assigning the poem to Rochester, in Bodl. MS. Rawl. Poet. 173, was probably copied from one of the 1680 editions. Aside from a worthless attribution to "Ephelia" in her *Female Poems*, 1682, no other early texts of "The Bully" carry ascriptions.

The Epsom affair also figures prominently in the passage which Sir Carr Scroope directed against Rochester in his "In defence of Satyr," probably written during the summer of 1676. Since this passage was quoted in full in the preceding chapter, it need not be given again. Scroope reproduces the usual mythic image of Rochester with a few inconspicuous additions and with a mild tone that is characteristic of his writing: Rochester is described as an irresponsible buffoon who is also malicious, scurrilous, treacherous to his friends, debauched, dangerously quarrelsome, and cowardly. Nevertheless, Scroope complains that Rochester is esteemed by the fashionable rakes as the pleasantest, wittiest man in town. After Rochester's scorching retort in "On the suppos'd Authour of a late Poem in defence of Satyr," Scroope's brief "Answer," probably written before the end of 1676, deftly dismisses Rochester as too disreputable, too cowardly, too pox-ridden, and too impotent in his malice to deserve any reply.

While Scroope and D'Urfey were planning their attacks, a far more ambitious verse assault on Rochester was brought to completion in a quiet town in Surrey. Fortunately for literary scholars, the date of *A Satyr against Vertue* can be established with certainty: John Oldham's poetical notebook (Bodl. MS. Rawl. Poet. 123) meticulously records that he composed this poem in "July 1676 at Croydon," where he was teaching school.

Though *A Satyr against Vertue*, like other lampoons considered in this chapter, was printed as Rochester's own composition in 1680, Thorpe is probably wrong in speculating that it was included in the Huntington edition because of an evident connection with Rochester (*Rochester's Poems*, p. 188). If this were true, we should expect to find it in the section of poems by or concerning Rochester; instead, it appears in the section of poems by miscellaneous authors. Evidently the fact that Oldham designed his poem as a satire on Rochester was unknown to the scribe of the archetype, as it was also unknown to the Restoration audience at large. The information was suppressed in all early printed texts of the poem and is, indeed, known today only because of notations in two manuscripts, one of them Oldham's holograph. Opposite the title of the poem, Oldham wrote, "Suppos'd to be spoken by a Court-Hector at Breaking of yᵉ Dial in Privy-Garden." Similarly, B. M. Add. MS. 14047 describes the poem as "Supposed to be spoken by yᵉ Court-Hector who demolished yᵉ sund-Diall." Both notations refer to an escapade which Rochester perpetrated on Friday, 25 June 1675. Bursting into the Privy Garden after a night's revelry, Rochester, Buckhurst, Fleetwood Shepherd, and several other Wits suddenly found themselves confronted by the King's sundial, an elaborate confection of glass spheres arranged in a phallic shape. Seized by a drunken inspiration, Rochester shouted, "What! Dost thou stand here to —— time?" and in a moment he had demolished the offending instrument.[8]

8. HMC, *Laing*, *1*, 405. John Aubrey, *Brief Lives*, ed. Andrew Clark (Oxford, Clarendon Press, 1898), *2*, 34. *The Poems and Letters of An-*

Besides being both horrified and fascinated by Rochester's personal life—lurid as it must have seemed from the perspective of Croydon—Oldham secretly admired Rochester's poetry, which at this stage of his career he studied and tried to imitate.[9] The technique of *A Satyr against Vertue* finds its closest analogues among Rochester's satires. Oldham's lampoon specially resembles the ironic structure which Rochester had used to satirize Mulgrave in "A very Heroical Epistle in Answer to Ephelia," written less than a year earlier; possibly Oldham was imitating this particular poem, though there is no documentary evidence that he was familiar with it. Drawing heavily upon the concepts of *le libertinage*,[1] Oldham depicts Rochester as *persona* arguing for a life of pure sensuality and repudiating all traditional social conventions, moral codes, and religious principles. When this kind of ironic technique is successful, as it is in Rochester's spoof of Mulgrave, the *persona* appears ridiculous by his implicit violation of the shared values of the contemporary audience. Regrettably, *A Satyr against Vertue* misses full effectiveness, partly because it tends to be pedantic, partly because Oldham lacked the requisite light touch, and partly because of his besetting sin of never saying in one line what he could say in two. Oldham succeeds, however, at one point where all other satirists failed: he endows the mythic image of Rochester with some of the

---

drew Marvell, ed. H. M. Margoliouth (Oxford, Clarendon Press, 1927), *I*, 190. Arthur Bryant, *King Charles II* (London, New York, and Toronto, Longmans, Green, 1932), p. 260. Wilson, *Court Wits*, pp. 37–38. The inventor of the sundial, Francis Hall (or Francis Line, or Franciscus Linus), published *An Explication of the Diall Sett up in the Kings Garden at London, an. 1669*, Liège, 1673; a drawing of the dial is included as a fold-out frontispiece.

9. In an undated satirical fragment in his notebook, Oldham apparently calls Rochester "our great witty bawdy Peer" (p. 225).

1. This aspect of Oldham's poem is discussed by Dale Underwood, *Etherege and the Seventeenth-Century Comedy of Manners* (New Haven, Yale Univ. Press, 1957), pp. 10 ff.

stature which the man possessed in real life. The ironic technique of Oldham's long lampoon is well illustrated by the first
of its twelve sections:

> Now curses on ye all, ye virtuous *Fools*,
>> Who think to fetter free born *Souls*,
> And tye 'em up to dull *Morality*, and *Rules*.
>> The *Stagyrite*, be damn'd, and all the Crew,
>> Of learned *Idiots*, who his steps pursue;
> And those more silly *Proselites*, whom his fond Precepts drew!
>> Oh had his *Ethicks*, been with their ⟨vile⟩ *Author* drown'd
>> Or a like fate, with those lost Writings found,
>> Which that grand *Plagiary*, doom'd to *Fire*,
>>> And made by unjust *Flames* expire,
>> They ne're had then seduc'd *Mortality*,
> Ne're lasted to debauch the *World*, with their lewd *Pedantry*.
> But damn'd and more (if *Hell* can do't) be that Thrice cursed
>> name,
>> Who e're the rudiments of Law design'd;
> Who e're did the First *Model* of *Religion*, frame,
> And by that double *Vassalage* enthrall'd *Mankind*;
> By nought before, but their own Pow'r, or will confin'd:
> Now quite abridg'd of all their Primitive liberty.
> And *Slaves*, to each capricious *Monarchs*, Tyranny.
> More happy *Brutes*! who the great Rule of sense observe,
>> And ne're from their First Charter swerve.
>> Happy whose lives are meerly to enjoy,
> And feel no stings of Sin, which may their Bliss annoy;
> Still unconcern'd, at *Epithets* of ill, or good,
> Distinctions unadult'rate *Nature*, never understood.[2]

---

2. A-1680-HU, p. 115. "Vile" in l. 7, the reading of Oldham's holograph draft, has been substituted for "wild."

In succeeding sections of the poem, "Rochester" envies the legendary exploits of such sinners as Nero, Guy Fawkes, and Satan.

Since the *persona* of *A Satyr against Vertue* represents Rochester, it is difficult to read Oldham's "Apology" for his lampoon without peculiar reference to the Earl. Speaking now in his own person, Oldham seemingly contrasts his poetical morality with Rochester's:

> Our *Poet*, has a diff'rent taste of Wit,
> Nor will to th' common Vogue, himself submit.
> Let some admire the *Fops*, whose Talents lye,
> In venting dull insipid *Blasphemy*; . . .
> Wits name, was never to profaness due,
> For then you see, he cou'd be witty too:
> He cou'd *Lampoon* the *State*, and *Libel Kings*,
> But that he's *Loyal*, and knows better things,
> Than *Fame*, whose guilty *Birth* from *Treason* springs. . . .
> He cou'd be *Baudy* toe, and nick the times,
> In what they dearly love, damn'd *Placket* Rhymes
> Such as our *Nobles* write————
> Whose nauseous *Poetry*, can reach no higher,
> Than what the *Cod-peice*, or its *God* inspire:
> So lewd they spend at Quill, you'd justly think,
> They wrote with something nastier than Ink.
>   (A-1680-HU, pp. 127, 128)

The phrase *"Libel Kings"* may allude to Rochester's "scepter" lampoon on Charles II, which was probably written during the preceding summer.

A fact little known to students of Rochester is that more than

a year after *A Satyr against Vertue,* Oldham again used the Earl
as *persona* in a long ironical satire in pindarics. This satire was
first published in Oldham's *Poems, and Translations,* 1683, as
"A Dithyrambick. The Drunkards Speech in a Mask" (p. 206).
As with *A Satyr against Vertue,* the early printed texts suppress
any indication that the poem satirizes Rochester. According to
Oldham's notebook, however, where it is headed "A Dithyram-
bique on Drinking" and includes some lines lacking in the printed
version, this poem is "Suppos'd to be Spoken by Rochester at yᵉ
Guinny Club" (p. 206). The printed version states that "A
Dithyrambick" was "Written in Aug. 1677"; the holograph text
dates it more precisely "Aug. 5. 1677." As an ironic defence of
drunkenness, "A Dithyrambick" has less range than *A Satyr
against Vertue* and is therefore markedly inferior. Since its
technique is otherwise identical with that of *A Satyr against
Vertue,* illustrative quotations would be superfluous.[3]

3. Passages on Rochester occur in two more lampoons written about this
date. One passage is not itself satirical, while the other is of slight importance.

The authorship of "Advice to Apollo" ("I've heard the Muses were still
soft and kind") is unknown, but its attitudes suggest an origin in Rochester's circle of Wits. Though many early texts assign it to 1678, internal
evidence shows that "Advice to Apollo" was composed during Dryden's
"retirement" from the stage between the production of *Aureng-Zebe* (17
Nov. 1675) and that of *All for Love* (12 Dec. 1677). As Wilson conjectured, the poem may have been a joint effort by the group of Rochester's cronies who assembled at Woodstock in autumn of 1677 (*Court Wits,*
p. 195). "Advice to Apollo" is a satire against satires in which Rochester
is praised for writing love poems:

> *Rochester*'s easie Muse does still improve,
> Each hour thy little wealthy World of Love,
> (That World in which each Muse is thought a Queen)
> That he must be forgiven in charity then;
> Though his sharp Satyrs have offended thee;
> In charity to Love who will decay,
> When his delightfull Muse (its only stay)
> Is by thy Power severely ta'ne away.

IV

After the concentrated satirical bombardment of Rochester between spring of 1676 and autumn of 1677, an unexplained two-year armistice set in until late 1679. Dryden's preface to *All for Love* was published in March 1678, but this attack is not in verse, and it owes little to the image of Rochester in the verse satires. Hostilities were resumed with Mulgrave's passage on Rochester in "An Essay upon Satyr," a copy of which was in Rochester's hands on 21 November 1679 (Wilson, *Rochester-Savile Letters*, p. 73). Familiar though this long passage is, it should be given in full to illustrate its continuity with the tradition:

> Roches⟨te⟩r I despise for his meer want of wit,
> Though thought to have a Tail and Cloven Feet;
> For while he mischief means to all mankind,
> Himself alone the ill effects does find;
> And so like Witches justly suffers shame,

Forbear (then) Civil Wars, and strike not down
Love, who alone supports thy tottering Crown.
    (*Poems on Affairs of State*, 1697 [Case 211-1-a], p. [1]212)

The other passage, written sometime during the middle 1670s, is found in James Carkesse's *Lucida Intervalla*, 1679 (p. 51), a collection of verses purportedly composed by an inmate of Bedlam. Carkesse whimsically predicts that he will soon be welcoming various authors of lampoons:

> *Bucks* both and *Rochester*, unless they mend,
> Hither the *King* designs forthwith to send:
> *Shepherd* and *Dreyden* too, must on 'em wait;
> For he's resolved at once to rid the State,
> Of this *Poetick*, *Wanton*, *Mad-like* Tribe,
> Whose *Rampant Muse* does *Court* and *City* Gibe.

For information on Carkesse, see Hugh Macdonald, "The Attacks on Dryden," *Essays and Studies by Members of the English Association*, 21 (1936), 41–74.

Whose harmless malice is so much the same;
False are his words, affected is his wit,
So often he does aim, so seldom hit;
To every face he cringes while he speaks,
But when the Back is turn'd the head he breaks;
Mean in each Action, lewd in every Limb,
Manners themselves are mischievous in him:
A proof that chance alone makes every Creature,
A very *Killig⟨re⟩w* without good Nature;
For what a *Bessus* has he always liv'd,
And his own *Kickings* notably contriv'd:
(For there's the folly that's still mixt with fear)
Cowards more blows than any Heroe bear;
Of fighting sparks some may her pleasures say,
But 'tis a bolder thing to run away:
The World may well forgive him all his ill,
For ev'ry fault does prove his penance still;
Falsly he falls into some dangerous Noose,
And then as meanly labours to get loose;
A life so infamous is better quitting,
Spent in base injury and low submitting:
I'd like to have left out his Poetry;
Forgot by all almost as well as me.
Sometimes he has some humour, never wit,
And if it rarely, very rarely hit:
'Tis under so much nasty rubbish laid,
To find it out's the Cinder-womans trade;
Who for the wretched remnants of a fire,
Must toil all day in ashes and in mire;
So lewdly dull his idle works appear,
The wretched Texts deserve no Comments here;
Where one poor thought sometimes left all alone,

> For a whole page of dulness to attone:
> 'Mongst forty bad, one tolerable line,
> Without expression, fancy, or design.[4]

Virtually every feature of this portrait, even the suggestion that Rochester was a devil, had appeared in earlier lampoons. Nevertheless, Mulgrave has arranged his inherited material so as to emphasize three alleged aspects of Rochester's character: (1) impotent malice, chiefly flattery as preparation for attempted treachery; (2) cowardice; (3) poor obscene poetry. Doubtless these three emphases were adopted partly to give coherence to the portrait, but it is interesting that each had a possible source in Mulgrave's personal experiences with Rochester. Since he cherished literary aspirations despite his limited talent, Mulgrave had reason to depreciate the poetry of an overpowering rival. Moreover, since Rochester was directly or indirectly responsible for attacks on Mulgrave in a multitude of lampoons, Mulgrave might well think it advantageous to accuse his adversary of malice, especially ineffectual malice. The charge of cowardice may allude to the brawl at Epsom, but it probably refers also to Rochester's behavior when Mulgrave challenged him to a duel in November 1669.

Similar in tone to Mulgrave's passage, though less artful, is a lengthy attack on Rochester in a Tory lampoon of unknown authorship written about two months later. This poem, which the manuscript text quoted below describes as "A Satyr ag^t. L^d. Roch. & Petitionings 1679/80," has hitherto escaped identification as a satire on Rochester. The date supplied in the manuscript is remarkably accurate, for internal evidence indicates that this lampoon was probably composed in January 1679/80. Both its title and its text mention Whig "Petitionings" for an early meet-

4. *The Fourth (and Last) Collection of Poems, Satyrs, Songs, &c.,* 1689 (Case 189–4), p. 31.

ing of Parliament, a political maneuver which Shaftesbury initiated about December 1679 and brought to a climax the following
month. Moreover, since the lampoon exhorts the King to "Call
home thy banish'd brother," it could scarcely have been written
after 28 January, when Charles announced in Council that he was
recalling James from Scotland. The passage on Rochester constitutes the first half of the poem:

> Amongst the Race of England's modern Peers,
> There's one whose looks, betray his lewder Years.
> Whome early Nature for all Ill did frame,
> And time increas'd not faster than his Fame.
> Unheard of vices were his studied care,
> The effects of which his rotten ruins wear.
> His sight's a terror to the boldest Punk,
> Who shunn's him more y^n. Pembroke, when hee's drunk.
> But tho' to Pox, & Impotence confin'd,
> His bodye's less corrupted then his Mind.
> Both Politick, & Heroe hee'd be thought,
> But Jamese's ruine has his Judgement bought,
> And Epsom Hedg can wittness how he fought.
> To a Soul so mean ev'n Shadwell is a stranger,
> Nay little Sid: (it seems) less values danger.
> (The most hen-heart-d wretches of the Age,
> Who ne're durst give offence but on ye stage,)
> But on such trash my time is ill bestow'd,
> Those Hackney Cowards in the comon Road.
> The man whose Caracter I would relate,
> From Infamy refin'd derives his Fate.
> As France can tell where he the broyl begann,
> Engaged his freind, & then away he ran.
> This is that worship'd Idoll who $w^{th's}$ Pen,

Detracts the best of Monarchs, best of Men.
Whose Libells wholly tend to move sedition,
(Like those good men who now adays petition.)
Falshood & knavery do his Moralls guide,
(A stain to Honor, & a slave to Pride.)
Yett courts & flatters you in ev'ry place
And all the while's designing y^r disgrace
The most Fantastick of all fools 'ith' Nation,
Industrious onely to be out of fashion.[5]

Despite the information in the heading of this lampoon, the passage may not at first look much like a description of Rochester, which is perhaps the reason why its subject has remained unidentified. Every detail is explicable as a reference to Rochester, however, and it is doubtful that any other contemporary noble-

5. B. M. Add. MS. 23722, fol. 73^r. The lampoon also appears in Folger MS. M. b. 12, fol. 2^r; B. M. Sloane MS. 655, fol. 8^r; Victoria and Albert Museum MS. Dyce 43, p. 8; Edinburgh MS. DC.1.3, p. 25; Vienna MS. 14090, fol. 10^v; and *Poems on Affairs of State*, 1704 (Case 211-3-a), p. 144, reprinted 1716 (Case 211-3-b), p. 128. None of these texts carries an ascription. The Folger, Dyce, and Vienna manuscripts may all be in the same handwriting.

The Tory lampoon was followed by "An Answer to the former Satyr" ("Amongst the writing race of Modern Witts"), whose unknown Whig author was so intent on echoing his opponent's phraseology that his passage on Rochester fails to offer anything new. Because of his wobbly irony, not even his real attitude toward Rochester is clear:

The first whose Character he would relate,
For want of Witt, & Fashion finds his Fate.
Theres not so false, so in famous a Thing,
So lew'd a Wretch ith' Court (God bless the King)
To Pox, & Impotence as much confin'd,
As little Politick, & no more refind.
In's heart the Honor, & in's Bones the dryness,
Just such a Heroe is his Royall Highness,
Had this dull wretch but his deserved fall,
Witt then and truth might flourish at Whitehall.

The quotation is from B. M. Add. MS. 23722, fol. 74^r. The poem is printed in *Poems on Affairs of State*, 1704 (Case 211-3-a), p. 147.

man could fill the specifications so well. Generally the portrait incorporates the features we have observed in earlier lampoons. Its subject is described as malicious, sycophantic, treacherous, cowardly, impotent, sexually perverted, and disfigured by venereal disease. He has written poetry, including at least one satire on King Charles—probably Rochester's "scepter" lampoon. He is admittedly a "worship'd Idoll," as Rochester was among such friends as Shadwell and Sedley ("little Sid," the nickname used also in "An Essay upon Satyr"). Possibly derived from Mulgrave's passage is the picture of this nobleman as a decayed gallant whose formerly fashionable manners now make him a parody of the true gentleman. Positive identification is afforded by the accusation that "Epsom Hedg can wittness how he fought": Rochester was the only peer who participated in the brawl at Epsom.

Other features of the portrait are more difficult. So far as is known, no single incident in Rochester's career fully satisfies the allegation that

> . . . France can tell where he the broyl begann,
> Engaged his freind, & then away he ran.

Most details in this couplet could refer to the Epsom affair: Rochester recommenced that "broyl" by drawing his sword, thereby fatally engaging his friend Downs, after which he ran away. But why "France"? Possibly the unknown satirist has tried to impose the circumstances of the Epsom brawl upon an earlier altercation in Paris which achieved international notoriety at the time, though Rochester's part in it was secondary. At the Paris opera in late June 1669, as Rochester was sitting on the stage with William Lord Cavendish (later Earl and Duke of Devonshire), one of a group of drunken French officers began to insult Cavendish, who thereupon struck the Frenchman in the face. Swords were quickly out of their sheaths, and Cavendish, badly outnumbered, found himself backed against the side scenes with several dangerous wounds. He was saved by a Swiss servant of Ralph Montagu (the English ambassador), who seized him and threw him into the pit. Rochester's actions during this melee are less fully recorded (he may have been slightly wounded while attempting to aid his companion), but the episode was widely remembered to Cavendish's credit.[6]

Equally problematic, but far more important, is the charge that Rochester was a moving spirit in the Whig campaign to exclude the Duke of York from the royal succession. This information, if true, would be highly significant. Throughout most of his life, Rochester seems to have avoided the quarrels of political parties. To be sure, there is no evidence that he ever broke off his close friendships with prominent Whigs like Dorset and Buckingham. Also, parliamentary records provide some support for the accusation in the lampoon: during 1679, Rochester voted consistently with the Whig leaders.[7] That Rochester helped to *lead* the fight for exclusion is, however, difficult to accept; such action on his part would inevitably be documented in numerous contemporary sources besides the lampoon. Possibly its Tory author, gambling that his readers would consider Rochester totally disreputable, hoped to convict the entire Whig party of guilt by association.

The two portraits just discussed are the work of an unimaginative prig and a party hack, but one may wonder whether their forbidding picture of Rochester as a superannuated debauchee

6. HMC, *Sixth Report*, p. 366; *Buccleuch and Queensberry*, *1*, 429–30. Sir William Temple, *Letters*, ed. Jonathan Swift, 1700, 2, 70–71. Grove, *The Lives of All the Earls and Dukes of Devonshire*, 1764, pp. 31–32. Francis Bickley, *The Cavendish Family* (London, Constable, 1911), pp. 150–51.

7. *Journals of the House of Lords*, *13*, 565, 587, 594.

was entirely the result of personal and political enmity. Rochester had little more than six months to live; by this time, his protracted devotion to Bacchus and Venus, attractive enough ten years before, may have left visibly repellent marks on the aging thirty-two-year-old libertine.

Apart from a possible allusion to Rochester as "*Lord Lampoon and Monsieur Song*" in Otway's *The Poet's Complaint of his Muse,* published about 22 January 1679/80,[8] no other satires on Rochester are known to have been written during his lifetime. His name turns up occasionally in lampoons composed after his death on 26 July 1680, but such references are better considered an aspect of his posthumous reputation and therefore find no place in this discussion.

V

A significant conclusion should emerge from the foregoing quotations of lampoons on Rochester: though the satirists created a consistent cartoon portrait of the Earl which developed discernibly over the years, it never approached the success of their characterizations of other Restoration figures like Mulgrave and Scroope. One aim of the satirists' rhetorical strategy was to persuade the reader to substitute their mythic image for the real person. Thus a measure of their failure with Rochester is that the man remains more fascinating than the myth.

Some understanding of the satirists' plight may be gleaned from Dryden's prose attack on the Earl in the preface to *All for Love,* which can scarcely be ignored in this chapter. Though

8. *The Works of Thomas Otway,* ed. J. C. Ghosh (Oxford, Clarendon Press, 1932), 2, 412. *Narcissus Luttrell's Popish Plot Catalogues,* intro. by F. C. Francis (Oxford, Basil Blackwell, 1956), p. [2]18. Otway's poem was advertised in the *Term Catalogues* in February 1679/80.

Dryden's partisans have doubtless felt obliged to defend it, his passage on Rochester suffers by comparison either with "An Allusion to Horace," which it answers, or with Dryden's own brilliant mythic portrayal of Shadwell in *Mac Flecknoe*, written about this same date. Whatever the root cause of Dryden's difficulty, one reason why Rochester's attack on the laureate is so convincing is that it mingles praise with its censure, whereas Dryden allows his opponent nothing. With ingratiating generosity (real or feigned), Rochester concedes Dryden's merits as a poet:

> But to be just, 'twill to his praise be found,
> His *Excellencies* more than faults abound
> Nor dare I from his sacred Temples tear,
> That *Lawrel*, which he best deserves to wear.
>
> (A-1680-HU, p. 43)

By contrast, Dryden's description of Rochester, "this Rhyming Judge of the Twelve-penny Gallery, this Legitimate Son of *Sternhold*" who allegedly cannot write his own name,[9] is so patently unfair that the objective reader could not accept it in imagination or as fact, especially if "An Allusion to Horace" lies open before him as implicit testimony against Dryden's accusations.

Various reasons may explain why Dryden and the verse satirists had such trouble creating a serviceable mythic image of Rochester. Twentieth-century readers forget too readily the commanding advantages which Rochester possessed over most of his opponents. Besides *scandalum magnatum*, not a risk to be taken lightly by a commoner, Rochester's position as literary dictator and arbiter of fashion was formidable, nor did he hesi-

9. *All for Love: or, The World well Lost*, 1678, sigs. b3ᵛ–b4ᵛ.

tate to crush an opposing satirist with the satirist's own weapons, if he thought the man worth the trouble. Possibly the danger of legal reprisal led Dryden, after meditating his attack a full two years, to portray Rochester's character in a form distorted almost beyond recognition. Similar fears may have cramped the creative urges of some of the verse satirists.

Along other lines, the satirists may have found an obstacle imposed by the origin of their mythic image of Rochester, which apparently began its existence among his cronies as a form of joshing. Once established, the clichés of this flippant characterization would be difficult to alter. Altered and developed they must be, however, if a hostile satirist expected his serious image of Rochester to carry conviction with an audience.

Even if these two causes were not operative, Restoration satirists would still have faced a severe challenge, for Rochester's real-life personality, especially as viewed by friendly observers, embodied unique qualities which only a very gifted writer could incorporate successfully into a satirical portrait. Most of the lampoons (D'Urfey's lyric, for example) tend to portray Rochester as little more than an ordinary rakehell who happened to be a peer—a mere bully like Philip Herbert, Earl of Pembroke, to whom Rochester is compared in the Tory tirade at the end of the preceding section of this chapter. Such a characterization impales the satirist on the horns of a dilemma: if Rochester is so insignificant, why bother to attack him? Only two poets apparently recognized the problem and took measures to solve it. Oldham, we have seen, tried to invest his mythic image of Rochester with some of the man's actual stature. Scroope took an opposite tack by denying, in a tone of sweet reasonableness, that Rochester possessed this stature. His epigrammatic "Answer" to Rochester's abuse of him beautifully illustrates his strategy:

> Raile on poore feeble *Scribler*, speak of me,
> In as bad Terms, as the *World* speaks of thee.
> Sit swelling in thy Hole, like a vext *Toad*,
> And full of *Pox*, and *Malice*, spit abroad.
> Thou can'st ⟨blast⟩ no *Mans Fame*, with thy ill word,
> Thy Pen, is full as harmless as thy Sword.[1]

Frustrating target that Rochester must have been for his fellow satirists, their final humiliation is that none of them equaled the skill of a brief poem in which he apparently satirized himself. In sixteen dramatically compressed lines, this poem presents a fictitious dialogue between Rochester and a postboy:

> [Rochester] Son of A whore God dam you can you tell
> A Peerless Peer the Readyest way to Hell
> Ive out swilld Baccus sworn of my own make
> Oaths wod fright furies & make Pluto quake
> Ive swived more whores more ways yⁿ Sodoms walls
> Ere knew or the College of Romes Cardinalls
> Witness Heroick scars, look here nere go
> sear cloaths & ulcers from yᵉ top to toe
> frighted at my own mischeifes I have fled
> and bravely left my lifes defender dead
> Broke houses to break chastity & died
> that floor with murder which my lust denyed
> Pox on it why do I speak of these poor things
> I have blasphemed my god & libelld Kings
> the readyest way to Hell come quick
> Boy   nere stirr
> The readyest way my Lords by Rochester [2]

1. A-1680-HU, p. 50. Since "blast" in l. 5 is the reading of all early manuscripts including the Yale MS., the reading of A-1680-HU, "hurt," must be a corruption.

2. The text is that of B. M. Harl. MS. 6914, fol. 21ʳ, with the fol-

Though several early texts assign the poem to 1674, this date can scarcely be correct, for the ninth and tenth lines almost certainly allude to the Epsom affair of 17 June 1676. While his "lifes defender," Downs, tried to quell the "mischeifes" which Rochester had set in motion by drawing his sword upon the constable, the "frighted" Rochester not very bravely fled, leaving Downs "dead" or at least mortally injured. This identification is further supported by marginal notations in three manuscripts: in Victoria and Albert Museum MS. Dyce 43, "lifes defender" is glossed as "Downs," in Vienna MS. 14090 as "Cap. Downs," and in B. M. Harl. MS. 6914 as "[C]aptn [D]owns" (with the initial letters of both words removed by trimming of the leaf).

lowing alterations: the heading, "To the Post Boy by L^d: Rochester 1674," is omitted, as is the marginal gloss opposite ll. 9–10; l. 15 is divided to signify the change of speakers; and the marginal note "Boy" is placed at l. 15 instead of l. 16.

The poem is headed "Verses to the Post Boy" in Victoria and Albert Museum MS. Dyce 43, p. 241, and "To y^e. Post Boy" in Vienna MS. 14090, fol. 128^r, where the table of contents lists it as "Verses to y^e. Postboy by Roch^r." Both of these manuscripts, which are probably in the same handwriting, drop the last word of the poem ("Rochester") below the line, evidently to make it serve as an ascription. The poem is headed "E: of Rochesters Conference With a Post Boy. 1674" in Bodl. MS. Firth C. 15, p. 15; "Earle of Rochester's Conference with a Post Boy. 1674" in the Ohio MS., p. 16 (the Wilson-Pinto text); and "Earle of Rochesters Conference with a Post Boy" in Taylor MS. 2, p. 8. These three manuscripts are almost certainly in the same handwriting. Taylor MS. 3, p. 254, gives the poem as "Roch: to a Post boy," and it appears as "To A Postboy: E: of R." in an uncatalogued manuscript at the University of Illinois.

Prinz published the first six lines of the poem as "Spoken to a Postboy, 1674" and described them as "Extempore to a Post-boy, reproduced from an old manuscript entry in vol. I of my copy of The Poetical Works of the Earls of Rochester, Roscomon, Dorset, etc. London, 1739" (*Rochesteriana: Being Some Anecdotes Concerning John Wilmot Earl of Rochester*, Leipzig, privately printed, 1926, pp. 9, 56). Hayward printed the same six lines and said of them: "These lines, spoken extempore, to a Post-boy, are attributed to him [Rochester] in a MS. commonplace book, and dated 1674" (*Collected Works*, p. xlix). Hayward does not identify his commonplace book.

Moreover, the succeeding couplet of the poem may be a lurid exaggeration of the portion of this episode in which Rochester and his companions, searching for a whore, broke into the constable's house and beat him. Since the verses to the postboy describe Downs as "dead," they were probably written after he finally succumbed on 27 June. Probably, too, they were not written much later, for they evidently figure in "In defence of Satyr" as the "*Buffoone* Conceit" with which (so Scroope alleges) Rochester attempted to shrug off his responsibility in the Epsom imbroglio. Very late June or early July 1676 seems the likeliest date for these verses, which, if Rochester wrote them, are surely one of the strangest acts of contrition on record.

The poem to the postboy has a curious textual history. Though it circulated in manuscript among Rochester's contemporaries, no portion of the poem reached print until 1926, nor has any twentieth-century editor of Rochester accorded it an unqualified status in the canon; indeed, its text has never before been published in full. Hayward and Prinz both printed only the first six lines, Hayward in the introduction to his edition and Prinz, using a different text, in his *Rochesteriana*. Subsequently, in an article, John Harold Wilson claimed the poem for Rochester but printed a version which lacks two lines. Pinto, adopting Wilson's version for his edition, nevertheless consigned it to his appendix of doubtful poems.[3]

These disagreements concerning the poem's authenticity may be due to titles in some early texts which could imply either that Rochester wrote the poem or that it was composed by some unnamed author as a lampoon on the Earl. Examples of these ambiguous titles are "Earle of Rochester's Conference with a Post Boy" and "Roch: to a Post boy." Other headings, however, seem

3. Wilson, "Rochester's 'Buffoon Conceit,'" *Modern Language Notes*, 56 (1941), 372–73. Pinto, *Poems*, p. 147.

to identify Rochester as author—for instance, "To the Post Boy by L^d: Rochester" and "Verses to y^e. Post-boy by Roch^r." Also, two texts drop the last word of the poem ("Rochester") below the line, apparently to make it serve as an ascription. There is no clear evidence that Rochester did not write the poem, nor is there any ascription to another author. Considerations of style further strengthen the case for Rochester's authorship: few poets writing in 1676 had such a flair for the dramatic or could reproduce Rochester's distinctive heroic-couplet manner so well. One can hardly quarrel with Wilson's judgment:

> Although it seems incredible that a poet could write so viciously of himself, I am persuaded that Rochester did so write. The poem is clearly his style of rough, vigorous verse, and his sense of irony was perfectly capable of such an attitude.

Pinto's inference that the poem is a kind of tape-recording of an actual episode—he printed it as an impromptu—scarcely merits serious attention. Experiences in real life do not occur in finished heroic couplets and perfect dramatic form, nor would postboys ordinarily be so clever.

An astonishing feature of these half-boastful, half-penitential verses is that Rochester is working in the tradition propagated by the lampoons written against him. Indeed, he composed his lines during a period when hostile lampoons were specially numerous. Rochester's poem focuses upon the Epsom affair, the incident most frequently cited to his disfavor by his enemies. He had "libelld Kings" in his "scepter" lampoon, mentioned by several satirists, and he possibly "blasphemed my god" in "A Satyr against Mankind," which called forth such lengthy disquisitions from Griffith and Lessey. Almost every detail of the familiar mythic image is here, slightly exaggerated: Rochester depicts

himself as blasphemer, drunkard, brawler, bully (even a mur-
derer), coward, whoremaster, and sexual degenerate covered with
sores from venereal disease. Rochester succeeds, however, in
transcending the limitations inherent in the traditional image of
himself. Following much the same line adopted by Oldham, but
far more effectively, Rochester infuses his self-portrait with
almost Satanic energy and grandeur. The result gives the elec-
trifying impression of being simultaneously in contact with both
myth and reality. It is as if Rochester turned to his brother
satirists with a mocking smile, saying, "Look! This is how it
should be done!"

7.

The Holograph Manuscript of Rochester's Poems

I

The publication in 1953 of virtually the full text of the so-called "Portland MS.," the only known manuscript of Rochester's poems in his own handwriting, was an event long awaited by students of Restoration literature. This manuscript was first reported by Francis Needham, at that time Librarian at Welbeck Abbey, who in 1934 printed two poems from Rochester's autograph in his *Welbeck Miscellany No. 2.*[1] In 1935, in his biography of Rochester, Vivian de Sola Pinto reprinted one of these poems and published for the first time four more poems and a fragment of a prose comedy in Rochester's hand, together with a single poem from the same manuscript in the hand of Rochester's

---

1. *Welbeck Miscellany No. 2. A Collection of Poems by Several Hands,* ed. Francis Needham (Bungay, Suffolk, R. Clay & Sons, 1934); hereafter called "Needham."

wife. Thereafter, for nearly twenty years, students of Rochester were left to speculate about the remaining poems in the Portland MS., until Pinto printed almost all of them in his edition of Rochester. Now that these texts are available, they invite an assessment of statements previously made concerning them as well as an attempt to determine what further conclusions they may support.[2]

On the whole, the new material from the Portland MS., when it finally appeared, was mildly disappointing—especially since this was claimed to be "the most important manuscript source for the text of Rochester's poems" (*Poems*, p. xlv). Of the poems in Rochester's hand, only two had not been printed in full or in part before 1953; one of these two is a rough fragment, and their combined length is only fourteen lines. The six new poems in Lady Rochester's hand are of relatively minor importance. Even the biographical interest of the poems in the Portland MS. is limited because, with one possible exception, their dates of composition cannot be established with any degree of precision.

The Portland MS., we are told, was once owned by Edward Harley, Earl of Oxford, who may have acquired it along with the Rochester correspondence still preserved in Harleian MS. 7003 in the British Museum (Needham, p. 51). At the time when Needham described the Portland MS., it was part of the Duke of Portland's collection at Welbeck Abbey; subsequently this volume was transferred to the library of the University of Nottingham, where it is now deposited. It is described as "a finely bound album in which there have been inserted drafts of a number of poems, some of which are in the autographs of

2. My remarks in following paragraphs are based on photostats and a microfilm of the Portland MS. In exchange for these photographs, which were supplied early in 1952 by the University of Nottingham, Professor Pinto was granted unrestricted permission to publish extensive Rochester material from a private collection of manuscripts in America.

Rochester and his wife" (*Poems*, p. xlv). The poems appear on scraps of paper of various shapes and sizes, most of them exhibiting fold-marks. In all, the Portland MS. contains nine poems and part of a prose comedy in Rochester's hand, eight poetical drafts including two copies of the same poem in Lady Rochester's hand, and one brief lyric in a third hand as yet unidentified. There is no reason to doubt the identifications of the first two hands. Both Rochester and his wife possessed rather distinctive styles of calligraphy—Rochester's the untutored scrawl of a Restoration nobleman, Lady Rochester's more disciplined—and comparisons can easily be made with the holograph letters in Harleian MS. 7003.

Unfortunately, the poems and the prose comedy are reproduced in scattered locations in Pinto's biography and edition. Discussion of their significance therefore requires a listing of all the items in the Portland MS. and the places where they may be found in print:

Fols. 1^r-1^v. Rochester's hand. No title. First line: "How perfect Cloris, & how free." Song of 32 lines in process of revision. Printed by Pinto, *Rochester*, p. 40, and *Poems*, p. 167; also printed in my article, "A Textual Paradox: Rochester's 'To a Lady in a Letter,' " *Papers of the Bibliographical Society of America, 54* (1960), 147–62.

Fols. 2^r-2^v. Rochester's hand. No title. First line: "T'was a dispute 'twixt heav'n & Earth." Lyric poem of 16 lines showing marks of revision. Printed by Needham, p. 51, and by Pinto, *Rochester*, p. 64, and *Poems*, p. 37.

Fol. 3^r. Rochester's hand. Title: "Song." First line: "Att Last you'l force mee to confess." Song of 8 lines containing one deletion and correction. Printed by Pinto, *Poems*, p. 38.

Fol. 4ʳ. Rochester's hand. No title. First line: "Leave this gawdy guilded Stage." Lyric poem of 10 lines containing one deletion and correction. Printed by Pinto, *Rochester*, p. 120, and *Poems*, p. 38.

Fol. 5ʳ. Rochester's hand. No title. First line: "Greate Mother of Eneas & of Love." Fragment of 8 lines of heroic couplets in process of composition and revision. Free translation of Lucretius, *De Rerum Natura*, 1.1–5. Printed by Pinto, *Poems*, p. 50.

Fol. 6ʳ. Rochester's hand. Title: "Sab: Lost." First line: "Shee yeilds, she yeilds, Pale Envy said Amen." Fragment of 12 lines in heroic couplets probably in process of composition. Printed by Pinto, *Rochester*, p. 49, and *Poems*, p. 61.

Fols. 7ʳ–7ᵛ. Rochester's hand. No title. First line: "Could I but make my wishes insolent." Ovidian love epistle of 26 lines in heroic couplets showing some marks of revision. Printed by Needham, p. 52, and Pinto, *Poems*, p. 42.

Fol. 8ʳ. Rochester's hand. No title. First line: "To forme a Plott." Epigram of 6 lines in rhymed pentameter verse. Printed by Pinto, *Poems*, p. 118.

Fols. 9ʳ–10ʳ. Rochester's hand. No title. First line: "What vaine unnecessary things are men." A rambling satirical fragment of 55 lines in heroic couplets; in process of composition and revision. Printed by Pinto, *Rochester*, p. 144 (opening lines only), and *Poems*, p. 116.

Fols. 11ʳ–11ᵛ. Rochester's hand. Part of the first scene of a prose comedy. Shows some marks of revision. Printed by Pinto, *Rochester*, p. 125.

Fol. 12ʳ. Lady Rochester's hand. Title: "Song." First line: "Nothing ades to loves fond fire." Song of 16 lines showing some marks of revision. Printed by Pinto, *Rochester*, p. 63, and *Poems*, p. 172.

Fol. 13ʳ. Lady Rochester's hand. Title: "Song." First line: "Phillis misfortunes that can be exprest." Song of 18 lines. Printed by Pinto, *Poems*, p. 143.

Fol. 14ʳ. Lady Rochester's hand. Title: "Song." First line: "Cloris misfortunes that can be exprest." Copy of the poem on fol. 13ʳ, differing only in accidentals and in the first line, where "Philis" has been deleted and "Cloris" substituted. Unpublished in this form.

Fol. 14ᵛ. Unidentified hand. No title. First line: "Your glory Phillis is in being lov'd." Lyric poem of 8 lines. Printed by Pinto, *Poems*, p. 144.

Fol. 15ʳ. Lady Rochester's hand. Title: "Song." First line: "Cloris to love without return." Song of 16 lines in process of revision. Printed by Pinto, *Poems*, p. 144.

Fol. 16ʳ. Lady Rochester's hand. No title. First line: "Continue still ingrate." Lyric poem of 8 lines. Probably a fragment, since part of a preceding line can barely be made out at the top of the sheet. Printed by Pinto, *Poems*, p. 145.

Fol. 17ʳ. Lady Rochester's hand. No title. First line: "Corrina vainly I pretend." Fragment of a song consisting of 15 lines in the early stages of composition and revision; the last 4 lines are a revised draft of the first 4. Printed by Pinto, *Poems*, p.145.

Fol. 17ᵛ. Lady Rochester's hand. No title. Single couplet: "Vertues my lawfull prince my tyrant love / His fauls dominion crulity [cruelty] does prove." Printed by Pinto, *Poems*, p. 146.

Fols. 18ʳ, 19ʳ–19ᵛ. Lady Rochester's hand. No title. First line: "Dearest Armilla could you once but guese." Fragment of a pastoral dialogue consisting of about 70 lines in the early stages of composition and revision; the deletions and corrections are so extensive that many of them are difficult to decipher. Approximately the first half of this draft is printed by Pinto, *Poems*, p. 146.

II

The authenticity of the ten pieces in Rochester's autograph seems beyond question. The prose comedy and six of the poems are probably or certainly in various stages of composition and revision, and two more poems exhibit a single deletion and correction each. Only one short poem, "To forme a Plott," appears to be a completed version bearing no marks of revision. Two of these poems are attributed to Rochester in other seventeenth-century sources. The initial poem in the Portland MS., the song beginning "How perfect Cloris, & how free," appears in the section of poems by or concerning Rochester in the Yale MS. and the Huntington edition of 1680 (A-1680-HU); it is also printed as Rochester's in Jacob Tonson's edition of 1691 (B-1691), and it is ascribed to him in Harvard MS. Eng. 636F. The brief lyric beginning "Att Last you'l force mee to confess" is printed as Rochester's in Tonson's *Examen Poeticum*, 1693, while in a miscellany published in 1676 it appears without ascription as an additional stanza to Rochester's famous song beginning "While on those lovely looks I gaze." [3] To my knowledge, none of the material in Rochester's hand has ever been attributed to another author.

The seven poems in Lady Rochester's autograph raise more difficult questions of authorship. The problem is neatly posed by the first poem in her hand, the song beginning "Nothing ades

3. See Part III for more detailed lists of the early texts and ascriptions of "While on those lovely looks I gaze" and "How perfect Cloris, & how free," which has the variant first line "How happy Cloris (were they free)." For the early texts and ascriptions of "Att Last you'l force mee to confess," see my article, "Two Rochester Songs," *Notes and Queries*, 201 (1956), 338–39.

to loves fond fire." This poem, the only one of the seven to be published before 1953, appears in the Yale MS. and the Huntington edition as "The Answer" to the song beginning "Give me leave to rail at you," which is probably genuine Rochester. Unhappily, the position of "The Answer" in the edition and the Yale MS. is ambiguous. Since it is part of the section of poems by or concerning Rochester, and since the Yale MS. gives no ascription for it, the scribe of the archetype of these two collections may have included it either as a poem by Rochester or as an answer to one of his by some other author (see Chapter 3). Other early texts of "The Answer" fail to resolve the ambiguity: either they carry no ascription or, like the text in Tonson's edition of 1691, they are probably descended from the Huntington edition.[4] Thus a decision as to whether this song is by Rochester, or by Lady Rochester, or even by an unidentified author must rest primarily on the evidence of the Portland MS.

When Pinto first published the Portland text of "The Answer" in 1935, he asserted that "a manuscript copy [of the poem] survives in Lady Rochester's handwriting and it is probably her own composition" (*Rochester*, p. 64). In 1950 James Thorpe, skeptical of this conclusion, ventured several objections which apply to all seven poems in Lady Rochester's autograph: "There is no other evidence that Lady Rochester courted the muses; Lady Rochester no doubt followed the fashion of making a copy of an appealing paper of verses that came to her hands; and Rochester did on other occasions assume more than one dramatic identity" (*Rochester's Poems*, p. 178). To these arguments one may add that Rochester could conceivably have composed and revised some of his poems, including "The Answer,"

---

4. See Part III for a more detailed list of the early texts and ascriptions of "Nothing ades to loves fond fire" (variant first line: "Nothing adds to your fond Fire").

by dictating them to his wife. In 1953, perhaps influenced by opinions such as Thorpe's, Pinto softened his earlier claim: "It is quite possible that Lady Rochester is the author of this poem." He concluded tentatively that the other six poems in Lady Rochester's hand, as well as the one in the unidentified hand, "may be either by Rochester or by Lady Rochester" (*Poems*, pp. 173, 228).

Sensible though Thorpe's position was under the circumstances, Lady Rochester's authorship of her seven poems is supported by evidence still withheld in 1950. Most important is a fact that is not indicated adequately even in Pinto's edition of 1953: four of the seven poems, including "The Answer," are unmistakably in the process of composition and revision. To be sure, the dictation theory could be invoked to explain how Rochester might be the author of two of these four poems as well as the three which exhibit no clear signs of revision. In the remaining two drafts, however—those beginning "Corrina vainly I pretend" and "Dearest Armilla could you once but guese"—the deletions, interlineations, and other evidences of revision are so complicated that it is difficult to believe the poems were composed by any hand other than the one which held the pen.

Moreover, the poems in Lady Rochester's autograph are differentiated from those in her husband's by considerations of theme, verse form, and esthetic quality. Lady Rochester's drafts are all love poems revealing no trace of the satirical emphasis so characteristic of Rochester, appearing frequently even in his lyrics; by contrast, two of the nine poems in his own hand are primarily satires, while several more are partially satirical in tone. No fewer than five of Rochester's nine poems are written in the heroic couplets which he elsewhere used so brilliantly, whereas only two of his wife's drafts employ this verse form, and their style is quite different. Taken as a whole, Lady Rochester's seven poems are noticeably inferior in quality to those in her husband's hand, even though some of the latter scarcely represent his best work.

In the face of this evidence, none of the remaining objections to Lady Rochester's authorship of the seven poems is effectual. The theory that she might have copied them from manuscripts in circulation fails to explain the revisions in four of her drafts. Also, except for "The Answer" and one special case to be discussed later, there is no contemporary record of her poems anywhere outside the Portland MS.: apparently six of the seven poems did not circulate. The fact that Lady Rochester is not otherwise known to have "courted the muses" will support no more than a weak *argumentum ex silentio*. Thus the conclusion seems inescapable that Lady Rochester is the author of the seven poems in her handwriting.

The authorship of the single poem in the unidentified hand, an eight-line love lyric beginning "Your glory Phillis is in being lov'd," must remain uncertain until new evidence appears. The mere fact of its presence in the Portland MS.—an assemblage of separate scraps of paper—is scarcely sufficient reason to attribute it either to Rochester or to his wife. Stylistically it is not unlike Lady Rochester's poems.

III

For most of the contents of the Portland MS., dates of composition cannot be determined even approximately. No date is available for the song in the unidentified hand, and virtually the same is true of all the poems in Lady Rochester's autograph. "The Answer" must, of course, have been written before its publication in the Huntington edition in late summer or early autumn of 1680, but all one can say of her other six poems is that they were composed after she reached the age of literary indiscretion and before her death in late July 1681.[5] Similarly undatable are Rochester's translation from Lucretius beginning "Greate Mother of Eneas & of Love" and his Ovidian love epistle beginning "Could I but make my wishes insolent." If the fragment with the cryptic title "Sab: Lost" refers to any particular woman in Rochester's life, there is apparently no way of discovering which one.

Other pieces in Rochester's hand seem to promise evidence of their dates of composition without really providing anything substantial. The fragment of a prose comedy, short though it is, contains so many clichés of Restoration comic plot structure that a date much before 1670 appears implausible. The lyric beginning "T'was a dispute 'twixt heav'n & Earth" is written in a quaint, old-fashioned style suggesting that it may be one of Rochester's early poems; such a conclusion could, however, be conjectural only. The lyric beginning "Leave this gawdy guilded Stage" may be addressed to an actress, but even if the recipient *was* Elizabeth Barry—Pinto's suggestion to that effect is not perhaps without merit—no precise date for the poem is forthcoming (*Rochester*, p. 119). Since the song "How perfect Cloris, & how free" is among Rochester's most mature lyrics, one may doubt Pinto's conclusion that it was "probably written not long after his return from his travels" in December 1664, when he was only seventeen years old (*Rochester*, p. 39). A *terminus ante quem* for its date of composition is furnished by its appearance (unnoticed by Pinto) in *A New Collection of the Choicest Songs*, 1676, which was licensed on 28 April 1676 and advertised in the *Term Catalogues* on 12 June 1676. This same volume (as

5. Narcissus Luttrell, *A Brief Historical Relation of State Affairs* (Oxford, 1857), *1*, 113; *Correspondence of the Family of Hatton*, ed. Edward Maunde Thompson (Westminster, Camden Society, 1878), *2*, 6. Lady Rochester's death date is sometimes given incorrectly as 20 August 1681.

Pinto also does not note) includes a text of "Att Last you'l force mee to confess."

Rochester's long satirical fragment in heroic couplets beginning "What vaine unnecessary things are men" offers a single topical allusion:

> 'Tis not the Player pleases but the Part
> Shee may like Rollo who despises Hart

The play in question is Beaumont and Fletcher's melodrama *The Bloody Brother,* usually known during the Restoration period as *Rollo Duke of Normandy* or simply *Rollo.* Unfortunately, Rochester's allusion does not help to date the poem, since *The Bloody Brother* was acted innumerable times during the Restoration, and Rollo was one of Charles Hart's most celebrated roles. Probably Rochester does not even refer to a specific series of performances. A tentative date for the poem may, however, be suggested by its similarities to Rochester's great heroic couplet satires of 1674–75, especially "Timon," "Tunbridge Wells," and "Artemisa to Cloe." As Pinto observes, a woman is the dramatic speaker in both "Artemisa to Cloe" and the fragment, and there are thematic resemblances (*Rochester,* p. 143).

The only poem in Rochester's hand which affords much opportunity for precise dating is the following six-line epigram:

> ————To forme a Plott,
> The blustring Bard whose rough unruly Rhyme
> Gives Plutarch's lives the lye in ev'ry Lyne
> Who rapture before nature does preferr
> And now himself turn'd his own Imager,
> Defaceth god's in ev'ry Character

The syntax of this epigram is not much clarified by Rochester's casual punctuation. The poem consists of a single periodic sentence whose main clause begins with the first three words of the second line and is completed by the last line; the fifth line is parenthetical. So interpreted, the epigram provides two pieces of information about the "blustring Bard" it satirizes. (1) He has written a narrative or dramatic work, based on Plutarch's *Lives* or bearing some relation to it, in which fidelity to his source and integrity of characterization are sacrificed to intrigue or incident. The work is written in ranting, bombastic rhymed verse. Almost certainly Rochester refers to a drama of the "heroic" species. (2) As indicated in the fifth line, the "blustring Bard" has also written some work conspicuously featuring a characterization of himself. The connective phrase "and now" implies that it is not the same work as his play but was written shortly afterward. These two conditions severely restrict the range of possible identifications, for they could scarcely be satisfied by more than one Restoration author.

Pinto suggests (*Poems*, pp. 213–14) that the ranting drama to which Rochester refers might be Dryden's *All for Love* (acted 12 Dec. 1677) or some play by Lee, who was a frequent borrower from Plutarch, notably in *The Rival Queens* (acted 17 Mar. 1676/7).[6] Both candidates seem unacceptable. Aside from the minor fact that *All for Love* is not in rhyme, neither writer had, before Rochester's death on 26 July 1680, followed up a play based largely on Plutarch with another work in which he obviously "turn'd his own Imager." The same is true of Sedley, whose *Antony and Cleopatra* (acted 12 Feb. 1676/7) uses Plutarch as its chief source. Shadwell, Settle, and Crowne do not fit Rochester's description. Also unfeasible is Pinto's further suggestion that the last two lines of the epigram allude to Mulgrave's "An Essay upon Satyr," which was being circulated in

6. In this chapter, all dates of dramatic performances and publication of plays are taken from Nicoll, *Restoration Drama*.

November 1679. Although Mulgrave included a character of himself in this poem, he is not known to have written any play prior to Rochester's death, let alone a play based on Plutarch. Moreover, if Rochester, like many of his contemporaries, believed that "An Essay upon Satyr" was wholly or partly written by Dryden, he would scarcely have supposed that it contained a self-portrait of its author.

The most likely candidate for identification as the "blustring Bard" seems to be Thomas Otway. Otway's first play, *Alcibiades* (acted 22 Sept. 1675), was based entirely on Plutarch, but Rochester probably refers to his later potboiler *The History and Fall of Caius Marius*, acted about September 1679 and published about November. Shortly thereafter, Otway "turn'd his own Imager" with a vengeance in *The Poet's Complaint of his Muse*, published about 22 January 1679/80.[7] Plutarch, along with Lucan and *Romeo and Juliet*, is a major source of *Caius Marius*, and the indebtedness to Plutarch is underlined by Otway's choice of ancient Rome for his setting. It is true that most of the play is in blank verse, but Rochester's term "Rhyme" could easily be a mistake on his part or a loose usage applied to poetry in general. Rochester's description of the "blustring Bard's" play is similar to the opinion of *Caius Marius* expressed by Otway's most recent editor, whose remarks are worth giving at length:

> Very little can be said in favour of this play. Otway has fallen between two stools and knocked his head against a third. The attempt to combine Shakespeare's romance with Plutarch's history has resulted in disaster to both, and mat-

7. *Caius Marius* is dated 1680 on its title page but was advertised in the *Term Catalogues* in November 1679. The *Poet's Complaint* is dated 1680 on its title page; though it was not advertised in the *Term Catalogues* until February 1679/80, it is dated 22 January by Narcissus Luttrell (*Narcissus Luttrell's Popish Plot Catalogues*, intro. by F. C. Francis, Oxford, Basil Blackwell, 1956, p. 218).

ters have been made worse by the attempt to make the feud between the rival Roman factions suggestive of the Whig and Tory controversy of Otway's time [cf. Rochester's "Plott"]. The different interests have not blended, and the play remains a clumsy patchwork with the seams staring. The characterization is crude, and the blank verse, in the adoption of which Otway follows the lead recently given by Dryden, is stiff and monotonous. Motives are left awaiting better explanation, and the plot merrily gads about wherever it will. For no earthly reason Martha drops from the clouds in one scene, only to disappear thither in a few moments. It seems as if, after returning from Flanders with a rough sketch of the historical part in his pocket, Otway, in the pressure of want, stitched it up with scenes and passages hurriedly rifled out of Shakespeare, and made over the piece to Betterton.[8]

In the *Poet's Complaint,* the "poet" is Otway himself, and he includes enough autobiographical material to make the poem an important source of information about his life. Though it is far from certain that he attacks Rochester in this poem, Otway's editors are agreed that the line *"Lord Lampoon* and *Monsieur Song"* refers to the Earl.[9] Whatever Otway's intentions may have been, it is possible that Rochester thought he had been attacked in the *Poet's Complaint* and that he composed his epigram as a reply during the early months of 1680.

If Rochester's epigram refers to Otway, it sheds new light on his relations with that distinguished dramatist during a period on which there has hitherto been no reliable information. The

8. *The Works of Thomas Otway,* ed. J. C. Ghosh (Oxford, Clarendon Press, 1932), *1,* 46.

9. Ghosh, *1,* 16; *2,* 412, 524. *The Complete Works of Thomas Otway,* ed. Montague Summers (London, Nonesuch Press, 1926), *3,* 310.

earliest record of any contact between the two men is Rochester's "An Allusion to Horace," written during the winter of 1675–76, in which Otway's *Alcibiades* deservedly receives unfavorable notice:

> Though ev'n that *Talent,* merits in some sort,
> That can divert the *Rabble,* and the *Court.*
> Which blundring S⟨*ettle*⟩, never cou'd attain,
> And puzling O⟨*tway*⟩, labors at in vain.
>   (A-1680-HU, p. 41)

This judgment of Otway's merits quickly altered, however, for Rochester took it upon himself to recommend Otway's second play, *Don Carlos* (acted 8 June 1676), to the King and the Duke of York, thus assuring its success. In his preface (pub. *c.* June 1676), Otway acknowledges his "unspeakable Obligations" to Rochester and shows the extent of his alliance with Rochester's literary faction by jeering at Dryden, hinting at a friendship with Shadwell, and boasting generally that "I had the greatest party of men of wit and sence on my side" (Ghosh, *1*, 174). Perhaps at Rochester's advice, Otway dedicated *Don Carlos* to the Duke of York, but he seized the next opportunity of giving credit to his real patron by dedicating to Rochester his third effort, *Titus and Berenice* with the *Cheats of Scapin* (pub. *c.* Feb. 1676/7).[1] A complicating development is Otway's alleged hopeless love affair with Elizabeth Barry, Rochester's mistress, on which there have been many romantic conjectures but few facts. It is not known certainly when this affair began, how it affected Rochester, or even whether it occurred at all.

---

1. The attack on Otway in "A Session of the Poets," written about November 1676, is not relevant to this discussion because there is no evidence that Rochester composed the poem (see Chapter 12).

After the publication of *Titus and Berenice,* silence descends upon the relationship between Otway and Rochester. Otway left for military service in Flanders early in 1678; his first comedy, *Friendship in Fashion,* was performed in April during his absence; he returned to England early in 1679; he overcame the future Duke of Marlborough in a duel in June; and *Caius Marius* was acted about September. Rochester's probable attack on Otway in his epigram, together with Otway's possible attack on his former patron in the *Poet's Complaint,* suggests that some kind of enmity sprang up between the two men before 1680. Future investigation may reveal whether this enmity stemmed from Otway's courtship of Elizabeth Barry, from Rochester's disappointment with Otway's plays, from Otway's strong Tory sympathies, or from some other cause as yet unknown.

IV

Returning now to the Portland MS., a few conclusions may be ventured concerning the new insights it affords into Rochester's relationship to his own poetry. The manuscript is, of course, uniquely valuable because it preserves the only known examples of Rochester's poems in the process of composition and revision. Perhaps the most important inference to be drawn is simply that Rochester *did* revise his work. Decades of scholarship have not yet dispelled the popular notion that he tossed off his verses during intervals of drunken frivolity with his fellow Wits, unconcerned for posterity or even for the fate of his productions beyond the night's debauch. Though his revisions in the Portland MS. could not be described as painstaking, they at least show that he took his poetry seriously. The manuscript reveals nothing unusual about his methods of composing and revising except the speed and facility with which he normally worked. For a first draft, he apparently began composition with the initial lines of a poem and proceeded consecutively as fast as inspiration permitted, sometimes returning to insert better readings directly over the words he wished to cancel or above the line. Next he seems to have written out a fair copy, revising both in the process of transcription and by making minor deletions and corrections after the copy was completed. Interestingly, Rochester's drafts, unlike those of his wife, include remarkably few "false starts" where a whole passage has been written down, crossed out, and then rewritten in slightly altered form.

A peculiar feature of the Portland MS. is that most of Rochester's drafts, even those which are virtually final recensions, give no titles. Though the manuscript contains nine Rochester poems as well as the prose comedy, the only headings are the cryptic "Sab: Lost" and a perfunctory "Song." This circumstance suggests that Rochester may not have been responsible for the clumsy titles by which some of his works were afterward known. It is not easy to believe that a poet who was usually a master of *le mot juste* would have perpetrated such outrages as "An Epistolary Essay from M. G. to O. B. upon their Mutual Poems" or "A Letter fancy'd from Artemisa in the Town, to Cloe in the Country"; these have the look of later scribal additions. Also, collation of the early manuscript versions of Rochester's poetry reveals that they are generally less consistent in their titles than the texts of other authors; scribes may have contributed different headings in different branches of a stemma. If Rochester did not ordinarily choose his own titles, a twentieth-century editor might feel justified in altering them where they do not seem suitable.

Individual works prompt further observations. The graceful

lyric beginning "T'was a dispute 'twixt heav'n & Earth" is almost unique among Rochester's poems in its use of an early seventeenth-century style of hyperbolic compliment. Its presence in the Portland MS. suggests that, like his contemporary Andrew Marvell, Rochester was not only a literary descendant of Cowley and Donne but also a son of the Sons of Ben.

At least two poems in the manuscript imply an attitude of veneration toward classical antiquity, especially Roman antiquity, which is inherent also in Rochester's "Allusion to Horace" and some of his other satires and translations. These two poems are the translation from Lucretius and the epigram on Otway, in which Rochester protests what he apparently considers an almost sacrilegious misuse of Plutarch. Though it is scarcely startling for an Augustan writer to show respect for Greek and Roman civilization, the popular notion persists that Rochester was a renegade who flouted all traditional standards. Outwardly rebellious he may have been, but his innermost values were as conservative as Pope's and more conservative, perhaps, than Dryden's.

The fragment of a prose comedy points up the central paradox of Rochester's relation to the drama of his day: despite his interest in the stage, his patronage of several major dramatists, his real-life role as prototype for innumerable witty young men in Restoration comedies, and his highly developed dramatic sense as shown in his poems, Rochester is not known to have written a single original play. The prose fragment may suggest some of the reasons. Though it begins attractively with a comic hero who is so fond of his own company that he cannot bear to sleep, it degenerates by the second page into a collection of clichés, after which it breaks off entirely. We need hardly regret that Rochester did not finish his comedy, for it promises nothing better than mediocrity. Like Henry James, whom he superficially resembles so little, Rochester seems to have been a gifted dramatist whose inability to write successfully for the stage forced him to sublimate his dramatic instincts in another literary genre.

V

Not the least disappointing feature of Pinto's treatment of the Portland MS. is the quality of the text. Nine points may be noted:

(1) In the first poem in the manuscript, the song of eight stanzas beginning "How perfect Cloris, & how free" (*Poems,* p. 167), Pinto omits important evidence showing the purpose of Rochester's revisions. Preceding the last two stanzas is a symbol consisting of a horizontal line twice looped back on itself. Between the second and third stanzas is a similar symbol apparently indicating that the last two stanzas were to be inserted here. That this was Rochester's intention is further shown by two circumstances. (a) The first six stanzas correspond to a complete six-stanza version of the poem appearing in the Yale MS. and the Huntington edition. (b) Two other stanzas corresponding to the last two in the Portland text appear after the second stanza of an eight-stanza version which is preserved in Harvard MS. Eng. 636F and in the uncanceled state of Tonson's edition of 1691; this longer version is also partially preserved in *A New Collection of the Choicest Songs,* 1676. Two deleted and corrected readings in the Portland text likewise indicate that the direction of change is from the six-stanza version to the one in eight stanzas. Evidently the six-stanza version is the earliest of the three, the Portland text is an intermediate version in process of revision, and the completed eight-stanza version repre-

sents Rochester's final thoughts. The early texts of this poem are discussed in detail elsewhere.[2]

(2) Pinto's reproduction of the fragment headed "Sab: Lost" distorts its character. To the left of this twelve-line text in the Portland MS. is a vertical list of eighteen abbreviations and sets of initials which seem to represent the names or positions of a retinue of servants in a typical seventeenth-century nobleman's household. Pinto prints the poem as if it were a sort of domestic conversation in which ten of the servants speak one or two lines each. On the strength of his textual treatment, he theorizes that the poem "possibly alludes" to Rochester's attempted abduction of Elizabeth Malet on 26 May 1665. "It may be conjectured," he continues, "that the list of abbreviated names represents the members of Rochester's household who formed the party that seized Miss Malet, and that 'Gill' and 'Doll' [two alleged names in the list] were the two women who were provided to look after her" (*Rochester*, pp. 49–50). Pinto further terms these verses a "strange dramatic fragment" and prints them in his edition as the first work in his section of "Dramatic Poetry" (*Poems*, pp. 61, 183).

To this handling of the poem several objections should be registered:

(a) Nothing about the poem itself suggests that it includes more than one speaker. It is not strikingly "dramatic," nor is it even particularly "strange."

(b) The list of servants is separated from the poem by a long vertical line apparently indicating that the two have no connection with each other. Pinto neither reproduces this line nor mentions it in his notes.

2. In my article, "A Textual Paradox: Rochester's 'To a Lady in a Letter,'" *Papers of the Bibliographical Society of America*, 54 (1960), 147–62, and its sequel, "An Unsuspected Cancel in Tonson's 1691 'Rochester,'" *PBSA*, 55 (1961), 130–33.

(c) Contrary to the way in which the list of servants is printed in Pinto's edition, most of the names in the list do not correspond spatially to the lines of the poem. Several occur opposite spaces between lines, and seven of them are above or below the poem.

(d) Without any warning in his notes, Pinto inserts colons after ten of the names in the list, thereby making it appear that these persons were intended to speak the lines which he prints after their names. In eight cases where colons actually occur after names in the manuscript, they are used according to normal seventeenth-century practice as a sign that the preceding word is abbreviated.

(e) It is even doubtful that the list contains any "Gill" or "Doll." Though not all the names can be deciphered with certainty, it is reasonably clear that some are not exactly as given by Pinto. Aside from punctuation, the first six names are correctly rendered by Pinto as "Blac," "Page," "Coach.," "Will," "Ja," and "Post:." The remaining twelve seem to be "Sill." or "Sin." (rather than "Gill:"), "S'ard:" (not "Gard:"), "But:," "Uphols:" (not "Upholst:"), "Cooke," "D'all:" (not "Doll:"), "C K.," "J. B.," "Sar:" (rather than "Gar:"), "Fr:," "Hm:," and "D. ch." (not "Dick:"). Not indicated in Pinto's text or his notes is the fact that a short horizontal line appears to the right of the list after every other name, dividing the servants into groups of twos.

Evidently there is no reason to link Rochester's twelve-line fragment with his attempted abduction of his future wife or even to suppose that it refers to her at all.

(3) In his text of the epigram on Otway, Pinto prints the short first line as if it were a title (*Poems*, p. 118). Despite his statement that "there is no punctuation in the MS." (*Poems*,

p. 213), this first line is preceded by a long dash and followed by a comma. Also, the line appears to the right of the page, not centered above the poem as in Pinto's text. There is no evidence that the epigram is a "fragment," as Pinto calls it (*Poems*, p. 213).

(4) Pinto prints the fragment beginning "Continue still ingrate" as if it were the third stanza of the "Song" beginning "Cloris to love without return" (*Poems*, pp. 144–45). Actually, the fragment (fol. 16ʳ) does not even appear on the same leaf as the "Song" (fol. 15ʳ). There are also differences in the verse forms used. The "Song" includes two eight-line stanzas, each consisting of four lines of iambic tetrameter rhymed *abab* followed by four lines of iambic pentameter rhymed *ccdd*. The fragment, on the other hand, consists of eight lines of iambic trimeter rhymed *ababcdcd*. Traces of a preceding line can be discerned at the top of the page on which the fragment occurs, and "Finish" is written below its last line, suggesting that it may be the conclusion of a much longer poem of which the rest is lost.

(5) Similarly, Pinto prints the couplet beginning "Vertues my lawfull prince" as if it were the last two lines of the song beginning "Corrina vainly I pretend" (*Poems*, pp. 145–46). Since the couplet occurs at the middle, not the top, of the verso of the leaf whose recto contains the song, it is evidently a separate poem.

(6) In the pastoral dialogue beginning "Dearest Armilla could you once but guese," Pinto omits an entire line which is not even scored out in the manuscript. Between Pinto's lines 26 and 27 (*Poems*, p. 147), the manuscript has: "your beauty yett exceeds your tyranny."

(7) In several instances Pinto misreads words in the manuscript. Five examples may suffice:

(a) In "How perfect Cloris, & how free" (*Poems*, p. 167), the first two words of line 13 are not "Nor ever" but "You never"—which is also the reading of the Yale MS. and the Huntington edition. The same error appears in the text of this poem in Pinto's biography (*Rochester*, p. 40).

(b) In "Could I but make my wishes insolent" (*Poems*, p. 42), the first word of line 11 is "Just," not "That." This error is strange, since Needham reproduces the correct reading (p. 52).

(c) In the epigram on Otway (*Poems*, p. 118), the second word of the second line is "blustring," not "Illustrius."

(d) In "What vaine unnecessary things are men" (*Poems*, p. 117), the word in line 53 which Pinto reads as "textes" is actually "trades."

(e) In "Dearest Armilla could you once but guese" (*Poems*, p. 146), line 5 reads "And more then you love fredome," not "And move you then some fredome."

(8) In numerous places Pinto fails to record deletions in the manuscript, thus concealing the extent of the revisions in Rochester's and Lady Rochester's hands. Since some of the deleted words can be made out even from a photograph, almost all of them could probably be deciphered with the aid of scientific tests. Pinto does not specify whether he has attempted such tests.

(9) Pinto's text in his edition departs from the spelling of the manuscript in at least fifty-five places, while in more than forty others it omits, alters, or otherwise misrepresents the punctuation. In a comparable number of cases it does not reproduce the capitalization accurately. A few illustrations of such errors can be observed at page 116 of Pinto's edition, where he includes a photograph of one page of the manuscript facing his transcription of it. Indeed, the texts from the Portland MS. which Pinto prints in his edition and his biography differ from each other almost as much as either of them differs from the original.

VI

Discussion of the Portland MS. would not be complete without attention to a group of seven poems in British Museum Harleian MS. 7316. Though these poems were brought to Pinto's notice shortly before his edition was published (*Poems*, p. xlv), he did not examine their significance. In the Harleian volume, which is a large bound manuscript miscellany in what seems to be an early eighteenth-century hand, the group occupies folios 20^r–23^v and is set off from the other contents by a blank page at either end (fols. 19^v, 24^r). The first six poems, carrying no ascriptions, consist of five which appear in the Portland MS. in Rochester's autograph and one appearing there in the hand of his wife. The seventh poem, not included in the Portland MS., is a three-line scrap of verse ascribed in the Harleian volume to Rochester. In order, the seven poems are: "Could I but make my wishes insolent" (fol. 20^r); a text of "What vaine unnecessary things are men" with the first forty lines in a different sequence and the last fifteen lines omitted (fols. 20^v–21^r); "How perfect Cloris, & how free" (fols. 21^v–22^r); " 'Twas a dispute t'wixt Heav'n & Earth" (fol. 22^v); "Att Last you'l force mee to Confess" (fol. 23^r); "Cloris to Love without return" (fols. 23^r–23^v); and the three-line scrap (fol. 23^v).

The first six poems in the Harleian group are almost certainly descended from the Portland text and are probably direct copies; the copying may have been done while both manuscripts were owned by the Harley family. The Harleian text follows the Portland MS. very closely in substantive readings, and there is even a general resemblance in accidentals. In places where the Portland MS. has readings deleted and corrected, the Harleian scribe usually adopts the corrected version but occasionally prefers the reading which has been scored out. Most important, all instances in which he departs from the readings of his source can be explained by peculiar features of the Portland MS. Two examples are of primary significance:

(1) The rearrangement of lines in "What vaine unnecessary things are men" is explicable in terms of the physical make-up of the Portland MS. In the holograph text, the poem begins with twenty lines on folio 9ʳ, continues with twenty more on the verso of the same leaf, and breaks off after fifteen lines on folio 10ʳ. The Harleian scribe, evidently thinking the poem started on folio 9ᵛ, begins his text with "E're beare this Scorne, I'de bee Shutt up at home" and the remaining nineteen lines on this page. Then, quite naturally, he continues with the twenty lines on the reverse side of the sheet. Apparently he omitted the fifteen lines on folio 10ʳ because he thought they belonged to a different poem.

(2) In the last line of the song "Cloris to love without return," the corruptions in the Harleian text were probably caused by failure to decipher Lady Rochester's revisions. The final version of the line is "your own ungratful hate has sett it free." Lady Rochester began, however, by writing "your own ungratful has." At this point she evidently perceived her omission of the noun and also decided to try another tense of the verb, for she wrote "hate" over part of "has" to cancel it and finished the line with "shall sett it free." Then she returned the verb to its original tense by writing "has" over the "hal" of "shall" and deleting the initial "s" and the second "l"; the resulting word, with its long "s," looks much like "hafe." The Harleian scribe apparently misunderstood this word, failed to realize that the first "has" was cancelled, and misread the word "hate": he wrote "Your own ungratfull Heart has halfe sett it free," thereby introducing an extra syllable into the line.

The probability that the first six poems in Harleian MS. 7316 were copied from the Portland MS. means, of course, that their value for study of the Rochester text is relatively slight. Nevertheless, they may be useful to an editor simply because they were copied some two centuries ago when the Portland MS. was in a more satisfactory state of preservation. In places where readings in the Portland MS. are difficult to decipher, the Harleian text may at least suggest what Rochester or Lady Rochester wrote. For example, on the second page of the Portland text of "What vaine unnecessary things are men," the right side of the sheet has been trimmed, removing the last letters of several lines. Line 36 reads "For our stol'n ravish'd men wee," followed by something illegible and not completely extant, with "sue" written in the space above. Pinto supposes the illegible word to be "next," possibly followed by "do" (*Poems*, pp. 117, 213). This cannot be correct, for the first two letters are "he." The Harleian text reads "hereby," a better possibility.

The Harleian text is also useful for study of typical scribal habits during the late seventeenth and early eighteenth centuries. In this period, most manuscripts of a given poem, if not derived from printed texts, are related to each other in a collateral fashion with all intermediaries lost. Examples of one extant manuscript which, like the Harleian text, is copied or even descended from another extant manuscript are quite rare. Thus it is difficult to formulate generalizations about contemporary scribal practices which would help to explain how variants in different manuscripts of a poem might have arisen. In view of the extensive textual variation exhibited by manuscript copies of some Restoration poems, the Harleian transcript is surprisingly accurate.

The virtual certainty that the first six poems in Harleian MS. 7316 derive from an authoritative source argues that the seventh poem of the group is probably genuine Rochester:

Under King Charles II^s. Picture,
  By Wilmot Earl of Rochester.

I John Roberts writ This same,
I pasted it, & plaister'd it, and put it in a Frame:
In Honor of my Master's Master, King Charles the Second
  by Name.

There is no evidence of the date at which Rochester may have
written these verses, nor has "John Roberts" been identified.
The phrase "my Master's Master" implies that he was one of
the Earl's servants. It seems impossible to determine at present
whether he was a relative of the Mrs. Roberts who was Rochester's mistress.

8.

Scroope's "I Cannot Change" and Rochester's Burlesque

Among the numerous lyrics preserved in the Yale MS. and the Rochester editions of 1680 is a delicately beautiful "Song" beginning "I cannot change as others do." This love lyric is immediately followed in the collection by a remarkably obscene burlesque in the same stanza form which begins "I swive as well as others do" and is usually titled "The Mock Song" (A-1680-HU, pp. 74, 75).

The "Song" has been universally accepted as Rochester's and has, indeed, been praised as one of his finest lyrics. Johannes Prinz listed it "among the most perfect of Rochester's songs," and Norman Ault selected it as one of seven poems to represent Rochester in his *Seventeenth Century Lyrics*. The "Song" was also printed as Rochester's in the editions of John Hayward, Quilter Johns, and Vivian de Sola Pinto, and it was accepted as genuine by John Harold Wilson and James Thorpe. By con-

trast, the "Mock Song" has received hardly any critical comment, and some scholars have considered it spurious. Though
Hayward, Johns, and Wilson assigned it to Rochester, its authenticity was doubted by Prinz and Thorpe, and it is omitted
from the most recent edition, that of Pinto (1953).[1] Thus it
is ironical that the much-admired "Song" is probably not by
Rochester at all, but by his archenemy Sir Carr Scroope, while
the despised "Mock Song" appears to be Rochester's burlesque
of Scroope's graceful lines.

This conclusion requires recognition of two key circumstances:
(1) all external evidence hitherto used to support Rochester's
authorship of either of the two songs occurs in printed texts
which probably descend from the Huntington edition of 1680
(A-1680-HU); and (2) the ascriptions in the Huntington edition must be interpreted in light of the ascriptions in the Yale
MS. and the arrangement of the collection as a whole.

Examination of the available evidence may conveniently begin
with the early printed texts of the "Song" and the "Mock Song."
Both poems are assigned to Rochester in the Huntington edition,
from which they were reprinted with the same ascription in the
other editions of 1680 and the later editions of 1685 (A-1685),
1701 (A-1701), 1713 (A-1713), and 1731 (A-1731). From one
of the 1680 editions, apparently, the "Mock Song" by itself
was reprinted with ascription to Rochester in Edmund Curll's
The Works Of the Earls of Rochester, Roscommon, Dorset, &c.,
1714 (C-1714-1).

Concurrently, Jacob Tonson included the "Song" without its
companion burlesque in his 1691 edition of Rochester (B-1691),
where it appears among a dozen or more lyrics which Tonson
probably printed from one of the 1680 editions. Tonson's text

1. See Part III for documentation of the previous scholarship on the
two songs.

of the "Song" is verbally identical with those in the 1680 editions; this fact may be specially significant because two early manuscript versions of the poem share variants against the printed texts (Osborn MSS. Chest II, Number 39 and Box III, Number 27).[2] Thus Tonson's attribution cannot be allowed much weight. The "Song" was reprinted with ascription to Rochester in the later Tonson editions of 1696 (B-1696), 1705 (B-1705), 1714 (B-1714), and 1732 (B-1732), and in the piracies of 1710 (B-1710-P) and 1718 (B-1718-P). The ascription of the "Song" to the mysterious "Ephelia" in her *Female Poems*, 1682 need not be taken seriously, since this text rather obviously derives from one of the 1680 editions. Other early printings of the two poems carry no ascriptions, nor do any occur in manuscripts outside the Yale MS. There is no further evidence that Rochester wrote the "Song." [3]

Since this evidence is ambiguous at best, special importance attaches to the information offered by the Yale MS. on the authorship of the two songs and on the reason why they came to be printed in the Huntington edition. The Yale MS. ascribes the "Song" to "Sr Carr Scr:" but unfortunately gives no explicit sign of authorship for the "Mock Song." As we have seen, however (Chapter 3), the position of these two lyrics in the collection is almost certainly in the section of poems by or concerning Rochester, at the very end of the subsection of songs. Evidently, therefore, they were included in the archetypal source of the Yale MS. and the Huntington edition as a song which Rochester burlesqued, together with the burlesque itself, and the scribe's intention was to assign the "Mock Song" to Rochester. The

2. In l. 9, the two manuscripts read "dies" for "lyes"; in l. 11, "Those" for "The"; in l. 12, "Those" for "The"; in l. 13, "my" for "this."

3. See Part III for a more detailed list of the early texts and ascriptions of the two songs.

single ascription to Scroope does not, to be sure, guarantee that he wrote the "Song," but the Yale MS. is unusually reliable in its testimony concerning authorship, and no other early ascription for the poem stands so good a chance of being correct.

On the face of the matter, the conclusion that Scroope and Rochester wrote the two songs is sufficiently plausible. Poetry of high quality like the "Song" was not beyond the reach of Scroope's abilities, which were more considerable than his present obscurity would suggest. Nor is the "Mock Song" unworthy of Rochester; despite the neglect it has suffered, perhaps because of its obscenity or the notion that it was spurious, it is a clever performance. Also, whereas the "Song" lacks the tendency to satire which is evident in so many of Rochester's genuine lyrics, the "Mock Song" is typically satirical in intention. Conversely, little plausibility can be granted to the implied conclusion of Prinz, Thorpe, and Pinto that Rochester wrote the "Song" and another poet then burlesqued it. Though Rochester's manner of life should have made him an ideal target for his fellow satirists, few of them in fact dared to provoke a man whose social prestige and literary skill enabled him to reduce an opponent to a pariah with a few strokes of his pen—who could, for example, permanently stigmatize Scroope as "an Ugly *Beau-Garcon*" or even Dryden as "*Poet Squab*." It is far more likely that Rochester would burlesque another poet's lyric than that the reverse should occur.

Though the argument that Scroope wrote the "Song" must rest primarily on the ascription in the Yale MS., his authorship is supported by other contemporary evidence of a more indirect kind. Such evidence is offered by the text of the poem in Osborn MS. Box III, Number 27. This text appears in a single sheet which has been folded once to form two leaves and which exhibits light traces of further foldings, suggesting that it may have been passed from hand to hand during the Restoration period. At the top of the recto of the first leaf, which is otherwise blank, are the title and ascription of the first poem on the verso, a version of "On Rome's Pardons" (see Chapter 14); the verso includes the text of this satire with the ascription repeated as heading, followed by a second short anti-Catholic satire beginning "Wⁿ God Almighty had his Palace framed," for which no title or ascription is given. The recto of the second leaf includes the last eight lines of "I cannot change" without title or ascription, followed by a satirical song on Cary Frazier headed simply "Another" and beginning "As Phrazier one Night at her Post in yᵉ Drawing Room stood." [4] At the top of the verso, which is otherwise blank, is written the title "A song on Mrs Phraziar."

Evidently the title on the verso of the second leaf means that "I cannot change" is addressed to Cary Frazier, and "Another" indicates that the succeeding poem also concerns her. If this interpretation is correct, the information in the Osborn manuscript is quite important, for Cary Frazier was the great romance of Sir Carr Scroope's life, whereas Rochester is not known to have had any amorous interest in her. Furthermore, an approximate date for the "Song" and the "Mock Song" would be supplied, since Sir Carr's affair with Cary was in progress between 2 November 1676 and 30 January 1676/7 and came to an abrupt end shortly thereafter, probably because she did not wish to marry him.[5]

4. For a discussion of this poem, see my article, "A 'Lost' Lampoon by Katherine Sedley?" *Manuscripts*, 6 (1954), 160–65. All subsequent biographical information on Scroope and Cary Frazier is taken from this article unless otherwise indicated.

5. Little help in identifying the subject of the "Song" is afforded by the text in B. M. Add. MS. 27408, which is headed "To Madam P ff G." Not only are these initials cryptic, but the text itself may have been copied from a printed source. It is probably not significant that the initials happen to be those of three women whom Scroope is said to have pursued: P(ortsmouth) ff(razier) G(wyn).

Similar evidence, though even less explicit, is provided by an apparent allusion to the "Song" in "A Familiar Epistle to Mr Julian Secretary of the Muses" ("Thou Comon Shore of this Poetique Towne"). The "Familiar Epistle," possibly written by Buckingham, is largely a satire on Scroope, whom it sarcastically addresses as "Strephon" (see Chapter 13). The first stanza of the "Song," in which the speaker claims he will remain constant even though his love is spurned, ends with the memorable refrain "Will still love on, will still love on, and dye." The "Familiar Epistle," commenting on Scroope's ill-success in love, possibly echoes this refrain in the following passage (the italics are mine):

> There's not a Nymph, in Citty, Town, or Court,
> But Strephons Billet Doux have beene her sport.
> *Still he loves on,* yet still as sure to misse,
> As they who wash an Ethiops face or his.
>
> (Yale MS., p. 356)

Admittedly such evidence is tenuous, but the "Familiar Epistle" is characteristically allusive in technique: it may also include echoes of two other poems connected with Scroope, Rochester's "On the suppos'd Authour of a late Poem in defence of Satyr" and Scroope's "Answer" (see Chapter 5). Needless to say, if the "Familiar Epistle" does allude to the "Song," it would imply that Scroope is the author.

Moreover, because of the date of the "Familiar Epistle"—spring or summer of 1677—such an allusion would tend to corroborate the implication of the Osborn manuscript that Scroope addressed the "Song" to Cary Frazier while he was courting her in late 1676 and early 1677. Scroope's affair with Nell Gwyn, the only other woman he is definitely known to have pursued, did not occur until spring of 1678, after the "Familiar Epistle" was composed. (The hint in this same satire that he was currently wooing the Duchess of Portsmouth finds little corroboration in other contemporary sources and may therefore be untrue.) After devoting much space to Scroope's frustrations in love, the "Familiar Epistle" pointedly concludes with a reference to "His Mistresse lost," who must be Cary Frazier, since Scroope was still courting her only a short time earlier.

A further argument that the two songs were written by Scroope and Rochester may be provided by a peculiar feature of the "Mock Song." Significantly, even though this poem is designed as a burlesque of its companion piece, it focuses primarily upon the alleged whorish qualities of the woman whom the "Song" addresses. That Rochester held a similar opinion of Cary Frazier is suggested by the following squib on her, which students of his poetry have not previously noticed. The only recorded text occurs in Osborn MS. Chest II, Number 14 (p. 1094):

> Her Father gave her Dildoes six
> Her Mother made 'um up a score
> But she loves nought but living pricks
> And swears by God sheel frig no more

In the Osborn manuscript, these verses are signed "Rochester" and headed "Upon Betty Frazer 1677." "Betty" is almost certainly a mistake for "Cary"; the Osborn manuscript elsewhere makes the same substitution.[6] No "Betty Frazer" who might be the subject of the lines seems to be known, whereas Cary was one of the Queen's Maids of Honor and a celebrated beauty of the Court of Charles II. The references to father and mother suggest Cary, both of whose parents were prominent at Court; her

6. In the lampoon beginning "As Colon drove his Sheepe along," the line which should read "In stept stately Cary Frazier" appears in this manuscript as "In stept stately Betty Frazer" (p. 1146).

father, Sir Alexander Frazier, was the King's principal physician, and her mother was one of the Queen's Dressers.[7] The date 1677 appended to the title is also noteworthy, for it points to exactly the period at which the "Song" and the "Mock Song" may have been composed.

Finally, the tentative dates of the "Song" and the "Mock Song," as well as the date given for the four-line squib, would relate all three poems to the literary quarrel between Rochester and Scroope which was at its height in 1676 and 1677. The quarrel began with Rochester's "An Allusion to Horace," composed during the winter of 1675–76, and continued with Scroope's retort in his "In defence of Satyr," written after June of 1676. Next followed Rochester's "On the suppos'd Authour of a late Poem in defence of Satyr" and Scroope's "The Answer," both probably in existence by the end of 1676 (see Chapter 5). The "Mock Song" and the four-line scrap of verse may have been Rochester's attempt to get at Scroope from a direction not used in his other satires, which contain no identifiable references to Cary Frazier. As for Scroope's contributions, the distinguished quality of his satires and his "Song" should suggest that his life and works deserve more scholarly attention than they have hitherto enjoyed.

7. For Lady Frazier's position at Court, see *CTB passim*.

9.

The Buckhurst-Etherege Epistles

An interesting, if minor, poetical tradition of the Restoration was the writing of informal letters in the verse form and style popularized by Samuel Butler in *Hudibras*. These hudibrastic epistles, as they may be called, usually employed rough iambic tetrameter couplets, comic rhymes, satirical wit, and outrageous bawdry. Among surviving examples are the ribald lines exchanged by Thomas Shadwell and William Wycherley in the spring of 1671, while Shadwell was visiting his friend Edmund Ashton in Lancashire. Less obscene but equally flippant are the two verse letters which George Etherege addressed to Lord Middleton from Ratisbon in 1686. Though Middleton himself apparently did not answer in kind, Etherege was favored early in 1687 with the well-known verse reply by John Dryden. The genre also includes several poems written in 1689 and 1690 by Matthew Prior, notably his famous epistle to Fleetwood Shepherd.[1]

1. *The Complete Works of Thomas Shadwell*, ed. Montague Summers

Bawdiest of the lot is a "linked group" of four hudibrastic epistles ascribed to Rochester in the first edition of 1680, the Huntington edition (A-1680-HU, pp. 77–87). The first and third of these poems, beginning "Dreaming last Night on Mrs Farley" and "If I can guess the Devil choak me," purport to be letters written by Charles Sackville, Lord Buckhurst, during a brief sojourn in the country. The second and fourth epistles, beginning "As crafty Harlots, use to shrink" and "So soft, and Am'rously you write," represent answers by George Etherege from London. In the first letter, Buckhurst instructs his friend to send down the latest copies of verses and to procure a suitable number of prostitutes for his imminent return to town. In his reply, Etherege encloses the verses and reports that he has secured the services of a strumpet named Cuffley, whom he and Buckhurst "had us'd too roughly" in a previous encounter, for she reduced her prices if treated in "a gentler way." The last two letters, in which Mistress Cuffley enjoys a remarkable share of attention, praise her charms and reveal that she has built up an enthusiastic clientele among the town gallants. The entire correspondence pokes fun at the conventions of romantic love and is distinguished by its youthful high spirits and disregard for the proprieties.

The authorship of these verse letters has caused much difficulty for students of Restoration poetry, who have generally hesitated to attribute them either to Rochester or to Buckhurst and Etherege. All four poems were omitted from the collections of Rochester edited by John Hayward, Quilter Johns, and

---

(London, Fortune Press, 1927), 5, 227–32. *The Letterbook of Sir George Etherege*, ed. Sybil Rosenfeld (London, Oxford Univ. Press, 1928), pp. 62–63, 79–82, 346–48. *The Literary Works of Matthew Prior*, ed. H. Bunker Wright and Monroe K. Spears (Oxford, Clarendon Press, 1959), *1*, 83, 85, 93, 103.

Vivian de Sola Pinto. On the other hand, A. Wilson Verity did not print any of them in his edition of Etherege. Johannes Prinz doubted that they were Rochester's but did not assign them to Buckhurst and Etherege because, he maintained, "there is no internal evidence that the *Epistles* are the joint production of two authors" (*Rochester*, p. 147). Brice Harris, in his biography of Buckhurst, was similarly noncommittal. Claiming, like Prinz, that "there is nothing in them to indicate that two different authors wrote them" and that "a consistency of style is noteworthy throughout," Harris strangely suggested "that Dorset [Buckhurst] himself composed the four letters"—adding, however, that this was "a possible, even probable solution, but not a demonstrable one." Elsewhere he remarked that "there seems to be no way of proving whether he [Buckhurst] wrote all or none of the fictitious rhymed correspondence" (*Dorset*, pp. 103, 238). James Thorpe also dealt cautiously with the epistles, observing that "it seems impossible to determine conclusively whether they were written by the alleged correspondents, or all of them by one of those correspondents, or all of them by Rochester or another." Nevertheless he found it "highly probable" that the epistles "were written, as their titles allege, by Buckhurst and Etherege" (*Rochester's Poems*, pp. 182–83). Somewhat earlier, John Harold Wilson had expressed the same opinion.[2]

Examination of the evidence supports Wilson's and Thorpe's conclusion that Buckhurst and Etherege composed the four hudibrastic epistles. Despite the ascriptions to Rochester in the Huntington edition, there is no valid reason to lay the poems at his door or to assign them to anyone other than Buckhurst and

2. See Part III for fuller documentation of the previous scholarship on the four epistles.

Etherege. All difficulties vanish with a proper understanding
of the arrangement of the Huntington edition and its counter-
part, the Yale MS. As we saw earlier (Chapter 3), the ascriptions in the edition are meaningless in this instance because the
epistles appear, not in the section of poems by or concerning
Rochester, but in the section of poems by miscellaneous authors.
All remaining sources ascribing the epistles to Rochester evidently descend from the Huntington edition. The poems were
reprinted as Rochester's in the other editions of 1680 and in the
later editions of 1685 (A-1685), 1701 (A-1701), 1713 (A-1713),
and 1731 (A-1731). From one of the 1680 editions they were
also reprinted under his name in Edmund Curll's *The Works
Of the Earls of Rochester, Roscommon, Dorset, &c.,* 1714
(C-1714-1), and succeeding editions of this collection. Little
help is afforded by an ambiguous note printed in the editions
of 1731 and later (C series): "The Four following *Epistles*
from *B.* to *E.* are supposed to be Written from the Lord *Buckhurst,* afterwards Earl of *Dorset,* to Mr. *Etherege,* afterwards
Sir *George Etherege.*"

Unfortunately, the sixth gap in the Yale MS. has removed
the first three epistles of the linked group and all but the concluding lines of the fourth, thereby eliminating any ascriptions
which were originally given. As Thorpe has pointed out, however, the text of the group in Harvard MS. Eng. 636F clearly
assigns the poems to Buckhurst and Etherege. Besides the in-
dications of authorship provided by the titles in this manuscript,
Buckhurst's name is signed to the first epistle and Etherege's
to the second and fourth. Also, unknown to Thorpe, similar ascriptions occur in two other independently descended texts in
early manuscripts. In Edinburgh MS. DC.1.3, which includes
the entire linked group, the titles of the first and third epistles

assign them to Buckhurst, while the second and fourth are attributed to Etherege both in their titles and in signatures appended to each poem. In National Library of Scotland MS. Advocate 19.3.4, which includes only the third epistle, the heading of the poem indicates that it was addressed by Buckhurst to Etherege.[3] This evidence supporting the authorship of Buckhurst and Etherege is unequivocal, nor is it contradicted by any other admissible testimony.

Further considerations suggest that the four verse letters were composed by Buckhurst and Etherege. In the first place, there is no good reason why anyone else should have written them. It is true, of course, that in the satirical poetry of this period one must constantly suspect the use of a *persona*, but the Buckhurst-Etherege epistles yield no evidence that such a technique is present. The *persona* is not employed in the similar hudibrastic epistles exchanged by Shadwell and Wycherley or those addressed by Etherege to Lord Middleton and by Dryden to Etherege; no one, to my knowledge, has seriously maintained that these other hudibrastic letters were not written by the correspondents themselves. Like these other verse letters, too, the Buckhurst-Etherege epistles are probably not a "fictitious rhymed correspondence," as Harris assumed, but a real one.

The attributions to Buckhurst and Etherege also seem plausible in view of Etherege's later behavior in Ratisbon, where he frequently tried to recapture the delights of his lost youth. His two hudibrastic epistles to Lord Middleton may well have been inspired by nostalgia for the wild days in London when he composed two similar poems in answer to Buckhurst. Moreover, in a letter to Buckhurst (now Earl of Dorset) dated 25 July

3. See Part III for a more detailed list of the early texts and ascriptions of the four epistles.

1687, Etherege reminisced about their earlier escapade with the Mistress Cuffley who figures so prominently in the four verse epistles:

> I have lost for want of exercise the use of fancy and imagination, and am grown so very stupid that when I read a new poem methinks the author should be invited to one of those reverend cells the hermit Lee has quitted. Lovers have been metamorphosed by the ancient poets, though churches have not yet; you and I were ne'er so bold to turn the fair Cuffle when she fled us into a tree, not dreaming she would grow as big as one of Evelyn's oaks, nor ourselves into bulls when we carried the two draggle-tailed nymphs one bitter, frosty night over the Thames to Lambeth. Sertorius aimed to make a milk-white hind an immortal dame, but his hint's improved by the lady of the spotted muff's ingracious son. I cannot guess on whom the Duke of Bucks' mantle is fallen, but it is MacFlecknoe with doubled portion of that prophet's art. There are many lucky hits, and Bishop Martin is a master stroke.[4]

This account is a useful gloss on the references to Cuffley in the poems, for it touches upon the circumstances under which the

4. Rosenfeld, *Letterbook*, pp. 239–40; the misreading of "Castle" for "Cuffle" has been corrected in accordance with H. F. B. Brett-Smith's review, *Review of English Studies*, 5 (1929), 227. Cuffley is mentioned in "The Session of Ladies 1688" ("A Session of Ladies was held on the Stage") in B. M. Harl. MS. 7319 (fol. 281ʳ):

> The Old & the Ugly, yᵉ Youthful & Fair
> All flew at the sound of Adonis his name
> Poor Cuffly alas, broke her neck in a Chair
> Making overmuch Hast to put in her Claim.

A marginal note beside the same quatrain in B. M. Harl. MS. 7317 (fol. 78ʳ) suggests that by this date Cuffley had graduated from a prostitute to "A Bawd." Etherege's statement that she had grown "as big as one of Evelyn's oaks" may mean that she had also become obese—or possibly that she was pregnant.

two gentlemen-rakes had "us'd her so offensively." It supplements the obscure lines in Buckhurst's second epistle which imply that when she was "tir'd with immoderate flight" from her pursuers, Cuffley had taken refuge "all Night" in the boughs of a *"Lofty Pine."*

Furthermore, the rather cryptic passage in Etherege's letter possibly alludes not only to the Cuffley incident but to the four hudibrastic epistles. The context of Etherege's remarks on Cuffley, referring specially to Dryden's *The Hind and the Panther,* pertains to poetry involving some sort of metamorphosis. Etherege may be saying by way of contrast that in their poems, he and Buckhurst had not transformed Cuffley into a tree nor themselves into bulls. If true, this interpretation would remove any remaining doubt that the four epistles were composed by Buckhurst and Etherege.

Stylistic considerations are generally a less satisfactory criterion of authenticity than other types of evidence, nor are they distinct enough to clarify the authorship of the Buckhurst-Etherege epistles. Though one may feel, like Prinz and Harris, that all four poems are similar in style, hudibrastic epistles tend to sound very much alike. The Shadwell-Wycherley epistles display this same stylistic consistency, as do the later verse letters written by Etherege and Dryden. The two poems ascribed to Buckhurst may, however, be differentiated from Etherege's answers by a greater ease of style as well as a broader range of allusion to classical literature and traditional love poetry.

No attempt has hitherto been made to date the Buckhurst-Etherege epistles, probably because of the confusion over their authorship. Oddly, they yield little evidence for assigning an exact date. They cannot, of course, have been written before Etherege and Buckhurst became acquainted, an event which occurred in connection with Etherege's first play, *The Comical*

Revenge, acted in March 1664; in Etherege's own words, "The Writing of it was a means to make me known to your Lordship." [5] Also, since all extant texts except the Edinburgh manuscript consistently designate one of the correspondents as "Buckhurst," the poems were probably composed by the time Buckhurst succeeded his uncle as Earl of Middlesex early in 1675, after which he would normally have been called by his new title (Harris, *Dorset,* pp. 60–62). Of the approximately eleven years between these terminal dates, three are eliminated because Etherege was absent on his diplomatic mission to Turkey from the summer of 1668 to the summer of 1671.[6]

Further conclusions must remain tentative, but a passage in Buckhurst's first epistle promises a more precise date for the four poems. He asks Etherege to send him

> any paultery *Poetry,*
> Tho from the *University.*
> Who when the *K——* and *Q——* were there,
> Did both their *Wit* and *Learning* spare;
> And have (I hope) endeavour'd since,
> To make the *World* some recompence.

The passage suggests that Buckhurst wrote it shortly after King Charles and his Queen made a formal visit to one of the two universities, where they could expect literary entertainment on the part of the scholars. This is not likely to be their retreat to Oxford during the winter of 1665–66 to escape the plague, for none of the four epistles mentions either the plague or the war then being waged against the Dutch. Nor is it likely to be

5. Nicoll, *Restoration Drama,* p. 410. *The Dramatic Works of Sir George Etherege,* ed. H. F. B. Brett-Smith (Oxford, Basil Blackwell, 1927), *1, 2.*

6. For a detailed account of this period in Etherege's life, see Thomas H. Fujimura, "Etherege at Constantinople," *PMLA, 71* (1956), 465–81.

Charles's visit to Cambridge in October 1671, for the Queen apparently did not accompany him. The only other recorded possibility seems to be the royal sojourn at Oxford at the end of September 1663, when the King and Queen "spent an edifying week of orations, Latin plays and sermons"—possibly the productions which Buckhurst dismisses so disparagingly.[7] The time of year is plausible, for both correspondents refer in their poems to the prevailing cold weather. Thus the four epistles may have been written during the winter of 1663–64. The Cuffley affair may belong to the same winter, for Etherege relates in his letter of 1687 that it took place "one bitter, frosty night." This dating of the poems seems to be supported by the position of the third epistle in the Advocate manuscript, the relevant portion of which consists of verses written during the early 1660s and transcribed in chronological order, perhaps very soon after their composition. In the chronological sequence of the manuscript, the third epistle appears after poems dated up to 1663 and before those dated 1664 or later.

If this surprisingly early date is correct—the youthful spirit of the poems suggests that it is—then the Buckhurst-Etherege epistles take on special significance. They would rank among the earliest productions of the two authors and among the first fruits of their friendship. Since Butler's *Hudibras* was not published until the end of 1662 (Pepys, *Diary*, 26 Dec. 1662), the four epistles might well have initiated the tradition of hudibrastic correspondence. They would also supply at least one

7. Arthur Bryant, *King Charles II* (London, New York, and Toronto, Longmans, Green, 1931), pp. 167, 179–80, 219. Other allusions in the four epistles fail to supply definite dates. Little help is offered by the references to various bawds and prostitutes—Farley, Roberts, Thomas, Dutton, Temple, and of course Cuffley. Buckhurst's reference to the Lord O'Brien who visited him in the country is similarly unpromising, for as Thorpe observes, at least two men bore this designation during the period in which the poems were probably written (*Rochester's Poems*, p. 173).

other item of new biographical information, for Etherege implies in his second answer that he has recently recovered from that standard ordeal of Restoration courtiers, a treatment for venereal disease.

Finally, if the four epistles were written during the winter of 1663–64, they could not possibly be Rochester's. He did not return to England from his Grand Tour until a full year later (Wilson, *Rochester-Savile Letters*, p. 4).

10.

Colonel Edmund Ashton

One of the satisfactions of literary research, especially in the unexplored territories of the Restoration, is the possibility of rescuing a hitherto unrecognized author from obscurity.[1] Such an author is the subject of this chapter. Though his name occurs in the biographies of a surprising number of major literary figures of the Restoration, students of this period know little about him and in some cases have even failed to identify him. His existence challenges attention, however, in connection with a group of three lampoons appearing in the Yale MS. and the Rochester editions of 1680. An account of his life and works must be prefaced by a discussion of the problems of authorship posed by this group of poems.

1. For a similar case of a previously unrecognized author (Edward Radclyffe, second Earl of Derwentwater), see my article, "Poems by 'My Lord R.': Rochester versus Radclyffe," *PMLA*, 72 (1957), 612–19.

I

Casual readers of Restoration literature, familiar with Dryden's great satire on Shadwell, are likely to assume that the consummate symbol of bad writing during the 1670s was Richard Flecknoe. A more notorious scribbler at this time, however, was the Honorable Edward Howard, author of six plays and much nondramatic verse, who may have escaped inclusion in *Mac Flecknoe* largely because he was Dryden's brother-in-law. About 1670, "Ned" Howard's writings were attacked in at least ten lampoons composed by various major and minor Wits at the Court of Charles II.[2] Of the ten poems, three were printed together under Rochester's name in the first edition of 1680, the Huntington edition (A-1680-HU, pp. 88–91).

The three lampoons printed in the Huntington edition may constitute a "linked group" of poems. In the order they assume in this group, their first lines are (1) "Come on ye Critticks! find one fault who dare," (2) "Thou damn'd Antipodes to common sense," and (3) "As when a Bully, draws his Sword." The existence of such a group is suggested by the fact that the three satires appear together in this order both in the Yale MS. and in *The Annual Miscellany: For The Year 1694,* 1694, where they were probably printed from a manuscript;[3] presumably they occupied this same order in the archetype of the Yale MS. and the Huntington edition. In the edition, however, the second and third poems are printed in reverse order. The first and third poems satirize Howard's epic *The Brittish Princes,* pub-

---

2. All ten poems are found in Bodl. MS. Eng. Poet. e. 4, pp. 188–98.

3. The linked group of three lampoons is reprinted in *The Annual Miscellany: For The Year 1694,* 1708, and in *The Third Part of Miscellany Poems,* 1716 and 1727. See Part III for a more detailed list of early texts and ascriptions of these poems.

lished about May 1669. The second poem ridicules his comedy *The Six days Adventure, or the New Utopia,* acted about March 1670/1.[4]

Despite the ascriptions to Rochester in the Huntington edition, there is no reason to suppose that he wrote any of the three satires on Howard. These ascriptions may, in fact, be dismissed as worthless. As we saw earlier (Chapter 3), the satires appear, not in the section of poems by or concerning Rochester, but in the section of poems by miscellaneous authors. Moreover, the Yale MS., which probably preserves the ascriptions given in the manuscript copytext of the Huntington edition, assigns the poems, not to Rochester, but to three other authors. All remaining sources which ascribe the poems to Rochester evidently descend from the Huntington edition. The poems were reprinted as Rochester's in the other 1680 editions and in the later editions of 1685 (A-1685), 1701 (A-1701), 1713 (A-1713), and 1731 (A-1731). From one of the 1680 editions they were also reprinted under his name in *The Works Of the Earls of Rochester, Roscommon, Dorset, &c.,* 1714 (C-1714-1), though two of the three texts in this edition include conflated readings probably taken from *The Annual Miscellany: For The Year 1694,* where the poems carry no ascriptions. Four lines of the first poem which are ascribed to Rochester in *The Agreeable Variety,* 1717 (reissued 1724 and 1742) were rather obviously printed from one of the Rochester editions. Gerard Langbaine, attributing the first two poems of the group to Rochester, cites one of the 1680 editions as his source. Indeed, Rochester apparently did not write any satire on Edward Howard; if he did, the poem is either un-

4. Nicoll, *Restoration Drama,* p. 414. *The Brittish Princes* was advertised in the *Term Catalogues* on 19 May 1669. A note in B. M. Add. MS. 18220 indicates that the first of the three lampoons was already in existence on 6 September 1669.

identified or no longer extant. Another lampoon which Rochester is alleged to have written against Howard, "On Poet Ninny,"
seems actually to satirize Sir Carr Scroope (see Chapter 13).

Aside from being wrongly ascribed to Rochester, the three
lampoons on Edward Howard present rather different problems of authorship. The first poem, beginning "Come on ye
Critticks! find one fault who dare," offers an unusually clear-
cut situation. It has generally been assigned to Charles Sackville, Lord Buckhurst, later Earl of Middlesex and Dorset,[5]
and a review of the evidence shows that this conclusion is undoubtedly correct. The poem is ascribed to Buckhurst in an impressive list of nine manuscript versions which apparently do
not derive either from printed texts or from each other: the
Yale MS., Harvard MS. Eng. 624, B.M. Sloane MS. 4455,
B. M. Add. MS. 18220, Bodl. MS. Rawl. D. 260, Bodl. MS.
Eng. Poet. e. 4, Bodl. MS. Don. b. 8, Bodl. MS. Douce 357, and
Edinburgh MS. D.C.1.3. To this list the printed texts add a
tenth ascription, in *Poetical Miscellanies: The Fifth Part,* 1704.
The 1704 miscellany is probably the source of all later ascrip-
tions to Buckhurst in printed texts, including those in *The Third
Part of Miscellany Poems,* 1716 and 1727, in editions of the
Works of Rochester, Roscommon, Dorset, etc. from 1718 on
(C series), and in *The Works of the most celebrated Minor
Poets,* 1749. Buckhurst's authorship of this lampoon seems to
have been common knowledge among his contemporaries, as is
shown by the ascriptions in manuscripts and also by the manner
in which Dryden assigns the poem to him in the dedication of
Examen Poeticum, 1693. Significantly, too, there is no valid evidence against Buckhurst's authorship. This popular satire is
probably the most important poem Buckhurst ever wrote; its

5. See Part III for documentation of the previous scholarship on these
three poems.

ironic structure is a noteworthy anticipation of the technique of Dryden's *Mac Flecknoe* and Pope's *Dunciad* (see Chapter 4).

If the authorship of the first lampoon on Howard is a simple matter, that of the second, beginning "Thou damn'd Antipodes to common sense," is chaos. Though this poem is generally assigned to Buckhurst, the evidence is far from clear. The case for Buckhurst's authorship rests on only two ascriptions, in Bodl. MS. Eng. Poet. e. 4 and in the *Miscellaneous Works* of Buckingham, 1704 (reprinted 1707). Buckingham's *Works* is the source of the text and ascription to Buckhurst in Bodl. MS. Rawl. Poet. 173, and it may be the source of the ascription in *The Works of the most celebrated Minor Poets,* 1749. Contradicting the attribution to Buckhurst are ascriptions to Henry Savile, in the Yale MS., and to "Witherley," presumably William Wycherley, in Harvard MS. Eng. 636F. Though the evidence favors Buckhurst's authorship, the ascriptions to Savile and Wycherley occur in sources which cannot be lightly disregarded. Moreover, the poem is markedly poorer in quality than Buckhurst's genuine satire. One may agree with Thorpe that "as the evidence now stands, it seems impossible to determine the author of this poem" (*Rochester's Poems,* p. 185). It includes an interesting comparison of Howard to Flecknoe as a bad writer ("Thou Foile to Flecknoe").[6]

The third lampoon on Howard—which supplies the *raison d'être* for the present chapter—poses still another type of problem. This poem, beginning "As when a Bully, draws his Sword," has generally been attributed to Rochester, though it is a weak performance on a subject which Rochester's satirical genius could surely have exploited more successfully. As we have seen, the

---

6. In some early texts, notably the 1680 editions, the reading "Flecknoe" has been corrupted to "*Fluence*"—a circumstance suggesting that at least one scribe was unfamiliar with Flecknoe's name.

early texts of the poem provide no valid evidence that Rochester wrote it. The situation has been confused, however, by A. J. Bull's contention that this satire is assigned to Rochester in Bodl. MS. Eng. Poet. e. 4.[7] The ascription in the Bodleian text consists of two initials, the second slightly smudged, which Bull evidently took to be "E. R." (Earl of Rochester). Comparison with the handwriting elsewhere in the manuscript reveals that the initials are not "E. R." but "E. A." This ascription is compatible with the one in the Yale MS., which assigns the poem to "Major Aston." When the two ascriptions are combined, the apparent author of the poem emerges as a certain "E. Aston," a military gentleman who possessed some literary pretensions and who must have been old enough in 1669 to compose the poem.

Such a person did in fact exist. He was Edmund Ashton, an officer for many years in the King's troop of Life Guards, a companion of the Court Wits, and a small poet in his own right.

II

The story of Ashton's life needs to be told, not only because his career touches those of more important men—he was a nobody who knew everybody who was anybody—but because it colorfully illustrates the existence led by a minor Wit at the Court of Charles II. Unfortunately, since Ashton is a fairly common family name, it is difficult to be certain that every bit of information in the following account applies to the same person.[8]

Edmund Ashton was born in 1643 or 1643/4 into an old family

7. A. J. Bull, "Thomas Shadwell's Satire on Edward Howard," *Review of English Studies*, 6 (1930), 312–15.

8. Ashton's surname is frequently given as "Ashton," "Assheton," or "Aston," his Christian name as either "Edmund" or (incorrectly) "Edward."

of Lancashire gentry who staunchly supported the Royalist cause during the Civil War. He was the oldest of the nine children of James Ashton of Chadderton, near Oldham; his father died in 1651 while Edmund was still a child. Edmund was admitted to Gray's Inn on 13 July 1659 and was called to the bar *ex gratia* on 9 November 1660. He matriculated at St. Edmund Hall, Oxford, on 11 April 1660 but left without taking a degree. By 17 March 1664/5 he had reached the age of 21 and assumed his position as a Lancashire country squire. On 15 April 1665 he was admitted to lands previously owned by his grandfather in a neighboring town. In a legal document dated 5 April 1666, the sheriff and "Edmund Assheton, Esquire" agreed to mitigate the punishment of a local gentleman convicted of barratry at the Lancaster assizes. The Ashton family seat, Chadderton Hall, was listed in 1666 as the largest house in Chadderton; it boasted thirteen taxable hearths, whereas its nearest competitor could claim only seven.[9]

Ashton's long career as a soldier evidently began early in 1667, during the closing months of the Second Dutch War. By 13 June he had bought a captain's commission in Sir Allen Apsley's regiment of foot. Among the lieutenants in Apsley's regiment was "Thos. Shadwell"; Ashton may at this time have formed his friendship with the famous dramatist, whose first

9. *The Visitation of the County Palatine of Lancaster, Made in the Year 1664–5, by Sir William Dugdale, Knight,* ed. F. R. Raines (Manchester, Chetham Society, 1872), p. 18. *The Victoria History of the County of Lancaster,* ed. William Farrer and J. Brownbill (London, Constable, 1906–14), 5, 116–18. Joseph Foster, *The Register of Admissions to Gray's Inn* (London, privately printed, 1889), p. 288; *Alumni Oxonienses* (Oxford and London, Parker, 1891–92), p. 38. *The Pension Book of Gray's Inn,* ed. Reginald J. Fletcher (London, Masters of the Bench, 1901–10), *1*, 434. HMC, *Kenyon,* p. 77. The approximate date of Ashton's birth, given incorrectly in the *Victoria History,* is supplied by Dugdale.

play, *The Sullen Lovers,* was acted the following year.[1] In May 1667 Ashton was in London helping the Earl of Castlehaven raise a regiment of foot to serve in Flanders under the King of Spain. Ashton, with the rank of captain, was to have a company of about 50 men ready for embarkation at Gravesend by 15 June. He and his company may have been among the 2400 recruits whom Castlehaven landed at Ostend in June and who served against the French until the Peace of Aix-la-Chapelle on 2 May 1668. I have discovered no record of Ashton's presence in England during this period.[2]

By 1669 Ashton had appeared at Court and begun to work his way into the select circle of Wits who surrounded Charles II. His success in this endeavor probably stemmed from a natural gregariousness and from an unusual facility for cultivating persons of fashion and influence—a fortunate gift, since his other talents seem to have been mediocre. At the outset, we find Ashton participating in two of the Wits' favorite occupations, dueling and the writing of verses. In November 1669 he was the "very mettled friend" who acted as Mulgrave's second in his abortive duel with Rochester. Ashton's role in this affair is known only from Mulgrave's biased narrative, written many years later. Mulgrave relates that he sent Ashton to call Rochester to account for some allegedly malicious remarks. On the night before the proposed duel Ashton accompanied Mulgrave to Knightsbridge, and on the following morning it was Ashton who snobbishly objected to Rochester's second as a person "whom no body knew." After Rochester pleaded illness as an excuse for not fighting, Ashton "thought himself obliged to write down

1. *CSPD,* 13 June 1667 (p. 181). Charles Dalton, *English Army Lists and Commission Registers* (London, Eyre and Spottiswoode, 1892–1904), *1,* 82.
2. HMC, *Kenyon,* p. 79. *DNB,* "Touchet."

every word and circumstance of this whole matter, in order to spread every where the true reason of our returning without having fought; which being never in the least either contradicted or resented by the Lord *Rochester*, intirely ruined his reputation as to courage." [3]

Late in 1669 Ashton added his uncertain voice to the chorus of abuse which greeted Edward Howard's perilous venture into heroic poetry. Ashton's satire, which mildly admonishes Howard on his behavior, was apparently written after other Wits like Buckhurst had shown the way. "And first the greater *Wits,* were at thee," wrote Ashton, adding with unconscious irony, "Now ev'ry little *Fool,* will pat thee." In 1670 Ashton sold one of his Lancashire estates; possibly he found, like many a fop in Restoration literature, that his attempt to emulate the fashionable life of the Wits was already a serious drain on his income. [4]

In May 1671 Ashton entertained his friend Thomas Shadwell at his home in Lancashire. From *"Hall* yclepped *Chaderton,"* as he facetiously called it, Shadwell sent William Wycherly a Rabelaisian epistle in hudibrastic verse which vividly describes the activities of himself and his host: drinking at the hall with the parson, whose large capacity for ale was matched by his small capacity for Latin; carousing with the local justices and squires at the village inn, where the conversation turned to hunting dogs; and soliciting the wholesome Lancashire lasses, whose favors could be purchased for a "Treat of Ale, or at most Brandy." Wycherley replied with a similar hudibrastic epistle in which he advised Shadwell to stick to his ale and leave the

3. Mulgrave's "Memoirs," in his *Works,* 1723, *2,* 8–10. HMC, *Seventh Report,* p. 488. *Journals of the House of Lords, 12,* 272–77.

4. *Victoria History, 5,* 101. A legal deed dated 1699 records another purchase of land from Edmund Ashton (*5,* 82). In 1669 Ashton granted a lease on the fulling mill in Chadderton (*5,* 16).

wenches to Ashton. On 25 May, while he was at Chadderton, Shadwell wrote the Duchess of Newcastle an urbane letter thanking her for her bountiful reward of his dedication to *The Humorists*. Ashton seems to have maintained a lifelong friendship with Shadwell. When Shadwell died in 1692, he bequeathed gold rings to Dorset, Sedley, William Jephson, and Ashton, "my most deare freinds by whome I have beene extreamely obliged." [5]

In September 1671, back in London, Ashton came to blows with George Etherege, who had just returned from his diplomatic duties in Turkey. This "furious combat," as reported to Rochester, took place "within the rayles of Covent Garden" and "ended hapily in a fall on Ashton's part." The assembled bystanders interposed and stopped the fight (HMC, *Bath, 2, 153*). Ashton's ill-success in his tussle with Etherege may have been due to his short stature; he was frequently called "little Ashton." About this time, he may have composed a rather graceful song which was printed anonymously early in 1672.

Surprisingly, Ashton next emerges at the beginning of the Third Dutch War as an English spy. At the formal outbreak of hostilities on 17 March 1671/2, he was operating out of Harwich with instructions to determine whether the Dutch were ready for war. If we can believe a co-worker, Captain Silas Taylor, Ashton's performance as a cloak-and-dagger agent was a failure. After one of Ashton's missions, Taylor saw "reason to question his information or his judgment." On a later mission, from which he returned on 1 April, Ashton traveled from Rotterdam to Amsterdam in what Taylor termed "a fruitless at-

---

5. *The Complete Works of Thomas Shadwell*, ed. Montague Summers (London, Fortune Press, 1927), *1*, lxxxv; *5*, 227–32. Albert S. Borgman, *Thomas Shadwell* (New York Univ. Press, 1928), p. 89.

tempt" to learn the names of the Dutch ships and their captains.[6]

In following weeks Ashton's fortunes evidently improved, for on 28 May 1672 he was attending the Duke of York at the battle of Sole Bay. When the flagship *Prince* was disabled by Dutch gunfire, Ashton, Henry Savile, and several others accompanied the Duke to the *St. Michael* in an open boat. Ashton's name figures in Savile's printed narrative of the engagement, which was being avidly read in London several days later.[7] Almost immediately, King Charles sent Ashton to deliver an account of the battle to Louis XIV, who was then marching triumphantly against the Dutch on the continent. Returning to England later in June, Ashton carried a letter from the Duke of Monmouth, who was serving with the French forces. For the expenses of his journey, he was generously granted 300 pounds.[8]

King Charles soon found other errands for Ashton, dispatching him on 29 June to Zeeland "with private instructions." Though the precise purpose of this mission is unspecified, it must have been important, and Ashton performed it to the King's satisfaction. Charles commended him for having "done his duty very well," hoped his mysterious mission would produce "very good success," and rewarded him in January 1672/3 with a free gift of 200 pounds. Ashton returned from the continent within a few weeks, and on 27 July the King sent him to the

---

6. *CSPD*, 26 Mar. 1672 (p. 238), 28 Mar. 1672 (p. 245), 2 Apr. 1672 (p. 267), 4 May 1672 (p. 463).

7. *CSPD*, 6 June 1672 (p. 164). HMC, *Dartmouth*, *3*, 21. *A True Relation of the Engagement of His Majesties Fleet*, 1672, p. 3.

8. *CSPD*, 10 June 1672 (pp. 193, 684), [19]/29 June 1672 (p. 250). *CTB*, 12 June 1672 (pp. 1082, 1252). *Correspondence of the Family of Hatton*, ed. Edward Maunde Thompson (Westminster, Camden Society, 1878), *1*, 91.

Duke of York to report his accomplishments in Zeeland and to deliver a letter of instructions for the disposition of the fleet. On 2 August he was in Harwich again, where, whatever King Charles might think, Captain Taylor continued to grumble about Ashton's performance.[9]

By late 1672 the war was no longer in vogue, and Ashton apparently took no further part in it. On his return to Court he seems to have enjoyed a measure of royal favor for several years. In March 1673 he purchased a commission as lieutenant and major in the fashionable King's own troop of Life Guards, commanded by the Duke of Monmouth. After some difficulties—the place he had bought was already full—his commission was confirmed in July, and at the same time he was promoted to lieutenant and lieutenant-colonel, a rank he continued to hold during the reigns of Charles II and James II.[1]

In July 1673 Ashton also obtained the post of Receiver of Hearthmoney for Lancashire. Sir Charles Sedley offered himself as surety for the new tax collector, which was hardly a judicious move, in view of Ashton's subsequent display of ineptness. In a few months Ashton was seriously behind in his accounts, and by March 1674 he owed the King 264 pounds. Two years later, after he lost his post, the amount had not yet been paid. Instructions were repeatedly issued to save him from prosecution.

Though 264 pounds was not an extraordinarily large sum, Ashton either was very short of cash or else hoped to get off

9. *CSPD*, 2 July 1672 (p. 303), 2 Aug. 1672 (p. 435), 5 Aug. 1672 (p. 446), 10 Jan. 1672/3 (p. 413). *CTB*, 7 Jan. 1672/3 (p. 27). *The Letters, Speeches and Declarations of King Charles II*, ed. Arthur Bryant (London, Cassell, 1935), pp. 253–55.

1. *CSPD*, 28 Mar. 1673 (p. 97), Apr. 1673 (p. 196), 26 July 1673 (p. 462; *Addenda*, p. 433). Dalton, *Army Lists, 1*, 140, 155, 252, 311; 2, 1, 115; 3, 173.

without paying. In December 1674 he sold a jewel to the King for the handsome price of 750 pounds, none of which seems to have been applied to his debt. Two months later he was playing the horses: a letter of 9 February reveals that he "has made two matches with the Duke of Albemarle, to be run at Newmarket, upon which he has bet a great deal of money." About March 1674/5, doubtless in an attempt to raise funds, he secured a promise of the next vacant post as Commissioner for Wine Licences. The promise was fulfilled in April 1676, but his salary of 200 pounds a year was not to commence until one of the other Commissioners died. In January 1675/6 he petitioned for a discharge of his arrear of 264 pounds, and in February for 300 pounds "to be allowed him upon his account he having given so many guineas lately for his brother's commission to be a lieutenant in the Guards who was soon after killed in the French service." The first of these two petitions was granted in March 1676, when King Charles indulgently canceled Ashton's debt of 264 pounds "in consideration of his good services and as a mark of royal favour." [2] By this date, too, Ashton's income may have been augmented by an appointment as Groom of the Bedchamber to the Duke of York, a position carrying an emolument of 200 pounds a year.[3]

Ashton's energies were not wholly engrossed by the trouble over the hearthmoney, for he still had time to carry more mes-

2. *CTB*, 3 July 1673 (p. 187), 5 July 1673 (p. 367), 10 Mar. 1673/4 (p. 489), 9 Nov. 1674 (p. 605), 2 Dec. 1674 (p. 267), 23 Dec. 1674 (p. 639), 8 Mar. 1674/5 (p. 700), 4 Feb. 1675/6 (p. 13), 26 Feb. 1675/6 (p. 138), 31 Mar. 1676 (p. 186), 26 Apr. 1676 (p. 197). *CSPD*, 15 Jan. 1675/6 (p. 514). HMC, *Kenyon*, p. 100.

3. Though Ashton is sometimes said to have been Gentleman of the Bedchamber to the Duke of York, I have discovered no evidence that he held this post. A certain "Ashton," presumably Edmund, is listed as Groom of the Bedchamber to the Duke of York in *Angliae Notitia; or, the Present State of England*, Part I, 9th ed., 1676, p. 200; 10th ed., 1677, p. 200; and 12th ed., 1679, p. 201.

sages and commit murder. Early in April 1675 he bore a letter from the Duke of York (later King James II) to the Prince of Orange (later King William III) expressing sympathy concerning the case of smallpox from which the Prince had just recovered. In July 1675 King Charles intervened to prevent Ashton and two others from being sentenced for killing a certain Peter Slater in Lancashire. Evidently the make-believe games of Restoration courtiers were not played for keeps if Charles could help it.[4]

References to Ashton's activities during the next decade are scattered and relatively unimportant. In April 1677 he entered a *caveat* concerning the estate of a certain Richard Aston, possibly a younger brother, who had killed a bailiff. He petitioned in December 1677 and June 1678 for grants of Irish lands, and in March 1679/80 "for a grant of the first of the five places of undersearcher that shall become void." About May 1678 the King granted him a forfeited estate in Lancashire. In November 1679 he was given leave from his duties in the Life Guards to go to Scotland for two months.[5] Ashton's name is connected with a coal-mining enterprise in Lancashire in a legal document dated 17 April 1682, and he helped settle a rather silly dispute which arose between the King's and Queen's troops of Life Guards on 7 May 1683. In 1684 the ancestral estate in Chadderton, including the hall where Shadwell stayed, passed out of the family. Though the sale was conducted by Ashton's youngest brother William, it is tempting to conjecture that the

4. *CSPD*, 31 Mar. 1675 (p. 47), 14 July 1675 (p. 212).

5. *CSPD*, 6 Apr. 1677 (p. 78), 3 Dec. 1677 (p. 489), 1 June 1678 (p. 201), 19 June 1678 (p. 233), 20 Nov. 1679 (p. 286), 4 Mar. 1679/80 (p. 408); see also 12 Sept. 1676 (p. 321). Ashton may have married early in 1679 (*Allegations for Marriage Licences Issued by the Dean and Chapter of Westminster*, ed. G. J. Armytage, London, Harleian Society Publications, 1886, p. 295).

transaction was necessitated by Edmund's expensive ambitions at Court.[6]

More interesting than these dry records are the contemptuous allusions to Ashton in satires written between 1675 and 1680. Though Sir Carr Scroope may not really have had Ashton in mind when he wrote "In defence of Satyr" in 1676, contemporary scribes applied these two couplets to him:

> There a vain *Fop*, *Mortgages* all his *Land*,
> To buy that gawdy *Play-thing*, a *Command*.

> Here one whom *God* to make a *Fool*, thought fit,
> In spight of *Providence*, will be a *Wit*.[7]

In 1677, in the lampoon beginning "Thou Comon Shore of this Poetique Towne," Ashton was numbered among those who contributed the verses hawked about London by "Captain" Robert Julian. Ashton's name was coupled with Scroope's, and both were compared unfavorably with Charles Sackville, Earl of Middlesex, soon to become Earl of Dorset:

> All mischeifs' thine, transcribeing thou wilt stoope
> From Lofty Middlesex to lowly Scroope.
> What tymes are these, when in that Heroes roome
> Bow-Bending Cupid does wth Ballads come,
> And little Aston offers to ye Bumm.

---

6. Giles Shaw, *Annals of Oldham* (Oldham, "Standard Office," 1904–06), *1*, 188–89, 193. HMC, *Montagu*, pp. 183–84.

7. A-1680-HU, p. 46. In Osborn MS. Chest II, Number 14 (pp. 1012–13), a marginal note identifies the subject of the first couplet as either "Capt: Aston" or "Sr Edward Bash:." Beside the second couplet in Harvard MS. Eng. 623F (p. 34) is written "Captain Aston."

> Can Two such Pigmyes such a weight support,
> Two such Tom Thumbs, of Satyr in a Court?
> (Yale MS., p. 353)

In *Mac Flecknoe*, written about this date, Dryden's satire on Ashton's friend Shadwell possibly alludes to Ashton also. The reference has never been satisfactorily explained:

> Echoes from *Pissing-Ally*, *Sh⟨adwell⟩* call,
> And *Sh⟨adwell⟩* they resound from *A⟨ston⟩ Hall*.

Late in 1679 Dryden's patron, Mulgrave, included his "very mettled friend" in "An Essay upon Satyr" among the small fry who did not merit serious attention from a satirist. Ashton is bracketed with Sir Thomas Armstrong, a fellow officer in the Guards:

> Besides, 'tis labour lost; for who would preach
> Morals to *Armstrong*, or dull *Aston* teach.[8]

No Restoration Wit could consider his career complete until he had patronized a professional poet, and in 1685 Ashton achieved this distinction, albeit in a modest way. Dedicating his unsuccessful farce *Cuckolds-Haven* to Ashton, Nahum Tate bestowed the customary eulogies on his patron, terming him "an Accomplisht Courtier, Souldier, and Scholar" and praising him for "that Justice, Courtesie, and Condescention, which (in relation to Inferiours) compleat the Character of a Gentleman." More important, Tate reveals that he owed his acquaintance with Ashton to the Earl of Roscommon, adding obsequiously that "while I have heard you discant together on your beloved Au-

---

8. *The Fourth (and Last) Collection of Poems, Satyrs, Songs, &c.,* 1689 (Case 189–4), sig. E1ᵛ. For a discussion of various aspects of Mulgrave's poem, see Maurice Irvine, "Identification of Characters in Mulgrave's 'Essay upon Satyr,'" *Studies in Philology, 34* (1937), 533–51.

thours, Time seem'd to me to be revolv'd, and I thought my self in the Court of *Augustus.*" It is possible, therefore, that Ashton participated in Roscommon's "academy" for the study and improvement of the English language, which flourished from about 1682 until Roscommon's death in January 1684/5. In this society Ashton would have known such men as Dryden, Dorset, Halifax, Lord Maitland (later Earl of Lauderdale), Lord Cavendish (later Duke of Devonshire), and Sir Charles Scarborough. Ashton was perhaps among the "few others of less note & Abilities" who belonged to the society.[9] About this time, he may have composed some verses which were copied into Etherege's letterbook in Ratisbon.

Despite his continuing friendship with Whigs like Shadwell, Ashton's actions when James II came to the throne suggest that he supported the new King wholeheartedly. One of James's first projects was to pack the House of Commons with his adherents, including Ashton. Urged by his commanding officer, the Duke of Albemarle, and by the King himself, Ashton stood for Clitheroe in Lancashire and was elected; his name appears occasionally in the records of James's one and only Parliament, which convened on 19 May 1685. In June he helped Albemarle raise the militia in Devonshire during Monmouth's ill-starred rebellion. In September his name appears in the secret service accounts for a payment of about 50 pounds. With the Revolution of 1688, Ashton's fortunes changed somewhat. He was not returned to Parliament in the elections of January 1688/9, and by 1 January 1689/90 he was discharged from the Life Guards with an allowance of 23 shillings per day and a statement that King William was "well satisfied" with his "good service."[1]

9. Carl Niemeyer, "The Earl of Roscommon's Academy," *Modern Language Notes, 49* (1934), 432–37.
1. HMC, *Kenyon,* pp. 177–80 and possibly p. 222; *Stopford-Sackville, 1,* 5. William Wardell Bean, *The Parliamentary Representation of the*

Ashton's life came to an end—appropriately, one may feel—
in a duel fought on Sunday morning, 1 December 1695, at Car-
shalton, in Surrey. His antagonist, a Mr. Nicholas Carew, was
convicted of manslaughter at the Surrey assizes but was par-
doned by King William.[2]

III

Few of Ashton's poems have survived the more than two and
a half centuries since his death. For obvious reasons, no collected edition of his works was ever issued, and I have discovered
only four poems which were assigned to him by his contemporaries. These include one prologue, one song, a paraphrase of
some lines from Horace, and the lampoon on Edward Howard
already discussed. Ironically, all four poems have been confused
with the productions of more famous writers.

One poem besides the satire on Howard was attributed to
Rochester. This is the prologue beginning "Gentle Reproofs
have long been try'd in vain," which John Hayward, Quilter
Johns, and Vivian de Sola Pinto printed in their editions of
Rochester, though its rather flaccid couplets are below his usual
quality.[3] The external evidence on the authorship of this poem
is deceptive, for the many ascriptions to Rochester may all de-

---

Six Northern Counties of England (Hull, privately printed, 1890), p.
252. *Journals of the House of Commons, 9* (1803), 727, 753, 761. *Moneys
Received and Paid for Secret Services,* ed. John Yonge Akerman (London,
Camden Society, 1851), p. 110. *CTB,* 27 Feb. 1689/90 (pp. 517–18)
and *passim.*

2. Narcissus Luttrell, *A Brief Historical Relation of State Affairs*
(Oxford, 1857), *3,* 557; *4,* 36. *CSPD,* 24 Dec. 1695 (p. 135), Mar.
1696 (p. 113), 20 Apr. 1696 (p. 138).

3. The prologue is printed as Rochester's by Hayward (*Collected
Works,* p. 121), Johns (*Poetical Works,* p. 132), and Pinto (*Poems,* p.

scend from the same unreliable source. The prologue was first assigned to Rochester in *Poems on Affairs of State,* 1697, which is notorious for its attempts to attribute spurious material to popular authors. From the numerous editions of this miscellany the poem was reprinted under his name in *A New Collection of Poems Relating to State Affairs,* 1705, and the *Miscellaneous Works* of Rochester and Roscommon, 1707 (C-1707-a). One of two manuscript versions carrying ascriptions to Rochester was probably copied from *Poems on Affairs of State;* in the second, though the text seems independent of printed sources, the ascription appears in a different ink and may therefore have been added from a printed version at a later date. Significantly, two other manuscripts which apparently do not derive from printed sources carry no ascriptions. Thus the case for Rochester's authorship can scarcely stand up against any substantial evidence favoring another author.

Strangely, Rochester's editors seem unaware that this prologue was ascribed to "Collonel Ashton" in Jacob Tonson's well-known *Sylvae: or, The Second Part of Poetical Miscellanies,* 1702. Though Tonson's text is five years later than the one in *Poems on Affairs of State,* it was evidently printed from a manuscript, and his volume is generally far more trustworthy than the earlier collection. Further evidence of Ashton's authorship may be provided by Tonson's very interesting procedure when he published the next edition of his miscellany in 1716. Instead of reprinting his own earlier text, he substituted the one in *Poems on Affairs of State,* apparently feeling that it was superior; thus he must have known of the ascription to Rochester. Nevertheless he retained his previous ascription,

---

54). J. W. Ebsworth, however, printed part of it as "Colonel Aston's Prologue" (*The Roxburghe Ballads,* 4 [Hertford, Ballad Society, 1883], 560).

though he altered its form to "Major Aston."[4] Unfortunately, there is no evidence as to the date of Ashton's prologue or the play it was designed to introduce.

Better in quality than Ashton's prologue or his lampoon on Howard is a song entitled "A farewel to Love," which begins "Once more Loves mighty chains are broke." This song was printed without ascription in Hobart Kemp's *A Collection of Poems, Written upon several Occasions, By several Persons*, 1672, a volume which includes poems by various Court Wits. From a later edition of this collection the song was reprinted under Sir Charles Sedley's name in his *Works* of 1722.[5] Pinto reports, however, that in a copy of Kemp's 1672 miscellany formerly owned by G. Thorn-Drury, a note in a contemporary hand assigns the song to "Capt. Aston." Since Sedley's 1722 *Works*

4. The poem is printed as "Prologue, by the E. of R———r" in *Poems on Affairs of State*, 1697 (Case 211-1-c), p. [2]214; 1699 (Case 211-1-d), p. [2]214; 1702 (Case 211-1-e), p. [2]214; 1703 (Case 211-1-f), p. [2]214; 1710 (Case 211-1-g), p. [2]214; 1716 (Case 211-1-h), p. [2]214; and in *A New Collection of Poems Relating to State Affairs*, 1705 (Case 237), p. 256. It is printed as Rochester's in C-1707-a, p. [1]75; C-1707-b, p. [2]75; C-1709, p. [2]123; C-1709-P, p. [4]1; C-1714-1, p. 57; and later editions of this collection. It appears without ascription in B. M. Add. MS. 21094, fol. 1[r], and B. M. Harl. MS. 6913, fol. 1[r], and as "Prologue by the E. of R———r" in B. M. Sloane MS. 655, fol. 3[r], which gives an incomplete text. In Taylor MS. 3, p. 1, the text is in brown ink while the signature "by y[e] E of Rochester" is in black ink; an inscription in the same black ink notes that the following poem in this manuscript is "in Print."

The poem is printed in *Sylvae*, 1702 (Case 172-2-d), p. 211, as "Prologue to the Young, Fluttering, Noisie Disturbers of the Pit. By Collonel Ashton," and as "Prologue, By Major Aston" in 1716 (Case 172-2-e), p. 314, and 1727 (Case 172-2-f), p. 309.

5. The song is printed without ascription in *A Collection of Poems*, 1672 (Case 151), p. [1]27; 1673 (Case 151-b), p. 27; 1693 (Case 151-c), p. 114; 1695 (Case 151-d), p. 114; 1701 (Case 151-e), p. 104; 1702 (Case 151-f), p. 104; and 1716 (Case 151-g), p. 83. From the 1701, 1702, or 1716 edition of this miscellany it was reprinted in *The Works Of the Honourable Sir Charles Sedley*, 1722, *1*, 9; it continues to appear in the editions of 1776 and 1778. Kemp's collection of 1672 was entered in the *Stationers' Register* on 28 October 1671 and advertised in the *Term Catalogues* on 7 February 1671/2.

presents a derivative text and is generally unreliable, its ascription can scarcely be trusted. Pinto is probably right in concluding that this song is Ashton's.[6]

Ashton's fourth poem, beginning "Upon the downs when shall I breathe at ease," is an eleven-line English paraphrase of a passage in Horace (*Satires*, 2.6, 60–62). These rather creditable verses appear in the letterbook of George Etherege, where they are signed "Coll. Ashton's." A. Wilson Verity printed them without explanation in his edition of Etherege. Sybil Rosenfeld, unable to identify the person whose name she found "so enigmatically appended" to the poem, suggested that Etherege might "have written it for, or at the request of, Ashton." She decided, however, that the lines were "probably" Ashton's, alleging that they were "far better than other occasional poems by Etherege." In his review of Rosenfeld's edition, H. F. B. Brett-Smith concluded that Ashton "pretty certainly" wrote the poem, citing as evidence an ascription "in another MS. of the period" which he did not specify; possibly he had in mind Bodl. MS. Firth C. 16, which assigns the poem to "M^{ur}: Aston" (p. 111).[7]

The verses in Etherege's letterbook may be one of Ashton's translations from the Latin which Nahum Tate mentions in his dedication to *Cuckolds-Haven*. After praising Roscommon's translations, Tate continues, "We likewise know, Sir, that you have not sate down with the bare knowledge of those ancient *Roman* Treasures, without giving some parts of them the *Eng-*

6. Pinto, *Works of Sedley*, *1*, xxiii, xxv; *2*, 240. Unfortunately, Pinto's statements are inconsistent. On *1*, xxiii, he speaks of the note in Thorn-Drury's copy as the only such ascription to Ashton, but on *2*, 240, he indicates that similar handwritten ascriptions occur in copies of the 1672 volume owned by Sir Charles Firth and H. F. B. Brett-Smith.

7. Verity, *Works of Etheredge*, p. 387. *The Letterbook of Sir George Etherege*, ed. Sybil Rosenfeld (London, Oxford Univ. Press, 1928), pp. 364–65. H. F. B. Brett-Smith, *Review of English Studies*, 5 (1929), 228. The poem appears without ascription in Harvard MS. Eng. 585, p. 403, and in *Poems on Affairs of State*, 1698 (Case 215), p. 222.

lish Stamp. And to hoard them in Secresy, is injury to your Country." If Ashton heeded Tate's plea to publish his lucubrations, I have been unable to locate them.

Ashton's surviving prose is even less considerable than his poetry. A few of his letters have been published.[8] A pamphlet on the French war, probably written late in life, affords an anecdote which typifies Ashton's rather pathetic and ineffectual career. As the foremost patron of the age, the Earl of Dorset was frequently asked to read the promising first drafts of authors who hoped to enjoy his benevolence. The best that Ashton could offer, however, was a rejected manuscript. In his covering letter to Dorset, Ashton explained that his pamphlet was refused because the printer "thought it wou'd give offence." "And so," he concluded plaintively, "I am disappointed of being an Author" (Harris, *Dorset*, p. 207). His pamphlet remains in manuscript to this day.

8. Letters written by Ashton are printed in full or in part in HMC, *Kenyon*, pp. 79, 100, 177; HMC, *Montagu*, p. 184; Harris, *Dorset*, p. 207.

II.

Rochester's "Timon" and "Tunbridge Wells"

I

In the past, Rochester has received equal praise for his satires and for his songs.[1] In the future, as nineteenth-century prejudices diminish and the predominantly satirical character of Augustan literature is better appreciated, Rochester's satires may well be recognized as his most substantial poetic achievement. This recognition should be forthcoming if only because satires are usually longer than lyrics, and a good long poem is more significant than a good short poem. In addition, Rochester's literary temperament was essentially satirical. Satires are his most numer-

1. As recently as 1959, the introduction to a paperback edition of Rochester's poetry insisted that his "positive achievement is his contribution to the tradition of SONG [*sic*]" (*Rochester*, ed. Ronald Duncan, London, Edward Hulton, 1959, p. 7).

ous compositions, they achieve higher quality than his work in other genres, and a tendency to satire is evident even in his lyrics. Also, unlike his lyrics, whose influence on contemporary practice was probably negligible, Rochester's satires contributed importantly in shaping the new Augustan sensibility as it emerged during the years around 1675.

Every reader will have his own preferences among Rochester's satires, and many lists of favorites would doubtless include such minor masterpieces as "Upon Nothing," "The Maim'd Debauchee," or "A very Heroical Epistle in Answer to Ephelia." The heart of Rochester's satirical achievement, however, is a series of five major satires probably composed between early 1674 and early 1676, a two-year period during which Rochester's creativity reached its peak. These five satires include "A Satyr against Mankind," Rochester's best-known poem, and "A Letter fancy'd from Artemisa in the Town, to Cloe in the Country," which is possibly his finest performance. Two other satires in the series are "An Allusion to Horace" and "Tunbridge Wells," both of which were widely read and highly influential. The fifth satire is the poem commonly known as "Timon," though this apt title was not used before 1704 and seems to possess no authority. Besides being written about the same time, the five satires form a group in other respects. Their length alone (ranging from 124 to 264 lines) sets them apart from Rochester's many short poems, and they are all written in his distinctive style of heroic couplets. They are linked by resemblances in their themes and by their structure, which is comparatively formal. This structure derives ultimately from Roman satire, though the relationship, very close in "An Allusion to Horace," is rather distant in "Artemisa to Cloe."

Since prior investigations have established Rochester's authorship of "A Satyr against Mankind," "Artemisa to Cloe," and "An Allusion to Horace," the authenticity of these three poems requires no further discussion; the new evidence offered by the present study is listed in Part III. Likewise, the present study adds little information on their dates of composition, to which we shall return briefly at the conclusion of this chapter. The case is different, however, with "Tunbridge Wells" ("At Five this Morne, when Phoebus raisd his head") and especially with "Timon" ("What Timon does old Age begin t' approach"). Though "Tunbridge Wells" has been attributed correctly to Rochester, the authenticity of "Timon" is in dispute, nor has the evidence on the authorship of either poem been examined in detail. The date of "Timon" has been determined precisely, but that of "Tunbridge Wells" remains unnecessarily vague.

"Timon" and "Tunbridge Wells" can conveniently be discussed together, for there is reason to suspect that they bear a special relationship to each other. One small similarity, the comparative weakness of the evidence supporting Rochester's authorship of these two poems, is suggested by the position they occupied in the archetypal source of the Yale MS. and the first edition of 1680, the Huntington edition. Though "A Satyr against Mankind," "Artemisa to Cloe," and "An Allusion to Horace" are found among the obviously genuine pieces in the section of poems by or concerning Rochester, "Timon" and "Tunbridge Wells" were relegated to the section of poems by miscellaneous authors. "Tunbridge Wells" appears in the Yale MS. without ascription, while "Timon" is actually assigned to another author. Evidently the scribe of the archetype, who was usually well-informed, did not know that they might be Rochester's. Moreover, though "Timon" found its way into the Huntington edition (A-1680-HU, p. 105), "Tunbridge Wells" was among the eleven or more poems from the original collection which the printer omitted.

II

The dates of "Timon" and "Tunbridge Wells" suggest some sort of connection between these two poems, for they seem to have been composed at almost exactly the same time.

The date of "Timon" was established in an article by Harold F. Brooks, who compared the following lines in the poem with dispatches in the *London Gazette:*[2]

> Will *Souches* this year any *Champoone* drink?
> Will *Turene* fight him? without doubt says *Huffe,*
> ⟨When⟩ [3] they Two meet, their meeting will be rough.

This passage refers to the war which Louis XIV was waging on the continent—specifically, to the situation on the Rhine during the spring of 1674. Souches, the Imperial general, took command in March, and news of his appointment reached England late in that month (*London Gazette,* 26–30 March and 30 March—2 April 1674). In April and May it appeared that Souches might join battle with Turenne, the French general on the Rhine, but by early June it was known in England that he was moving his army to Flanders, where there was little chance that he and Turenne would clash (*London Gazette,* 4–8 June 1674). In October, Souches was relieved of his command (*London Gazette,* 12–15 and 19–22 Oct. 1674). Accordingly, "Timon" must have been composed during April, May, or early June of 1674, while Souches and Turenne still faced each other on the Rhine.

Other topical allusions in the poem corroborate the date proposed by Brooks without rendering it more precise. "Timon"

2. "The Date of Rochester's 'Timon,'" *Notes and Queries,* 174 (1938), 384–85.
3. Since "When" is the reading of all early manuscripts including the Yale MS., the reading of A-1680-HU, "If," must be a corruption.

contains specific references to Dryden's *The Indian Emperour* (acted *c.* April 1665); to Etherege's first two plays (acted March 1664 and Feb. 1667/8); to Orrery's *Mustapha* (acted April 1665) and *The Black Prince* (acted Oct. 1667); to Crowne's *Pandion and Amphigenia* (pub. 1665) and *The History of Charles the Eighth* (acted *c.* Dec. 1671); to charges that Shadwell received assistance in writing *Epsom-Wells* (acted Dec. 1672); and to Settle's *The Empress of Morocco* (probably acted at Court during spring of 1672/3).[4] The only later reference is the passage on Souches and Turenne. At the opposite limit, the poem speculates on the future actions of Turenne, who died on 27 July 1675. Among Timon's friends it names *"Buckhurst,"* who became Earl of Middlesex early in 1675, after which he would normally have been called by his new title (Harris, *Dorset,* pp. 60–62).

The date of "Tunbridge Wells," like that of "Timon," is established primarily by internal evidence, though this poem mentions fewer contemporary events. A reference to Etherege's

---

4. Dates of dramatic performances are taken from Nicoll, *Restoration Drama,* except that of *The Empress of Morocco,* for which see Eleanore Boswell, *The Restoration Court Stage* (Cambridge, Harvard Univ. Press, 1932), pp. 131–33. The dating of "Timon" has been needlessly complicated by the following couplet, describing the beef served by the "dull dining *Sot*":

> Hard as the *Arse* of M——, under which,
> The *Coachman* sweats, as ridden by a *Witch.*

Some editors (Hayward, Johns, Pinto) have filled out the blank with "Mazarin" (who did not reach England until December 1675) or "Mordaunt." In four independently descended manuscripts, however, the reading is "Mosely." Other contemporary references suggest that Mistress Moseley, whose name is sometimes linked with Shaftesbury's, operated a house of prostitution about this time. She is mentioned by Thomas Duffet in *Psyche Debauch'd,* 1678, p. 23, and possibly in *The Empress of Morocco. A Farce,* 1674, p. 34; in "Advice to a C——t Monger" ("Fucksters, you y[t]. will be happy"), Yale MS., p. 395; and in "Satyr. 1688/9" ("Long had my Pen lay'n dull and useless by"), Bodl. MS. Firth C. 15, pp. 312, 315.

The Comical Revenge (acted March 1664) is too early to afford much help, but a firm *terminus post quem* is provided by the following passage, which is a tissue of allusions to the two parts of Andrew Marvell's *The Rehearsal Transpros'd:*

> Listning I found yᵉ Cobb of all this Rabble
> Pert Bayes, wᵗʰ his Importance Comfortable:
> He being rais'd to an Arch-Deaconry,
> By trampling on Religion Liberty;
> Was growne too great, & look'd too fat & Jolly,
> To be disturb'd wᵗʰ care, or Melancholly,
> Tho' Marvell has enough, expos'd his Folly.
> He dranke to carry off some old remaines,
> His Lazy dull distemper, left in's Veines:
> Let him drinke on, but 'tis not a whole Flood,
> Can give sufficient sweetnesse to his blood,
> To make his Nature, or his Manners good.
> Importance dranke too, tho' she'd beene noe Sinner
> To wash away some Dreggs, he had spewd in her.⁵

From 1670 to 1672, Samuel Parker, who was "rais'd to an Arch-Deaconry" (of Canterbury) in June 1670, published several books advocating an extreme Erastian control of religious affairs by the state. About autumn of 1672,⁶ Marvell defended religious liberty in Part I of *The Rehearsal Transpros'd,* where he whimsically satirized Parker as "Mr. Bayes" —referring, of course, to Buckingham's famous burlesque. When Parker and others angrily replied, Marvell again ridiculed the archdeacon and his theories in Part II of *The Rehearsal*

5. In this chapter, "Tunbridge Wells" is quoted from the text in the Yale MS., p. 251. The passage on Parker is discussed by Pierre Legouis, "Three Notes on 'Rochester's' Poems," *Modern Language Notes, 69* (1954), 502-06.

6. *The Complete Works of Andrew Marvell,* ed. Alexander B. Grosart (London, 1873), *3,* 244.

Transpros'd. According to its title page, this work was written partly as an answer to a letter of 3 November 1673; since several weeks at least would be required to write and print such a lengthy volume, it can scarcely have reached the public much before early 1674. Also, since the date of its imprint is 1673, it was probably not published later than 24 March 1673/4, the last day of the year Old Style.

In one of his earlier publications, Parker alleged cryptically that he was "much concerned . . . in matters of a closer and more comfortable importance to himself and his own affairs." In Part I of *The Rehearsal Transpros'd*, after speculating facetiously on the nature of these mysterious "matters," Marvell concludes that Parker must be involved with a woman, to whom he refers thereafter as "comfortable importance." [7] In "Tunbridge Wells," the phrase is inverted to "Importance Comfortable." Similar treatment is accorded a phrase in Parker's rejoinder to Marvell, where the archdeacon claimed that he planned to reply sooner but had "been prevented by a dull and lazy distemper." Marvell picks up "dull and lazy distemper" and repeats it frequently in Part II of *The Rehearsal Transpros'd;* [8] in "Tunbridge Wells" it becomes "Lazy dull distemper." Marvell also scolds Parker for his venal ambitions, glances at his obesity, and rebukes him for railing. [9] "Tunbridge

---

7. *Works of Marvell*, ed. Grosart, 3, 9–10, 12, 34, 62, 86, 94, 118, 132, 234, 319, 339, 409, 455, 474. The phrase became a commonplace in contemporary satire. See, for example, Thomas Duffet's *Psyche Debauch'd*, 1678, p. 60; Dryden's *Limberham* (*The Works of John Dryden*, ed. Sir Walter Scott and George Saintsbury, Edinburgh, William Paterson, 1882–93, 6, 118); and the "Epistle to the Tories" prefixed to *The Tory-Poets* (*The Complete Works of Thomas Shadwell*, ed. Montague Summers, London, Fortune Press, 1927, 5, 277).

8. *Works of Marvell*, ed. Grosart, 3, 233, 236, 238, 246, 312, 337, 362, 441.

9. *Works of Marvell*, ed. Grosart, 3, 118–22, 263–65, 336–37, 313, 315.

Wells" apparently echoes these charges in its statements that
Bayes "Was growne too great, & look'd too fat & Jolly" and
that not even "a whole Flood, / Can give sufficient sweetnesse
to his blood, / To make his Nature, or his Manners good."

The phrase "Lazy dull distemper" in "Tunbridge Wells"
demonstrates that the poem was written after Part ii of *The
Rehearsal Transpros'd* was published early in 1674. Moreover,
the character of the lines on Parker argues that they were composed very soon afterward, for they reflect a recent close study
of Marvell's work and would lose much of their point if that
work were not still fresh in the public consciousness. Support
for this early date is provided by the version of "Tunbridge
Wells" in Osborn MS. Chest ii, Number 13, where the poem is
assigned to "An°. 1673"—that is, before 25 March 1674.
Though such dates are often only approximate, the agreement of
external and internal evidence implies that this one is fairly accurate. Three other early texts contain notes specifying exact
days, probably days on which the poem was transcribed and thus
already in existence: the date *"June 30. 1675"* appears in *Poems
on Affairs of State* and Taylor MS. 3, while Bodl. MS. Douce
357 records the date "Sept 20: 81."

The evidence therefore suggests that "Timon" and "Tunbridge Wells" were both written during the spring of 1674.

III

"Tunbridge Wells" has been regarded as authentic by every
student of Rochester who has dealt with it—by John Hayward,
Johannes Prinz, Quilter Johns, Vivian de Sola Pinto, John
Harold Wilson, and Pierre Legouis.[1] Despite this unanimity,

1. Hayward, *Collected Works*, p. 122. Prinz, *Rochester*, pp. 125–27.
Johns, *Poetical Works*, p. 106. Pinto, *Rochester*, pp. 149–53; *Poems*, p.

the external evidence hitherto used to support Rochester's authorship is limited almost entirely to ascriptions in early printed texts of the poem, all of which may derive wholly or in part from the same unreliable source. Pinto alone cites an ascription to Rochester in a manuscript (Bodl. MS. Douce 357). Thus the case for Rochester's authorship of "Tunbridge Wells" is weaker than is traditionally assumed.

After circulating in manuscript for twenty-three years—a remarkably long delay, in view of its popularity—"Tunbridge Wells" was finally printed under Rochester's name in *Poems on Affairs of State*, 1697, which is notorious for its attempts to attribute spurious material to well-known authors. The poem was reprinted with ascription to Rochester in the many later editions of this miscellany and in *A New Collection of Poems Relating to State Affairs*, 1705. "Tunbridge Wells" was again printed as Rochester's in Benjamin Bragge's *Miscellaneous Works* of Rochester and Roscommon, 1707 (C-1707-a), where the text is conflated from a manuscript and some edition of *Poems on Affairs of State*.[2] Bragge's text was reissued by Edmund Curll in 1707 (C-1707-b) and reprinted with ascription to Rochester in Curll's editions of 1709 (C-1709) and 1714

---

87. Wilson, *Court Wits*, pp. 132–33. Legouis, in the article previously cited.

2. The conflated character of this text is implicitly recognized in the preface which Curll inserted in his reissue of Bragge's edition: "If any Gentleman should make it an Objection, that several Pieces in this Volume, have been already Printed, that will be easily answer'd, by assuring the World how widely different they will appear, by comparing 'em together; what has been Printed before, being only spurious, and mangled, and these true and perfect Copies. As for Instance; my Lord *Rochester's Tunbridge-Wells*, is Printed in the *State Poems*, which, when compar'd with the true Copy in this Collection, there will be found above twenty additional Lines and Alterations, which are mark'd with an inverted Comma, for Distinction; and so throughout the whole Book, where there are any new Lines; which, 'tis hop'd, will be a full Satisfaction to those Gentlemen, who shall make such Objections" (C-1707-b, sig. A1ᵛ).

(C-1714-1) and in later editions of this collection. From the edition of 1709, in turn, the poem was printed as Rochester's in the piracy of the same year (C-1709-P), in his *Poems On Several Occasions,* 1713 (A-1713), and in *The Works of the Right Honourable John Earl of Rochester,* 1718 (B-1718-P), which is largely a piracy of one of Jacob Tonson's editions. Giles Jacob also lists "Tunbridge Wells" as Rochester's, but his list, as shown by the poems he includes and by the forms of his titles, almost certainly derives from Curll's edition of 1714.[3]

Since these ascriptions in printed sources all appear to descend from the one in *Poems on Affairs of State,* the case for Rochester's authorship of "Tunbridge Wells" must rest primarily on ascriptions in manuscript versions which the evidence suggests are independently derived. Five of these texts ascribe the poem to Rochester: Osborn MS. Chest II, Number 13 (vol. II, p. 164), Taylor MS. 3 (p. 213), Harvard MS. Eng. 636F (p. 131), B. M. Add. MS. 4456 (fol. 201[r]), and Bodl. MS. Douce 357 (fol. 136[v]). Other independently descended manuscripts, including the Yale MS., unfortunately give no ascriptions.[4] The only testimony against Rochester's authorship is a note in which Alexander Pope denies that "Tunbridge Wells" is Rochester's, but without assigning the poem to another author.[5]

3. "Tunbridge Wells" is printed as Rochester's in *Poems on Affairs of State,* 1697 (Case 211-1-c), p. [2]218, 1699 (Case 211-1-d), p. [2]218, 1702 (Case 211-1-e), p. [2]218, 1703 (Case 211-1-f), p. [2]218, 1710 (Case 211-1-g), p. [2]218, and 1716 (Case 211-1-h), p. [2]218; in *A New Collection of Poems Relating to State Affairs,* 1705 (Case 237), p. 258; in C-1707-a, p. [1]35, C-1707-b, p. [2]35, C-1709, p. [2]57, C-1709-P, p. [2]13, and C-1714-1, p. 26; in A-1713, p. 152, and A-1731, p. 140; and in B-1718-P, p. 11. Jacob, *Poetical Register,* 2, 232.

4. B. M. Add. MS. 34362, fol. 22[r]; Victoria and Albert Museum MS. Dyce 43, p. 234; Lambeth Codices Manuscripti Gibsoniani 941, item 115; Edinburgh MS. DC.1.3, p. 66; Vienna MS. 14090, fol. 124[r]; Yale MS., p. 251; Osborn MS. Box XXII, Number 3, p. 17; and Osborn MS. Chest II, Number 3, p. 123, which gives an incomplete text.

5. This is a manuscript note on p. 258 of Pope's copy of *A New Collec-*

Pope's note is necessarily late in date, while in any event his statement is outweighed by the other evidence. In the absence of further arguments to the contrary, the six independent ascriptions in early texts—five manuscripts and *Poems on Affairs of State*—support the conclusion that Rochester probably composed "Tunbridge Wells." It seems superfluous to cite stylistic similarities between this poem and others which are certainly genuine—notably "A Satyr against Mankind," "Artemisa to Cloe," and "An Allusion to Horace."

Greater difficulties are encountered in determining the authorship of "Timon." This poem has generally been attributed to Rochester, or to Rochester in collaboration with George Villiers, Duke of Buckingham, with a confidence scarcely warranted by the evidence hitherto available.[6] Hayward printed "Timon" in his edition of Rochester with a statement that it was "written jointly" by Rochester and Buckingham (*Collected Works*, p. 331). Subsequently, Prinz and Johns attributed the poem to Rochester alone, as did Pinto in his biography of the Earl. Wilson assigned "Timon" to Rochester, "perhaps in collaboration with Buckingham" (*Court Wits*, p. 182), while Pinto in his edition of the Earl's poems, revising his own earlier opinion, concluded that "Timon" was probably "written by Rochester in collaboration with one or more of his friends" (*Poems*, p. 197). James Thorpe, cautiously recognizing that "Timon" might represent "composite authorship," classified it as a doubtful poem "probably at least in large part Rochester's composition." Quite rightly, he observed that "the evidence

---

tion of Poems Relating to State Affairs, 1705 (Case 237), now in the British Museum. In the title of the poem, which reads "Tunbridge-Wells. *By the Earl of* Rochester, *June* 30. 1675," Pope has inserted the word "Not" before the word "*By*." See W. J. Cameron, "Pope's Annotations on 'State Affairs' Poems," *Notes and Queries, 203* (1958), 291–94.

6. See Part III for fuller documentation of the previous scholarship on "Timon."

for Rochester's authorship of this poem is not so positive as is usually supposed" (*Rochester's Poems*, pp. 186–87).

Examination of the known data on the authorship of "Timon" leads to several striking conclusions: the premise that Buckingham was either sole or part author of the poem has no valid basis; the external evidence hitherto adduced for Rochester's authorship is inadmissible; the many ascriptions in early printed sources provide no reliable testimony; and the available external evidence favors, not Rochester or Buckingham, but Sir Charles Sedley, whose possible authorship of the poem has not previously received serious consideration. Under the circumstances, this chapter cannot pretend to identify the author of "Timon" with full certainty. Investigation of the evidence will clarify the situation, however, and it may offer a new and firmer basis for the traditional view that "Timon" was written by Rochester.

The evidence for Buckingham's authorship of "Timon" does not survive a close scrutiny.[7] The poem was first printed as Buckingham's in his *Miscellaneous Works* of 1704 (reprinted 1707), where it is headed "Timon, a Satyr, In Imitation of Monsieur Boleau [*sic*], upon several Passages in some new Plays then Acted upon the Stage." This ascription deserves little respect. Not only is the *Miscellaneous Works* generally untrustworthy, but its text of "Timon" was apparently printed from one of the Rochester editions of 1680, where the poem is assigned to the Earl alone. Nothing about the 1704 version suggests that it incorporates any reliable testimony independent of its textual source. Evidently John Nutt, the publisher of the 1704 *Works*, raided the earlier Rochester edition to pad out his slender list of Buckingham's poems. The same source supplied

7. See Part III for a more detailed list of the early texts and ascriptions of "Timon."

him with Scroope's "In defence of Satyr" and the anonymous "A Session of the Poets," which he likewise assigned wrongly to Buckingham.

From Buckingham's *Miscellaneous Works*, 1704 or 1707, "Timon" was reprinted in his *Works* of 1715, where it is assigned to both Buckingham and Rochester. Again the ascription seems to provide no information not taken from earlier printed texts. Probably the publisher of the 1715 *Works*, Samuel Briscoe, tried to reconcile the conflicting attributions in his printed sources by listing the poem under both names. He used the same dual ascription for "In defence of Satyr" and "A Session of the Poets," also reprinted from the *Miscellaneous Works*, and even for Rochester's "Upon Nothing," though he evidently printed it from a manuscript. Later ascriptions of "Timon" to Buckingham or to Buckingham and Rochester seem to derive from the editions of 1704, 1707, or 1715. Jacob's ascription to Buckingham and Rochester was taken from the 1715 *Works*, as is shown by the title he uses for the poem. The similar title and ascription given by Theophilus Cibber may derive from Jacob or directly from the volume of 1715. Horace Walpole, attributing "Timon" to Buckingham and Rochester, cites the 1715 *Works* as his source. Apparently there is no further evidence that Buckingham participated in the writing of "Timon" or even that the poem is a product of joint authorship. As Prinz observed, "Timon" possesses a structural unity and a homogeneous style which argue for a single author (*Rochester*, p. 99).

If the ascriptions in early printed texts furnish no substantial support for Buckingham's authorship, they also afford little for Rochester's. "Timon" was first printed under the Earl's name in the Huntington edition of 1680, where it bears the colorless title "Satyr." As we have seen (Chapter 3), this ascription is invalid because "Timon" appears, not in the section of poems by or concerning Rochester, but in the section of poems by miscellaneous authors. Moreover, the Yale MS., which probably preserves the ascriptions given in the archetype and in the manuscript copy-text of the Huntington edition, assigns this satire, not to Rochester, but to Sedley.

All other printed sources ascribing "Timon" to Rochester evidently descend from the Huntington edition. The poem was reprinted as Rochester's in the other 1680 editions and in the later editions of 1685 (A-1685), 1701 (A-1701), 1713 (A-1713), and 1731 (A-1731). From one of the 1680 editions, "Timon" was also reprinted as Rochester's in Curll's *The Works Of the Earls of Rochester, Roscommon, Dorset, &c.*, 1714 (C-1714-1), and succeeding editions of this collection; the title introduced in the 1714 text, "The Rehearsal. A Satire," possibly glances at Buckingham's play and the ascription of this poem to him in his *Miscellaneous Works*. Gerard Langbaine, attributing "Timon" to Rochester, cites one of the 1680 editions as his source. As shown by the title he uses, Jacob's similar ascription in his list of Rochester's poems almost certainly derives from Curll's edition of 1714. Likewise, Dean Lockier's ascription to Rochester cannot be assumed to represent independent testimony. Hence these printed ascriptions, which have heretofore been the only external evidence cited in support of Rochester's authorship, provide no real reason to suppose that "Timon" is his composition.

With the evidence of the early printed sources disqualified, attention may next be directed to ascriptions in independently descended manuscript versions of "Timon." At least three such ascriptions exist, two of them previously unknown: the poem is assigned to Rochester in Harvard MS. Eng. 623F and to Sedley in Harvard MS. Eng. 636F and the Yale MS. Another independently descended text, in Edinburgh MS. DC.1.3, lacks ascription, as does a manuscript reported by Pinto. Though these ascriptions in manuscripts may appear to favor Sedley's authorship, actually they yield no clear conclusion. Harvard MS. Eng. 623F is a reliable source, so that its ascription to Rochester can scarcely be disregarded. Evidence of other kinds must therefore be invoked to determine whether "Timon" was written by Rochester, Sedley, or some author as yet unidentified.

Before we proceed to this other evidence, brief mention should be made of two arguments which students of Rochester have advanced in support of his authorship of "Timon." Though neither argument carries much weight, the unsatisfactory state of the external evidence requires that all relevant points be considered. Thorpe has emphasized that "Timon" is adapted from Boileau's third satire, just as "A Satyr against Mankind" is to some extent based on his eighth satire. Rochester seems to have been specially fond of Boileau's poetry. According to Burnet, *"Boileau* among the *French,* and *Cowley* among the *English* Wits, were those he admired most." Dennis remarked that Rochester "was very well acquainted with *Boileau"* and "defer'd very much to his Judgment." [8]

The second argument concerns the character of Timon, who speaks all but the first four lines of the poem. According to Wilson, Timon is "Rochester, of course" (*Court Wits,* p. 130), while Thorpe similarly felt that "Timon is supposed to represent Rochester himself" (*Rochester's Poems,* p. 186). This identifica-

8. Gilbert Burnet, *Some Passages of the Life and Death Of the Right Honourable John Earl of Rochester,* 1680, p. 8. *The Critical Works of John Dennis,* ed. Edward Niles Hooker (Baltimore, Johns Hopkins Press, 1939–43), *1,* 8. On the sources of "A Satyr against Mankind," see S. F. Crocker, "Rochester's *Satire against Mankind:* A Study of Certain Aspects of the Background," *West Virginia University Studies: III, Philological Papers,* 2 (1937), 57–73; John F. Moore, "The Originality of Rochester's *Satyr against Mankind,"* PMLA, *58* (1943), 393–401; Dale Underwood, *Etherege and the Seventeenth-Century Comedy of Manners* (New Haven, Yale Univ. Press, 1957), pp. 10 ff.

tion may be too positive, for Augustan writers frequently employed the device of the *persona*. Sometimes the *persona* is the butt of the satire, as in Rochester's "A very Heroical Epistle in Answer to Ephelia" and "An Epistolary Essay from M. G. to O. B." (see Chapter 4). Far from being satirized, however, Timon represents the norm of values by which judgment is passed upon other characters in the poem—the host, his wife, and the four hectors. Timon's function is something like that of the "gentlemen of wit and sense" in the comedies of Shadwell, who embody the standards violated by the humor characters. Thus Timon may be a projection of the values, and conceivably the identity, of the author of the poem.

The identification of Timon with Rochester is at least plausible. Timon's personality resembles Rochester's, and his name as well as his attitudes suggest the misanthropy which was associated with the Earl. Timon cannot be Sedley, for Sedley, Buckhurst, and Henry Savile are the wits of Timon's acquaintance whom he was to meet at the house of the "dull dining *Sot*." Savile, of course, was one of Rochester's closest friends.

IV

Because they are unavoidably subjective, considerations of style are among the least desirable criteria of the authenticity of a work. When other types of evidence prove inadequate, however, as they do with "Timon," an appeal to style may become necessary. Fortunately, the verse style of "Timon," like that of the four major satires which can be accepted as Rochester's, is unusually distinctive. Indeed, this style may have been an important, if intangible, reason for the consensus among students of Rochester that part or all of "Timon" is probably his.

A general argument for Rochester's authorship of "Timon" is

its literary excellence, which is specially evident in comparison with the satire by Boileau on which it is based. In "Timon," Boileau's poem is so skillfully adapted to English idiom and circumstances that a reader would hardly suspect a French original. "Timon" even improves upon its model in some ways. In place of Boileau's elaborate descriptions, for example, "Timon" artfully utilizes a few suggestive details. In other respects, too—reflected in the fact that it is sixty-one lines shorter than Boileau's version—"Timon" exhibits the precise, economical technique which characterizes Rochester's work.

Few poets writing in England in 1674 could have produced so good a poem as "Timon," and Rochester was certainly among them. On the other hand, there is reason to doubt that Sedley could or would have composed such a poem. Sedley's collected works include only one formal satire in heroic couplets, evidently written a quarter of a century after "Timon." This poem, *The Happy Pair*, does not resemble "Timon" and is inferior to it (Pinto, *Works of Sedley*, *1*, 63). Despite his gifts as a lyrist, Sedley possessed no outstanding talent as a satirist and no particular skill in writing heroic couplets. By contrast, satire was Rochester's forte, and his couplet style was both brilliant and individualistic.

Possibly the best argument for Rochester's authorship of "Timon" is its similarity to "Tunbridge Wells," which, we have seen, was composed at almost the same date. Though the strongest part of the argument involves the verse styles of these two satires, their resemblances in structure deserve comment. The structure of "Timon" centers upon its dramatic speaker, and the poem achieves unity through its narrative element, consisting of Timon's dramatically rendered account of his visit to the "dull dining *Sot*" and the incidents he observed during the meal. Thematically the poem is unified by the social and intellectual norms which are implied in Timon's attitudes and violated by the opinions and actions of the host, his wife, and the four bullies, as well as by the dramatists whose works are cited.

"Tunbridge Wells" employs a dramatic speaker in much the same way, though he bears no name and there is no trace of the interlocutor who speaks the first four lines of "Timon." The narrative element, if less prominent than in "Timon," is nevertheless present in several forms. For example, the most obvious linkage of the satirical vignettes which make up the body of the poem is that the speaker witnesses them during his perambulations about the fashionable watering place. Also, the vignettes themselves are dramatically conceived, especially those involving the "Gallant" and "young Damsell" (to be quoted presently) and the "Two Wives, wth ⟨girl⟩ just fit for Man." The norms of value in "Tunbridge Wells" resemble those of "Timon," though they are more profound and pervasive. Throughout most of the poem, they are established indirectly, concretely, and imaginatively by the satirical vignettes and directly, if less fully, by the comments of the speaker. In the last ten lines the speaker posits the norms explicitly. The initial couplet of this proto-Swiftian passage states the principal theme of the poem:

> Blesse me thought I, what thing is Man that thus
> In all his shapes, he is rediculous?

The preceding vignettes have depicted various "shapes" in which mankind is absurd.

The similarities between the verse styles of "Timon" and "Tunbridge Wells" are fully evident only when the poems are studied in their entirety. Nevertheless, three sample passages, from these two poems and from *The Happy Pair*, may suggest grounds for concluding that "Timon" was written by Rochester rather than by Sedley or some other author. In all three passages, accidentals have been modernized so that details of spelling, punctuation, and capitalization will not distract attention from the main concern. The first passage is from "Timon":

> And now the bottle briskly flies about,
> Instead of ice, wrapped ⟨up⟩ [9] in a wet clout.
> A brimmer follows the third bit we eat;
> Small beer becomes our drink, and wine our meat.
> The table was so large that in less space
> A man might, safe, six old Italians place;
> Each man had as much room as Porter, B⟨lount⟩,
> Or Harris had in Cullen's bushel c——t.
> And now the wine began to work, mine host
> Had been a colonel; we must hear him boast,
> Not of towns won, but an estate he lost
> For the King's service, which indeed he spent
> Whoring and drinking, but with good intent.
> He talked much of a plot and money lent
> In Cromwell's time. My lady, she
> Complained our love was coarse, our poetry
> Unfit for modest ears; small whores and players
> Were of our harebrained youth the only cares,
> Who were too wild for any virtuous league,
> Too rotten to consummate the intrigue.
> Falkland she praised, and Suckling's easy pen,
> And seemed to taste their former parts again.
> Mine host drinks to the best in Christendom,
> And decently my lady quits the room.

9. This word is omitted in A-1680-HU and the Yale MS. but appears in the other manuscript versions of the poem.

From "Tunbridge Wells":

Here waiting for gallant, young damsel stood
Leaning on cane and muffled up in hood.
The would-be wit, whose business was to woo,
With hat removed and solemn scrape of shoe
Advanceth bowing, then genteelly shrugs
And ruffled foretop into order tugs
And thus accosts her: "Madam, methinks the weather
I⟨s⟩ ¹ grown much more serene since you came hither!
You influence the heavens, but should the sun
Withdraw himself to see ⟨his⟩ ² rays outdone
By your bright eyes, they could supply the morn
And make a day before the day be born."
With mouth screwed up, conceited winking eyes,
And breasts thrust forward, "Lord, sir!" she replies.
"It is your goodness and not my deserts
Which makes you show this learning, wit, and parts."
He, puzzled, bites his nail, both to display
The sparkling ring and think what next to say,
And thus breaks forth afresh: "Madam, egad!
Your luck at cards last night was very bad.
At cribbage fifty-nine, and the next show
To make the game, and yet to want those two.
God damn me, madam, I'm the son of a whore
If in my life I saw the like before!"
To peddler's stall he drags her, and her breast
With hearts and such-like foolish toys he dressed,

1. "Is" is the reading of all early texts except the Yale MS., which reads "I."
2. "His" is the reading of all early texts except the Yale MS., Harvard MS. Eng. 636F, and B. M. Add. MS. 4456, which read "its."

And then more smartly to expound the riddle
Of all his prattle, gives her a Scotch fiddle.

From Sedley's *The Happy Pair:*

We mind not now the merits of our kind,
Curious in gold, but to the persons blind.
The man ne'er minds his love, for money still
Is the base thirsted object of his will.
Upon condition of a promised store,
He'll hug a thing that crawls upon all four.
Bring him an old rich corpse with grim death's head,
He'll swear she's young, and her complexion red;
Or if you could bring one without a face,
He'll praise her conquering eyes and charming grace.
The woman too, by such affections led,
Contemns the living to embrace the dead;
And rather than not covet, basely bold,
Would wed a coffin, were the hinges gold.
Nature's apostate, active youth she scorns;
Will long for oxen if you gild their horns.
Say he's deform'd, has neither eyes nor nose—
Nay, nothing to bespeak him man but clothes—
Straight she replies he's rich, so passes down;
There's nothing ugly but a poor baboon.
Thus might she clasp a loathsome toad in bed
Because he bears a pearl within his head.
And gilded pills, though bitter, may delight
The lickerish lust of wavering appetite.

Full understanding of Rochester's distinctive style of heroic couplets would require an exhaustive analysis of better texts than are yet available for his poetry. Nevertheless, even a cursory examination of these three specimens should show that the style of "Timon" closely resembles that of "Tunbridge Wells" and differs appreciably from Sedley's style. The lines from "Timon" and "Tunbridge Wells" are notable for their racy conversational phrasing, whereas Sedley's diction is more formal, sometimes almost stiff (e.g. "base thirsted object"). Sedley adheres rather slavishly to the closed couplet, producing a monotonous effect even in this brief passage; he uses enjambment only twice and usually concludes every second line with a full stop. The passages from "Timon" and "Tunbridge Wells," on the other hand, employ enjambment very freely, and the sense may flow on without end-stopping for three or four lines. Sedley's use of balance, parallelism, antithesis, and chiasmus conforms to the couplet rhetoric that had become standard by the end of the seventeenth century. "Timon" and "Tunbridge Wells," by contrast, exploit these rhetorical devices with subtlety and originality. Indeed, their verse style, unlike Sedley's, is remarkable for its rhythmic flexibility and variety, resulting partly from a skillful displacing of accents for rhetorical emphasis. (By such means, Rochester—whose ear was unusually sensitive—characteristically produces on extreme tension between the prose cadence of the syntax and the set rhythmic pattern of the pentameter couplet.)

Apart from the style of their verse, the passages from "Timon" and "Tunbridge Wells" display a dramatic quality that is largely lacking in Sedley's lines. Also, their light comic irony contrasts with Sedley's heavy sarcasm. Arguments like these are essentially subjective, of course, so that the reader must judge their validity according to his own lights. At a minimum, however, they suggest that "Timon" should be retained in the Rochester canon until new evidence either confirms or disproves his authorship.

V

The similar style and structure of "Timon" and "Tunbridge Wells," together with the probability that both poems were composed during the spring of 1674, point to some further conclusions. It is possible that these two poems should be viewed as pendant pieces. If this is so, "Timon" may well have been written first, with "Tunbridge Wells" following after Rochester's initial success in adapting Boileau had encouraged him to try his hand at an original poem of the same kind.

An analogous situation may be presented by "A Satyr against Mankind" and "Artemisa to Cloe." The themes of these two satires exhibit complex resemblances which would repay much further study. The most obvious structural similarity is that each poem involves a contrast between two characters, one representing conventional Christian values, the other expressing attitudes which might loosely be termed libertine, Hobbist, or materialist. The conventional position is represented in "A Satyr against Mankind" by the "formal Band, and Beard" and in "Artemisa to Cloe" by Artemisa herself; the libertine characters are the principal speaker in "A Satyr against Mankind" and the "fine *Lady*" of "Artemisa to Cloe." Though their dates of composition are not entirely certain, "A Satyr against Mankind" and "Artemisa to Cloe" may have been composed about the same time, probably between the middle of 1674 and the end of 1675. Their complex structure and maturity of style suggest a date after "Timon" and "Tunbridge Wells," while "A Satyr against Mankind" is dated 1674 in a manuscript version and was certainly in existence by 23 March 1675/6.[3]

---

3. "A Satyr against Mankind" is dated "Anno. 74" in Bodl. MS. Tanner 306 (fol. 414ʳ) and mentioned in a letter dated 23 March 1675/6 (HMC, *Seventh Report*, p. 467). "Artemisa to Cloe" may be echoed by

These tentative conclusions bear importantly on the development of Rochester's own poetry and that of Restoration literature generally. Prior to 1674, Rochester was essentially a writer of short poems, chiefly songs and some lampoons following native traditions. Examples of the latter include the hudibrastic "A Ramble in St. James's Park" and the anapestic couplets of the satire beginning "Too long the wise commons have been in debate," both apparently composed early in 1673. So far as is known, Rochester had not yet written any formal satires along classical Roman lines. His desire to attempt this more ambitious genre may have been prompted by the example of Boileau, whose satires began to attract attention in England about 1673. Before he composed a wholly original poem in an unaccustomed form, Rochester possibly wished to follow a model (much as Boileau himself followed Horace and Juvenal), thereby producing "Timon," which may be the earliest extant imitation of Boileau's satires in the English language; probably "Tunbridge Wells" came shortly afterward. During the next year and a half, he may have repeated the process with "A Satyr against Mankind" and "Artemisa to Cloe."

John Oldham in "An Apology to the fore-going Satyr by way of Epilogue," probably composed in July 1676 or shortly thereafter. Rochester wrote:

> *Woman*, who is an Arrant *Bird* of Night,
> Bold in the duske, before a *Fools* dull sight,
> Must fly, when *Reason* brings the blazing light.
>   (A-1680-HU, p. 23)

Oldham, possibly imitating Rochester, wrote:

> But Criminal *Writers*, like dull *Birds* of Night,
> For weakness, or for shame, avoid the light.
>   (A-1680-HU, p. 128)

Though the parallel is not very convincing by itself, Oldham was much influenced by Rochester at this early stage of his career, and a copy of "Artemisa to Cloe" appears in his own handwriting in his poetical notebook (Bodl. MS. Rawl. Poet. 123, p. 116).

In the winter of 1675–76, led on perhaps by his experience with Boileau, Rochester tried a new and more sophisticated kind of adaptation. Unlike "Timon" and "A Satyr against Mankind," which do not require a familiarity with Boileau's satires, "An Allusion to Horace" assumes a knowledge of the Latin poem. Some of its subtler satirical effects are achieved through implicit parallels and contrasts with its original, often carrying an ironic connotation. In a sense, Horace's poem becomes an integral part of Rochester's. This technique of "imitation," which Pope later refined to its ultimate, seems to have originated with Rochester.[4] Evidently Rochester's contact with Boileau stimulated some of his own best poetry, thus giving a notable impetus to the development of formal satire in Augustan England.

4. For a valuable study of the development of this genre, see Harold F. Brooks, "The 'Imitation' in English Poetry, Especially in Formal Satire, before the Age of Pope," *Review of English Studies*, 25 (1949), 124–40. The date of "An Allusion to Horace" is discussed in Chapter 5.

12.

"A Session of the Poets"
Reconsidered

I

Among the approximately 250 poems which have been attributed to Rochester at one time or another, none has stimulated more discussion of its authorship than "A Session of the Poets" ("Since the Sons of the Muses, grew num'rous, and loud"), printed in the Huntington edition of his works in 1680 (A-1680-HU, p. 111). Indeed, this lampoon constitutes one of the best-known problems of authorship in Restoration literature. Such concern may seem excessive, in view of the meager esthetic merits of the poem, especially its crude versification. Nevertheless, "A Session" arouses interest for several reasons. Like other examples of the "sessions" genre, which was popular during the seventeenth and early eighteenth centuries, it portrays a group of contemporary writers vying for the award of the bays from Apollo, god of poetry.[1] In the process, it provides well-informed satirical comments on many dramatists of the mid-seventies: Dryden, Etherege, Wycherley, Shadwell, Lee, Settle, Otway, Crowne, Aphra Behn, Ravenscroft, Rawlins, D'Urfey, and Betterton. Also, "A Session" is distinguished by a few memorable phrases which have furnished at least one book title.[2]

Strangely, though much evidence on "A Session" has been assembled, its authorship remains in dispute. The ascription to Rochester, sanctified by tradition until the 1920s, was accepted rather uncritically by John Hayward (1926) and Quilter Johns (1933) in their editions of Rochester's works, and by Vivian de Sola Pinto in his biography of the poet (1935). Johannes Prinz questioned Rochester's authorship, however (1927), and in an important series of studies (1926–33), Roswell G. Ham collected extensive evidence and arguments for assigning the poem to Elkanah Settle. Meanwhile, casual contributors to the controversy expressed differing opinions. Graham Greene (1931) claimed the poem for George Villiers, Duke of Buckingham; he was answered by D. M. Walmsley (1931), who restored it to Rochester. J. C. Ghosh in his edition of Otway (1932), though cognizant of most of Ham's evidence, preferred Rochester's authorship; Hugh Macdonald (1937) similarly dissented from Ham's conclusions. Recently, the most significant contribution has been an article by John Harold Wilson (1946) in which he analyzed Ham's case and argued for assigning "A Session" to Rochester, or Rochester in collaboration with a group of other Court Wits. Wilson's arguments were accepted without

1. For an account of other works belonging to the "sessions" genre, see Hugh Macdonald, *A Journal from Parnassus* (London, P. J. Dobell, 1937), Introduction.

2. Willard Connely, *Brawny Wycherley* (New York and London, Charles Scribner's Sons, 1930).

independent inquiry by James Thorpe (1950) and Pinto (1953) in their editions of Rochester's poems.[3]

Now that a decade and a half has passed since Wilson first presented his views, the case of "A Session of the Poets" needs to be reconsidered. Despite the favor they have found, Wilson's conclusions are open to difference of opinion. The authorship of "A Session" apparently resolves itself into four possibilities: the poem may have been composed (1) by Buckingham, or Buckingham assisted by Rochester; (2) by Rochester, or Rochester in collaboration with other Court Wits, as Wilson concluded; (3) by Settle, as Ham argued; (4) by some other poet as yet unidentified. Examination of the available evidence yields little or no support for Rochester or Buckingham and points clearly toward Settle or some author unknown. Moreover, even though such an examination utilizes little new data and does not conclusively establish the author of "A Session," it may help to clarify the relevant facts, which have sometimes been obscured by the persuasive rhetoric of previous treatments.

II

Investigation of the authorship of "A Session of the Poets" may conveniently begin with the ascriptions which accompany early texts of the lampoon in manuscripts and printed books. Proper evaluation of these texts and ascriptions serves to discredit virtually all evidence connecting either Rochester or Buckingham with the composition of the poem.[4]

"A Session" was first printed under Buckingham's name in his *Miscellaneous Works*, 1704 (reprinted 1707), where it is

3. See Part III for documentation of the previous scholarship on "A Session."

4. See Part III for a more detailed list of the early texts and ascriptions of "A Session."

headed "A Tryal of the Poets for the Bays, in Imitation of a Satyr in Boileau." This ascription deserves little respect. Not only is the *Miscellaneous Works* generally untrustworthy, but its text was apparently printed from one of the Rochester editions of 1680, where the poem is assigned to the Earl alone. Nothing about the 1704 version suggests that it incorporates any reliable testimony independent of its textual source; it even errs in describing "A Session" as an imitation of Boileau. Evidently John Nutt, the publisher of the *Miscellaneous Works*, pilfered from the earlier Rochester edition to augment his slender list of Buckingham's poems; the same source supplied him with Scroope's "In defence of Satyr" and Rochester's "Timon," which he likewise assigned wrongly to Buckingham. A single manuscript version ascribing "A Session" to Buckingham, in Bodl. MS. Rawl. Poet. 173, was copied from the 1704 or 1707 *Miscellaneous Works* and therefore furnishes no additional evidence.

From the 1707 *Miscellaneous Works*, "A Session" was reprinted in Buckingham's *Works* of 1715, where it is assigned to both Buckingham and Rochester. Again the ascription seems to embody no reliable information not taken from earlier printed sources. Probably the publisher of the 1715 *Works*, Samuel Briscoe, adopted the clumsy premise of joint authorship to resolve the conflicting attributions he found in earlier printed texts of the lampoon. He used the same dual ascription for "In defence of Satyr" and "Timon," also reprinted from the *Miscellaneous Works*, and even for Rochester's "Upon Nothing," though he evidently printed it from a manuscript. Later texts in Buckingham's works, which assign "A Session" either to Buckingham and Rochester or to Buckingham alone, seem to derive from the editions of 1704, 1707, and 1715. Horace Walpole, attributing the lampoon to Buckingham and Rochester,

cites the 1715 *Works* as his source. Apparently there is no
further evidence that Buckingham participated in the writing
of "A Session." Nor does there seem to be any other real indication that the poem was not composed by a single author.

If the early texts of "A Session" furnish no substantial support for Buckingham's authorship, they likewise afford little
for Rochester's. No weight can be given to the ascription in the
Huntington edition, which is the earliest printed appearance of
the poem. As we have seen (Chapter 3), this ascription is meaningless because "A Session" occurs, not in the section of poems
by or concerning Rochester, but in the section of poems by miscellaneous authors. Moreover, the Yale MS., which probably
preserves the ascriptions given in the manuscript source of the
Huntington edition, assigns "A Session," not to Rochester, but
to another poet.

All other sources ascribing the lampoon to Rochester—indeed,
all other printed texts, including those which assign it to Buckingham—evidently descend from the Huntington edition. "A
Session" was reprinted as Rochester's in the other 1680 editions
and in the later editions of 1685 (A-1685), 1701 (A-1701),
1713 (A-1713), and 1731 (A-1731). From one of the 1680
editions it was also reprinted under his name in Edmund Curll's
*The Works Of the Earls of Rochester, Roscommon, Dorset,
&c.,* 1714 (C-1714-1), and succeeding editions of this collection.
The 1714 *Works* was the source of the text in Jacob Tonson's
The Second Part of Miscellany Poems, 1716 (reprinted 1727),
where—significantly, perhaps—the ascription to Rochester is
omitted. From some later edition of the 1714 *Works* (C series),
"A Session" was reprinted without ascription in *A Collection of
Merry Poems,* 1736. A single manuscript version, in B. M.
Lansdowne MS. 1039, was copied without ascription from one
of the 1680 editions. Though "A Session" is several times men-

tioned as Rochester's in Anthony Wood's *Athenae Oxonienses*, the information is invariably credited to one of the 1680 editions and therefore seems to possess no independent standing. Similarly, the ascriptions to Rochester by Giles Jacob and Theophilus Cibber appear to be taken from earlier printed texts.

The only other early texts of "A Session" are seven manuscripts which evidently do not derive from printed sources. Unfortunately, ascriptions are lacking in six of these: Osborn MS. Chest 11, Number 14, Harvard MS. Eng. 623F, Harvard MS. Eng. 636F, Bodl. MS. Rawl. Poet. 159, Bodl. MS. Don. b. 8, and Edinburgh MS. DC.1.3. In the remaining manuscript, however—the Yale MS.—the heading of the poem states that it was "Suppos'd to be written by Elk: Settle." The form of this ascription, to be sure, implies reservations about Settle's authorship; the copyist merely indicates that common report assigned "A Session" to Settle. Nevertheless, this is the only early text of the lampoon whose ascription promises any degree of reliability.

III

The foregoing account of ascriptions in early texts of "A Session" is accepted in substance by Wilson, whose case for Rochester rests on other grounds. Conceding that "little evidence for authorship can be drawn from contemporary attributions," Wilson nevertheless maintained that Rochester was the principal author of the poem, and that he may have been assisted by a group of Court Wits, meeting perhaps at the lodge at Woodstock, which since early 1674 had been Rochester's official residence as Ranger and Keeper of Woodstock Park. From these conclusions, Wilson conjured up an attractive vision of the Wits seated about a long table before the fire in the great hall, drinking their bumpers of wine while they scribbled their joint lampoon on the popular playwrights of the day. As the most recent contribution to our knowledge of "A Session," Wilson's brief for Rochester's authorship deserves detailed scrutiny. His intricate argument may be fairly reduced to the following five points and accompanying critiques:

(1) Observing that "A Session" deals harshly with some professional dramatists but leniently with two gentleman playwrights, Wilson contends that its author was therefore a gentleman and a courtier—possibly Rochester. Etherege, denied the bays because of his laziness, is praised for his "fancy, sense Judgment, & *Wit*," and Wycherley is "too good for the Place":

> No *Gentleman Writer*, that office shou'd bear
> 'Twas a *Trader* in *Wit*, the *Lawrel* shou'd wear,
> As none but a *Citt*, e're makes a *Lord Major*.

Conversely, the professional playwrights, Wilson alleges, are treated with the tone of "sarcastic superiority" one might expect from a nobleman like Rochester—the tone of his answer to a letter from Henry Savile:

> For the Libel you speak of, upon that most unwitty Generation the present Poets, I rejoice in it with all my Heart, and shall take it for a Favour, if you will send me a Copy. He cannot want Wit utterly, that has a Spleen to those Rogues, tho' never so dully express'd (Wilson, *Rochester-Savile Letters*, p. 50).

This argument scarcely carries much weight. Surely it is hazardous to assume that gentle and noble authors would be praised, and professional poets vilified, only by the gentle and noble authors themselves. There is little evidence that literary divisions during the 1670s followed class lines. At the time "A

Session" was composed (*c.* Nov. 1676), the province of wit was generally divided into two factions which included noblemen and commoners in similar proportions; one faction was headed by Rochester (nobleman) and Shadwell (commoner), the other by Dryden (commoner) and Mulgrave (nobleman). Moreover, even if the attitudes expressed in the lampoon *did* indicate a nobleman to be its author, such evidence would not identify that nobleman as Rochester. Wilson himself admits that his argument "is no proof that Rochester wrote the 'Session.'"

(2) Wilson maintains that "certainly the 'Session' is consistent with Rochester's expressed attitudes toward the poets of the day." In works written before the date of "A Session," he argues, Rochester had censured Shadwell, Settle, Crowne, Dryden, Otway, and Lee; these same authors are satirized in "A Session."

To this argument one may object that it distorts the facts. Two dramatists attacked in "A Session," Shadwell and Otway, will serve to illustrate. It is true that Rochester's "Timon" (written spring of 1674) contains a derisive couplet on Shadwell, and that in his epilogue to Sir Francis Fane's *Love in the Dark* (acted May 1675),[5] Rochester ridiculed Shadwell's dramatic opera *Psyche*. Shortly thereafter, however, he must have revised his estimate of the popular playwright's merits, for "An Allusion to Horace" (written winter of 1675–76) is highly complimentary:

> Of all our *Modern Wits*, none seems to me,
> Once to have toucht, upon true *Comedy*,
> But hasty *Shadwel*, and slow *Wicherley*
> *Shadwells* unfinish'd works do yet impart,
> Great proofs of force of *Nature*, none of Art:

5. In this chapter, all dates of dramatic performances and publication of plays are taken from Nicoll, *Restoration Drama.*

With just bold strokes he dashes here, and there,
Shewing great *Mastery*, with little Care;
And scorns to varnish his good Touches o're,
To make the *Fools*, and *Women*, praise 'em more.
                                    (A-1680-HU, p. 42)

This is better than "grudging praise," as Wilson calls it,
especially when bestowed by a severe critic like Rochester.
Equally favorable are Rochester's concluding lines, where
Shadwell is elevated to the select company of gentlemen and
noblemen who are true judges of wit:

I loath the *Rabble*, 'tis enough for me,
If S⟨edley⟩, S⟨hadwell⟩, S⟨hepherd⟩, W⟨ycherley⟩,
G⟨odolphin⟩, B⟨utler⟩, B⟨uckhurst⟩, B⟨uckingham⟩,
And some few more, whom I omit to name,
Approve my sense, I count their censure *Fame*.
                                    (A-1680-HU, p. 44)

There is no evidence that Rochester had altered his high opinion
by the end of 1676, when Shadwell was attacked in "A Session."
Shadwell and Rochester apparently continued in alliance against
the faction led by Dryden, who soon afterward took separate
revenges against his two adversaries in *Mac Flecknoe* and the
preface to *All for Love* (pub. March 1678).

Otway seems to have enjoyed similar favor from Rochester
at the time "A Session" was written. Though Rochester's "An
Allusion to Horace" sneered at "puzling O⟨tway⟩" for his poor
first play, *Alcibiades*, the Earl evidently perceived the greater
merits of Otway's next venture, *Don Carlos* (acted June 1676),
for he used his influence to insure its success on the stage.
Otway's preface to the play (pub. summer or autumn of 1676)
acknowledged his "unspeakable Obligations" to Rochester,

crossed swords with Dryden, and hinted at a friendship with Shadwell [6]—as does "A Session," where Otway is introduced as "*Tom S⟨hadwell's⟩, dear Zany.*" About three months after he was coarsely abused in "A Session," Otway dedicated to Rochester his *Titus and Berenice* with the *Cheats of Scapin* (pub. *c.* Feb. 1676/7).

The remarkable feature of the attitudes expressed in "A Session" is their lack of partisan purpose. They favor neither the Rochester-Shadwell nor the Dryden-Mulgrave faction, nor do they support either of the two playhouses against the other.

(3) On 1 November 1677, Henry Savile wrote his friend Rochester:

> and now I am upon poetry I must tell you the whole tribe are alarumed att a libell against them lately sent by the post to Will's coffe house. I am not happy enough to have seen it but I heare it commended and therefore the more probably thought to be composed att Woodstock, especially considering what an assembly either is yett or att least has been there, to whom my most humble service, if they are yett with you (Wilson, *Rochester-Savile Letters*, p. 49).

As Wilson was the first to note, the verses "lately sent by the post to Will's" cannot be "A Session," which was composed nearly a year earlier and would no longer have "alarumed" the tribe of poets in October of 1677. Nevertheless, Wilson argues, Savile's letter implies that such lampoons had previously been written at Woodstock during convivial gatherings of the Wits, and "A Session" could have been one of them.

Wilson's inference seems valid, unless Savile's speculation on the authorship of the "libell" is merely a deft compliment to

6. *The Works of Thomas Otway*, ed. J. C. Ghosh (Oxford, Clarendon Press, 1932), *1*, 174.

the talents of Rochester and the visiting Wits. Even if poems were composed when the Wits assembled at Woodstock, however, this does not show that "A Session" was among them or that Rochester had any hand in it.

(4) In an undated letter to his wife, Rochester wrote:

> I feare I must see London shortly, & begin to repent I did not bring you wth mee for since these rakehells are nott here to disturb us you myght have past y^r devotions this Holy season as well in this place as att Adderbury (Prinz, *Rochester*, p. 267).

Apparently Rochester was writing from Woodstock at Christmastime after a group of the "rakehells" had left. Wilson suggests that this was 1676, and that the departed Wits had just produced "A Session," which originated during the last few weeks of that year.

Wilson's argument would be strong if Rochester's letter could be dated 1676, for it would place a group of Wits at Woodstock at the exact time "A Session" was composed. Unfortunately for his case, however, there is no special reason to assign Rochester's letter to this year; it could equally well have been written in 1677, after the gathering mentioned in Savile's letter. Thus it provides no support for Rochester's authorship.

(5) The passage on Settle in "A Session" includes the following lines:

> God damme, cryes S⟨*hadwell*⟩, he cannot write sense,
> And Ballocks cry'd *Newport*, I hate that dull *Rogue*.

Wilson identifies "Newport" as Frank Newport (son of Francis, Lord Newport), a minor Wit notable chiefly for his drunken misbehavior. As Wilson observes, Frank Newport's presence in the poem would be an anomaly, since all other contenders for the bays are dramatists. Indeed, it would be "difficult to explain," he argues, unless we assume that while the Wits were composing "A Session" at Woodstock, Frank blurted out an obscene remark which amused the company so much that it was written into the poem.

Wilson's explanation is more ingenious than convincing. Though the line on Newport is admittedly puzzling, it is a long leap from this detail to the conclusion that Rochester had a major hand in "A Session." Even if Frank Newport was the person intended, and even if his presence in the poem suggested group authorship, this would not show that the group was meeting at Woodstock, or that it included Rochester, or that Rochester helped compose the poem.

In summary, Wilson produces no evidence indicating a direct connection between Rochester and the composition of "A Session." Even a single ascription in an early manuscript would be stronger testimony. One should add, however, that Wilson's arguments for Rochester's authorship, which he generally presents with suitable reservations, are only the least impressive part of his contribution. Of greater value are his analysis of the work of his predecessors, chiefly Ham, and his clarification of earlier misconceptions about several important items of evidence.

IV

Immediately after its composition, and for several years thereafter, "A Session of the Poets" was popularly attributed to Settle and Settle alone. This much is demonstrated by evidence which, though ultimately contradictory and therefore incapable of establishing Settle as the author, nevertheless possesses a cogency lacking in Wilson's tenuous arguments and in the illusory ascriptions accompanying many early texts of the lampoon. The relevant facts, which are deeply entangled in literary and political feuds of the day, can best be presented in a chronological account beginning with the year 1673.

Late in this year Elkanah Settle, flushed with the success of his heroic tragedy *The Empress of Morocco,* published the play with gorgeous "sculptures" and a bumptious prefatory epistle ridiculing the dedications of his less fortunate brother playwrights. For obscure reasons, Settle's onslaught greatly alarmed the brethren, especially Dryden, who several months earlier had dedicated to Sedley his unsuccessful comedy *The Assignation.* In 1674 Dryden joined Shadwell (with whom he had just conducted a spirited controversy) and John Crowne in writing the exhaustively abusive pamphlet *Notes and Observations on the Empress of Morocco. Or, Some few Errata's to be Printed instead of the Sculptures with the Second Edition of that Play.*[7] Unabashed, Settle effectively retorted in kind early in 1675 with his *Notes and Observations On the Empress of Morocco Revised. With Some few Errata's to be Printed instead of the Postcript, with the next Edition of the Conquest of Granada.*[8]

Here the quarrel might have ended, for Dryden and Crowne took no further part in it. Shadwell, however, (so Settle later charged) inserted into Newcastle's *The Triumphant Widow* (acted Nov. 1674) a scene ridiculing Settle as the "silly Heroick Poet" Crambo.[9] Then Settle, in his postscript to *Love and Re-*

7. As Wilson noted, a parody included in this pamphlet addresses Settle as "Great Boy," a phrase echoed in "A Session" by "And bid the great *Boy,* shou'd be sent back to *School.*"

8. Dated 1674 on its title page but advertised in the *Term Catalogues* on 15 February 1674/5.

9. In his preface to *Ibrahim,* Settle related of Shadwell that "Having a Play, call'd the *Triumphant Widdow,* given him to bring into the Duke's Playhouse, he spitefully foists in a Scene of his own into the Play, and makes a silly Heroick Poet in it, speak the very words he had heard me say, and made reflexions on some of the very Lines he had so sencelesly

venge (pub. *c.* May 1675), castigated the impudence of dramatists who (like Shadwell) excused poor plays by claiming they
were "Written in three Weeks, or a Months time"; in his dedication of *The Conquest of China*, early in 1676, he commented
further upon "the common Vanity of our Tribe" and "the general Style of my Brethren." Shadwell, feeling injured by these
remarks, retaliated in February 1675/6 with his preface to *The
Libertine*, where after several paragraphs of billingsgate he refused to take any more notice of Settle. Apparently he kept his
word, for the last shots of the battle were fired in Settle's notorious preface to *Ibrahim* (pub. summer or autumn of 1676),
which is a vituperative survey of Shadwell's entire dramatic
career. Mysterious circumstances surround this preface, which
is lacking in most copies of the play; either it was suppressed, or
there was originally no intention of binding it into more than a
few copies.

In this atmosphere "A Session of the Poets" came to birth
about November 1676. Wilson neatly established its date on
grounds that it mentions events of early November but ignores
later occurrences which might have claimed the satirist's attention. The poem refers to Ravenscroft's *The Citizen turn'd Gentleman* (acted July 1672), later reissued as *Mamamouchi*
(1675); [1] to Etherege's "long Seav'n years silence" between
She wou'd if she cou'd (acted Feb. 1667/8) and *The Man of
Mode* (acted March 1675/6); to Rawlins's *Tom Essence* (acted

---

prated on before in his *Notes*" (Hugh Macdonald, *The Preface to Ibrahim*,
Oxford, Basil Blackwell, 1947, p. 5). But Dryden as well as Settle may
be represented by Crambo, who hates Ben Jonson for having "no Wit"
(*The Triumphant Widow*, 1677, p. 61); Shadwell had attributed this
opinion to Dryden during his earlier controversy with the laureate.

1. In place of the "Anababaluthu" of the printed texts, several manuscripts read "At last Mamamouchi." "Anababaluthu" may echo the gib-
berish that Ravenscroft had used in his play.

c. Aug. 1676); to the ill-fated preface of Settle's *Ibrahim* (pub. summer or autumn of 1676) [2] but not his *Pastor Fido* (acted *c.* Dec. 1676); to Otway's *Don Carlos* (acted June 1676) and its preface (pub. summer or autumn of 1676) [3] but not his *Titus and Berenice* and *Cheats of Scapin* (acted *c.* Dec. 1676); to D'Urfey's *Madam Fickle* (acted 4 Nov. 1676) but not his *The Fool Turn'd Critick* (acted 18 Nov. 1676). Lee is said to have "hit once in Thrice": his first three attempts were *Nero* (acted May 1674), *Sophonisba* (acted April 1675), and *Gloriana* (acted Jan. 1675/6), to which there is additional reference ("He made him his *Ovid* in *Augustus's Court*"). No mention is made of Lee's successful fourth play, *The Rival Queens* (acted March 1676/7). Wilson's date for "A Session" is roughly corroborated by Bodl. MS. Rawl. Poet. 159 and Osborn MS. Chest 11, Number 14, which assign it to 1676 and 1676/7 respectively.

The earliest indication that "A Session" was being attributed to Settle is an anonymous play, *Wits Led by the Nose*, acted at the King's house less than a year after the poem was written (*c.* July 1677). This play is a reworking of William Chamberlayne's tragicomedy *Loves Victory* (1658), with a new comic subplot portraying the quarrels of two country gentlemen and

2. In "A Session," Settle submits "an *Ibrahim*, with the Preface torn out." Also, in this preface Settle complained of Shadwell that "he makes it his business before he sees a Line of any of my Plays, to cry 'em down; and long before they are Acted to make Factions and Cabals to damn them: and in all Companies, he cries *God damme I* [Settle] *can't write Sence nor Grammar*" (Macdonald, *The Preface to Ibrahim*, p. 13). This is echoed in "A Session" by "God damme, cryes S⟨*hadwell*⟩, he cannot write sense."

3. In "A Session," Otway "swears for *Heroicks*, he writes best of any," an allusion to the following statement in the preface to *Don Carlos:* "I dare not presume to take to my self what a great many, and those I am sure of good Judgement too, have been so kind to afford me (*viz.*) That it is the best Heroick Play that has been written of late" (*Works of Otway*, ed. Ghosh, *1*, 174).

would-be wits, Sir Jasper Sympleton and Sir Symon Credulous. Ham, who first noted the significance of the play, identified Sir Jasper and Sir Symon with Settle and Otway—a doubtful inference, since no friction is recorded between these two dramatists at the time. With better reason, Wilson suggested that the subplot glances at the recently concluded feud between Settle and Shadwell. Probably Settle is burlesqued as Sir Jasper, though in later scenes he may be represented by Sir Symon also; little attempt is made to differentiate the two poetasters.[4] Settle and Shadwell were both playwrights for the rival (and more prosperous) Duke's house.

Early in the play, Sir Jasper and Sir Symon quarrel over their mutual mistress, Theocrine, and decide to fight each other—not with swords, but with verses. Sir Jasper boasts of his performance with an unmistakable reference to "A Session of the Poets":

> By my Fathers Soul I've done, and without Ostentation, to as great a height, as—*When the Sons of the Muses grew Numerous and loud,* and so forth (p. 19).

A few lines later he says to Sir Symon,

> Villain you have abus'd Poetry it self, and I will be reveng'd, I will have a Session of Poets shall damn thee Ibraimattically, lead thee to School by the Nose and Chastise thy Insolence (p. 21).

---

4. For example, Sir Symon (rather than Sir Jasper) is asked, "And what makes your name Sir, crowded on the Title Page of several Plays in splendid Characters, as if that Ostentation did proclaim thee a man of wit and merit?" This, Ham observes, may allude to the sumptuous printing of *The Empress of Morocco.* In Sir Symon's reply Ham noted a possible reference to documents like the preface to *Ibrahim:* ". . . those Dedications writ by us . . . tending to down right rayling at the Age, or finding fault perhaps with the best Poets" (p. 48).

The second speech clearly connects the satire of "A Session" with that of the preface to *Ibrahim*, in which Settle had attacked Shadwell. Evidently the anonymous playwright expected his audience to be familiar with the lampoon and know that it was being attributed to Settle. This is important evidence, for *Wits Led by the Nose* must have been written only a few months after "A Session" made its appearance.

Wits Led by the Nose may also contain the earliest trace of an elusive duel which complicates the authorship of "A Session." As this doubtful tale was later told (in *A Character of the True Blue Protestant Poet*, 1682), Otway challenged Settle because of the abusive lines the latter had directed at him in the lampoon; Settle, refusing to act the part of a gentleman, abjectly signed a paper stating, "I confess I Writ the *Sessions of the Poets*, and am very sorry for't, and am the Son of a Whore for doing it."

In the play, Sir Jasper and Sir Symon fight a comic duel ending with both of them in cowardly flight. Afterward, each is accused of abusing the other, and "all the Poets of the Age," in a lampoon resembling "A Session." Their clever servants in disguise, Drayner and Slywit, force the two scribblers to put their names to a confession similar to the one Settle reportedly signed:

> *Dra.* Come Sir, dispatch, we are in hast.
> *Jas.* So am I to be gone.   [*Aside.*
> *Sly.* Swear Sir.
> *Sym.* Swear what?
> *Sly.* Either you did, or did not write the Verses.
> *Sym.* I vow to Gad, and all that, I am Innocent.
> *Sly.* That's but a weak Oath, and shows too must [*sic*] of Cowardize to gain belief, swear me a full mouth'd Oath like a true *Englishman.*

Sym. Then on the Vertue of a Gentleman, and Honour of Sir *Symon Credulous,* I am not Guilty.

Sly. Honour and Vertue are two mighty strangers to an Ignoble breast; I cannot in the least Imagine they are lodg'd in your's. Come Gentlemen, here's Pen Ink and Paper, write ev'ry Letter that we shall command you, or die in disobeying.

Sym. Was ever poor Pretended led by the Nose before? Honour begone, to save my Life I'le do it; we are ready Sir.

> [*Sir* Jasper *and Sir* Symon *go to the Table, and prepare to write.*

Sly. Write this then,—I am a Coward.

Sym. All the World knows that already, it needs no publication.

Sly. Write I Command you.

Both. I am a Coward.——   [*Write:*

Sly. An Arrand stinking Coward.

Both. An Arrand stinking Coward.——   [*Write:*

Dra. A Poetical Thief.

Jas. Not I by Heav'n.

Dra. Write I say.

Both. A —— —— —— —— —— —— ——   [*Write.*

Sly. And a damm'd Son of a Whore, if ever I writ these Verses.

Both. And a —— —— —— ——   [*Write.*

(pp. 48–9)

Significantly, Sir Jasper and Sir Symon *deny* their authorship of the lampoon, whereas Settle allegedly was forced to *admit* he had written "A Session."

The second piece of evidence for Settle's authorship is a passage in Otway's Tory poem *The Poet's Complaint of his Muse* (pub. *c.* 22 Jan. 1679/80), in which he took revenge for the earlier attack on him in "A Session":

Next him appear'd that blundring Sot
Who a late *Session of the Poets* wrote.
Nature has markt him for a heavy Fool;
  By's flat broad Face you'l know the Owl.
The other Birds have hooted him from light;
Much buffeting has made him love the Night,
    And onely in the dark he strays;
Still Wretch enough to live, with worse Fools spends his days,
  And for old Shoes and Scraps repeats dull Plays.[5]

Though it is not quite certain that these lines refer to Settle, the evidence suggests that they do. Neither Rochester nor Buckingham can be intended. The passage plainly does not describe a nobleman; Rochester's face was not "flat" and "broad"; neither man was a "heavy Fool" or a social outcast, and neither had been reduced to reciting "dull Plays" for "old Shoes and Scraps." Settle's circumstances fit the description, however, for he produced no new play between his *Pastor Fido* (acted *c.* Dec. 1676) and *The Female Prelate* (acted *c.* Sept. 1679), and at all periods of his life his unengaging personality left him few friends. It was a commonplace of contemporary satire that Settle was ostracized by his fellow poets; the "other Birds" had indeed "hooted him from light." [6] The last line of Otway's pas-

---

5. *Works of Otway*, ed. Ghosh, *2*, 411–12. Though Otway's poem was not advertised in the *Term Catalogues* until February 1679/80, it is dated 22 January by Narcissus Luttrell (*Narcissus Luttrell's Popish Plot Catalogues*, intro. by F. C. Francis, Oxford, Basil Blackwell, 1956, p. 218).

6. F. C. Brown, *Elkanah Settle: His Life and Works* (Univ. of Chicago Press, 1910), p. 9. Possibly another satirical commonplace characterized Settle as an owl. Ham noted the following couplet in "Satyr against the

sage should be compared with a sentence in *Remarks upon E. Settle's Narrative* (1683): "Had he repeated his *Narrative*, as he was wont to do his Tragic Scenes, by bits and Scraps to the Scullers in R*offee's* Ale-Boxes, they would have given him better advice then he has taken" (p. 2).

Wilson is scarcely justified in doubting the honesty of Otway's attribution because "Settle and Otway were then engaged in vicious political writing, the first for the Whigs, the second for the Tories, and each snatched at any weapon with which to injure his opponents." Whatever his political temperature, Otway seems to have been a man of honor. Also, despite the Tory sentiments of Otway's poem, his lines on Settle appear, not in the invective against the Whigs, but between two nonpolitical passages, one on the author of *Sodom* and the other on *"Lord Lampoon* and *Monsieur Song."* Conspicuously absent from the Settle passage is any allusion to the supposed duel, which Otway might well have mentioned if it had really occurred.

The third piece of evidence is the statement in the Yale MS. that "A Session" was "Suppos'd to be written by Elk: Settle." This tentative ascription at least indicates that common report placed the lampoon at Settle's door. Though the exact date of the Yale MS. is uncertain, it was probably transcribed during the first half of 1680; at any rate, the collection it represents must have been assembled by autumn of that year, when most of it was printed as the first edition of Rochester's poems (A-1680-HU).

The fourth and last piece of evidence for Settle's authorship is an anonymous attack in the Tory pamphlet *A Character of*

Poets" ("Wretch whosoe'er thou art that longs for praise"), B. M. Harl. MS. 7317, fol. 36^v:

> But Settle that incorrigable Owl,
> That Composition of a knave and Fool . . .

the True Blue Protestant Poet, published in April 1682 while
Settle was busily feeding the Whig propaganda mills (Macdonald, *Dryden Bibliography,* p. 239). Besides assigning "A
Session" to Settle, this pamphlet gives the story of the duel in
its fullest form:

> It happened about four years ago, there came out a Copy
> of Verses, of the same *Libellous nature* of *Azaria, and
> Hushai,* (which by the greatest part of the Town has been
> accounted his;) but since the *Illegitimate Brat* had not
> strength to Support it self, and he found its deformity,
> and weakness, gave no credit to the *Vigorous Abilities* of
> the Father; He (tis said) has laid it at an Impotent, Lame
> Mans door, who because he never had any of his own, he
> gladly *Adopted* the *Bastard;*) But our *Malicious Buzzard*
> did not in those days Soar so high, he only did abuse the
> *Poets* then, into whose number he would fain have crept,
> which because they always scorn'd, and lookt with Con-
> tempt upon him, He endeavours thus to revenge himself;
> but it fell out most unluckily, for a discovery was soon
> made of our *Author.*
>
> And Mr. *O.* a Man of the Sword, as well as the Pen,
> finding himself most coursly dealt withal, immediately
> call'd him to an account, and required the satisfaction of
> a Gentleman from him: This I must confess was some-
> thing unreasonable, and did by no means agre with our
> *Scriblers Constitution,* who had much rather *Rail* than
> *Fight;* and being at this news as much surprized, and in
> little better pickle, than *Alderman Atkins* would have been
> upon the like occasion, beg'd he would spare his Life, and
> he would give him any other satisfaction he could desire;
> and presently taking, *Pen, Ink,* and *Paper* out of his Pocket,

> he writ these following words, (*viz.*) *I confess I Writ the*
> Sessions of the Poets, *and am very sorry for't, and am the*
> Son of a Whore for doing it*; Witness my hand* E. S.
> This he delivered to Mr. *O.* which it seems saved his
> Throat for that time; but I am affraid for a worse hand
> (p. 2).

Unfortunately, this account may not be trustworthy. Since its
author was a party hack bent on exhuming every unflattering
aspect of Settle's past, he might well have resorted to malicious
fiction if the truth was inadequate. It is possible that he fabri-
cated his yarn from a variety of sources: from the popular ru-
mor that Settle wrote "A Session," from circumstances of Otway's career, and from the earlier burlesque of Settle in *Wits
Led by the Nose.* Settle's "confession" that he was "the Son of
a Whore" is similar to the statement which Sir Jasper and Sir
Symon are obliged to sign, and the expression "pen, ink, and
paper" (though it was a cliché) figures rather suspiciously in
both the play and the later prose narrative. Otway might have
been selected as Settle's triumphant antagonist because he was
attacked in "A Session," because of his lines on Settle in the
Poet's Complaint, because he was a political ally of the author
of *The True Blue Protestant Poet,* and because he was known
as a formidable swordsman, having in June 1679 administered
to John Churchill, the future Duke of Marlborough, what Ham
terms "the first and last military reverse of a great soldier's
career."

True or not, the tale of the Otway-Settle duel obtained wide
currency. In an ironical passage in *The Tory-Poets* (pub. *c.*
4 Sept. 1682), Dryden is depicted as saying,

> But though I have no Plot, and Verse be rough,
> I say 'tis Wit, and that sure is enough.

> The Lawrel makes a Wit; a Brave, the Sword;
> And all are wise men at a Councel board;
> S——le's a Coward, 'cause fool *Ot*——*y* fought him,
> And *Mul*——*ve* is a Wit because I taught him.

In *The Second Part of Absalom and Achitophel* (pub. *c.* 10 Nov. 1682), Dryden included in his portrait of Doeg (Settle) the line "For almonds he'll cry whore to his own mother." As late as June 1683, the anonymous author of *Remarks upon E. Settle's Narrative* commented: "He has twice given it under his hand that his Mother was a *Whore*. Once to Mr. *O.* as not finding himself any way prepar'd to die . . ." (p. 7).[7] Probably all three of these references derive from *The True Blue Protestant Poet*.

In the absence of further data, the evidence presented thus far, despite its shortcomings, would warrant the conclusion that Settle probably wrote "A Session." Two additional points prevent such a conclusion, however. The first is Settle's own denial of his authorship and the duel story in *A Supplement to the Narrative*, written in summer or autumn of 1683 after he had deserted the Whigs and crossed to the other side of the political fence. In language notable for its incoherent fury, he denounced *Remarks upon E. Settle's Narrative* for its "Villanous Forgeries"

> taken out of a certain inveterate Filthy Libel against me, called the *Character of a true Blue Protestant Poet*, where

7. For the dates of these three references to the Otway-Settle duel, see Macdonald, *Dryden Bibliography*, pp. 31, 235, 239. The lines from *The Tory-Poets* (doubtfully attributed to Shadwell) are quoted from *The Complete Works of Thomas Shadwell*, ed. Montague Summers (London, Fortune Press, 1927), 5, 282. Missing the irony in this passage, Ham assumed that it supported the truth of the duel story; Wilson, though he noted its irony, suggested without warrant that it implied skepticism about the reliability of the tale.

amongst the Impudent Lyes and Detraction that fills that Paper, I was accused of being the Author of a Scandalous Copy of Verses call'd the *Sessions of the Poets,* an ill-natured scurrilous Lampoon, written some years since, and now laid as believed at the Fathers Door, being Printed amongst the Lord *Rs.——* Poems. Amongst the other Extravagancies in that Base and Malicious Libel against me. [*sic*] It was said that I gave it under my Hand to Mr. *O——* a Gentleman highly wronged and affronted in that Paper of Verses, that *I was the Author of that Sessions of Poets, and that for which I was the Son of a Whore* [*sic*].

Which is so damnable a Falshood, and so publickly known to be so too, that on the quite contrary I disown'd and abjured the writing so much as one Syllable of it: and to vindicate my self from the scandal of such a Lampoon, at that time so unjustly and so universally laid at my Door, and so much to my disreputation, if to clear my self by no less a Potestation [*sic*] then that *I was the Son of a Whore if I wrote one word of it,* when indeed *I did not* write one word of it, be calling a Mothers Honesty into Question, let the World Judge (p. 17).

Settle's sincerity might be doubted, for his conscience was pliable, as shown by his recent switch from the Whigs to the Tories, and he doubtless had something to gain by denying the authorship of "A Session" and the story of Otway's challenge. Nevertheless, the best possible testimony in a question of authorship is a direct statement from the reputed author himself, and the other evidence in the case scarcely outweighs Settle's own words. The truth of his denial is perhaps argued by the fact that (in Wilson's phrase) "Otway was still alive, and still wore a sword"; if Settle had earlier admitted his authorship when threatened with death, Otway was capable in 1683 of repeating that threat. But it is conceivable that Settle wrote "A Session" even if the duel story is a forgery. A noteworthy detail in Settle's statement is the information that "A Session" had been "universally laid at my Door"; other evidence, we have seen, also indicates that the lampoon was commonly credited to Settle from the time it first appeared. Settle's attempt to shift the poem to Rochester deserves little respect, since he bases his attribution on the unreliable testimony of the 1680 editions and qualifies even this claim with an "as believed."

The remaining evidence against Settle's authorship is the passage in "A Session" which attacks him. As Wilson maintained, Settle would scarcely subject himself to these corrosive lines, which read in full:

> *Poet S⟨ettle⟩*, his Tryal, was the next came about,
> He brought him an *Ibrahim*, with the Preface torn out;
> And humbly desir'd, he might give no offence;
> God damme, cryes *S⟨hadwell⟩*, he cannot write sense,
> And Ballocks cry'd *Newport*, I hate that dull *Rogue*;
> Apollo, consid'ring he was not in vogue,
> Wou'd not trust his dear *Bays*, with so modest a *Fool*,
> And bid the great *Boy*, shou'd be sent back to *School*.

Arguing for Settle's authorship, Ham found this passage relatively inoffensive and suggested that Settle included it to divert suspicion from himself. (Mulgrave used a similar ruse three years later in "An Essay upon Satyr.") But the lines are far from mild, and it is difficult to see what Settle could gain by a lampoon which handles him with a harshness lacking even in some passages on his enemies—notably the genial Rabelaisian passage on Shadwell, whom Settle had abused only a few months earlier in the preface to *Ibrahim*. On the other hand, Settle's contemporaries must have known that he was attacked in "A Session" when they ascribed it to him, and Settle himself does not cite the passage as an argument against his own authorship. Moreover, the lines lose some of their sting when one realizes that the worst barbs are indirect. The one bawdy comment is voiced by an inconsiderable witling, Shadwell's profanity is lifted from Settle's own preface to *Ibrahim,* and the phrase "great *Boy*" derives from the Dryden-Shadwell-Crowne *Notes and Observations*. Little else is left except the innocuous charges that Settle is "not in vogue," is "so modest a *Fool*," and "shou'd be sent back to *School.*"

The findings in this chapter may be summarized in a three-fold conclusion: (1) there is no valid reason to assign "A Session" to Rochester or Buckingham; (2) all admissible testimony connects the satire with Elkanah Settle; (3) Settle's authorship is unacceptable because of his own denial and the lines in the poem which attack him. Very possibly the lampoon was composed by some poet for whom no evidence has yet appeared; in any event, the ascriptions to Buckingham and Rochester are mere bibliographical accidents. If "A Session" must have a home, it can best find shelter among the doubtful poems in the edition of Settle's works which one hopes some scholar will eventually undertake.

13.

Problems of a Linked Group:
Satires on Scroope and Mulgrave

Of the various "linked groups" of poems preserved in the Yale MS. and the Rochester editions of 1680, the most complex is a series of five satires on John Sheffield, Earl of Mulgrave, and Sir Carr Scroope. This group poses problems involving dates of composition, identification of persons satirized, and authorship. Though the subjects of four of the satires have been properly identified, the remaining poem has hitherto been wrongly interpreted as a satire on Edward Howard and has, as a result, been dated seven or eight years too early. Evidence of various kinds suggests not only that it is a satire on Scroope, but that it may be a poem by Rochester which has been presumed lost. All five satires raise puzzling questions of authorship. The traditional view assigns the first poem to Etherege, the second, third, and fourth poems to Rochester, and the fifth poem to Buckingham. Though this chapter does not propose to challenge

322

the traditional attributions, there is need to re-examine the underlying problems, which students of the Restoration have not, in general, faced squarely.

I

The five satires in the linked group include, in order, (1) "Ephelia to Bajazet" ("How far are they deceiv'd who hope in vain"), (2) "A very Heroical Epistle in Answer to Ephelia" ("If your deceiv'd, it is not by my Cheat"), (3) "On Poet Ninny" ("Crusht by that just contempt his Follys bring"), (4) "My Lord All-Pride" ("Bursting with Pride, the loath'd Impostume swells"), and (5) "A Familiar Epistle to Mr Julian Secretary of the Muses" ("Thou Comon Shore of this Poetique Towne").[1]

Despite the problems they raise, the conclusion that these satires constitute a linked group is unusually well authenticated. The best evidence is a manuscript pamphlet, bound into B. M. Egerton MS. 2623, which is entirely occupied by these five poems in order; this pamphlet exhibits the fold-marks characteristic of manuscript sheets which were passed from hand to hand during the Restoration period. Additional evidence that the five satires circulated as a linked group is their occurrence, in exactly the same order, in Osborn MS. Chest ii, Number 14, and the Yale MS.[2] Presumably the group passed into these

---

1. For the first four poems, the titles and texts used are those of A-1680-HU (Thorpe, *Rochester's Poems*, pp. 138–45). For the epistle to Julian, the title and text are those of the Yale MS., p. 352.

2. See Part iii for a detailed list of the early texts and ascriptions of the first four poems. Part or all of the linked group may be preserved in the "Portland Miscellany," since Pinto reports that the first four poems appear there, and that the second poem immediately follows the first (*Poems*, pp. 178, 211, 212). Such a conclusion must remain conjectural, however, until this manuscript is released for proper analysis.

two larger collections by way of manuscript pamphlets similar to the one preserved in the Egerton volume. Though the Rochester editions of 1680 include only the first four poems, it is probable that the entire group occurred in the lost copy-text of the Huntington edition (A-1680-HU), and that the fifth poem, the epistle to Julian, was omitted in the process of printing (see Chapter 3). In other instances, especially in its later pages, the Huntington edition omits poems which appear in the Yale MS. and which were therefore probably present in the archetype of the collection.

Portions of the linked group are found in three more early texts. Two of these texts suggest that the first four satires may have circulated as a group by themselves; perhaps the epistle to Julian was a later addition to an original group of four satires, or it may have dropped out of the five-poem series because it was the last poem in this abnormally large group and because it is substantially longer than the other poems. The first four satires appear together and in order in Huntington MSS. Ellesmere 8736–38. University of Edinburgh MS. DC.1.3 similarly gives these four poems together and in order but also includes the epistle to Julian five pages earlier; since manuscript versions of the epistle are fairly common, such a situation might be explained on the theory that the scribe initially copied this satire from another source and then, to avoid repetition, omitted it when he came to transcribe the five-poem linked group. Also apparently derived from a four-poem or five-poem manuscript text of the group is the broadside *A Very Heroical Epistle from My Lord All-Pride to Dol-Common*, 1679. This broadside prints the second and fourth poems in order, and the "Argument" prefixed to the second poem refers to "a most lamentable Letter" which is recognizable as the first poem of the group. Possibly the publisher was interested only in these three satires on Mulgrave and therefore omitted all reference to the two on Scroope.

Various reasons may explain why the five satires were originally brought together as a linked group. The first two poems are specially linked because the second, "A very Heroical Epistle in Answer to Ephelia," is unquestionably a reply to the first, "Ephelia to Bajazet." In the group as a whole, the most obvious connection is that each of the five poems is a satire on one of two persons: the first, second, and fourth poems satirize Mulgrave, while the third and fifth satirize Scroope. Such a bracketing of Mulgrave and Scroope suggests still another possible linkage, for in the late 1670s, the period during which the five satires were written, both men were associated with the literary faction which also included Dryden. Thus the satires might all have been composed by members of the opposing faction, whose chief figure was Rochester. This hypothesis would seem to support the traditional attribution of the five poems to Etherege, Rochester, and Buckingham.

A major puzzle is presented by the arrangement of the poems within the linked group—unless, of course, we assume that this order is merely fortuitous. If the five poems were originally brought together because of the two persons they satirize, one would expect the three satires on Mulgrave to be located contiguous to one another, and the same with the two satires on Scroope. Actually, the first satire on Scroope intervenes between the second and third satires on Mulgrave. As we shall see later in this chapter, the dates at which the five poems were composed seem to have no significant bearing on their order within the linked group. A better possibility is that the poems are arranged according to authorship, with the three Rochester attributions located contiguously, the Etherege poem placed first to keep the two Bajazet-Ephelia epistles in proper relation to each other, and the Buckingham poem placed last to avoid interrupting the sequence of Rochester poems.

The most probable explanation, however, is suggested by the circumstance that except for the first poem, the group as a whole exhibits a pattern of alternation: the second poem satirizes Mulgrave, the third Scroope, the fourth Mulgrave, and the fifth Scroope. External evidence which correlates with this pattern is provided by Edinburgh MS. DC.1.3, whose ascriptions postulate the linked group as a literary feud between Scroope and Mulgrave. After the first poem, which carries no ascription, the Edinburgh manuscript describes the second as "The answer by S^r. Charles Scroope." The third poem, apparently credited to Mulgrave, is headed "on S. C. S. For Answering Ephelia to Bajazett," and the fourth is titled "Ansuerd againe by S^r. CR: Scroope on y^e. l^d. Alpride" (i.e. Mulgrave). If we continue this pattern by a process of induction, the fifth satire (which is separated from the linked group in the Edinburgh manuscript) might be a rejoinder to Scroope written by Mulgrave or one of his friends—perhaps Dryden, to whom the poem is assigned in several other early sources. Further corroboration of the pattern might be found in the fact that the third poem seems to answer an earlier satire by Scroope, and the fourth poem an earlier satire by Mulgrave.

Probably the ascriptions in the Edinburgh manuscript reflect the intentions of the scribe responsible for the archetypal version of the linked group, since no other hypothesis seems to account so well for its arrangement. Superficially plausible though these ascriptions may appear, however, other evidence casts doubt on the assumption that Mulgrave or Scroope wrote any of the five satires. Most of this evidence will be discussed later, but it is noteworthy in passing that all other manuscript copies of the linked group, as well as the broadside of 1679, fail to provide ascriptions. Thus, if ascriptions to Mulgrave or Scroope occurred in the archetype of the group, they were evidently distrusted by several scribes who made subsequent copies. Such a situation would help to explain why all five satires are plagued with serious problems of authorship. In any event, the authorship of the poems can probably be established only by seeking evidence in sources which are independent of the linked group. This is a severe limitation, since for the first four poems, very few texts which do not derive from the group are known to have survived.

II

Before we consider the authorship of the five poems, it is desirable to review their dates of composition and the identity of the persons they satirize. This is especially true of the third poem, "On Poet Ninny," whose subject has heretofore been identified incorrectly.

Investigation of the dates and subjects of the five satires can best begin with the epistle to Julian, which presents a clearer case than the other four poems. External evidence consistently identifies the principal subject of this satire as Sir Carr Scroope, even though the poem itself calls him "Strephon," a pastoral pseudonym often reserved for Rochester. Four early manuscript copies contain an appended note specifying that "The Knight which is the Subject of this Satyr is S^r. Car. Scroop: who dyed 1680." Another manuscript gives a marginal gloss identifying the "Knight" as "Sr Car. Scroop." [3] John Aubrey quotes the

---

3. The appended note is quoted from the text in B. M. Harl. MS. 7319, fol. 28^v. Other texts giving virtually the same note are found in Bodl. MS. Firth C. 15, p. 31; the Ohio MS., p. 25; and Taylor MS. 2, p. 22. These last three texts are, however, all in the same hand, and the

concluding couplet of the poem and describes it as "the bitter satyricall verses made on Sir Carre Scroop." [4]

Even without this testimony, internal evidence shows that the epistle to Julian satirizes Scroope. Numerous details in the poem correspond to known facts of Scroope's career and to standard charges made against him in other contemporary lampoons. The poem refers to his bad eyesight (Rochester termed him "the Pur-blind *Knight*"), to his ugly face, to his inordinate devotion to rhyming, to his inclination to defend himself with his pen rather than his sword, to his amorous pursuit of all the girls in town, whom he bombarded with his verses, and to his ill-success in love because of his repulsive appearance. More specifically, the poem twice calls its subject "Knight" (Scroope was a baronet) and alludes to his mother's promiscuity, the death of his brother in a playhouse brawl, and his failure to win the hand of Cary Frazier, daughter of the King's physician. Furthermore, the subject's personality is described as an amalgam of contradictory qualities, "like Aesops Batt, half Bird, half Beast." In manners he is half a fool, half a wit, and therefore a fop; in morals he is half a knave, half a poet. With this characterization should be compared the following passage on Scroope in Rochester's "On the suppos'd Authour of a late Poem in defence of Satyr":

> 'Twere labour lost, or else I wou'd advise.
> But thy half *Wit*, will ne're let thee be wise.
> Half-witty, and half-mad, and scarce half-brave,
> Half-honest (which is very much a *Knave*.)

first may be. The marginal gloss accompanies the text in National Library of Scotland MS. Advocate 19.1.12, fol. 87^r.

4. John Aubrey, *Brief Lives*, ed. Andrew Clark (Oxford, Clarendon Press, 1898), 2, 279.

> Made up of all these Halfs, thou can'st not pass,
> For any thing intirely, but an *Asse*.
>
> $$\text{(A-1680-HU, p. 50)}$$

The epistle to Julian is assigned to 1677 in four early manuscripts,[5] and internal evidence corroborates this date. Since the poem refers to "Lofty Middlesex," it could not have been written before the early part of 1675, when Charles Sackville, Lord Buckhurst, became Earl of Middlesex; nor can it be dated much after 27 August 1677, when he became Earl of Dorset (Harris, *Dorset*, pp. 60–62, 73). A more precise *terminus post quem* is provided by the concluding couplet:

> His Brother Murder'd, & his Mother Whor'd
> His Mistresse lost, & yet his Pen's his Sword.

Scroope's younger brother was killed by Sir Thomas Armstrong in an altercation at the Duke's House on 28 August 1675.[6] At the approximate date of the epistle to Julian, Scroope's mother was mistress to Rochester's close friend Henry Savile. Scroope's courtship of Cary Frazier, the "Mistresse lost," was still in progress on 30 January 1676/7:[7] evidently the epistle to Julian was composed some time later, after Scroope abandoned his hopes of Cary Frazier and possibly transferred his attentions to Louise de Keroualle, Duchess of Portsmouth, who is twice mentioned in the poem ("great Lovisas grace"). Significantly, there is no reference to Nell Gwyn, whom Scroope was pur-

---

5. These are the first four manuscripts cited above in footnote 3.

6. HMC, *Seventh Report*, p. 465; *Le Fleming*, p. 121. *CSPD*, 9 Sept. 1675 (p. 289), 8 Oct. 1675 (p. 339). Gerard Langbaine, *An Account of the English Dramatick Poets*, 1691, p. 460.

7. HMC, *Rutland*, 2, 37. For a fuller account of the affair between Scroope and Cary Frazier, see my article, "A 'Lost' Lampoon by Katherine Sedley?" *Manuscripts*, 6 (1954), 160–65.

suing in the spring of 1678.[8] Thus the epistle to Julian can be dated spring or summer of 1677. Interestingly, one couplet refers to Dryden's "retirement" from the stage between the production of *Aureng-Zebe* (17 Nov. 1675) and that of *All for Love* (12 Dec. 1677):

> Lesse art thou helpt from Drydens Bed-rid Age,
> That Drone, has left his Sting upon y[e] Stage.

With the epistle to Julian as background, attention may be focused on the third poem of the group, "On Poet Ninny." Wilson supposed that this poem satirizes Edward Howard and that it was written about 1670, when Howard was under fire from various Court Wits (*Court Wits*, pp. 179–80). His conclusion apparently derives from only two facts: Poet Ninny in Shadwell's play *The Sullen Lovers* (acted 2 May 1668) is a caricature of Howard, and the comedian James Nokes, who created the role, is mentioned in the poem.[9] Wilson's interpretation ignores the possibility that the epithet Poet Ninny might be applied to some other person, thereby transferring to him the pejorative associations with Howard that Shadwell had given it. Thorpe, while not proposing another candidate, remarked that "some exceptions can be made to the traditional view, Edward Howard" (*Rochester's Poems*, p. 190).

Evidence both external and internal suggests that "On Poet Ninny," like the epistle to Julian, is a satire on Sir Carr Scroope. External evidence is provided by two early texts. In Curll's

8. John Harold Wilson, *Nell Gwyn: Royal Mistress* (New York, Pellegrini and Cudahy, 1952), p. 288.

9. *The Complete Works of Thomas Shadwell*, ed. Montague Summers (London, Fortune Press, 1927), *1*, 5. A third use of Edward Howard in "On Poet Ninny" is the allusion to Buckhurst's well-known satire, discussed below on p. 336.

The Works Of the Earls of Rochester, Roscommon, Dorset, &c., 1714 (C-1714-1), a footnote to the title of the poem identifies its subject as "Sir C. Scroop." Similarly, the heading in Edinburgh MS. DC.1.3, already mentioned, describes the poem as written "on S. C. S. For Answering Ephelia to Bajazett." The edition of 1714 is not, to be sure, very reliable, and the ascriptions in the Edinburgh manuscript are suspect. Nevertheless, the fact that these two sources agree on the person satirized may argue that their testimony deserves some consideration.

Moreover, internal evidence tends to corroborate this testimony. Much of the art of personal satire during the Restoration period consisted of forming a colorful caricature of the person satirized—of creating what was essentially a half-real, half-fictional figure. Once the details of this semimythic characterization had been established by its creator, they could be, and were, endlessly duplicated by other satirists. With some Restoration personalities such as Rochester, the satirists were less than successful; Scroope, however, was one of their conspicuous triumphs. Close examination of "On Poet Ninny" shows that it is made up almost exclusively of features which were part of the standard satirical picture of Scroope. The point can be illustrated by comparing the poem with several other lampoons, all written during 1675–80, in which Scroope is attacked. These include the epistle to Julian, Rochester's "An Allusion to Horace" and "On the suppos'd Authour" ("To rack, and torture thy unmeaning Brain"), "Advice to Apollo" ("I've heard the Muses were still soft and kind"), "A Satyr" ("Of all the Wonders since the World began"), "The Answer" ("Among the writing Race of Modern Wits"), "The Cabal" ("Now the Reformer of the Court and Stage"), and "Tunbridge Lampoon" ("England by all thought Beautyes naturall Soyle").[1]

A common charge leveled at Scroope by the satirists was that his face was ugly. "On Poet Ninny" calls its subject "a hideous sight" and "a nauseous *Creature*," refers to his "ugliness" and his "Face of *Farce*," and advises him, "Thou canst not ev'n offend, but with thy Face." Similarly, Rochester's "On the suppos'd Authour" mentions Scroope's "grizly *Face*," terms him "a lump deform'd, and shapeless . . . hideous to the sight," and asserts that his physiognomy is God's satire on the human race. The epistle to Julian, which devotes no fewer than nineteen lines to Scroope's forbidding appearance, banters him on his "hard favour'd Face," his "unfinish'd Face," and his swarthy complexion, "made of Adams owne red Clay." "Advice to Apollo" dubs him "that Knight o' th' wither'd Face," "A Satyr" mentions his swarthy skin, and "The Answer" sarcastically congratulates him on his "Beauty."

A related legend perpetuated by the satirists was that Scroope pestered every woman in town with his amorous attentions but was doomed eternally to failure because of his ugliness. "On Poet Ninny" describes its subject as "a sad example . . . of hopeless love" because of his face, and

> The just reverse of *Nokes*, when he wou'd be,
> Some mighty *Heroe*, and makes love like thee!

1. For "An Allusion to Horace," the text used is that in Thorpe, *Rochester's Poems*, p. 40; for "On the suppos'd Authour," the text in Thorpe, p. 49; for "Advice to Apollo," the text in *Poems on Affairs of State*, 1697 (Case 211-1-a), p. [1]211; for "A Satyr," the text in *Poems on Affairs of State*, 1697 (Case 211-1-c), p. [2]35; for "The Answer," the text in *Poems on Affairs of State*, 1704 (Case 211-3-a), p. 147; for "The Cabal," the text in *Poems on Affairs of State*, 1697 (Case 211-1-c), p. [1]261; for "Tunbridge Lampoon," the text in B. M. Add. MS. 34362, fol. 86[r].

Rochester's "On the suppos'd Authour" develops this same theme more fully in a corrosive passage claiming that though Scroope was "begot in *Loves* despight,"

> Yet *Love's* thy bus'ness, *Beauty* thy delight.
> Curse on that silly hour, that first inspir'd,
> Thy madness, to pretend to be admir'd;
> To paint thy grizly *Face*, to dance, to dress,
> And all those Awkward *Follies* that express,
> Thy loathsome Love, and filthy daintiness.
> Who needs will be an Ugly *Beau-Garcon*,
> Spit at, and shun'd, by ev'ry *Girl* in *Town*;
> Where dreadfully *Loves Scare-Crow*, thou art plac'd
> To fright the tender *Flock*, that long to taste:
> While ev'ry coming *Maid*, when you appear,
> Starts back for shame, and strait turns chaste for fear,
> For none so poor, or *Prostitute* have prov'd,
> Where you made love, t' endure to be belov'd.

The epistle to Julian labels Scroope "Bow-Bending Cupid" and extends mock sympathy for his inability to gain a mistress by his love poems:

> There's not a Nymph, in Citty, Town, or Court,
> But Strephons Billet Doux have beene her sport.
> Still he loves on, yet still as sure to misse,
> As they who wash an Ethiops face or his.
> What Fate unhappy Strephon does attend
> Never to get a Mistresse, or a Friend?

"A Satyr" similarly rallies Scroope on his fruitless expectation that "the *Women* all / Should breathless at his feet admiring fall."

"On Poet Ninny" terms its subject "the Melancholly *Knight*" and refers to his "dismal look, and Melancholly *Meene.*" Apparently these phrases reflect a standard accusation that Scroope affected a pose of melancholy as part of his absurd devotion to the writing of verses. The charge is best explained by the passage on Scroope in "Advice to Apollo":

> First, strike Sir *Carr*, that Knight o' th' wither'd Face,
> Who (for th' reversion of a Poet's place)
> Waits on *Melpomene*, and sooths her Grace;
> That angry Miss alone he strives to please,
> For fear the rest should teach him Wit and Ease,
> And make him quit his lov'd laborious Walks,
> When sad or silent o'er the Room he stalks,
> And strives to write as wisely as he talks.

Three other lampoons mention Scroope's lugubrious expression as he walks along mentally composing his verses: "A Satyr" describes the "hanging Look on's Brows," the epistle to Julian jeers at his "squeezing lookes," and "Tunbridge Lampoon" relates how a lonely "Contemplation workes his brain." Along the same lines, Scroope's "Head with Whimseys fill'd" in "A Satyr" matches Poet Ninny's "craz'd *Head*" and "Head *Romancy.*"

As the preceding paragraphs suggest, "On Poet Ninny," like most of the lampoons on Scroope, ridicules its victim as a fop. Apparently Scroope possessed no outstandingly vicious traits which the satirists could single out; consequently, they were reduced to calling him fool and coxcomb, too ineffectual to do anything really evil. Poet Ninny is dismissed as "a sad example . . . of harmless malice" who can offend only with his face, reference is made to his *"Cap'ring Person,"* and he is further addressed in these terms:

> There are some ⟨modish⟩ [2] *Fools*, we dayly see,
> Modest, and dull, why they are *Wits*, to thee!
> For of all *Folly*, sure the very top,
> Is a conceited *Ninny* and a *Fop*.
> With Face of *Farce*, joyn'd to a Head *Romancy*,
> There's no such *Coxcomb* as your *Fool* of fancy.

Similarly, the epistle to Julian maintains that Scroope is half fool, half wit, and therefore "hangs betweene 'em both, & is a Fopp." Rochester's "On the suppos'd Authour," in a passage previously quoted, describes Scroope's "Awkward *Follies*" in his role of "Ugly *Beau-Garcon*." "The Cabal" asks, "Who'd not be as affected as Sir *Carr?*" Other satires on Scroope likewise contain charges of foppery.

Two additional parallels suggest that Poet Ninny is Scroope. The poem calls its subject "*Knight*," just as Scroope receives this title in "An Allusion to Horace," the epistle to Julian, "Advice to Apollo," "A Satyr," and "Tunbridge Lampoon." Moreover, the statement that Poet Ninny, in his "harmless malice," can offend only with his face may allude to the conventional charge that Scroope was afraid to use his sword in defence of his honor. This accusation, which occurs too frequently to require extensive documentation, is memorably expressed in the concluding lines of the epistle to Julian:

> Strephon's a very Draggon at his Pen.
> His Brother Murder'd, & his Mother Whor'd
> His Mistresse lost, & yet his Pen's his Sword.

Aside from its many parallels with lampoons known to be aimed at Scroope, the opening lines of "On Poet Ninny" may

2. Since "modish" is the reading of all early manuscripts including the Yale MS., the reading of A-1680-HU, "Modest," must be a corruption.

help to identify its subject. Evidently Poet Ninny has written a satire replying to an attack on him:

> Crusht by that just contempt his *Follys* bring,
> On his craz'd *Head*, the *Vermin* fain wou'd sting.
> But never *Satyr*, did so softly bite,
> Or gentle *George* himself, more gently write.

The third line alludes to the last couplet of Buckhurst's famous satire on Edward Howard:

> Thou sett'st thy Name, to what thy self dost write,
> Did ever *Libell*, yet so sharply bite?
>
> (A-1680-HU, p. 89)

The point, of course, is that Poet Ninny's retort, contrary to his intention, is written in a soft, gentle, innocuous manner. This accusation suggests Scroope, for his contemporaries apparently considered that he wrote in a "soft" style. Aphra Behn, for one, praised him highly for the "natural softness" of his poems.[3] The meaning of her observation can be seen in such a delicate lyric as Scroope's "I cannot change as others do" or in satires like his "In defence of Satyr" and "The Answer" ("Raile on poore feeble Scribler, speak of me"), whose restraint is a marked contrast to the savage attacks characteristic of most Restoration lampoons.

Though these many items of internal evidence carry little weight individually, their collective cogency, especially in combination with the external evidence of the Edinburgh manuscript and Curll's 1714 edition, leaves little question that "On Poet Ninny" is a satire on Scroope. The date of the poem will be discussed later along with its authorship: it may have been written early in 1678.

3. *Miscellany, Being A Collection of Poems*, 1685 (Case 177), sig. XI[v].

The dates and subjects of the first two satires of the linked group are inseparably connected. The first poem purports to be a letter of complaint from an abandoned woman to her lover, while the second is her lover's haughty reply. The second poem was clearly designed as a response to the first. In many early texts, either the two poems appear together or a note is included indicating their relationship. The most common (and probably correct) titles are "Ephelia to Bajazet" and "A very Heroical Epistle in Answer to Ephelia." Internal correspondences, too intricate to demonstrate fully, further suggest that the first poem is answered in the second. To cite just one example, Ephelia laments, "How far are they deceiv'd who hope in vain, / A lasting *Lease* of joys from *Love* t' obtain," to which Bajazet retorts, "Madam, / If your deceiv'd, it is not by my Cheat." As we saw earlier (Chapter 4), Bajazet is a *persona* and the object of the satire. Probably Ephelia is a *persona* too, since her epistle lightly satirizes Bajazet and seems, on the whole, too mannered to be an outpouring of personal grief. Evidently Ephelia's complaint was modeled upon Ovid's *Heroides*, which was very popular and much imitated during the seventeenth century; the title of the second poem, "A very Heroical Epistle," implies that this was the case.

Bajazet is unquestionably a satirical portrait of John Sheffield, Earl of Mulgrave. Like Scroope, Mulgrave was among the more successful creations in the secular mythology of Restoration satire; in its inverted pantheon, he occupied a central and easily recognizable eminence. To the satirists he was the epitome of arrogance and egotism, especially as regarded his more or less imaginary achievements as soldier and lover. A characterization embodying such traits, as Bajazet does, would not have been mistaken by the Restoration audience for anyone else. The name "Bajazet," which derives from the haughty

Turkish emperor in Marlowe's *Tamburlaine,* is applied to Mulgrave in other lampoons of the period; so are the similar epithets
"My Lord All-Pride" and "King John." In the two epistles,
Ephelia calls Bajazet "great Man," remarks how "great his
passion was," and refers to his "Noble *Bed,*" while Bajazet
complacently considers himself one of "the Great." Allusions to
Mulgrave's Order of the Garter occur in both poems: Bajazet
mentions his "blazing *Star*" of the Garter, and Ephelia more
indirectly comments that "y'ave been the *Star,* by which I
steer'd." Moreover, the title of "My Lord All-Pride" in Edinburgh MS. DC.1.3, "Ansuerd againe by S^r. CR: Scroope on
y^e. l^d. Alpride," implies that "A very Heroical Epistle" is a
satire on the same person. Similarly, the broadside of 1679 calls
the subjects of both of these poems Lord All-Pride. External
evidence is provided by Narcissus Luttrell's copy of the broadside, on which he wrote "Ag^t ye Ld Mulgrave." [4]

Since the Bajazet-Ephelia epistles refer to Mulgrave's Order
of the Garter, they must have been composed after 23 April
1674, the date on which Mulgrave received that honor.[5] At the
opposite limit, "Ephelia to Bajazet" is evidently the "Ephelias
Lamentation" mentioned in the epistle to Julian and was therefore probably in existence by the middle of 1677. More precisely, evidence of the events which occasioned the two poems,
as well as additional evidence on the identities of Ephelia and
Bajazet, is furnished by the concluding lines of "A very Heroical
Epistle." Bajazet envies the "happy *Sultan*" because

> Thou fear'st no injur'd *Kinsmans* threatning Blade,
> Nor Mid-night Ambushes, by *Rivals* laid;

    4. C. H. Wilkinson, "Lord Rochester," *London Times Literary Supple-
ment,* 11 July 1935, p. 448.
    5. William A. Shaw, *The Knights of England* (London, Sherratt and
Hughes, 1906), *1,* 37.

> While here with aking Hearts, our joys we tast,
> Disturb'd by Swords, like *Democles* his Feast.

As Wilson first observed, these lines allude to Mulgrave's widely publicized and rather ridiculous affair with Mall Kirke, one of the Duchess of York's Maids of Honor. The affair was in progress in September 1674, when the Duke of Monmouth, one of Mulgrave's rivals in Mall's affections, laid a "midnight ambush" at her chamber door and had Mulgrave apprehended by the guard as he was departing. Approximately nine months later, Mall gave birth to a boy. Though it was far from certain that Mulgrave was its father, Mall's brother, the ferocious Percy Kirke, took the "injured kinsman's" part and challenged Mulgrave. In the duel, fought on 4 July 1675, Mulgrave was worsted.[6] Presumably the two Bajazet-Ephelia epistles were written shortly afterward.

As for "My Lord All-Pride," external evidence that it satirizes Mulgrave includes Luttrell's note on the broadside and a similar note in the Sterling copy of the 1680 editions (A-1680-S-S) indicating that the subject of the poem was "now D. of Bucks," a title bestowed on Mulgrave in 1703. As we have noted, the headings in both the broadside and the Edinburgh manuscript imply that Lord All-Pride is the same person as Bajazet. Also, the text of the poem, like its title, reflects the standard satirical conception of Mulgrave as an almost allegorical figure of conceit.

Other internal evidence supports this identification. Lord All-Pride has written a lampoon, but

6. HMC, *Rutland*, 2, 27. *Essex Papers*, ed. Osmund Airy (Westminster, Camden Society, 1890), *1*, 261. *The Bulstrode Papers*, ed. Alfred Morrison (London, privately printed, 1897), *1*, 303–05. *Savile Correspondence*, ed. William Durrant Cooper (Westminster, Camden Society, 1858), p. 39. Mulgrave, "Memoirs," in his *Works*, 1723, 2, 14. Wilson, *Court Wits*, pp. 30–31, 117–18.

> his *Brain*'s so weak,
> That his starved fancy, is compell'd to ⟨rake⟩,[7]
> Among the *Excrements* of others wit,
> To make a stinking *Meal* of what they shit.
> So *Swine*, for nasty *Meat*, to *Dunghil* run,
> And toss their gruntling *Snowts* up when they've done.

This passage repeats a conventional accusation against Mulgrave: that the verses he passed off as his own were written wholly or in part by others, especially by Dryden. Later in the poem, Lord All-Pride is ridiculed, as Mulgrave was, for his conceit concerning his accomplishments in love and war. He "sets up for a *Spark*," and

> With equal self conceit too, he bears Arms,
> But with that vile success, his part performs,
> That he *Burlesques* his Trade, and what is best
> In others, turns like *Harlequin*, ⟨to⟩ [8] jeast.
> So have I seen at *Smithfields* wondrous *Fair*,
> When all his *Brother Monsters*, florish there;
> A *Lubbard Elephant*, divert the *Town*,
> With making *Legs*, and shooting off a *Gun*.

Like the Bajazet-Ephelia epistles, "My Lord All-Pride" includes star imagery which may allude to Mulgrave's Order of the Garter: "Against his *Stars*, the *Coxcomb* ever strives."

The date of "My Lord All-Pride" is a puzzle. Wilson's conclusion that it was written in answer to Mulgrave's "An Essay

---

7. "Rake" is the reading of the broadside of 1679, A-1680-PF, and all early manuscripts except the Yale MS. A-1680-HU and the Yale MS. read "take," an obvious corruption.

8. Since "to" is the reading of the broadside of 1679 and of all early manuscripts including the Yale MS., the reading of A-1680-HU, "in," must be a corruption.

upon Satyr" (*Court Wits*, p. 118) seems supported by internal evidence. The opening lines state that

> Bursting with *Pride*, the loath'd *Impostume* swells,
> Pr——k him, he sheds his *Venom* strait, & smells.

The inference is that Mulgrave, "pricked" by satires on him, has "shed his venom" in a lampoon written in reply. These circumstances fit "An Essay upon Satyr," in which Mulgrave retaliated against the Wits who had been sniping at him for at least four years. The charge that Lord All-Pride's lampoon was not entirely his own composition is also relevant, since assumptions that Mulgrave received help from Dryden and others tended to center on "An Essay upon Satyr." Rochester, for example, apparently makes such an assumption in "An Epistolary Essay from M. G. to O. B."

The difficulty is that "An Essay upon Satyr" was not in circulation until November 1679 (Rochester had a copy on 21 November),[9] whereas "My Lord All-Pride" was printed, possibly from a text of the linked group of five satires, in *A Very Heroical Epistle*, 1679. Since Narcissus Luttrell dated his copy 1679, even though the date is printed, this broadside must have been in existence by 24 March 1679/80, the last day of the year Old Style. Thus, if "My Lord All-Pride" is an answer to "An Essay upon Satyr," it was written, put into circulation, gathered into the linked group, and printed, all within three months—a possible, but not a very probable interval. "My Lord All-Pride" may therefore refer to some earlier lampoon by Mulgrave which remains unidentified. The problem is not likely to be solved until a definitive account of Mulgrave's life and works is written.

9. Wilson, *Rochester-Savile Letters*, p. 73. Anthony Wood, *Athenae Oxonienses*, 4, 210. HMC, *Seventh Report*, p. 477.

III

Unfortunately, the evidence now available does not support a conclusive case for the authorship of any of the five satires belonging to the linked group. Examination of the known data may, however, provide a basis for trustworthy conclusions at some future time.

All external evidence traditionally used to argue for Rochester's authorship of the first four satires must be disregarded, since this evidence derives from the Rochester editions of 1680, where the satires appear, not in the section of poems by or concerning Rochester, but in the section of poems by miscellaneous authors (see Chapter 3). Moreover, as we have seen, these satires were evidently taken into the archetype of the Huntington edition and the Yale MS. from a linked group assembled on the premise that the poems represented a literary quarrel between Scroope and Mulgrave which did not involve Rochester. The first four satires were reprinted as Rochester's in the edition of 1685 (A-1685); the first three continue to appear under his name in the editions of 1701 (A-1701), 1713 (A-1713), and 1731 (A-1731). From one of the 1680 editions, the first two satires were reprinted in Bragge's *Miscellaneous Works* of Rochester and Roscommon, 1707 (C-1707-a), though only the second is there assigned to Rochester; similarly ascribed, they continue to appear in Curll's second issue (C-1707-b), his edition of 1709 (C-1709), and the piracy of 1709 (C-1709-P). In Curll's edition of 1714 (C-1714-1), all four satires are attributed to Rochester; the third and fourth are reprinted from one of the 1680 editions, while the first two seem to be conflated texts derived partly from the 1680 edition and partly from Curll's edition of 1709. Later editions in this series (C series) reprint the first two poems as Rochester's but omit the others. A single manuscript version ascribing the first poem to Rochester, in Bodl. MS. Rawl. Poet. 173, was probably copied from a printed text. Thorpe, recognizing the weakness of these ascriptions, remarked that "it is lack of evidence to contradict Rochester's authorship rather than positive proof . . . which allows [the second, third, and fourth poems] to be attributed to Rochester" (*Rochester's Poems*, p. 190).

The hypothesis that the linked group preserves a feud between Mulgrave and Scroope, though supported by its arrangement and by the ascriptions in Edinburgh MS. DC.1.3, must also be viewed skeptically. Arguments based on style are perhaps most convincing here. It is scarcely plausible that a mediocre versifier like Mulgrave, whose ineptness is abundantly evident in "An Essay upon Satyr," could have written the skillful couplets of "On Poet Ninny." Similarly, one may doubt that Scroope's literary abilities, though not negligible, were sufficient to produce the delicate sustained irony of "A very Heroical Epistle," nor is the savage abuse of Mulgrave in "My Lord All-Pride" commensurate with Scroope's "natural softness." Indeed, "On Poet Ninny" and "My Lord All-Pride" are so much alike in style and structure that it is difficult to believe they were composed by two different authors. Furthermore, though these two poems allude to earlier lampoons by Scroope and Mulgrave respectively, there is no internal indication that "On Poet Ninny" specifically answers "A very Heroical Epistle," or that "My Lord All-Pride" answers "On Poet Ninny"—or, for that matter, that the epistle to Julian answers "My Lord All-Pride." The dates of the five satires, if they could be established more firmly, might furnish additional arguments that these poems do not represent a quarrel between Scroope and Mulgrave.

The five poems may now be considered individually. Two ascriptions for "Ephelia to Bajazet," if they can be called that, need hardly be taken seriously. In the broadside *A Very Heroi-cal Epistle*, 1679, the second poem of the linked group is pre-ceded by this explanation: "Dol-Common being forsaken by my Lord All-pride, and having written him a most lamentable Let-ter, his Lordship sends her the following answer." It is un-certain whether "Dol-Common" is intended to be the author or merely the *persona* (Ephelia) of the "most lamentable Letter," but in any case the name is generic, probably deriving from the principal female character of Jonson's *The Alchemist*. In Curll's edition of 1709, the poem is headed "A Letter From the Lady K. S—— To the Right Honourable the Earl of Rochester. Which occasion'd that Preceding" (i.e. "A very Heroical Epistle"). Apparently this ascription confuses *persona* and author for both "Ephelia to Bajazet" and its answer. The identity of "the Lady K. S——" is academic, since the edition of 1709 is unreliable and there is no other evidence connecting the poem with such a person. Possibly the reference is to Katherine Sedley, whose illegitimate daughter by King James II became Mulgrave's third wife on 16 March 1705/6.[1]

More serious difficulty is caused by the inclusion of "Ephelia to Bajazet" in *Female Poems On several Occasions. Written by Ephelia*, 1679. The Ephelia of *Female Poems* remains one of the more intriguing mysteries of Restoration literature; Ed-mund Gosse fancifully supposed she might be Joan Philips, only daughter of the "matchless Orinda," and Thorn-Drury attempted to reconstruct an account of her life from auto-biographical details in her poems.[2] Probably the ascription for the epistle to Bajazet could be evaluated more certainly if we

    1. G.E.C., *The Complete Peerage,* ed. Vicary Gibbs, 2 (London, St. Catherine Press, 1912), 399.
    2. Edmund Gosse, *Seventeenth Century Studies* (4th ed., London, W. Heineman, 1913), pp. 255–58. Macdonald, *Dryden Bibliography,* p. 123.

knew who the poetess Ephelia was, and especially whether she exercised any supervision over the printing of her work. Apparently she authorized the publication of *Female Poems*, since it includes a verse dedication to "Princess Mary, Dutchess of *Richmond* & *Lenox*," which is signed "Ephelia."

"Ephelia to Bajazet" may, however, have been foisted into *Female Poems* by the publisher, James Courtney, partly because extra material was needed to fill out the last gathering, in which the poem is printed, and partly because the name of the *persona* happened to coincide with the pseudonym of his author. Such a possibility gains support from the title given for the poem: "In the Person of a Lady to Bajazet, Her unconstant Gallant." Though this heading clearly recognizes that the speaker of the poem is a *persona*, it attempts to transfer the name Ephelia from *persona* to author. To the second edition of *Female Poems* (actually second issue), which he published in 1682, Courtney similarly added many spurious pieces. "Ephelia to Bajazet" seems somewhat out of place among the other poems in the first edition, most of which tell an intensely personal, continuous love story in which real-life figures bear pastoral pseudonyms. Ephelia falls in love with Strephon, whose actual initials are given as "J. G.," she grows jealous of an unattractive rival named Mopsa, she is courted by Clovis, she loses Strephon when he marries an African lady in Tangier, and she finally loses Clovis too when he falls in love with Marina. The name Bajazet occurs nowhere among these other poems, nor can the details specified concerning "J. G." be construed to fit Mulgrave.

The traditional ascription to Etherege, who still seems the most satisfactory contender, is found in the epistle to Julian:

Poor George, grows old, his Muse worne out of fashion
Hoarsly she sung Ephelias Lamentation.

Almost certainly "Ephelia to Bajazet" is meant: the phrase "Ephelias Lamentation" describes its contents accurately, and no other poem is known which fits the description so well. That the reference is also to Etherege may be less certain, since other Georges who wrote verse were alive at the time—for example, George Villiers, Duke of Buckingham. The text in Taylor MS. 2, however, glosses "Poor George" as "Sr George Etheridge." The ascription to Etherege is strengthened by the circumstance, hitherto unknown, that the epistle to Julian belongs to the same linked group as "Ephelia to Bajazet"; the ascription in the epistle can be dated two years earlier than any other, and only two years after "Ephelia to Bajazet" was probably composed. Etherege's authorship is plausible. The author of "Ephelia to Bajazet" displays the interests of a dramatist rather than those of a satirist, and the style of the poem is not unlike Etherege's.

For the second poem of the group, "A very Heroical Epistle," the usable external evidence of authorship is limited to two manuscript texts. One is found in Edinburgh MS. DC.1.3, which assigns the poem to Sir Carr Scroope; further evidence of Scroope's authorship was possibly possessed by Ebsworth, but since he cites no source, he may refer to the Edinburgh manuscript.[3] The other text occurs in Bodl. MS. Don. b. 8, which ascribes the poem to Rochester. Though these contradictory attributions might seem roughly equal in value, closer examination shows that the evidence favors Rochester. As we have seen, the ascriptions in the Edinburgh manuscript are suspect in this instance, and considerations of style cast doubt on Scroope's authorship. The Bodleian manuscript, by contrast, is unusually

3. *The Roxburghe Ballads*, ed. J. W. Ebsworth, *4* (Hertford, Ballad Society, 1883), 568, 576.

reliable in its ascriptions. More important, it appears to preserve the only known text and ascription for the poem which are independent of the linked group and the questionable assumptions of authorship on which the arrangement of this group was probably based. Thus its testimony deserves special respect.

The ascription to Rochester is also supported by strong internal evidence. Detailed analysis in a previous chapter (Chapter 4) suggests that "A very Heroical Epistle" employs the same complex ironic technique as Rochester's "An Epistolary Essay from M. G. to O. B.," and that the latter poem, like the former, is a satire on Mulgrave. In both poems, Mulgrave as *persona* represents an inversion of traditional values; he expresses attitudes which, by violating conventional standards of conduct and morality, are made to appear self-centered, vainglorious, and finally ridiculous. This technique—which is basically the same as that of *Mac Flecknoe* and *The Dunciad*, not to mention Rochester's own "Upon Nothing"—is not only distinctive but difficult to use successfully, especially with the comic artistry displayed in "A very Heroical Epistle." Even so good a poet as John Oldham fails to exploit such ironic devices with full effectiveness in his famous *A Satyr against Vertue*. Very few poets writing in 1675 (the probable date of the poem) could have composed "A very Heroical Epistle," and Rochester was certainly one of them.

"Ephelia to Bajazet" and its answer, "A very Heroical Epistle," may stem from a collaboration between Etherege and Rochester. Apparently these two friends were much together during 1675–76. Both participated in the notorious brawl at Epsom in June 1676, and several parallels in ideas between Rochester's "Artemisa to Cloe" (written *c.* 1675) and Etherege's *The Man of Mode* (acted 11 March 1675/6) may have resulted from casual conversations between the two men.[4] As is well known, the character of Dorimant in *The Man of Mode* was probably modeled upon Rochester.

Little external evidence of authorship is available for the third and fourth poems of the group. Aside from the printed texts, which provide no admissible testimony, the only ascriptions are the questionable ones in Edinburgh MS. DC.1.3, which assigns "My Lord All-Pride" to Scroope and implies that "On Poet Ninny" was written by Mulgrave. No texts independent of the linked group are known to exist. Considerations of style and structure suggest, however, that Rochester composed these two poems. Both represent a type of satire which, though less common in Restoration literature than might be supposed, is illustrated by a genuine Rochester poem, "On the suppos'd Authour." The usual Restoration lampoon is the long-winded "catalogue" variety, which satirizes perhaps a dozen different persons seriatim, each receiving only a few lines. Instead of peppering a multitude of victims with buckshot, each of these three poems concentrates its satirical firepower into a short, withering blast at a single person. Such a lampoon, to be as effective as these, requires the precise, economical diction and the controlled versification which are conspicuous features of Rochester's style. A slight additional argument that Rochester may have written "On Poet Ninny" and "My Lord All-Pride" is their position in the linked group contiguous to "A very Heroical Epistle," which is probably his. Scroope and Mulgrave, the subjects of these three poems, were of course Rochester's favorite satirical targets.

Moreover, "On Poet Ninny" may be Rochester's "lost" attack on Scroope to which Wilson called attention. In a letter dated 25 April 1678, John Verney wrote to Sir Ralph Verney,

4. See my article, "Etherege's 'Man of Mode' and Rochester's 'Artemisa to Cloe,'" *Notes and Queries*, 203 (1958), 473–74.

"Lord Rochester has been very ill and very penitent, but is now bettering.—Here enclosed are his verses on Sir Car. Scroope at large." [5] As Wilson observed, Verney is not likely to refer to "On the suppos'd Authour," which Rochester wrote in answer to Scroope's "In defence of Satyr." Scroope's poem was probably in circulation soon after the Epsom brawl in June 1676, and "On the suppos'd Authour" is scarcely the kind of retort which Rochester would have lingered over. Moreover, since "On the suppos'd Authour," as well as Scroope's subsequent reply, seems to be echoed in the epistle to Julian (see Chapter 5), it was evidently in existence by the summer of 1677 and could hardly have been newsworthy almost a year later. No other "verses on Sir Car. Scroope at large" are found among Rochester's demonstrably genuine poems. I propose, therefore, that "On Poet Ninny" be accepted as Rochester's "lost" lampoon until a better possibility appears.

If, as seems probable, "On Poet Ninny" is the satire mentioned by Verney, it was evidently composed early in 1678. This date is supported in a general way by the opening lines of the poem, which allude to one or more previous lampoons on Scroope and at least one of his satirical answers. The earliest known attack on Scroope occurs in Rochester's "Allusion to Horace," which was composed during the winter of 1675–76 and seems to have led the way for other satirists. Scroope's earliest known reply is "In defence of Satyr," which must have been written after June 1676. A probable *terminus ante quem* for the date of "On Poet Ninny" is the publication of *A Very Heroical Epistle*, 1679, for which a manuscript version of the linked group may have served as copy-text.

The case for Rochester's authorship of "My Lord All-Pride" is perhaps strengthened somewhat by the chance that "On Poet

5. Wilson, *Court Wits*, p. 233. HMC, *Seventh Report*, p. 470.

Ninny" is his "lost" lampoon on Scroope. Since conclusive
evidence on "My Lord All-Pride" is lacking, a very minor circumstance may be worth recording. The phrase "looby *Meene*"
in this poem is echoed in the following couplet in "Rochester's
Ghost" ("From the deep-vaulted Den of endless Night"),
which was written about 1682:

> I'll speak not of his slouching Looby Mien,
> Altho it is the worst that e'er was seen.[6]

The couplet appears in a passage which represents Rochester's
ghost speaking about Mulgrave; hence it seems to imply that
"My Lord All-Pride" was written by Rochester. Evidently the
reader was expected to understand this reference, since similar
echoes of "An Allusion to Horace" and the preface to *All for
Love* are also included; after the reference to Dryden the
poet comments, "I use his words." The unknown author of
"Rochester's Ghost" may, however, have derived his knowledge
of "My Lord All-Pride" from the Rochester editions of 1680.

So far as I am aware, the fifth satire of the linked group, the
epistle to Julian, has never been attributed to Rochester. Many
contemporaries evidently believed, rather implausibly, that Dryden wrote it. It is ascribed to him in five early manuscript
versions; none of these texts appears in combination with the
linked group and, significantly, four of them may be in the
same handwriting. The poem is also assigned to Dryden in *The
Sixth Part of Miscellany Poems*, 1716, which was published by
Jacob Tonson.[7] Anthony Wood thought the poem was written
"by Driden or somebody else." In *Satyr to His Muse*, 1682
(doubtfully attributed to Shadwell), Dryden as *persona* is made
to say,

6. *Poems on Affairs of State*, 1703 (Case 211-2-a), p. 131.
7. The manuscripts are the same ones cited in footnote 3 at the beginning of this chapter. The epistle to Julian is ascribed to Dryden in
The Sixth Part of Miscellany Poems, 1716 (Case 172-6-b), p. 359, and
1727 (Case 172-6-c), p. 288.

I like *Borosky* by the false *Count* hir'd,
On *Scroop* my Blunderbuss of Satyr fir'd,
In cool Blood call'd him Fool, Knave, Coward too.[8]

Probably the epistle to Julian is meant.

With good reason, Dryden's editors have consistently refused to accept the epistle to Julian as authentic. It includes a couplet mentioning Dryden in the third person; thus, if we suppose that he wrote the poem, we must assume against probability that this couplet represents an unsuccessful attempt to conceal his authorship. More important, Sir Carr Scroope, the primary target of the lampoon, was a special enemy of Rochester and his circle of Wits. Scroope seems, indeed, to have been intimate with Dryden's circle at the time the epistle to Julian was composed (spring or summer of 1677). He contributed the prologue to Lee's *The Rival Queens* (acted 17 March 1676/7), which was dedicated to Mulgrave and for which Dryden wrote commendatory verses. He also contributed a song to Lee's *Mithridates* (acted Feb. 1677/8), for which Dryden wrote the epilogue used at the first performance.[9]

Most other early texts of the epistle to Julian carry no ascriptions. The poem is, however, assigned to Buckingham in the second volume of his *Miscellaneous Works*, 1705.[1] Unreliable though this edition is, the ascription to Buckingham is at least

8. *Works of Shadwell*, ed. Summers, 5, 266. Wood's remark appears in Aubrey, *Brief Lives*, 2, 279.

9. *The Works of Nathaniel Lee*, ed. Thomas B. Stroup and Arthur L. Cooke (New Brunswick [N.J.], Scarecrow Press, 1954–55), 1, 219–24, 344–45, 364.

1. The poem appears without ascription in the Yale MS., p. 352; Osborn MS. Chest II, Number 14, p. 1184; Osborn MS. Box XXII, Number 3, p. 43; Taylor MS. 3, p. 52; B. M. Sloane MS. 655, fol. 45ʳ; B. M. Harl. MS. 6913, fol. 25ʳ; B. M. Egerton MS. 2623, fol. 81ʳ; Bodl. MS. Douce 357, fol. 65ʳ; Victoria and Albert Museum MS. Dyce 43, p. 176; Edinburgh MS. DC.1.3, p. 17; Vienna MS. 14090, fol. 96ʳ; *Poems on Affairs of State*, 1704 (Case 211-3-a), p. 156, and 1716 (Case 211-3-b), p. 139. It is printed in the folio leaflet *An Exclamation Against Julian*,

plausible. Buckingham's poetical talents were more than sufficient to write the epistle to Julian, which is above average in quality for Restoration lampoons. Buckingham spent much time with Rochester and his friends during 1677, when the poem was composed, and he might have written it as a result of this association. After Buckingham was sent to the Tower for insisting that Parliament had been automatically dissolved, his release was obtained by Rochester and other cronies in midsummer of 1677, whereupon he proceeded to make merry at Rochester's lodgings in Whitehall. In October and November, Buckingham was Rochester's guest at a convivial gathering at Woodstock. Several letters from Buckingham to Rochester, mostly written in 1677, further illustrate their close friendship at this period.[2]

Many of the conclusions offered in this chapter must, of course, remain tentative until more evidence comes to light. Such evidence will, one hopes, not only clarify the nature of the linked group but solve the problems of authorship which beset the five satires.

Secretary to the Muses; With the Character of a Libeller. By a Person of Quality, [1679] (Macdonald 191). It is attributed to Buckingham in *The Second Volume of Miscellaneous Works, Written by George, Late Duke of Buckingham,* 1705 (Case 232-2), p. [1]90, and reprinted with this ascription in *The Works Of His Grace, George Villiers, Late Duke of Buckingham,* 1715, 2, 221. The 1715 *Works* is probably the source of ascriptions to Buckingham by Jacob (*Poetical Register,* 2, 218), Cibber (*Lives of the Poets,* 2, 323), and Walpole (*Catalogue of Royal and Noble Authors,* 2, 78).

The poem is tentatively assigned to Buckingham by Brice Harris ("Captain Robert Julian, Secretary to the Muses," *English Literary History, 10* [1943], 294–309), Wilson (*Court Wits,* pp. 116, 233–34), Thorpe (*Rochester's Poems,* pp. 189–90), and Pinto (*Poems,* pp. 178–79).

2. *The Poems and Letters of Andrew Marvell,* ed. H. M. Margoliouth (Oxford, Clarendon Press, 1927), 2, 329. HMC, *Seventh Report,* p. 469; *Le Fleming,* p. 141. Prinz, *Rochester,* pp. 276–81.

14.

"On Rome's Pardons": An Unsolved Problem of Authorship

The last poem in the Rochester editions of 1680, a brief anti-Catholic lampoon titled "On Rome's Pardons," is unique in its apparent lack of relationship to the manuscript collection from which the earliest of the editions, the Huntington edition, was largely printed. "On Rome's Pardons" is classified as genuine by every previous student of Rochester who has dealt with it—by Johannes Prinz, John Hayward, Quilter Johns, James Thorpe, and Vivian de Sola Pinto.[1] Though this unanimity is impressive, the basis for it is less than clear; indeed, the evidence now available seems inadequate to solve the problem of authenticity posed by "On Rome's Pardons." Unhappily, therefore, this chapter cannot pretend to offer definite conclusions. Investigation of the known data will clarify the situation, however,

---

1. See Part III for documentation of the previous scholarship on "On Rome's Pardons."

and may ultimately help to determine the author of the poem when new evidence comes to light.

The crux of the problem is a sharply defined conflict between external evidence which seems to support Rochester's authorship and internal evidence which seems to deny it. Most of the difficulty is caused by the external evidence, consisting entirely of numerous ascriptions in early texts of "On Rome's Pardons." This evidence raises two questions: (1) whether the ascription to Rochester in the Huntington edition is trustworthy, and (2) whether the many other ascriptions to Rochester possess any authority independent of the Huntington edition. The first question requires examination of the circumstances under which "On Rome's Pardons" came to be printed in the Huntington edition. Thus the Yale MS. must be inspected to ascertain what position, if any, the poem may have occupied in the archetype from which both the manuscript and the Huntington edition are descended.

Apparently the archetype did not contain "On Rome's Pardons." The Yale MS., which probably preserves the arrangement and contents of the archetype, fails to include the poem either in the position it occupies in the Huntington edition or anywhere else. Nor is "On Rome's Pardons" likely to have been removed from the Yale MS. by any of the seven gaps. The nearest gap, the seventh and last, is fifteen poems distant in the Huntington edition and twenty-one poems away in the manuscript. If "On Rome's Pardons" was excised by this gap or an earlier one, its present location in the edition would represent an unparalleled departure from the order of the Yale MS.; the most nearly comparable case is "To all curious Criticks and Admirers of Meeter," whose respective locations in the edition and the Yale MS. are separated by only three poems in the manuscript and two in the edition. Other aspects of the gaps also suggest that "On Rome's Pardons" was not among the excised poems. The first three gaps were almost certainly occupied by the missing portions of poems still partially extant in the Yale MS., and the same is probably true of the seventh gap; similarly, the sixth gap would be filled completely by the poems in the corresponding pages of the Huntington edition. Though the fourth and fifth gaps evidently included several poems besides those in the corresponding portions of the edition, they occur in the subsection of songs, where "On Rome's Pardons" would be an anomaly unless it too is a song: it does not appear to be, and no early text indicates that it is.

Even if there were reason to suppose that "On Rome's Pardons" was among the poems removed by the gaps, such evidence would be ambiguous unless we also knew which gap it formerly occupied. For example, if it was excised by the fourth or fifth gaps, which are in the first half of the Yale MS., this would mean that the scribe of the archetype probably thought Rochester wrote it; by contrast, if it was removed by the seventh gap, in the second half of the Yale MS., he evidently believed the poem was by someone else. Moreover, even if the lost copy-text of the Huntington edition, or the archetype, differed in contents from the Yale MS. and included "On Rome's Pardons" where it now appears in the edition, this circumstance would argue against Rochester's authorship because the poem would then be in the section of poems by miscellaneous authors. Consequently, neither the Yale MS. itself nor the arrangement of the collection provides any usable evidence that Rochester composed "On Rome's Pardons."

A simple circumstance in the Huntington edition further supports the conclusion that "On Rome's Pardons" was printed from some source other than the lost manuscript which served as copy-text for the preceding sixty poems in the volume. The position of this poem at the end of the edition (A-1680-HU, p. 151) points to a familiar bibliographical situation. The signatures in the book run A-I⁸K⁴. The last poem which the edition shares with the Yale MS., "Captain [Radcliffe's] Ramble," continues only through the first four lines on the recto of K4. If nothing else followed, most of the recto and all of the verso of this leaf would remain blank. Frequently an attempt would be made to fill such a space, but in the Yale MS., and presumably in the lost copy-text of the Huntington edition, all the remaining poems in the latter part of the collection would be too long. Hence it is probable that "On Rome's Pardons" was taken from some other manuscript source, not because it was by Rochester, but because it was approximately the required length. Since the printer of the Huntington edition does not elsewhere show much concern for the authenticity of the poems he assigns to Rochester, there is scant reason to suppose that he did so in this instance.

The case for Rochester's authorship of "On Rome's Pardons" therefore hinges on the second question raised by the external evidence: whether any ascriptions in other early texts are independent of the ascription in the Huntington edition. This question is more complicated than the first. Later printed texts ascribing the poem to Rochester pose few problems, to be sure, since they all probably descend from the Huntington edition. Thus their testimony cannot be allowed much weight.[2] The poem is reprinted with ascription to Rochester in the other 1680 editions and in the later editions of 1685 (A-1685), 1701 (A-1701), 1713 (A-1713), and 1731 (A-1731). It is also assigned to him in two seventeenth-century miscellanies, *Rome Rhym'd to Death*, 1683 and *A Second Collection of The Newest and Most Ingenious Poems, Satyrs, Songs, &c. against Popery*

2. See Part III for a more detailed list of the early texts and ascriptions of "On Rome's Pardons."

and Tyranny, 1689. These two texts are verbally identical with those in the majority of the 1680 editions; indeed, the textual variation is too slight to determine whether the later miscellany derived its text from the earlier miscellany or directly from one of the 1680 editions. Both miscellanies attribute the poem to "the E. of R.," a form which may have been borrowed from the title pages of the 1680 editions.

In the eighteenth century, "On Rome's Pardons" was assigned to Rochester in Benjamin Bragge's *Miscellaneous Works* of Rochester and Roscommon, 1707 (C-1707-a); except for a one-letter misprint, this text is verbally identical with most of the earlier printed versions, any one of which might therefore have been the copy-text. The poem was reissued in 1707 (C-1707-b) and reprinted with ascription to Rochester in the edition of 1709 (C-1709), the piracy of 1709 (C-1709-P), the edition of 1714 (C-1714-1), and later editions in this series (C series). The text in *A Collection of Merry Poems*, 1736 probably derives from an earlier printed source though it carries no ascription.

Unlike the printed texts, the early manuscripts of "On Rome's Pardons" present a situation which is indeterminate. No fewer than thirteen manuscript versions are now known to exist, eight ascribing the poem to Rochester and five carrying no ascriptions. Unfortunately, the textual evidence fails to reveal how many of these versions may have been copied from printed sources. If any two or more of the thirteen manuscripts represent a line of textual transmission independent of the Huntington edition, they should ordinarily share variants against all the printed versions. This condition is not fulfilled to any significant extent, even though several of the manuscripts exhibit a surprising amount of variation for a poem only fifteen lines long; the few concurrences against the printed texts could scarcely support any conclusions. If the textual theory advanced in

Chapter 2 is rigidly applied, such a situation probably means that all or all but one of the manuscripts descend from the Huntington edition.

Moreover, three manuscript versions of "On Rome's Pardons" occur in bound volumes containing other material probably copied from printed sources. These are the texts in Bodl. MSS. Add. B. 106 and Sancroft 53, which ascribe the poem to Rochester, and in Bodl. MS. Rawl. Poet. 173, which carries no ascription. Indeed, the title in the latter text includes a corruption ("Pardon" for "Pardons") which originated in one of the 1680 editions (A-1680-F) and was transmitted to most of its descendants (A-1680-HA, A-1685, and all later editions in the A series). The same corrupt reading appears in the titles in Osborn MS. Box LVIII, Number 4, which carries an ascription to Rochester, and Bodl. MS. Rawl. Poet. 152, which gives no ascription. Three further texts are identical or almost identical with the Huntington edition in all substantive readings exclusive of the title of the poem; these texts are found in Harvard MSS. Eng. 586 and 606, both of which assign the poem to Rochester, and Bodl. MS. Don. e. 23, which lacks ascription.[3]

3. For three of the manuscript copies carrying ascriptions to Rochester, suspicion of descent from the Huntington edition is strengthened by the existence of a two-poem "linked group." This group consists of "On Rome's Pardons" followed by another short anti-Catholic satire beginning "When God Almighty had his Palace fram'd." The group is found in Osborn MS. Box III, Number 27, Harvard MS. Eng. 586, and Folger MS. M. a. 187, while in *A Second Collection*, 1689, "On Rome's Pardons" (p. 18) is the third poem following "When God Almighty" (p. 17). These three manuscripts of "When God Almighty" are closely related to the text of 1689 and may descend from it: though they exhibit some slight agreement with each other against this printed text, they almost invariably agree with it against texts which are independent of it (B. M. Sloane MS. 1731A, fol. 152^r; B. M. Add. MS. 29497, fol. 37^v; *The Muses Farewel to Popery and Slavery*, 1689 [Case 191-1-a], p. 74; *Poems on Affairs of State*, 1704 [Case 211-3-a], p. 1).

Moreover, if—as seems virtually certain—the text of "On Rome's Pardons" in *A Second Collection* derives from an earlier printed source, the

Conceivably so many manuscript versions might have been copied from printed sources because the anti-Catholic sentiments of "On Rome's Pardons" appealed to popular sympathies during the interval after the poem was first published in 1680.

On the other hand, it is scarcely probable that at least twelve of the thirteen manuscripts should derive from printed sources, especially since the evidence pointing to such a conclusion is not extensive. Theoretically at least, the puzzling textual situation could be explained on the premise that the version in the Huntington edition, which contains no recognizably corrupt readings, preserves the poem as its author wrote it, and that most of the manuscripts descend in radial fashion from one authorial draft. Also, several individual manuscripts yield additional evidence that they were not copied from printed versions. The texts in B. M. Sloane MS. 1731A and Bodl. MS. Smith 27, carrying no ascriptions, occupy single loose sheets which exhibit fold-marks and may therefore have passed from hand to hand during the Restoration period; possibly some variants in the British Museum version are authoritative. Similarly, the text in Osborn MS. Box III, Number 27, carrying an ascription to Rochester, occurs in a single sheet which has been folded once to form two leaves and shows traces of further folding. Other poems in this same sheet appear to be independent of printed texts; one is the

---

copy-text for the two poems in this miscellany cannot, of course, have been a manuscript version of the linked group. Hence the group itself must probably derive from *A Second Collection*. Some scribe, attracted by the anti-Catholic character of these two poems in the miscellany, may have made a transcript from which the three extant texts of the group are descended. If this theory is correct, only one of the many manuscripts assigning "On Rome's Pardons" to Rochester, Osborn MS. Chest II, Number 4, offers no substantial hint of derivation from the Huntington edition.

On the other hand, for reasons given in Chapter 2, it would be quite unusual for three manuscripts to descend from the same copy of a printed text. In any event, finespun reasoning is rather futile when the external evidence as a whole is so inconclusive.

second stanza of Sir Carr Scroope's lyric "I cannot change as others do" (see Chapter 8), while another is a satirical song which remained unpublished until 1954.[4] A further text ascribing "On Rome's Pardons" to Rochester appears in a bound manuscript volume, Osborn MS. Chest 11, Number 4, which does not otherwise seem to derive its contents from printed sources. On the whole, then, it is difficult to deny that some ascriptions in these manuscripts may be independent of the Huntington edition and may therefore support the conclusion that Rochester wrote "On Rome's Pardons."

Internal evidence tends, however, to reverse this conclusion. The anti-Catholic sentiments of "On Rome's Pardons" raise doubts concerning Rochester's authorship, for there is good reason to believe that his feelings toward the Church of Rome, unlike those of most contemporary Englishmen, were tolerant and even favorable. His demonstrably genuine poems not only include no other anti-Catholic satires but fail to reveal any specifically anti-Catholic opinions. The closest that Rochester comes to a hostile attitude is a single couplet in "A Ramble in St. James's Park" which mentions sodomy among the Jesuits, and another in "To the Post Boy" referring to similar sexual perversity in the College of Cardinals; in both couplets, the sexuality rather than the Catholicism is of primary importance.[5] Such an absence of anti-Catholic feeling is noteworthy in a writer who lived through the hysteria of the Popish Plot.

4. See my article, "A 'Lost' Lampoon by Katherine Sedley?" *Manuscripts*, 6 (1954), 160–65.

5. In "A Ramble in St. James's Park" (A-1680-HU, p. 18):

> The *Jesuits Fraternity*,
> Shall leave the use of *Buggery*.

In "To the Post Boy" (B. M. Harl. MS. 6914, fol. 21^r):

> Ive swived more whores more ways y^n Sodoms walls
> Ere knew or the College of Romes Cardinalls.

Furthermore, it is virtually certain that Rochester's wife was a Catholic during all but a few months of their married life, and that she was converted to Catholicism by his own wish and design. Part of the story of her conversion came out in connection with the trial of Stephen College, the "Protestant Joiner," in August 1681. Though some of the witnesses at this trial were probably unreliable, considerable weight must be allowed the testimony of William Clarke of Sandford, trustee and steward of Rochester's estate, who deposed:

> I do not know that College was a Papist, but have heard him say that, being about 14 years since a trooper under the Earl of Rochester, my lord employed him to bring Thomson, a priest, to his lady to pervert her, and that he did so several times and by means of that priest she was perverted.[6]

These events must have occurred about June 1667, a few months after Rochester's marriage, when he held a commission as captain of horse under Prince Rupert.[7] Rochester's reconversion of his wife to Protestantism took place in late May 1680 during his last illness, as many contemporaries noted.[8]

6. *CSPD*, 24 Aug. 1681 (p. 416). For corroborating testimony, see *CSPD*, 16 Aug. 1681 (p. 406), 20 Aug. (p. 409), 20 Aug. (p. 410), 24 Aug. (pp. 415–16), 24 Aug. (p. 416), 26 Aug. (p. 420); this evidence is discussed briefly by Wilson, who finds it "incredible" (*Rochester-Savile Letters*, p. 5). See also HMC, *Rutland*, 2, 56; *A true Copy of the dying Words of Mr. Stephen Colledge*, 1681; *The Speech and Carriage of Stephen Colledge before the Castle at Oxford*, 1681; *Notes upon Stephen College . . . By Roger L'Estrange*, 1681, pp. 5–6, 16–19.

7. *CSPD*, 13 June 1667 (pp. 179, 183). Charles Dalton, *English Army Lists and Commission Registers* (London, Eyre and Spottiswoode, 1892–1904), *1*, 76. *The Arraignment, Tryal and Condemnation of Stephen Colledge for High-Treason*, 1681, p. 72.

8. *The Camden Miscellany*, *11* (London, Royal Historical Society, 1907), 32. Margaret M. Verney, *Memoirs of the Verney Family* (London and New York, Longmans, Green, 1899), p. 245. *Some Account of the Life of Rachael Wriothesley Lady Russell* (London, 1819), p. 219.

Burnet says of her original conversion to Catholicism that
Rochester "himself had been not a little Instrumental in pro-
curing it, as he freely acknowledged." Rochester's motives in
this affair remain obscure, but it is clear that he would never have
persuaded his wife to become a Catholic, nor permitted her to
remain one for thirteen years, if he held strong anti-Catholic
convictions.

Stylistic considerations shed little light on the authorship of
"On Rome's Pardons." It is a cool, clever *reductio ad absurdum*
of the Catholic system of pardons, not unworthy of Rochester's
talents. Since the tone of the satire is detached rather than bit-
terly involved, Rochester might conceivably have composed it
as a *jeu d'esprit* despite his usual favorable attitude toward
Catholicism. On the other hand, there is nothing specially
Rochesterian about "On Rome's Pardons." I am not convinced
that he wrote it.

Robert Parsons, *A Sermon Preached At the Funeral of the R^t Honorable
John Earl of Rochester*, 1680, p. 28. Gilbert Burnet, *Some Passages of the
Life and Death Of the Right Honourable John Earl of Rochester*, 1680,
p. 143. B. M. Add. MS. 6269, fol. 33ᵛ; Huntington MS. HA 13404.

PART III

Lists of Early Texts and Ascriptions

Introduction

Part III offers a comprehensive list of the early texts of the sixty-one poems which were printed in the Rochester editions of 1680, together with the external evidence of authorship preserved either in these texts or in other early sources. Besides providing detailed documentation for much of the discussion in Parts I and II, Part III assembles all the known information on the authorship of those poems which are not singled out for special studies. Incidentally it affords a rough index of the popularity of the poems among Rochester's contemporaries. Also cited are the more important conclusions which students of Restoration literature have hitherto formulated concerning the authorship of the poems. The sixty-one poems are listed by first lines in the order they occupy in the 1680 editions. After the first line of each poem is a note of its authorship, with a cross-reference, if necessary, to the appropriate chapter in Part II. Together with the discussions of authorship in Part II, Part III is designed to supersede Thorpe's Appendix C (*Rochester's Poems*, pp. 169–91).

For each text, the following facts are normally recorded: identification of the source in which the text appears, the number (if any) of the page or folio on which it begins, the title and ascription if either is included, all notations indicating dates, and other types of information which may be important in individual cases. When a text was reprinted in successive editions of the same book, its title and ascription are usually reproduced only for the earliest text in the series. Line divisions are not indicated in quotations of titles, ascriptions, dates, and the like. Quotations of this kind of information from printed texts do not reproduce italics, small capitals, or full capitals other than initial letters of words: these typographical features have little significance for the present study.

Wherever practicable, the texts of each poem are listed in the order of their dates so as to clarify the notes on their derivation. The manuscripts cannot, of course, be dated precisely, nor would a rigidly chronological arrangement be desirable in cases where a poem was reprinted concurrently in successive editions of several different books. Manuscripts are listed first because most of them are independently descended. The order within each list of manuscripts is, however, arbitrary.

Editions of Rochester's works are identified by the symbols which are explained in Chapter 1 and enumerated in the third section of Appendix B. Texts in the 1680 editions are represented by a reference to A-1680-HU alone, but other appearances of the sixty-one poems are listed in full for editions in the A, B, and D series. Editions in the C series are cited only up to 1714, since later volumes in this series have not yet been adequately investigated. Texts in miscellanies are recorded up to 1750, the terminal date of Case's bibliography. Texts in song-books are recorded up to 1702, the terminal date of the bibliography by Day and Murrie; listings of later texts in song-books would be useful but do not seem feasible in the absence of a satisfactory bibliography. A few other printed volumes are cited by the numbers assigned to them in Macdonald's bibliography of Dryden.

Though they rarely possess much value, statements concerning authorship are recorded from sources like Gerald Langbaine's *Account of the English Dramatick Poets,* Giles Jacob's *Poetical Register,* Theophilus Cibber's *Lives of the Poets,* and Horace Walpole's *Catalogue of Royal and Noble Authors.* Most such collections derive their information from earlier printed books—at least for poems attributed to Rochester. The page numbers cited by Langbaine indicate that he used one of the Rochester editions of 1680. As is shown by the items he includes and by the forms of his titles, Jacob's list of Rochester's poems comes almost entirely from an edition in the C series, probably C-1714-1. Walpole acknowledges that his list of the Earl's poems is taken mostly from Anthony Wood's *Athenae Oxonienses.* Wood's testimony, on the other hand, is sometimes important, especially because he is careful to identify his sources.

Each text in the following lists carries an explicit or implicit indication of its probable derivation. The absence of a note indicating derivation—as with most of the manuscripts—signifies independent descent. No note of derivation is given for texts in A-1680-HU, since this edition was printed entirely from manuscript sources. Nor is a source specified for the earliest printed text, if any, which antedates A-1680-HU. All conclusions concerning derivation of texts are based on the methods outlined in Chapter 2. Except for a few unimportant eighteenth-century printings which were not accessible, the verbal variants in all texts have been collated in full. Because of the great quantity of this textual evidence, it cannot be presented in detail, nor would citation of selected variants have much value.

Extensive though the following lists may appear, the reader should not suppose that they are, or can be, complete. Experience with the Rochester text over the past ten years suggests that, in the future, manuscripts containing versions of his poems will con-

tinue to be discovered at frequent intervals.[1] Indeed, one purpose of these lists is to bring such new material to light, for the
evidence preserved in Restoration manuscripts offers the most
promising means of solving the remaining problems of the
Rochester canon.

1. Regrettably, it has not been possible to include in the following lists
a manuscript volume at the University of Nottingham, designated rather
oddly as the "Portland Miscellany," which was used by Pinto for his edition
of Rochester (*Poems,* pp. xlvi, 163, and *passim*). Over the past several
years, repeated inquiries concerning this volume have, when acknowledged
at all, failed to elicit satisfactory answers. Though the "Portland Miscellany" evidently contains few ascriptions, it may be valuable for its texts of
Rochester's songs, most of which did not circulate widely in manuscript.

In the absence of firsthand knowledge, the "Additional Notes" in the
following lists record whatever information Pinto gives concerning appearances in the "Portland Miscellany" of the sixty-one poems printed in
the Rochester editions of 1680. I am not, of course, responsible for errors
and omissions in this information. There is no indication that the "Portland Miscellany" has been investigated to determine how much of its text
was copied from printed sources.

DEAR FRIEND. I HEAR THIS TOWN DOES SO ABOUND

Author: Rochester.

Texts:

Yale MS., p. 1: "An Epistolary Essay very delightfull and solid from ye L^d: R: to ye L^d: M: upon their mutuall Poems."

Osborn MS. Chest 11, Number 28: "A Letter from My Lord Rochester to the Earl of Mi——." Appears in a single loose sheet folded once and bearing marks of further folding.

Harvard MS. Eng. 584, p. 147: "On Common Fame by ye late Earl of Rochester." Fragment of 8 lines beginning "Ther's nothing in ye world which I can name." (Possibly copied from a printed text.)

Harvard MS. Eng. 602F: no title; no ascription. (Copied from one of the A-1680 editions.)

Harvard MS. Eng. 623F, p. 39: "A Letter To My Lord Mulgrave"; signed "Rochester."

Harvard MS. Eng. 636F, p. 4: "To My Lord Mulgrave, from Rochester. An Epistolary Essay From M. G. to O. B. Upon their Mutuall Poems"; signed "Rochester."

Bodl. MS. Rawl. Poet. 173, fol. 132^r. Two fragments, the first of 14 lines, the second of 10 lines. The first fragment, beginning "Perhaps Ill verses ought to be confin'd," is headed "A Fragment out of L^d. Rochester's, which may serve as an apology for the whole Collection." The second, beginning "There's not a thing on Earth that I can name," is headed "Upon Fame. by the same." (Copied from an edition in the A series.)

A-1680-HU, p. 3: "An Epistolary Essay from M. G. to O. B. upon their Mutual Poems"; ascribed to Rochester. Reprinted with ascription to Rochester in the other A-1680 editions and

in A-1685, p. 3; A-1701, p. 3; A-1713, p. 3; A-1731, p. 3.
B-1691, p. 82: "An Epistolary Essay: From M. G. to O. B.
Upon their Mutual Poems"; ascribed to Rochester. Reprinted
with ascription to Rochester in B-1696, p. 78; B-1705, p. 78;
B-1714, p. 46; B-1732, p. 46; B-1710-P, p. 33; B-1718-P,
p. 41. (The text in B-1691 was printed from one of the
A-1680 editions.)

ADDITIONAL NOTES: Pinto reports that a text of this poem,
headed "From E. R. to E. M.," appears in the "Portland
Miscellany" (*Poems*, p. 191).

In the entry for his "lost" edition in the *Stationers' Register* under 19 November 1690, Francis Saunders described this
poem as "An Epistolari essay from E. R. to E. M."

PREVIOUS SCHOLARSHIP: Printed as Rochester's by Hayward
(*Collected Works*, p. 33), Johns (*Poetical Works*, p. 55),
and Pinto (*Poems*, p. 92). Attributed to Rochester by Prinz
(*Rochester*, pp. 118, 176, 186, 210–11, 244), Wilson (*Court
Wits*, pp. 8, 73, 174), and Thorpe (*Rochester's Poems*, pp.
172–73).

WERE I (WHO TO MY COST ALREADY AM

AUTHOR: Rochester.

TEXTS:

Yale MS., p. 8: "A Satyr. Against Man. By yᵉ E: of R:." Includes the epilogue.

Osborn MS. Chest II, Number 3, p. 124: "A Satyr against Mankind by the Ld R:." Lacks the epilogue.

Osborn MS. Chest II, Number 28: "A Satyr"; no ascription.
Lacks the epilogue. Appears on a single loose sheet.

Harvard MS. Eng. 584, p. 151: ". . . yᵉ Earl of Rochesters

Satyr against Man, which begins thus." First 13 lines only. (The ascription to Rochester was probably copied from the pamphlet *Corinna; or, Humane Frailty,* 1699. The source of the thirteen-line text, which does not appear in the pamphlet, is uncertain.)

Harvard MS. Eng. 623F, p. 12: "Satyr On Man"; signed "Rochester." Includes the epilogue.

Harvard MS. Eng. 636F, p. 80: "A Satyre. Agst: Man"; both main part of poem and epilogue signed "Rochester." The epilogue has separate title "An Addition to the Satyr Against Man."

Folger MS. 4108: no title. Written in margin: "E of Rochest. Poem. p. 11." Fragment of 9 lines beginning "Honesty is against all common sense." (Evidently copied from one of the editions in the A series, several of which print the passage on p. 11.)

Illinois MS. (uncatalogued): "A Satyr against man by the Earl of Rochester." Includes the epilogue.

B. M. Sloane MS. 1458, fol. 16^r: "A Satyre agst Reason & mankind by my Ld Rochester." Lacks the epilogue.

B. M. Add. MS. 4456, fol. 204^r: "Satyr"; no ascription. Lacks the epilogue.

B. M. Add. MS. 14047, fol. 130^r: "A Satyr on Man:—By ye Ld Roch:." Includes the epilogue.

B. M. Burney MS. 390, fol. 6^r: "A Satyr against Man, & Reason"; signed "E: of Rochest^r." Lacks the epilogue.

Bodl. MS. Rawl. Poet. 81, fol. 23^r: "A Satyr on Man"; no ascription. Lacks the epilogue.

Bodl. MS. Rawl. Poet. 123, p. 110: "Satyr upon Man"; no ascription. This text, in the handwriting of John Oldham, lacks the epilogue and the last 8 lines of the main part of the poem. It gives variant readings in the margin.

Bodl. MS. Eng. Poet. d. 152, fol. 70ʳ: "Satyre agˢᵗ Mankind";
signed "Ld Roch:." Incomplete text ending with the line
"Where actions cease thoughts are impertinent."

Bodl. MS. Eng. Poet. e. 4, p. 181: "A Satyre against Mankind";
signed "John E. Rochester." Includes the epilogue, separately
titled "Addition."

Bodl. MS. Add. B. 106, fol. 20ᵛ: "A Satyr against Reason &
Mankinde." In margin beside title: "Rochester." Includes the
epilogue. Variant readings are supplied as interlinear corrections.

Bodl. MS. Tanner 306, fol. 414ʳ: "A Satyr on Man. Anno. 74";
signed "By Lᵈ of Rochester" ("of Dorcester" scored out).
On outside of formerly folded sheet: "Of Man." Lacks the
epilogue. Variant readings are supplied as interlinear corrections.

Bodl. MS. Don. b. 8, p. 495: "A Satyre. by the earl of Roches-
ter." Lacks the epilogue. On p. 498 is written in the margin:
"This satyre is supposed to be a Translation of yᵉ Earle of
Rochesters out of Italian."

Cambridge MS. Add. 6339, fol. 16ʳ: no title; no ascription. Incomplete text beginning "Though one's a Statesman, t' other
but a Hound" and continuing to the end of the main part of
the poem.

Edinburgh MS. DC.1.3, p. 19: "Apologie"; no ascription. Includes epilogue only.

Edinburgh MS. DC.1.3, p. 25 (should be p. 27): "A Satyre
against Mankind"; signed "By the Earl of Rochester." Includes main part of poem and epilogue, which is separately
titled "The Apology."

A Satyr against Mankind. Written by a Person of Honour,
[1679]. Lacks the epilogue. (For a discussion of the text of
this folio leaflet, see W. D. Paden, "Rochester's Satyr," *Books*

and Libraries at the University of Kansas, 1, no. 3 [April 1953], pp. 8–11.)

A-1680-HU, p. 6: "Satyr"; ascribed to Rochester. Includes the epilogue. Reprinted with ascription to Rochester in the other A-1680 editions and in A-1685, p. 6; A-1701, p. 6; A-1713, p. 6; A-1731, p. 6. (The text in A-1701, which is reprinted in A-1713 and A-1731, introduces several corrected readings probably taken from B-1691, B-1696, or the folio leaflet of 1679.)

B-1691, p. 89: "A Satyr against Mankind"; ascribed to Rochester. Reprinted with ascription to Rochester in B-1696, p. 86; B-1705, p. 85; B-1714, p. 50; B-1732, p. 50; B-1710-P, p. 36; B-1718-P, p. 3. The epilogue is omitted in B-1691, B-1696, B-1705, B-1710-P, and B-1718-P but is included in B-1714 and B-1732 under the separate title "Postscript." (The text in B-1691 is taken from the folio leaflet of 1679 with numerous corrected readings probably introduced from one of the A-1680 editions. The text of the epilogue in B-1714 is conflated from one of the A-1680 editions and some later edition in the A series.)

C-1707-a, p. [1]1: "An Addition to the Satyr against Man"; ascribed to Rochester. Includes epilogue only. (Derived from a manuscript, with some readings probably introduced from one of the A-1680 editions.)

C-1707-b, p. [1]1: "A Satyr against Man. Imitated from Monsieur Bolieu. (Never before Printed entire.)"; ascribed to Rochester. Includes main part of poem and epilogue. Reprinted with ascription to Rochester in C-1709, p. [2]1; C-1709-P, p. [1]13; C-1711-P, p. 19; C-1714-1, p. 1; and later editions in this series. (In C-1707-b, the main part of the poem derives from one of the A-1680 editions, with some readings probably introduced from an edition in the B series. Up to the line "Who for Re-

proof of Sins does Man deride," the epilogue is conflated from
C-1707-a and one of the A-1680 editions; thereafter it appears
on the reissued sheets of C-1707-a.)

ADDITIONAL NOTES: Pinto reports that texts of the main part of
the poem and the epilogue appear in the "Portland Miscellany" (*Poems*, pp. 214–15).

The poem is ascribed to Rochester in a letter from John
Verney to Sir Ralph Verney dated 23 March 1675/6: "I have
a sheet or two of Verses (s^d to be Rochesters) of Faith & Rea-
son, much after ye sense of his Satyr ag^t man, If you have
not seen them I'le next weeke send you a coppy" (V. de Sola
Pinto, "An Unpublished Poem Attributed to Rochester," *Lon-
don Times Literary Supplement*, 22 November 1934, p. 824;
HMC, *Seventh Report*, p. 467). For the verses on "Faith &
Reason," which are not by Rochester but by Sir William
Davenant, see also Pinto, "A Poem Attributed to Rochester,"
London Times Literary Supplement, 6 December 1934, p.
875, and "Rochester and the Deists," *London Times Literary
Supplement*, 13 December 1934, p. 895.

Alexander Radcliffe apparently attributes this poem to
Rochester in his "News from Hell," published in *The Ramble: an Anti-Heroick Poem*, 1682, p. 4:

> A Lord who was in Metre wont
> To call a Privy Member C——
> Whose Verse, by Women termed lewd,
> Is still preserv'd, not understood.
> But that which made 'em curse and ban,
> Was for his Satyr against Man.

The poem is assigned to Rochester by Anthony Wood, who
nevertheless adds that it was "ascribed by some to the duke of

Buckingham" (*Athenae Oxonienses, 3,* 1229). Horace Walpole's attribution to Rochester derives from Wood (*Catalogue of Royal and Noble Authors, 2,* 39). Giles Jacob's similar ascription, together with the 61 lines he quotes from the poem, may derive from an edition in the C series (*Poetical Register, 2,* 232, 233–35). Also probably taken from printed sources are attributions to Rochester by Dean Lockier and Alexander Pope (Joseph Spence, *Anecdotes,* ed. Samuel Weller Singer, London, 1820, pp. 66, 136).

PREVIOUS SCHOLARSHIP: Attributed to Oldham by Percy L. Babington ("Dryden not the Author of 'MacFlecknoe,' " *Modern Language Review, 13* [1918], 25–34). Printed as Rochester's by Hayward (*Collected Works,* pp. xiii, 35) and Johns (*Poetical Works,* p. 59). Attributed to Rochester by Prinz (*Rochester,* pp. 59–60, 98–99, 122–24, 126, 189), Pinto (*Rochester,* pp. 59–60, 174–83; *Poems,* p. 118), Wilson (*Court Wits,* pp. 133–37, 140–41, 214, 236; *Rochester-Savile Letters,* pp. 14–15), and Thorpe (*Rochester's Poems,* p. 173).

MUCH WINE HAD PAST
WITH GRAVE DISCOURSE

AUTHOR: Rochester.

TEXTS:

Yale MS., p. 34: "A Ramble in St James's Parke. By ye E: of R:." All but the title and first 13 lines have been removed by the first gap, pp. 35–44.

Osborn MS. Chest II, Number 3. The table of contents in this manuscript lists "A Sayter on S^t. Jameses Parke by L^d: Rochester" as appearing on p. 112, but the leaves containing the poem have been cut out.

Harvard MS. Eng. 636F, p. 12: "Upon y^e. Night walkers in S^t. James Parke"; signed "Rochester."

B. M. Sloane MS. 2332, fol. 5^v: "Poems by ye E. of R." Consists of two fragments totaling 18 lines. (Probably copied from one of the A-1680 editions, with the heading taken from the title page.)

B. M. Harl. MS. 6057, fol. 60^r: "Lord Rochester." Incomplete text ending "You may go mad for ye North Wind."

Edinburgh MS. DC.1.3, p. 90: "L. Rochester on St James's Park."

A-1680-HU, p. 14: "A Ramble in St. James's Park"; ascribed to Rochester. Reprinted with ascription to Rochester in the other A-1680 editions and in A-1685, p. 14; A-1701, p. 13; A-1713, p. 14; A-1731, p. 13.

C-1714-1, p. 79: "A Ramble in St. James's Park"; ascribed to Rochester. Reprinted with ascription to Rochester in later editions in this series. (The 1714 text was printed from one of the A-1680 editions.)

ADDITIONAL NOTES: Pinto reports that a text of this poem, headed "A Ramble in ye Park," appears in the "Portland Miscellany" (*Poems*, p. 211).

In a postscript to a letter dated 20 March 1672/3 (Huntington MS. HA 12525), Godfrey Thacker wrote from London to his cousin, the Earl of Huntingdon: "I send your L^{d}ship a copy of verses of my Ld Rochers makeing though inferiour to those of St James his Parke." There follows a full eighteen-line text of the satire beginning "Too long the wise commons have been in debate" (see "Special Note" below). For further information on Thacker's letter, see Lucyle Hook, "Something More About Rochester," *Modern Language Notes*, 75 (1960), 478–85.

Referring to the poems in the A-1680 editions, Anthony Wood says (*Athenae Oxonienses, 3,* 1230):

> Among them is a poem entit. *A Ramble into St. James's Park,* p. 14, which I guess is the same with that which is meant and challenged in the preface to the poems of Alexander Radcliff of Greys inn entit. *The Ramble, an anti-heroick Poem, together with some terrestrial Hymns, and carnal Ejaculations.* Lond. 1682. oct. as the true composure of the said Radcliff, but being falsly and imperfectly published under the earl's name, is said there to be enlarged two thirds, above what it was, when before in print.

Wood is mistaken; he has confused Rochester's poem with Alexander Radcliffe's *The Ramble,* an entirely different work. Wood's error is reproduced by Horace Walpole (*Catalogue of Royal and Noble Authors, 2,* 39).

PREVIOUS SCHOLARSHIP: Omitted from their editions of Rochester by Hayward (*Collected Works*) and Johns (*Poetical Works*). Attributed to Rochester by Prinz (*Rochester,* p. 144), Thorpe (*Rochester's Poems,* p. 173), and Pinto (*Poems,* p. 114).

SPECIAL NOTE: Thacker's ascription (see "Additional Notes" above) indicates that Rochester is the author of the brief satire beginning "Too long the wise commons have been in debate." The poem is also ascribed to Rochester in Bodl. MS. Don. b. 8, p. 409. It was first printed under his name in *Poems on Affairs of State,* 1704 (Case 211-3-a), p. 73, and reprinted in 1716 (Case 211-3-b), p. 65. It was again printed as Rochester's from a manuscript source in C-1707-a, p. [1]10. This latter text was reissued in C-1707-b, p. [2]10, and reprinted with ascription to Rochester in C-1709, p. ²94; C-1709-P, p. ³8; C-1714-1, p. 93; and later editions in the C series. There are no ascriptions to any other author. The poem exhibits the high-spirited wit characteristic of some of Rochester's writing during the early 1670s; evidently it was composed just before the date of Thacker's letter.

The poem appears without ascription in Victoria and Albert Museum MS. Dyce 43, p. 223; Edinburgh MS. DC.1.3, p. 77 and p. 98; Vienna MS. 14090, fol. 119ʳ; Taylor MS. 1, p. 112; Taylor MS. 3, p. 103; and Osborn MS. Chest 11, Number 3, p. 167. It was printed as Rochester's by Hayward (*Collected Works*, p. 98) and Johns (*Poetical Works*, p. 153) and attributed to Rochester by Prinz (*Rochester*, p. 145) and Wilson (*Court Wits*, pp. 124, 132). Pinto omitted it from his edition (*Poems*) without explanation.

CLOE, BY YAUR COMMAND IN VERSE I WRITE

AUTHOR: Rochester.

TEXTS:

Yale MS., p. 45: "A Letter fancy'd from Artemisa in yᵉ Towne to Cloe in yᵉ Countrey. By yᵉ E: of R:."

Harvard MS. Eng. 623F, p. 1: "A Letter from Artemisia In the Town, to Chloe in the Country"; signed "Rochester."

Harvard MS. Eng. 636F, p. 20: "A Letter From Artemisa in the Towne to Chloe in yᵉ Country"; signed "Rochester."

Folger MS. M. b. 12, fol. 10ᵛ: "Satyr By Lᵈ: Rochester." Fragment of 92 lines beginning "You smile to see me (whom the World perchance."

Huntington MS. Ellesmere 8793: "A Letter from Artemiza In the Towne to Chloe In the Country"; no ascription.

B. M. Add. MS. 27408, fols. 8ᵛ, 10ᵛ: no title; no ascription. Fragment of 89 lines beginning "Who had prevail'd on her through her own Skill."

Bodl. MS. Rawl. Poet. 123, pp. 108–09, 116–23: "A Letter from Artemiza in yᵉ Town to Chloe in yᵉ Country"; no ascription. This text, in the handwriting of John Oldham, gives variant readings in the margin.

Bodl. MS. Rawl. Poet. 152, fol. 50ʳ: "A letter ffrom Artimiza in yᵉ town to Cloe in yᵉ Country"; no ascription.

Bodl. MS. Rawl. Poet. 173, fols. 65ᵛ, 132ʳ. Two fragments, the first of 77 lines, the second of 22 lines. The first fragment, beginning "This in my time was an observed Rule," is headed "The Cheating Whore. or, a Caveat to Young Fops. Out of Ld Roch.'s Poems." The second, beginning "I took this time to think, what nature meant," is headed "On a Witty Whore." (Copied from one of the A-1680 editions.)

Bodl. MS. Don. b. 8, p. 490: "A Letter from Artemiza in the Towne to Chloe in the Countrey." On p. 494 is written in the margin: "This poeme is supposed, to bee made by yᵉ Earle of Rochester, or Mʳ Wolseley."

Bodl. MS. North b. 24, fol. 60ʳ: "A Letter of Artemisa in the towne, to Chloe in the Countrey"; no ascription. Incomplete text ending with the line "Of such whome witts undoe, and Fools repaire."

Cambridge MS. Add. 29, fol. 33ʳ: no title; no ascription. Fragment of 125 lines beginning "[As if 't had been] yᵉ Lady of y[ᵉ house]."

Cambridge MS. Add. 6339, fol. 4ʳ: "A letter from Artemisia in the Town to Cloe in the Countrey by Lᵈ Rochester."

Victoria and Albert Museum MS. Dyce 43, p. 61: "Satyr"; signed "E. Rochestʳ." Fragment of 92 lines beginning "You smile to see me (whom the world perchance."

Edinburgh MS. DC.1.3, p. 60: "A Letter from Artemisa in ye towne To Cloe in the Conntrey"; no ascription.

Vienna MS. 14090, fol. 35^v: "Satyr"; signed "Rochester." Fragment of 89 lines beginning "You smile to see me (whom y^e. world pchance."

Artemisa to Cloe. A Letter from a Lady in the Town, to a Lady in the Country; Concerning The Loves of the Town: By a Person of Quality, 1679. (Printed from a manuscript.)

A Letter From Artemiza in the Town, to Chloë in the Country. By a Person of Honour, [1679]. (Printed from a manuscript.)

Peter Murray Hill Ltd. Catalogue No. 67, spring 1959 (item 42, p. 34), describes a copy of this folio leaflet in which "By Rochest'" is written on the first page in a contemporary hand.

A-1680-HU, p. 19: "A Letter fancy'd from Artemisa in the Town, to Cloe in the Country"; ascribed to Rochester. Reprinted with ascription to Rochester in the other A-1680 editions and in A-1685, p. 19; A-1701, p. 18; A-1713, p. 19; A-1731, p. 18. (A few readings in A-1701 have been corrected from another source, probably B-1691 or B-1696.)

The Triumph of Wit, 1688 (not in Case), p. 203: no title; no ascription. Fragment of 12 lines beginning "You smile to see me, whom the World perchance." (Possibly printed from A-1685.)

B-1691, p. 65: "A Letter, From Artemisa In the Town, To Cloe In the Country"; ascribed to Rochester. Reprinted with ascription to Rochester in B-1696, p. 62; B-1705, p. 62; B-1714, p. 36; B-1732, p. 36; B-1710-P, p. 26; B-1718-P, p. 29. (The text in B-1691 is conflated from one of the A-1680 editions and some other source or sources, probably a manuscript.)

Poems on Affairs of State, 1698 (Case 215), p. 25: "Satyr by the Lord Rochester." Fragment of 83 lines beginning "You Smile to see me (whom the World per chance." (Printed from a manuscript.)

ADDITIONAL NOTES: Pinto reports a text of this poem in the "Portland Miscellany" (*Poems*, p. 186).

Giles Jacob ascribes the poem to Rochester and quotes 6 lines of its text (*Poetical Register*, 2, 235). The source of his information is uncertain.

PREVIOUS SCHOLARSHIP: Printed as Rochester's by Hayward (*Collected Works*, p. 26) and Johns (*Poetical Works*, p. 45). Attributed to Rochester by Prinz (*Rochester*, p. 147), Pinto (*Rochester*, pp. 136–43; *Poems*, p. 79), Wilson (*Court Wits*, pp. 73, 131, 136), and Thorpe (*Rochester's Poems*, p. 173).

NAKED SHE LAY, CLASPT IN MY LONGING ARMS

AUTHOR: Rochester.

TEXTS:

Yale MS., p. 62: "The Imperfect Enjoyment By ye E: of R:." All but the title and first 12 lines have been removed by the second gap, pp. 63–66.

Harvard MS. Eng. 636F, p. 114: "Imperfect Enjoyment"; signed "Rochester."

Bodl. MS. Add. B. 106, fol. 39^r: "The Imperfect Enjoym^t."; ascribed to Rochester. (Copied from one of the A-1680 editions.)

Edinburgh MS. DC.1.3, p. 16: "The Imperfect Injoyment"; no ascription.

A-1680-HU, p. 28: "The Imperfect Enjoyment"; ascribed to
   Rochester. Reprinted with ascription to Rochester in the
   other A-1680 editions and in A-1685, p. 28; A-1701, p. 26;
   A-1713, p. 28; A-1731, p. 26.

C-1714-1, p. 114: "The Disappointment"; ascribed to Rochester. Reprinted with ascription to Rochester in later editions
   in this series. (The 1714 text was printed from one of the
   A-1680 editions.)

ADDITIONAL NOTES: Pinto reports a text of this poem in the
   "Portland Miscellany" (*Poems*, p. 179).
     The poem is attributed to Rochester by Giles Jacob, whose
   information almost certainly derives from an edition in the
   C series (*Poetical Register*, 2, 233).

PREVIOUS SCHOLARSHIP: Printed as Rochester's by Hayward
   (*Collected Works*, pp. xiii, 71) and Johns (*Poetical Works*,
   p. 166). Attributed to Rochester by Prinz (*Rochester*, p.
   144), Wilson (*Court Wits*, pp. 100–01), Thorpe (*Rochester's Poems*, p. 173), and Pinto (*Poems*, p. 44).

OH LOVE! HOW COLD, AND
SLOW TO TAKE MY PART

AUTHOR: Rochester.

TEXTS:

Yale MS., p. 67: "To Love. By yᵉ E: of R: O! Nunquam pro
   me satis indignate Cupido."

Harvard MS. Eng. 636F, p. 58: "To Love. Cunnquam pme
   Satis indignate Cupido"; signed "Rochester."

Illinois MS. (uncatalogued): "Ovid: Amor: lib: 2ᵈ. Eleg: 9
   O nunquam pro me satis indignate Cupido!"; no ascription.

Bodl. MS. Rawl. Poet. 173, fol. 48ᵛ: "Lib: 2. Eleg: 9ᵗʰ. To

Love. By L^d. Rochester." (Probably copied from a printed text.)

Cambridge MS. Add. 6339, fol. 20^r: "A Translation of the 9th Elegy of Ovids 2^d Book of Amorum. O nunquam pro me satis indignate Cupido. By Ld Rochester."

A-1680-HU, p. 30: "To Love. O! nunquam pro me satis indignate Cupido"; ascribed to Rochester. Reprinted with ascription to Rochester in the other A-1680 editions and in A-1685, p. 30; A-1701, p. 28; A-1713, p. 31; A-1731, p. 29.

Miscellany Poems, 1684 (Case 172-1-a), p. [1]135: "Elegy the Ninth. Englished By the late Earl of Rochester. To Love." Reprinted with ascription to Rochester in 1692 (Case 172-1-b), p. 133, and 1692 (Case 172-1-c), p. 133. (Though the textual evidence is inconclusive, the 1684 version may be conflated from one of the A-1680 editions and a manuscript.)

B-1691, p. 111: "The Ninth Elegy In the second Book of Ovid's Amours, Translated. To Love"; ascribed to Rochester. Reprinted with ascription to Rochester in B-1696, p. 108; B-1705, p. 107; B-1714, p. 73; B-1732, p. 73; B-1710-P, p. 47; B-1718-P, p. 58. (The text in B-1691 was printed from *Miscellany Poems,* 1684. Both volumes were published by Jacob Tonson.)

Ovid's Epistles: with His Amours, 1725 (Case 165-k), p. 282: "Elegy IX. To Love. By the late Earl of Rochester." Reprinted with ascription to Rochester in 1727 (Case 165-l), p. 263; 1729 (Case 165-m), p. 281; 1736 (not in Case), p. 280; 1748 (Case 165-n), p. 280. Wilson (*Court Wits,* p. 90) states incorrectly that the poem appears in the first edition, 1680 (Case 165). (The 1725 text derives from the version in *Miscellany Poems,* 1684, or one of its printed descendants—all issued, like the volume of 1725, by the Tonson publishing house.)

ADDITIONAL NOTES: Pinto reports that a text of this poem, headed "Ovid," appears in the "Portland Miscellany" (*Poems*, p. 179).

Anthony Wood, attributing the poem to Rochester, cites B-1691 and *Miscellany Poems*, 1684, as his sources (*Athenae Oxonienses*, 3, 1232).

PREVIOUS SCHOLARSHIP: Printed as Rochester's by Hayward (*Collected Works*, p. 47), Johns (*Poetical Works*, p. 76), and Pinto (*Poems*, p. 47). Attributed to Rochester by Prinz (*Rochester*, p. 111), Wilson (*Court Wits*, p. 90), and Thorpe (*Rochester's Poems*, p. 174).

AS SOME BRAVE ADMIRAL, IN FORMER WAR

AUTHOR: Rochester.

TEXTS:

Yale MS., p. 71: "Upon his lyeing in & cou'd not drinke. By ye E: of R:."

Osborn MS. Chest 11, Number 3, p. 178: "L^d: R:^{s} Ghost."

Harvard MS. Eng. 636F, p. 1: "The Disabled Debauchee"; signed "Rochester."

B. M. Add. MS. 14047, fol. 130^v: "By my L^d. Buckhurst:—."

B. M. Add. MS. 23722, fol. 52^r: "The Disabled Debauchee by ye E. of Rochester 1675."

Bodl. MS. Rawl. Poet. 81, fol. 22^r: "My Ld Rochest^{rs}." This text is followed by a Latin translation of the poem, beginning "Qualis abexacto Dux classis marte solutus."

Bodl. MS. Eng. Poet. e. 4, p. 187: "The disabled Debauchee"; signed "John E Rochester."

Bodl. MS. Don. b. 8, p. 409: "The disabled Debauchee by ye same" (Rochester).

Edinburgh MS. DC.1.3, p. 77: "The Disabled Debauch"; no ascription.

A-1680-HU, p. 32: "The Maim'd Debauchee"; ascribed to Rochester. Reprinted with ascription to Rochester in the other A-1680 editions and in A-1685, p. 32; A-1701, p. 30; A-1713, p. 33; A-1731, p. 31.

Female Poems On Several Occasions. Written by Ephelia, 2d ed., 1682, p. 142: "The Maim'd Debauchee"; ascribed to Ephelia. (Printed from one of the A-1680 editions.)

B-1691, p. 100: "The Maim'd Debauchee"; ascribed to Rochester. Reprinted with ascription to Rochester in B-1696, p. 97; B-1705, p. 96; B-1714, p. 66; B-1732, p. 66; B-1710-P, p. 41; B-1718-P, p. 46. (The text in B-1691 was printed from one of the A-1680 editions with some readings corrected from a manuscript.)

ADDITIONAL NOTE: Pinto reports that a text of this poem, headed "The Disabled Debauch," appears in the "Portland Miscellany" (*Poems,* pp. 184, 185).

PREVIOUS SCHOLARSHIP: Printed as Rochester's by Hayward (*Collected Works,* p. 41) and Johns (*Poetical Works,* p. 66). Attributed to Rochester by Prinz (*Rochester,* pp. 107, 127–28), Pinto (*Rochester,* pp. 134–36; *Poems,* p. 75), and Thorpe (*Rochester's Poems,* p. 174).

SAY HEAV'N-BORN MUSE, FOR ONLY THOU CANST TELL

AUTHOR: Uncertain; not Rochester (see Chapter 6).

TEXTS:

Yale MS., p. 76: "The Argument"; no ascription. All but the title and first 12 lines have been removed by the third gap, pp. 77–86. (In section of poems by or concerning Rochester.)

Harvard MS. Eng. 636F, p. 220: "The Argument"; signed "Rochester."

A-1680-HU, p. 35: "The Argument"; ascribed to Rochester. Reprinted with ascription to Rochester in the other A-1680 editions but omitted from A-1685, A-1701, A-1713, and A-1731.

In A-1680-S-S (Sterling copy), a marginal note in a contemporary hand identifies "R——" in l. 15 as "Rochester."

C-1714-1, p. 85: "Bath Intrigues. The Argument"; ascribed to Rochester. Reprinted with ascription to Rochester in later editions in this series. (The 1714 text was printed from one of the A-1680 editions.)

ADDITIONAL NOTE: Attributed to Rochester by Giles Jacob, whose information derives from an edition in the C series (*Poetical Register*, 2, 232).

PREVIOUS SCHOLARSHIP: Omitted by Hayward (*Collected Works*, p. xiii), Johns (*Poetical Works*), and Pinto (*Poems*). Rochester's authorship doubted by Prinz, who suggests that Alexander Radcliffe might have written the poem (*Rochester*, p. 150). Rochester's authorship doubted by Thorpe (*Rochester's Poems*, p. 174).

WELL SIR, 'TIS GRANTED, I SAID D—— RHIMES

AUTHOR: Rochester (see Chapter 5).

TEXTS:

Yale MS., p. 87. The title and first 4 lines of this text have been removed by the third gap, pp. 77–86. (In section of poems by or concerning Rochester.)

Osborn MS. Chest II, Number 14, p. 974: "A Satyr against the present poetts Being an Allusion to Horrace Satyr: x: Booke: 1: Nempe in composito Dixi pedi: &c: Written by the Earle of Rochester 1677." Includes marginal notations identifying some of the persons satirized.

Harvard MS. Eng. 623F, p. 28: "A Satyr On the Poets"; signed "Rochester."

Harvard MS. Eng. 636F, p. 40: "An Imitation of the 10th Satire Hor: 1th. Lib. Nempe Incomposito dixi pede currere &c."; signed "Rochester."

Illinois MS. 30 Je 45 Stonehill, p. 209: "Rotchestrs censures of the poets."

B. M. Sloane MS. 655, fol. 51^r: "An Allusion to Horace, The xth: Satyr: of the 1st: Booke. Nempe incomposito dixi dede &c"; no ascription.

B. M. Sloane MS. 1504, fol. 69^r: "An allusion to Horace the 10th: Satyr of the first Booke.—Nempe incomposito dixi pede"; no ascription. At end of poem: "Amsterdam. Oct: 8 / 79 Capt: Stead gave ye Copy:."

B. M. Add. MS. 18220, fol. 121^r: "Nempe incomposito dixi pede currere versus Lucili &c"; signed "Ld Rochester."

B. M. Add. MS. 34362, fol. 84^r: "An Allusion to Horace y° 10th Satyr Nempe incomposito dixi pede &c."; no ascription.

B. M. Harl. MS. 6947, fol. 199^r: "An Allusion to Horace, The xth Satyr of the first Book. Nempe incomposito dixi pede, &c."; no ascription. Includes only the first 62 lines of the poem.

Bodl. MS. Add. B. 106, fol. 5^r: "By the E. of Rochester In imitation of the tenth Satyr of the first booke of Horace's Sermons Nempe incomposito dixi pede currere versus." (The ascription, title, and first 85 lines of this copy are apparently independent of printed texts. Another hand, or the same hand at a later date, has added the rest of the poem and corrected some readings in ll. 1–85, probably from one of the A-1680 editions.)

Cambridge MS. Add. 42, fol. 106^r: "An Alusion to Horace: Sermon: lib: ye session of the poetes"; no ascription.

Cambridge MS. Add. 6339, fol. 13^r: "The Session of Poets by Ld Rochester."

A-1680-HU, p. 40: "An Allusion to Horace. The 10th Satyr of the 1st. Book. Nempe incomposito Dixi pede &c."; ascribed to Rochester. Reprinted with ascription to Rochester in the other A-1680 editions and in A-1685, p. 35; A-1701, p. 32; A-1713, p. 35; A-1731, p. 33.

C-1707-a, p. ^{1}18: "Horace's 10th Satyr of the First Book Imitated. Nempe incomposito Dixi Pede, &c."; ascribed to Rochester. Reissued in C-1707-b, p. ^{2}18, and reprinted with ascription to Rochester in C-1709, p. ^{2}15; C-1709-P, p. ^{2}1; C-1714-1, p. 10; and later editions in this series. (The text in C-1707-a was printed from a manuscript.)

B-1714, p. 87: "An Allusion to The 10th Satyr of the 1st Book of Horace"; ascribed to Rochester. Reprinted with ascription to Rochester in B-1732, p. 87. (The text in B-1714 is conflated from an edition in the C series, probably C-1709, and from A-1685, A-1701, or A-1713, probably A-1685.)

The Odes and Satires of Horace, 1715 (Case 286), p. 169: "Satyr x. Nempe Incomposito dixi Pede currere Versus Lucili"; no ascription. Reprinted with the additional note "Printed in Rochester's Poems in Twelves" in 1715 (Case 287), p. 161; 1717 (Case 287-b), p. 161; 1721 (Case 287-c), p. 161; 1730 (Case 287-d), p. 161; Dublin 1730 (not in Case), p. 170. (The text in Case 286 was printed from an edition in the C series. "Rochester's Poems in Twelves" is evidently B-1714, which, like Case 287, was published by Jacob Tonson.)

B-1718-P, p. 19: "Horace's Nempe incomposito dixi pede, &c. Imitated"; ascribed to Rochester. (Printed from an edition in the C series.)

ADDITIONAL NOTES: Pinto reports a text of this poem in the "Portland Miscellany" (*Poems*, p. 192).

Dryden evidently attributes "An Allusion to Horace" to Rochester in the preface to *All for Love*, 1678, sigs. b3ᵛ–b4ᵛ (pub. March 1678). Years later, in his dedication to Dorset of *The Satires of Decimus Junius Juvenalis*, 1693 (p. iii), Dryden ascribes the poem to "an Author of your own Quality, (whose Ashes I will not disturb,)."

The passage on Dryden in "Rochester's Ghost" ("From the deep-vaulted Den of endless Night"), written about 1682, implies both that Rochester wrote "An Allusion to Horace" and that Dryden had attributed it to him in the preface to *All for Love* (*Poems on Affairs of State*, 1703 [Case 211-2-a], pp. 130–31).

"An Allusion to Horace" is assigned to Rochester in *The Medal of John Bayes*, 1682, probably by Shadwell (*The Complete Works of Thomas Shadwell*, ed. Montague Summers, London, Fortune Press, 1927, 5, 254); in *The Tory-Poets*, 1682, doubtfully attributed to Shadwell (Summers, *Works of Shadwell*, 5, 281); and in Crowne's "The Epistle to the Reader" prefixed to his *Caligula*, 1698 (*The Dramatic Works of John Crowne*, ed. James Maidment and W. H. Logan, Edinburgh, W. Paterson, 1873–74, 4, 353–54).

Giles Jacob includes "An Allusion to Horace" in his list of Rochester's poems, which he apparently copied from C-1714-1 (*Poetical Register*, 2, 232; see also 1, 242–43 and 2, 174). Also probably derived from earlier printed sources are the ascriptions to Rochester by Gerard Langbaine (*An Account of*

the English Dramatick Poets, 1691, pp. 325–26, 486–87);
by George Granville, Lord Lansdown (*Genuine Works,*
1732, *1,* 433, 434); by Theophilus Cibber (*Lives of the
Poets, 3,* 97, 255–56); and by Alexander Pope (Joseph
Spence, *Anecdotes,* ed. Samuel Weller Singer, London, 1820,
pp. 200–01, 281).

PREVIOUS SCHOLARSHIP: Printed as Rochester's by Hayward
(*Collected Works,* p. 55) and Johns (*Poetical Works,* p. 91).
Attributed to Rochester by J. Woodfall Ebsworth (*Roxburghe
Ballads, 4* [Hertford, Ballad Society, 1883], 569–70), Prinz
(*Rochester,* pp. 69–70, 72–73, 74–75, 84, 85, 98, 102, 111,
116–18, 142, 159, 162, 199), Pinto (*Rochester,* pp. 154–58;
Poems, pp. xxiv, xxvi, xxix, 95), Wilson (*Court Wits,* pp. 9,
99, 114, 147, 154–55, 182, 185–90, 237; "Rochester, Dryden,
and the Rose-Street Affair," *Review of English Studies, 15*
[1939], 294–301), and Thorpe (*Rochester's Poems,* pp.
174–75).

WHEN SHAKES. JOHNS. FLETCHER, RUL'D THE STAGE

AUTHOR: Sir Carr Scroope (see Chapter 5).

TEXTS:

Yale MS., p. 95: "In defence of Satyr"; no ascription. (In
section of poems by or concerning Rochester.)

Osborn MS. Chest 11, Number 14, p. 1011: "The occasion off S^r
Car Scroops writing this ensuing poem, was upon a satyr off
the Lord Rochesters against the poetts, in which he abuses
him: vid: pag: 977: In Defence of Satyr, writt by Sr Carr
Scroope 1677." Includes marginal notations identifying some
of the persons satirized.

Harvard MS. Eng. 623F, p. 33: "In Defence of Satyr"; signed "Scroop." Includes marginal notations identifying some of the persons satirized.

Harvard MS. Eng. 636F, p. 46: "In Defence of Satyre"; indirectly attributed to Scroope, since "The Answer" is ascribed to him in this manuscript (p. 53). Includes marginal notations identifying some of the persons satirized.

Folger MS. 789.4: "In Defence of Satyr"; no ascription. Includes marginal notations identifying some of the persons satirized.

B. M. Add. MS. 34362, fol. 82^r: "In Defence of Satyr"; no ascription.

B. M. Egerton MS. 2623, fol. 87^r: "In defence of Satyr"; no ascription.

Bodl. MS. Rawl. Poet. 172, fol. 108^r: no title. In the righthand margin near the end of this copy, another hand, or possibly the same hand at a later date, has written what appears to be "Satyre by E. Rochr." (Though this text is independent of printed sources, the ascription must be suspected of derivation from some edition which assigns the poem to Rochester.)

Bodl. MS. Rawl. Poet. 173, fol. 135^r: "A Satyr upon the Follies & vices of the Age By the D. of B." Omits the last 4 lines. (Copied from Buckingham's *Works*, 1704 or 1707.)

Bodl. MS. Add. B. 106, fol. 42^v: "In Defence of Satyr"; ascribed to Rochester. (Probably copied from one of the A-1680 editions.)

Bodl. MS. Don. b. 8, p. 710: "In defence of Satyrs"; no ascription.

Bodl. MS. Rawl. A. 341, fol. 133^v: "In Defence of Satyr"; no ascription.

Bodl. MS. Ballard 50, fol. 134^r: "In Defence of Satyr"; no ascription. Includes only the first 47 lines.

Edinburgh MS. DC.1.3, p. 12: "In defence of satyr"; indirectly attributed to Scroope, since "Answer'd By Sʳ Charles
scroop" is the second poem following in this manuscript
(p. 14).

A-1680-HU, p. 45: "In defence of Satyr"; ascribed to Rochester.
Reprinted with ascription to Rochester in the other A-1680
editions and in A-1685, p. 39; A-1701, p. 36; A-1713, p. 40;
A-1731, p. 37.

William Winstanley, *The Lives Of the most Famous English
Poets*, 1687, p. 198: "in Defence of Satyr"; ascribed to
Rochester. Includes only the first 45 lines. (Probably derived
from one of the A-1680 editions.)

Thomas Pope Blount, *De Re Poetica*, 1694, p. 44. Includes
only the first 13 lines of the poem, after which is printed:
"Earl of Rochester in Defence of Satyr." (Probably derived
from an edition in the A series.)

*Miscellaneous Works, Written by His Grace, George, Late
Duke of Buckingham*, 1704 (Case 232-1-a), p. ¹47: "A Satyr
upon the Follys of the Men of the Age. By the Duke of
Buckingham. Ascrib'd falsly to the Earl of R." Reprinted
with ascription to Buckingham in 1707 (Case 232-1-b), p. ¹47.
Reprinted with ascription to "the Duke of Buckingham, and
the Earl of Rochester" in *The Works Of His Grace, George
Villiers, Late Duke of Buckingham*, 1715, *1, 155*. Reprinted
in later editions of this collection with ascriptions to Buckingham and Rochester or to Buckingham alone. (The 1704 text
was printed from one of the A-1680 editions.)

B-1714, p. 96: "The following Verses were written by Sir Car.
Scrope, on his being reflected upon at the latter End of the
foregoing Copy. In Defence of Satyr." Reprinted with ascription to Scroope in B-1732, p. 96. (The text in B-1714 was

conflated from a manuscript, from A-1685, and possibly also from A-1701 or A-1713.)

C-1714-1, p. 75: "In Defence of Satire." Though this text includes no direct indication that the poem is not by Rochester, the same volume elsewhere ascribes to him "An Answer to the Defence of Satire, written by Sir C. Scroop" (p. 59). Later editions in this series reprint "In Defence of Satire" with ascription to Scroope. (The text in C-1714-1 was printed from one of the A-1680 editions.)

ADDITIONAL NOTES: Pinto reports that a text of this poem in the "Portland Miscellany" carries an ascription to "Scroop" (*Poems*, p. 224).

C-1707-a prints, from a manuscript source, "An Answer to the Defence of Satyr Written by Sir C. Scroop" (p. ¹12).

In Anthony Wood's *Fasti Oxonienses* (*4*, 294), a passage added in the posthumous 2d ed., 1721, attributes "In Defence of Satyr" to Scroope. The source of the ascription is said to be a "MS. in Mr. Sheldon's libr."

Giles Jacob (*Poetical Register*, *2*, 232–33) lists "A Defence of Satire" among Rochester's poems but immediately afterward attributes to Rochester the "Answer to the Defence of Satire, written by Sir C. S." Jacob's information is, in any case, almost certainly derived from C-1714-1.

Horace Walpole attributes the poem to Buckingham and Rochester but indicates Buckingham's 1715 *Works* as his source (*Catalogue of Royal and Noble Authors*, *2*, 77, 79).

PREVIOUS SCHOLARSHIP: Omitted by Johns (*Poetical Works*). Attributed to Scroope by J. Woodfall Ebsworth (*Roxburghe Ballads*, *4* [Hertford, Ballad Society, 1883], 570), Hayward (*Collected Works*, pp. xxxii, 361), Prinz (*Rochester*, pp. 97–

98, 119, 154), Wilson (*Court Wits*, pp. 112–13, 114–15, 224), and Thorpe (*Rochester's Poems*, pp. 174–75). Attributed by Pinto to "Rochester in collaboration with Buckingham" (*Poems*, pp. 137, 223–25).

TO RACK, AND TORTURE
THY UNMEANING BRAIN

Author: Rochester (see Chapter 5).

Texts:

Yale MS., p. 102: "On ye suppos'd Author of a late Poem in defence of Satyr"; no ascription. (In section of poems by or concerning Rochester.)

Osborn MS. Chest 11, Number 14, p. 1021: "on the Supposed Author off the Defence off Satyr: vid: pag: 1012: 1677." At end of poem: "writt by the Lord Rochester."

Harvard MS. Eng. 623F, p. 37: "On the Author of the Defence of Satyr"; signed "Rochester."

Harvard MS. Eng. 636F, p. 51: "To the Supposed Author of A Late Poem in Defence of Satyre"; signed "Roch."

Bodl. MS. Rawl. D. 1171, fol. 40^v: "On a Poet who writ in Praise of Satyr, by ye Earl of Rochet." (Copied from *A Collection of Poems By Several Hands*, 1693, or a later edition of this miscellany.)

Edinburgh MS. DC.1.3, p. 13: "Answer to the Defence of Satyr"; signed "Rochester."

A-1680-HU, p. 49: "On the suppos'd Authour of a late Poem in defence of Satyr"; ascribed to Rochester. Reprinted with ascription to Rochester in the other A-1680 editions and in A-1685, p. 43; A-1701, p. 39; A-1713, p. 44; A-1731, p. 41.

A Collection of Poems By Several Hands, 1693 (Case 151-c), p. 111: "On a Poet Who Writ in the Praise of Satyr. By the

Earl of Rochester." Reprinted with ascription to Rochester
in 1695 (Case 151-d), p. 111; 1701 (Case 151-e), p. 101;
1702 (Case 151-f), p. 101; 1716 (Case 151-g), p. 82. (The
1693 text was printed from a manuscript.)

C-1707-a, p. [1]12: "An Answer to the Defence of Satyr Written
by Sir C. Scroop"; ascribed to Rochester. Reissued in C-
1707-b, p. [2]12, and reprinted with ascription to Rochester in
C-1709, p. [2]96; C-1709-P, p. [3]8; C-1714-1, p. 59; and later
editions in this series. (The text in C-1707-a was printed from
a manuscript with some readings possibly corrected from one
of the A-1680 editions.)

B-1714, p. 100: "On the suppos'd Author of a late Poem in
Defence of Satyr"; ascribed to Rochester. Reprinted with
ascription to Rochester in B-1732, p. 100. (The text in B-1714
was printed from one of the A-1680 editions.)

ADDITIONAL NOTES: Pinto reports a text of this poem in the
"Portland Miscellany" (*Poems*, p. 223).

In Anthony Wood's *Athenae Oxonienses* (*3*, 1232), a
passage added in the posthumous 2d ed., 1721, lists "On the
supposed Author" among Rochester's unpublished satires.
Since this listing errs in describing the poem as unpublished,
its ascription apparently derives from a manuscript source
and therefore represents independent testimony.

Horace Walpole attributes "On the supposed Author" to
Rochester but indicates *Athenae Oxonienses* as his source
(*Catalogue of Royal and Noble Authors*, *2*, 38–39, 41). Giles
Jacob's ascription to Rochester apparently derives from an
edition in the C series (*Poetical Register*, *2*, 233).

PREVIOUS SCHOLARSHIP: Printed as Rochester's by Hayward
(*Collected Works*, p. 62) and Johns (*Poetical Works*, p. 135).
Attributed to Rochester by J. Woodfall Ebsworth (*Rox-*

burghe Ballads, 4 [Hertford, Ballad Society, 1883], 570–71),
Prinz (*Rochester,* pp. 119–20), Wilson (*Court Wits,* pp.
115, 233), and Thorpe (*Rochester's Poems,* pp. 174–75). Attributed by Pinto to Rochester or "some collector of Rochesteriana like the editor of 1680" (*Poems,* pp. 141, 223–25).

RAILE ON POORE FEEBLE SCRIBLER, SPEAK OF ME

AUTHOR: Sir Carr Scroope (see Chapter 5).

TEXTS:

Yale MS., p. 105: "The Answer"; no ascription. (In section of
poems by or concerning Rochester.)

Osborn MS. Chest II, Number 14, p. 1022: "The Authors
Reply"; indirectly attributed to Scroope, since the title refers
to the "author" of "In Defence of Satyr," which is assigned
to Scroope in this manuscript (p. 1011).

Harvard MS. Eng. 623F, p. 38: "Answer to the foregoing
verses"; signed "Scroop."

Harvard MS. Eng. 636F, p. 53: "The Answer by S^r. S: C."

Edinburgh MS. DC.1.3, p. 14: "Answer'd By Sr Charles
scroop"; signed "S. C. S."

A-1680-HU, p. 50: "The Answer"; ascribed to Rochester. Reprinted with ascription to Rochester in the other A-1680
editions and in A-1685, p. 44; A-1701, p. 41; A-1713, p. 45;
A-1731, p. 42.

ADDITIONAL NOTE: Pinto reports a text of this poem in the
"Portland Miscellany" (*Poems,* p. 223).

PREVIOUS SCHOLARSHIP: Omitted by Johns (*Poetical Works*).
Attributed to Scroope by J. Woodfall Ebsworth (*Roxburghe
Ballads, 4* [Hertford, Ballad Society, 1883], 571), Hayward

(*Collected Works,* pp. 313, 361), Prinz (*Rochester,* p. 120), Wilson (*Court Wits,* p. 115), and Thorpe, "although the evidence is thin" (*Rochester's Poems,* pp. 175–76). Attributed by Pinto to Rochester or "some collector of Rochesteriana like the editor of 1680" (*Poems,* pp. 142, 223–25).

AFTER DEATH, NOTHING IS, AND NOTHING, DEATH

AUTHOR: Rochester.

TEXTS:

Yale MS., p. 106: "Senecas Troas Act 2ᵈ Chor:"; no ascription. (In section of poems by or concerning Rochester.)

Osborn MS. Chest II, Number 28: "Seneca: Tros: Act: 2. Chorus"; no ascription. Appears on a single loose sheet.

Osborn MS. Box XXII, Number 8, p. 10: "On Death by my Lord Rochester." (Possibly copied from one of the A-1680 editions.)

Harvard MS. Eng. 586: "Seneca's Troas, Chorus of the 2ᵈ Act Post Mortem nihil est, ipsaque Mors nihil &c. Translated by yᵉ Earl of Rochester." (Probably copied from an edition in the B series.)

Harvard MS. Eng. 636F, p. 79: "A Paraphrase upon Seneca Trag. Act: 2ᵈ. Chorus Finem Versus. Post Mortam nihill est, ipsaqᵉ morse nihill &c."; signed "Rochester."

Harvard MS. Eng. 652F, fol. 61ʳ: no title; no ascription.

Bodl. MS. Don. b. 8, p. 498: "Seneca's Troas. Act. 2. Chorus"; no ascription.

Edinburgh MS. DC.1.3, p. 17: "Post Nihil Mortem &ᶜ."; no ascription.

A-1680-HU, p. 50: "Seneca's Troas, Act. 2. Chorus"; ascribed to Rochester. Reprinted with ascription to Rochester in the

other A-1680 editions but omitted from A-1685, A-1701,
A-1713, and A-1731.

B-1691, p. 119: "The latter end of the Chorus of the second
Act of Seneca's Troas translated"; ascribed to Rochester. Reprinted with ascription to Rochester in B-1696, p. 116;
B-1705, p. 115; B-1714, p. 79; B-1732, p. 79; B-1710-P,
p. 51. Omitted from B-1718-P. (The 1691 text was probably
printed from one of the A-1680 editions.)

ADDITIONAL NOTES: Pinto reports that a text of this poem,
headed "Seneca's Troas, Act 2, Chorus," appears in the
"Portland Miscellany" (*Poems*, p. 179).

Charles Blount, writing to "Strephon" (Rochester) on 7
February 1679/80, unmistakably refers to this poem as
Rochester's (*The Miscellaneous Works of Charles Blount,
Esq.*, 1695, p. [1]117):

> I Had the Honour Yesterday to receive from the Hands
> of an Humble Servant of your Lordship's, your most
> incomperable Version of that Passage of *Seneca*'s, where
> he begins with,—*Post mortem nihil est, ipsaque mors
> nihil*, &c.—and must confess, with your Lor[d]ship's
> Pardon, that I cannot but esteem the Translation to be,
> in some measure, a confutation of the Original; since
> what less than a divine and immortal Mind could have
> produced what you have there written? Indeed, the
> Hand that wrote it may become *Lumber*, but sure, the
> Spirit that dictated it, can never be so: No, my Lord,
> your mighty Genius is a most sufficient Argument of its
> own Immortality; and more prevalent with me, than
> all the Harangues of the Parsons, or Sophistry of the
> Schoolmen.

PREVIOUS SCHOLARSHIP: Attributed to Rochester by Hayward (*Collected Works*, p. 48), Johns (*Poetical Works*, p. 80), Prinz (*Rochester*, pp. 111, 232–33), Pinto ("Rochester and the Deists," *London Times Literary Supplement*, 13 December 1934, p. 895; *Rochester*, pp. 210–13; *Poems*, pp. xxxii, 49), Wilson (*Court Wits*, p. 202), and Thorpe (*Rochester's Poems*, p. 176).

NOTHING THOU ELDER BROTHER EV'N TO SHADE

AUTHOR: Rochester.

TEXTS:

Yale MS., p. 108: "Upon Nothing"; no ascription. (In section of poems by or concerning Rochester.)

Osborn MS. Chest 11, Number 4, p. 25: "Upon Nothing, by ye Earl of Rochester."

Osborn MS. Chest 11, Number 13, volume 2, p. 173: "Upon Nothing—Composed by ye Earle of Rochester." At end of poem: "from Tho: Rainton. 14th. May. 1678."

Harvard MS. Eng. 623F (bound volume), p. 10: "Upon Nothing"; signed "Rochester."

Harvard MS. Eng. 623F (loose sheet): "Uppon Nothing"; no ascription.

Harvard MS. Eng. 636F, p. 55: "Upon Nothing"; signed "Rochester."

Illinois MS. (uncatalogued): "Upon Nothing by y^e. E. of R."

B. M. Add. MS. 4457, fol. 43^r: "On Nothing"; signed "Rochester." At end of poem: "This Autograph of the eminent D^r. John Nalson was given me by his Son the Rev^{ed}. & Ingenious M^r. Val: Nalson Preb: of York 1710."

B. M. Add. MS. 29497, fol. 48ʳ: "Uppon Nothing"; no ascription.

B. M. Add. MS. 30162, fol 1ᵛ: "Upon Nothing—by Lord Rochester."

Bodl. MS. Rawl. Poet. 90, fol. 106ʳ: "Upon Nothinge"; no ascription.

Bodl. MS. Rawl. Poet. 173, fol. 151ᵛ: "Upon Nothing. By Lᵈ. Rochᵗʳ:." (Probably copied from an edition in the B series, though two readings may have been corrected from another source.)

Bodl. MS. Add. B. 106, fol. 19ᵛ: "Upon Nothing, or Somewhat of Nothing." In margin beside title: "Rochester." (Though this copy includes interlinear corrections evidently taken from one of the A-1680 editions, its original text and probably its title and ascription derive from a manuscript source.)

Bodl. MS. Tanner 306, fol. 410ʳ: "Upon Nothing"; no ascription.

Bodl. MS. Don. b. 8, p. 654: "Rochesters Verses upon nothing."

Bodl. MS. Sancroft 53, p. 68: "E. R. Upō Nothḡ, aftʳ much Ateism, ends thus:." Last 6 lines only. (Possibly copied from a printed source.)

Cambridge MS. Add. 6339, fol. 12ʳ: "Upon Nothing Lᵈ Rochester."

Lambeth Codices Manuscripti Gibsoniani 941, item 116: "Upon Nothing"; no ascription.

Edinburgh MS. DC.1.3, p. 11: "on Nothing"; no ascription.

Upon Nothing. A Poem. By a Person of Honour, [1679].

In a copy of this broadside at the University of Texas, a contemporary hand has glossed *"a Person of Honour"* as "John Earl of Rochester."

Upon Nothing A Poem. By a Person of Honour, [1679]. Differs from the other broadside of 1679 in reading "Life" instead of "Light" in l. 15. Though the two broadsides exhibit few verbal variants, they were printed from entirely separate settings of type. (Probably one of these two broadsides was printed from the other, or both were set from the same manuscript. In its variants against the "Light" broadside, the one reading "Life" usually presents a deteriorated text.)

In a copy of this broadside at the University of Texas, a contemporary hand has glossed *"a Person of Honour"* as "L^d. Rochester."

A-1680-HU, p. 51: "Upon Nothing"; ascribed to Rochester. Reprinted with ascription to Rochester in the other A-1680 editions and in A-1713, p. 129, and A-1731, p. 117. Omitted from A-1685 and A-1701.

Wit and Drollery, 1682 (Case 114-c), p. 120: "The New Nothing"; no ascription. (Probably printed from one of the A-1680 editions.)

Rome Rhym'd to Death, 1683 (Case 170), p. 126: "Upon Nothing. By the E. of R." (Printed from the "Life" broadside of 1679. The ascription may derive from the A-1680 editions.)

Poems by Several Hands, and on Several Occasions Collected by N. Tate, 1685 (Case 181), p. 5: "Upon Nothing, By the Late Earl of Rochester." (Printed from one of the A-1680 editions.)

B-1691, p. 104: "Upon Nothing"; ascribed to Rochester. Reprinted with ascription to Rochester in B-1696, p. 101; B-1705, p. 100; B-1714, p. 68; B-1732, p. 68; B-1710-P, p. 43; B-1718-P, p. 49. (The 1691 text was printed from one of the A-1680 editions.)

Upon Nothing. A Poem. By the Right Honourable, John late Earl of Rochester, 1711, p. 5: "Upon Nothing. A Poem."

(Printed from one of the broadsides of 1679 with a few readings probably corrected from one of the editions in the B series, which are violently attacked in the "Advertisement," pp. [3]–[4].)

C-1714-1, p. 72: "Upon Nothing"; ascribed to Rochester. Reprinted with ascription to Rochester in later editions in this series. (The 1714 text was printed from one of the A-1680 editions, though one or two readings may have been corrected from another source.)

The Works Of His Grace, George Villiers, Late Duke of Buckingham, 1715, *1*, 149: "Upon Nothing: A Poem. By the Duke of Buckingham, and the Earl of Rochester." Reprinted in at least one later edition of this collection (1775) with ascription to Buckingham and Rochester. (Though it is closely related to the broadsides of 1679, the 1715 text was probably printed from a manuscript.)

The Windsor Medley, 1731 (Case 371), p. 49: "Upon Nothing"; no ascription. (Derived from A-1680-HU or one of its descendants, though a few readings may have been corrected from another source.)

ADDITIONAL NOTES: Pinto reports a text of this poem in the "Portland Miscellany" (*Poems,* p. 185).

"Upon Nothing" is attributed to Rochester in Anthony Wood's *Athenae Oxonienses* (*3*, 1230). Joseph Addison's ascription to Rochester in *Spectator* No. 305 probably derives from a printed source. Giles Jacob's similar ascription almost certainly derives from an edition in the C series (*Poetical Register,* 2, 233). Horace Walpole assigns the poem to Rochester and cites Wood as his source; elsewhere he ascribes it to Buckingham and Rochester and cites Buckingham's

1715 *Works* as his source (*Catalogue of Royal and Noble Authors*, 2, 39, 77, 79).

Previous Scholarship: Attributed to Rochester by Hayward (*Collected Works*, p. 43), Johns (*Poetical Works*, p. 69), Prinz (*Rochester*, pp. 94–97, 107), Pinto (*Rochester*, pp. 128–30; *Poems*, pp. xliii, 79), Wilson (*Court Wits*, pp. 137–38), and Thorpe (*Rochester's Poems*, p. 176).

'TIS NOT THAT I'M WEARY GROWN

Author: Probably Rochester.

Texts:

Yale MS., p. 113: "Upon his leaving his Mistresse"; no ascription. (In section of poems by or concerning Rochester.)

Harvard MS. Eng. 636F, p. 61: "Upon his Leaveing his M^{ris}."; signed "Roch."

A-1680-HU, p. 54: "Upon his leaving his Mistriss"; ascribed to Rochester. Reprinted with ascription to Rochester in the other A-1680 editions and in A-1685, p. 44; A-1701, p. 41; A-1713, p. 46; A-1731, p. 42.

Female Poems On Several Occasions. Written by Ephelia, 2d ed., 1682, p. 145: "Upon his leaving his Mistress"; ascribed to Ephelia. (Probably printed from one of the A-1680 editions.)

Poems by Several Hands, and on Several Occasions Collected by N. Tate, 1685 (Case 181), p. 8: "Upon his leaving his Mistress. By the same Author" (Rochester). (Probably printed from one of the A-1680 editions.)

The Triumph of Wit, 1688 (not in Case), p. 157: "The Parting Farewell: A Song"; no ascription. Reprinted without ascription in the 2d ed., 1692 (not in Case), p. 157. (The 1688 text was probably printed from A-1685.)

B-1691, p. 49: "Upon his Leaving his Mistress"; ascribed to Rochester. Reprinted with ascription to Rochester in B-1696, p. 46; B-1705, p. 46; B-1714, p. 26; B-1732, p. 26; B-1710-P, p. 19; B-1718-P, p. 82. (The 1691 text probably derives from one of the A-1680 editions.)

PREVIOUS SCHOLARSHIP: Printed as Rochester's by Hayward (*Collected Works*, p. 20), Johns (*Poetical Works*, p. 33), and Pinto (*Poems*, p. 27). Attributed to Rochester by Prinz (*Rochester*, p. 114), Wilson (*Court Wits*, p. 104), and Thorpe (*Rochester's Poems*, p. 176).

IN THE FIELDS OF LINCOLNS INN

AUTHOR: Probably Sir Charles Sedley (see Chapter 6).

TEXTS:

[Yale MS.] This poem was probably among those removed by the fourth gap, pp. 115–32. (In section of poems by or concerning Rochester.)

Harvard MS. Eng. 636F, p. 10: "A Song"; signed "Rochester."

Bodl. MS. Eng. Poet. d. 152, fol. 79^r: no title; no ascription. (Probably copied from one of the A-1680 editions.)

Bodl. MS. Don. b. 8, p. 586: no title; signed "Sr Charles Sidley."

A-1680-HU, p. 55: "Song"; ascribed to Rochester. Reprinted with ascription to Rochester in the other A-1680 editions but omitted from A-1685, A-1701, A-1713, and A-1731.

PREVIOUS SCHOLARSHIP: Rochester's authorship doubted by Prinz (*Rochester*, p. 151). Omitted from their editions of Rochester by Hayward (*Collected Works*), Johns (*Poetical*

Works), and Pinto (*Poems*). Attributed to Rochester by Thorpe (*Rochester's Poems*, p. 176). Sedley's authorship doubted by Pinto (*Works of Sedley, 1*, xxvii).

VULCAN CONTRIVE ME SUCH A CUP

AUTHOR: Probably Rochester.

TEXTS:

[Yale MS.] This poem was probably among those removed by the fourth gap, pp. 115–32. (In section of poems by or concerning Rochester.)

Harvard MS. Eng. 636F, p. 62: "Upon drinking of A Bowle"; signed "Roch."

Illinois MS. 20 D 43 Ellis: "An Address to Vulcan"; no ascription. Omits lines 9–16. Includes music. (Possibly derived from printed text.)

Bodl. MS. Rawl. Poet. 173, fol. 141^r: "upon drinking in a Bowl"; no ascription. (Probably copied from printed text.)

Bodl. MS. Add. B. 106, fol. 42^r: "Upon his drinking bowl"; ascribed to Rochester. (Probably copied from one of the A-1680 editions.)

A-1680-HU, p. 56: "Upon his Drinking a Bowl"; ascribed to Rochester. Reprinted with ascription to Rochester in the other A-1680 editions and in A-1685, p. 45; A-1701, p. 42; A-1713, p. 47; A-1731, p. 43.

Female Poems On Several Occasions. Written by Ephelia, 2d ed., 1682, p. 152: "Upon a Drinking Bowle"; ascribed to Ephelia. (Probably printed from one of the A-1680 editions.)

The Triumph of Wit, 1688 (not in Case), p. 158: "The Jolly Fellow's good Wish: A Song"; no ascription. (Probably printed from A-1685.)

B-1691, p. 51: "Upon drinking in a Bowl"; ascribed to

Rochester. Reprinted with ascription to Rochester in B-1696, p. 48; B-1705, p. [48]; B-1714, p. 27; B-1732, p. 27; B-1710-P, p. 20; B-1718-P, p. 84. (The 1691 text probably derives from one of the A-1680 editions.)

The Works of Anacreon, and Sappho, 1713 (Case 271), p. 17: "The Cup." According to the preface of this volume (sig. a2ʳ), "the excellent Imitations of my Lord *Rochester*, and Mr. *Oldham* of the two *Cups*, are inserted as we found them in their respective Works."

A Collection of Bacchanalian Songs, 1729 (Case 357-b), p. 137: "Song xcvi"; no ascription. Thorpe (*Rochester's Poems*, p. 177) incorrectly lists a text in *The Triumphs of Bacchus*, 1729 (Case 357). (The 1729 version probably derives from an earlier printed text.)

A Complete Collection of Old and New English and Scotch Songs, 1735 (Case 400–2), p. 14: "Song xv. Ring, ring the Bar Bell, &c."; no ascription. (Probably derived from earlier printed text.)

The Merry Companion, 1739 (Case 424), p. 341: "Song vi. Ring, ring the bar bell, &c."; no ascription. Reprinted without ascription in 1742 (Case 424-b), p. 202. (The 1739 version probably derives from an earlier printed text.)

ADDITIONAL NOTES: Pinto reports a text of this poem, headed "Nestor," in the "Portland Miscellany" (*Poems*, p. 169).

Evidently this song is attributed to Rochester in Lee's *The Princess of Cleve* (acted Aug. or Sept. 1680), in which Rochester is represented as "Count Rosidore": "Therefore the Fury of Wine and Fury of Women possess me waking and sleeping; let me Dream of nothing but dimpl'd Cheeks, and laughing Lips, and flowing Bowls, Venus be my Star, and Whoring my House, and Death I defie thee. Thus sung

Rosidore in the Urn . . ." (*The Works of Nathaniel Lee,* ed. Thomas B. Stroup and Arthur L. Cooke, New Brunswick, [N. J.], Scarecrow Press, 1954–55, 2, 149, 188).

PREVIOUS SCHOLARSHIP: Printed as Rochester's by Hayward (*Collected Works,* p. 21) and Johns (*Poetical Works,* p. 34). Attributed to Rochester by Prinz (*Rochester,* p. 112), Pinto (*Rochester,* pp. 82–84; *Poems,* p. 28), Wilson (*Court Wits,* pp. 89, 231), and Thorpe (*Rochester's Poems,* pp. 176–77).

AS CLORIS FULL OF HARMLESS THOUGHTS

AUTHOR: Probably Rochester.

TEXTS:

[Yale MS.] This poem was probably among those removed by the fourth gap, pp. 115–32. (In section of poems by or concerning Rochester.)

B. M. Sloane MS. 1009, fol. 389^v: no title; no ascription. Includes only the first 8 lines.

Bodl. MS. Rawl. Poet. 173, fol. 71^r: "The Yielding Nymph. a Song. by L^d. Ro:." (Probably copied from an edition in the A series.)

Corydon and Cloris or, The Wanton Sheepherdess, [1677?]: "To a pleasant Play-house new Tune: Or, Amorett and Phillis"; no ascription. Adds 8 lines which are lacking in other versions. (Probably printed from a manuscript source.)

The Wits Academy, 1677 (not in Case), p. ^{2}115: "Song CXXIX"; no ascription. (Probably printed from a manuscript source.)

The Last and Best Edition of New Songs, 1677 (Case 163), sig. B3^r: "A Song"; no ascription. (Probably printed from a manuscript source.)

New Ayres and Dialogues, 1678 (Day and Murrie 46), p. 14:

"While Cloe full of harmless thoughts"; no ascription. Includes music ascribed to "James Hart." (Possibly printed
from a manuscript source.)

Choice Ayres & Songs, 1679 (Day and Murrie 48), p. 8: no
title; no ascription. Includes music ascribed to "Mr. James
Hart." (Possibly printed from a manuscript source.)

A-1680-HU, p. 58: "Song"; ascribed to Rochester. Reprinted
with ascription to Rochester in the other A-1680 editions and
in A-1685, p. 46; A-1701, p. 43; A-1713, p. 48; A-1731, p. 44.

Female Poems On Several Occasions. Written by Ephelia, 2d
ed., 1682, p. 154: "Song"; ascribed to Ephelia. (Probably
printed from one of the A-1680 editions.)

The Triumph of Wit, 1688 (not in Case), p. 140: "The Conquest of Coyness: A Song"; no ascription. Reprinted without
ascription in the 2d ed., 1692 (not in Case), p. 144, and the
5th ed., 1707 (Case 244-e), p. 143. According to Thorpe
(*Rochester's Poems,* p. 177), the poem also appears without
ascription in the 4th ed., 1702 (not in Case). (The 1688 text
was probably printed from A-1685.)

B-1691, p. 53: "A Song"; ascribed to Rochester. Reprinted with
ascription to Rochester in B-1696, p. 50; B-1705, p. 50;
B-1714, p. 28; B-1732, p. 28; B-1710-P, p. 21; B-1718-P,
p. 86. (The 1691 text probably derives from one of the A-1680
editions.)

The Hive, 1724 (Case 331-2-a), p. 29: no title; no ascription.
Reprinted without ascription in 1727 (Case 331-2-c), p. 28,
and 1733 (Case 331-2-d), p. 28. (The 1724 version probably
derives from an earlier printed text.)

The Choice, 1729 (Case 353-1-a), p. 28: "Song xxvi"; no ascription. Reprinted without ascription in 1732 (Case 353-1-b),
p. 28, and 1737 (Case 353-1-c), p. 28. (The 1729 version
probably derives from an earlier printed text.)

The Vocal Miscellany, 1734 (Case 388-1-b), p. 135: "Song CLII. Lucky Minute"; no ascription. Reprinted without ascription in 1738 (Case 388-1-c), p. 135, and 1738 (Case 388-1-d), p. 135. (The 1734 version probably derives from an earlier printed text.)

A Complete Collection of Old and New English and Scotch Songs, 1735 (Case 400-1), p. 104: "Song LXXXIII. Lucky Minute"; no ascription. (Probably derived from an earlier printed text.)

The Cupid, 1736 (Case 404), p. 220: "Song XVIII"; no ascription. Reprinted without ascription in 1739 (Case 404-b), p. 241. According to Thorpe (*Rochester's Poems*, p. 177), the poem also appears without ascription in Dublin 1737 (not in Case). (The 1736 version probably derives from an earlier printed text.)

The Syren, 2d ed., 1738 (not in Case), p. 29: "Song XXIV. Lucky Minute"; no ascription. Reprinted without ascription in 1739 (Case 423-c), p. 29. (The 1738 version probably derives from an earlier printed text.)

The Merry Companion, 1739 (Case 424), p. 78: "Song XXXII. Lucky Minute"; no ascription. Reprinted without ascription in 1742 (Case 424-b), p. 88. (The 1739 version probably derives from an earlier printed text.)

Philomel, 1744 (Case 444), p. 16: "Song XXIII"; no ascription. (Probably derived from an earlier printed text.)

ADDITIONAL NOTES: According to J. Woodfall Ebsworth (*Roxburghe Ballads*, 6 [Hertford, Ballad Society, 1889], 133), this poem is printed with music in *The Merry Musician*, 2, 73; Watts's *Musical Miscellany*, 1, 146; *An Antidote against Melancholy*, 1749, p. 118; and *The Convivial Songster*, February 1782, p. 89.

Evidently this song was used in Otway's comedy *Friend-ship in Fashion*, acted in April 1678 (*The Works of Thomas Otway*, ed. J. C. Ghosh, Oxford, Clarendon Press, 1932, *1*, 43–44, 347; *2*, 493).

PREVIOUS SCHOLARSHIP: Printed as Rochester's by Hayward (*Collected Works*, p. 22) and Johns (*Poetical Works*, p. 36). Attributed to Rochester by Pinto (*Rochester*, pp. 65–66; *Poems*, p. 29), Wilson (*Court Wits*, p. 100), and Thorpe (*Rochester's Poems*, p. 177).

QUOTH THE DUTCHESS OF CL——,
TO MRS. KN——

AUTHOR: Probably Rochester.

TEXTS:

[Yale MS.] This poem was probably among those removed by the fourth gap, pp. 115–32. (In section of poems by or concerning Rochester.)

Osborn MS. Chest II, Number 3, p. 110: "A Dialogue betweene Mall: Knight and the Dut: of Cleaveland"; no ascription. This text, of which only the title and first 3 lines are extant, appears on a small piece of p. 110 which is pinned to p. 108.

Harvard MS. Eng. 636F, p. 277: "M^rs: Knights Advice to the Dutchess, of Cleavland, in Distress For A Prick"; no ascription.

Edinburgh MS. DC.1.3, p. 110: "Song by ye D^cs. of Cleavland & Mrs Knight"; no ascription.

A-1680-HU, p. 59: "Song"; ascribed to Rochester. Reprinted with ascription to Rochester in the other A-1680 editions but omitted from A-1685, A-1701, A-1713, and A-1731.

PREVIOUS SCHOLARSHIP: Rochester's authorship doubted by Prinz (*Rochester*, p. 151). Omitted by Hayward (*Collected Works*), Johns (*Poetical Works*), and Pinto (*Poems*). Attributed to Rochester by Thorpe (*Rochester's Poems*, p. 177).

I RISE AT ELEVEN, I DINE ABOUT TWO

AUTHOR: Probably Charles Sackville, Lord Buckhurst, Earl of Middlesex and Dorset (see Chapter 6).

TEXTS:

[Yale MS.] This poem was probably among those removed by the fourth gap, pp. 115–32. (In section of poems by or concerning Rochester.)

Bodl. MS. Rawl. Poet. 152, fol. 89^v: "The Debauch"; no ascription.

Edinburgh MS. DC.1.3, p. 95: "Regine &. vive"; no ascription.

A-1680-HU, p. 59: "Song"; ascribed to Rochester. Reprinted with ascription to Rochester in the other A-1680 editions and in A-1685, p. 47; A-1701, p. 44; A-1713, p. 49; A-1731, p. 45.

C-1714-1, p. 147: "The Debauchee"; ascribed to Rochester. Reprinted with ascription to Rochester in later editions in this series. (The 1714 text probably derives from one of the A-1680 editions.)

ADDITIONAL NOTE: In a postscript to a letter dated 20 March 1672/3 (Huntington MS. HA 12525), Godfrey Thacker wrote from London to his cousin, the Earl of Huntingdon:

> My Lord Buckhurst and Lord Rochester being in company, a suddaine Malancholly possest him Rochester inquiring the reason hee answered hee was troubled at Rochesters

lude way of living, and in thes verses over the leafe exprest it

> you rise at Eleaven
> And dine at two
> you get drunk at seaven
> And have nothing to doe
> you goe to a wentch but for feare of a clapp
> you spend in your hand or spue in her lapp

For further information on Thacker's letter, see Lucyle Hook,
"Something More About Rochester," *Modern Language
Notes*, 75 (1960), 478–85.

PREVIOUS SCHOLARSHIP: Printed as Rochester's by Hayward
    (*Collected Works*, p. 66) and Johns (*Poetical Works*, p. 102).
    Attributed to Rochester by Prinz (*Rochester*, pp. 93, 144)
    and Thorpe (*Rochester's Poems*, p. 177). Omitted from his
    edition by Pinto (*Poems*).

LOVE A WOMAN! Y'ARE AN ASS

AUTHOR: Probably Rochester.

TEXTS:

[Yale MS.] This poem was probably among those removed by
    the fourth gap, pp. 115–32. (In section of poems by or con-
    cerning Rochester.)

Harvard MS. Eng. 636F, p. 247 (misnumbered 147): "Song";
    signed "Roch."

A-1680-HU, p. 60: "Song"; ascribed to Rochester. Reprinted
    with ascription to Rochester in the other A-1680 editions and
    in A-1685, p. 48; A-1701, p. 44; A-1713, p. 50; A-1731, p. 46.

B-1691, p. 44: "A Song"; ascribed to Rochester. Reprinted with ascription to Rochester in B-1696, p. 41; B-1705, p. 42; B-1714, p. 23; B-1732, p. 23; B-1710-P, p. 18; B-1718-P, p. 79. (The text in B-1691 derives partially or wholly from a manuscript source. For the readings of uncanceled leaf D7, which includes the obscene fourth stanza of the poem, see my note, "An Unsuspected Cancel in Tonson's 1691 'Rochester,'" *Papers of the Bibliographical Society of America*, 55 [1961], 130–33.)

ADDITIONAL NOTE: Pinto reports a text of this poem in the "Portland Miscellany" (*Poems*, p. 169).

PREVIOUS SCHOLARSHIP: Printed as Rochester's by Hayward (*Collected Works*, p. 18), Johns (*Poetical Works*, p. 30), and Pinto (*Poems*, p. 25). Attributed to Rochester by Prinz (*Rochester*, p. 142), Wilson (*Court Wits*, p. 104), and Thorpe (*Rochester's Poems*, p. 177).

FAIR CLORIS IN A PIG-STYE, LAY

AUTHOR: Probably Rochester.

TEXTS:

Yale MS., p. 133: "Song to Cloris"; no ascription. (In section of poems by or concerning Rochester.)

Osborn MS. Chest 11, Number 32: no title; no ascription. Appears on a single loose sheet exhibiting fold-marks. Lacks the last 3 stanzas.

Harvard MS. Eng. 636F, p. 77: "A Song"; signed "Roch."

A-1680-HU, p. 61: "Song to Cloris"; ascribed to Rochester. Reprinted with ascription to Rochester in the other A-1680 editions and in A-1685, p. 49; A-1701, p. 45; A-1713, p. 51; A-1731, p. 46.

B-1691, p. 59: "A Song. To Cloris"; ascribed to Rochester. Reprinted with ascription to Rochester in B-1696, p. 56; B-1705, p. 56; B-1714, p. 32; B-1732, p. 32; B-1710-P, p. 23; B-1718-P, p. 91. All but B-1718-P omit the last stanza. (The 1691 text probably derives from one of the A-1680 editions. The 1718 text may derive primarily from A-1685, A-1701, or A-1713.)

D-1718, p. 70: "A Song"; ascribed to Rochester. Reprinted with ascription to Rochester in D-1761, p. 246. (The 1718 text was probably printed from a manuscript.)

The Muse in Good Humour, 1745 (Case 450-1-d), p. 145: "Chloris in a Pig-stye"; no ascription. (Derived from earlier printed text.)

ADDITIONAL NOTE: Pinto reports a text of this poem in the "Portland Miscellany" (*Poems,* p. 173).

PREVIOUS SCHOLARSHIP: Printed as Rochester's by Hayward (*Collected Works,* p. 24), Johns (*Poetical Works,* p. 41), and Pinto (*Poems,* p. 32). Attributed to Rochester by Prinz (*Rochester,* pp. 107, 141), Wilson (*Court Wits,* p. 100), and Thorpe (*Rochester's Poems,* p. 178).

GIVE ME LEAVE TO RAIL AT YOU

AUTHOR: Probably Rochester.

TEXTS:

Yale MS., p. 136: "Song"; no ascription. (In section of poems by or concerning Rochester.)

Folger MS. M. b. 12, fol. 31ᵛ: "Song"; no ascription.

Victoria and Albert Museum MS. Dyce 43, p. 105: "Song"; no ascription.

Songs for i 2 & 3 Voyces, [1677] (Day and Murrie 44), p. 31:
no title; no ascription. First 8 lines only. Includes music by
Henry Bowman. Reissued without ascription in 1678 (Day
and Murrie 47), p. 31, and 1679 (Day and Murrie 50), p. 31.

In the British Museum copy of *Songs for i 2 & 3 Voyces*,
[1677], a contemporary hand has written in the lefthand
margin "words by y°: L:ᵈ Rochester."

A-1680-HU, p. 63: "Song"; ascribed to Rochester. Reprinted
with ascription to Rochester in the other A-1680 editions and
in A-1685, p. 51; A-1701, p. 47; A-1713, p. 53; A-1731, p. 48.

Female Poems On Several Occasions. Written by Ephelia, 2d
ed., 1682, p. 159: "Song"; ascribed to Ephelia. (Printed from
one of the A-1680 editions.)

Pastoralle, [1684] (Day and Murrie 71), p. 41: no title; no
ascription. Last 8 lines only, beginning "Kindness hath re-
sistles charms." Music by Louis Grabu. (Derived from manuscript source.)

*Valentinian: A Tragedy. As 'tis Alter'd by the late Earl of Roch-
ester*, 1685, p. 75: "A Song"; possibly attributed to Rochester.
Last 8 lines only. (Derived from manuscript source.)

The Triumph of Wit, 1688 (not in Case), p. 160: "The Debate:
A Song"; no ascription. Reprinted without ascription in the
2d ed., 1692 (not in Case), p. 159. (The 1688 text was
probably printed from A-1685.)

B-1691, p. 55: "A Song"; ascribed to Rochester. Reprinted with
ascription to Rochester in B-1696, p. 52; B-1705, p. 52;
B-1714, p. 29; B-1732, p. 29; B-1710-P, p. 22; B-1718-P, p.
88. (The 1691 text was probably printed from one of the
A-1680 editions.)

B-1691, p. 455: "A Song"; possibly attributed to Rochester. Reprinted in B-1696, p. 216; B-1705, p. 216; B-1714, p. 302;

B-1732, p. 301; B-1710-P, p. 154. Last 8 lines only. (The 1691 text was printed from *Valentinian*, 1685.)

The Agreeable Variety, 1717 (Case 293), p. 148: "From the Lord Rochester." Reissued with ascription to Rochester in 1724 (Case 293-b), p. 148, and 1742 (Case 293-c), p. 148. Fragment of 4 lines beginning "Kindness has resistless Charms." (The 1717 version probably derives from an earlier printed text, as its title suggests.)

The Choice, 1733 (Case 353-3), p. 109: "Song xcvii"; no ascription. Last 8 lines only. (Probably derived from earlier printed text.)

A Complete Collection of Old and New English and Scotch Songs, 1735 (Case 400-2), p. 12: "Song xii. Give me leave to rail at you"; no ascription. (Probably derived from earlier printed text.)

A Complete Collection of Old and New English and Scotch Songs, 1736 (Case 400-7), p. 180: "Song clxxv. Kindness hath resistless, &c."; no ascription. Last 8 lines only. (Probably derived from earlier printed text.)

The Syren, 2d ed., 1738 (not in Case), p. 295: "Song cccxlv"; no ascription. Reprinted without ascription in 1739 (Case 423-c), p. 295. Last 8 lines only. (The 1738 version probably derives from an earlier printed text.)

ADDITIONAL NOTE: According to Pinto, a text of this poem, headed "To Thirsis," appears in the "Portland Miscellany," p. 58 (*Poems*, p. 171).

PREVIOUS SCHOLARSHIP: Printed as Rochester's by Hayward (*Collected Works*, p. 23), Johns (*Poetical Works*, p. 38), and Pinto (*Rochester*, p. 63; *Poems*, p. 30). Attributed to Rochester by Thorpe (*Rochester's Poems*, p. 178).

NOTHING ADDS TO YOUR FOND FIRE

AUTHOR: Probably Rochester's wife (see Chapter 7).

TEXTS:

Yale MS., p. 137: "The Answer"; no ascription. (In section of poems by or concerning Rochester.)

Folger MS. M. b. 12, fol. 32ʳ: "The Answer"; no ascription.

Victoria and Albert Museum MS. Dyce 43, p. 106: "The Answer"; no ascription.

Portland MS., fol. 12ʳ: "Song." This text, in the handwriting of Rochester's wife, includes minor revisions in the form of deletions and interlinear corrections.

A-1680-HU, p. 63: "The Answer"; ascribed to Rochester. Reprinted with ascription to Rochester in the other A-1680 editions and in A-1685, p. 51; A-1701, p. 47; A-1713, p. 54; A-1731, p. 49.

Female Poems On Several Occasions. Written by Ephelia, 2d ed., 1682, p. 160: "The Answer"; ascribed to Ephelia. (Probably printed from one of the A-1680 editions.)

The Triumph of Wit, 1688 (not in Case), p. 161: "The Reply: A Song"; no ascription. Reprinted without ascription in the 2d ed., 1692 (not in Case), p. 159. (The 1688 text was probably printed from A-1685.)

B-1691, p. 56: "The Answer"; ascribed to Rochester. Reprinted with ascription to Rochester in B-1696, p. 53; B-1705, p. 53; B-1714, p. 30; B-1732, p. 30; B-1710-P, p. 22; B-1718-P, p. 89. (The 1691 text was probably printed from one of the A-1680 editions, though it is barely possible that one or two readings were corrected from a manuscript source.)

A Complete Collection of Old and New English and Scotch Songs, 1735 (Case 400-2), p. 13: "Song XIII. The Answer"; no ascription. (Printed from B-1691.)

ADDITIONAL NOTE: Pinto reports a text of this poem in the "Portland Miscellany" (*Poems*, p. 171).

PREVIOUS SCHOLARSHIP: Printed as Rochester's by Hayward (*Collected Works*, p. 23) and Johns (*Poetical Works*, p. 39). Attributed to Rochester's wife by Pinto (*Rochester*, pp. 63–64; *Poems*, pp. 31, 173). Regarded by Thorpe as "a poem of doubtful authorship, possibly by Lady Rochester" (*Rochester's Poems*, p. 178).

PHILLIS, BE GENTLER I ADVICE

AUTHOR: Rochester.

TEXTS:

Yale MS., p. 139: "Song"; no ascription. (In section of poems by or concerning Rochester.)

Harvard MS. Eng. 636F, p. 64: "Song"; signed "Roch."

Folger MS. M. b. 12, fol. 32ᵛ: "Song"; no ascription.

Phillipps MS. 9500, p. 160: "A Song"; no ascription. (Possibly copied from printed text.)

B. M. Add. MS. 27408, fol. 9ᵛ: "To Phillis"; no ascription. (Possibly copied from printed text.)

Victoria and Albert Museum MS. Dyce 43, p. 107: "Song"; no ascription.

Edinburgh MS. DC.1.3, p. 67: "Song By the L: Rochester."

Vienna MS. 14090, fol. 60ʳ: "Song"; no ascription.

A-1680-HU, p. 65: "Song"; ascribed to Rochester. Reprinted with ascription to Rochester in the other A-1680 editions and in A-1685, p. 54; A-1701, p. 49; A-1713, p. 56; A-1731, p. 50.

Female Poems On Several Occasions. Written by Ephelia, 2d
ed., 1682, p. 168: "Song"; ascribed to Ephelia. (Probably
printed from one of the A-1680 editions.)

The Theater of Music, 1685 (Day and Murrie 79), p. 43: no
title; no ascription. Includes music ascribed to "Mr. Thomas
Tedway" (Tudway). Reissued without ascription in *The New
Treasury of Musick,* 1695 (Day and Murrie 134), p. ²43.
(The 1685 text may derive from one of the A-1680 editions.)

The Triumph of Wit, 1688 (not in Case), p. 165: "On Fading
Beauty: A Song"; no ascription. Reprinted without ascription
in the 2d ed., 1692 (not in Case), p. 162, and the 5th ed.,
1707 (Case 244-e), p. 156. This version adds 8 lines which are
lacking in other early texts. (The 1688 text was probably
printed from A-1685.)

B-1691, p. 34: "A Song"; ascribed to Rochester. Reprinted with
ascription to Rochester in B-1696, p. 31; B-1705, p. 31;
B-1714, p. 18; B-1732, p. 18; B-1710-P, p. 14. Omitted from
B-1718-P. (The 1691 text probably derives from one of the
A-1680 editions.)

Deliciae Poeticae, 1706 (Case 240), p. 79: "A Song"; no ascription. Reissued without ascription in *Mirth Diverts all Care,*
1708 (not in Case), p. 79, and 1709 (not in Case), p. 79. (The
1706 version probably derives from an earlier printed text.)

The Hive, 1724 (Case 331-2-a), p. 103: no title; no ascription.
Reprinted without ascription in 1727 (Case 331-2-c), p. 99,
and 1733 (Case 331-2-d), p. 100. (The 1724 version probably
derives from an earlier printed text.)

*A Complete Collection of Old and New English and Scotch
Songs,* 1735 (Case 400-2), p. 20: "Song XXII. Thus Kitty beautiful and young"; no ascription. (Probably derived from
earlier printed text.)

ADDITIONAL NOTE: Pinto reports a text of this poem in the "Portland Miscellany" (*Poems*, p. 166).

PREVIOUS SCHOLARSHIP: Printed as Rochester's by Hayward (*Collected Works*, p. 15) and Johns (*Poetical Works*, p. 24). Attributed to Rochester by Pinto (*Rochester*, p. 67; *Poems*, p. 21), Wilson (*Court Wits*, p. 97), and Thorpe (*Rochester's Poems*, pp. 178–79).

WHAT CRUEL PAINS CORINNA, TAKES

AUTHOR: Probably Rochester.

TEXTS:

Yale MS., p. 140: "Song"; no ascription. (In section of poems by or concerning Rochester.)

Bodl. MS. Rawl. Poet. 173, fol. 71^v: "Woman's Frailty. A Song. by L^d. Ro:." (Probably copied from an edition in the A series.)

A-1680-HU, p. 65: "Song"; ascribed to Rochester. Reprinted with ascription to Rochester in the other A-1680 editions and in A-1685, p. 55; A-1701, p. 50; A-1713, p. 57; A-1731, p. 51.

The Theater of Music, 1685 (Day and Murrie 78), p. 57: "Words by the late Earl of Rochester." Includes music ascribed to "Mr. Snow" (Moses Snow). Reissued with ascription to Rochester in *The New Treasury of Musick*, 1695 (Day and Murrie 134), p. ^{1}57. (The 1685 text may derive from one of the A-1680 editions.)

The Triumph of Wit, 1688 (not in Case), p. 164: "She wou'd seem Angry: A Song"; no ascription. Reprinted without ascription in the 2d ed., 1692 (not in Case), p. 162, and the 5th ed., 1707 (Case 244-e), p. 155. According to Thorpe (*Rochester's Poems*, p. 179), the poem appears without ascription in the 4th ed., 1702 (not in Case). (The 1688 text was probably printed from A-1685.)

B-1691, p. 30: "To Corinna. A Song"; ascribed to Rochester. Reprinted with ascription to Rochester in B-1696, p. 27; B-1705, p. 27; B-1714, p. 16; B-1732, p. 16; B-1710-P, p. 12; B-1718-P, p. 69. (The 1691 text probably derives from one of the A-1680 editions.)

A Complete Collection of Old and New English and Scotch Songs, 1735 (Case 400-2), p. 24: "Song xxix. What cruel pains, &c."; no ascription. (Probably derived from earlier printed text.)

ADDITIONAL NOTE: According to Pinto, a text of this poem, lacking the third stanza, appears on p. 56 of the "Portland Miscellany" (*Poems*, p. 166).

PREVIOUS SCHOLARSHIP: Printed as Rochester's by Hayward (*Collected Works*, p. 13), Johns (*Poetical Works*, p. 21), and Pinto (*Poems*, p. 19). Attributed to Rochester by Thorpe (*Rochester's Poems*, p. 179).

LOVE, BAD ME HOPE, AND I OBEY'D

AUTHOR: Probably Rochester.

TEXTS:

Yale MS., p. 142: "Womans Honour"; no ascription. (In section of poems by or concerning Rochester.)

Harvard MS. Eng. 636F, p. 65: "Womans Honour"; signed "Roch."

Victoria and Albert Museum MS. Dyce 43, p. 108: "Womans Honour A Song"; no ascription.

Vienna MS. 14090, fol. 61ᵛ: "Woman's Honour. A Song"; no ascription.

A-1680-HU, p. 66: "Womans Honor"; ascribed to Rochester. Reprinted with ascription to Rochester in the other A-1680 editions and in A-1685, p. 56; A-1701, p. 50; A-1713, p. 58; A-1731, p. 52.

Female Poems On Several Occasions. Written by Ephelia, 2d ed., 1682, p. 166: "Womans Honour"; ascribed to Ephelia. (Probably printed from one of the A-1680 editions.)

B-1691, p. 22: "Womans Honour. A Song"; ascribed to Rochester. Reprinted with ascription to Rochester in B-1696, p. 19; B-1705, p. 19; B-1714, p. 11; B-1732, p. 11; B-1710-P, p. 9; B-1718-P, p. 62. (The 1691 text probably derives from one of the A-1680 editions.)

The Hive, 1724 (Case 331-2-a), p. 143: "Woman's Honour"; no ascription. Reprinted without ascription in 1727 (Case 331-2-c), p. 147, and 1733 (Case 331-2-d), p. 147. According to Thorpe (*Rochester's Poems,* p. 179), the poem also appears without ascription in the 2d ed., 2, 1724 (not in Case). (The 1724 version probably derives from an earlier printed text.)

The Choice, 1732 (Case 353-1-b), p. 258: "Song ccxxxvii"; no ascription. Reprinted without ascription in 1737 (Case 353-1-c), p. 258. (The 1732 version probably derives from an earlier printed text.)

A Complete Collection of Old and New English and Scotch Songs, 1735 (Case 400-2), p. 23: "Song xxvii. Love bid me hope"; no ascription. (Probably derived from earlier printed text.)

ADDITIONAL NOTE: Pinto reports a text of this poem in the "Portland Miscellany" (*Poems,* p. 166).

PREVIOUS SCHOLARSHIP: Printed as Rochester's by Hayward (*Collected Works,* p. 10), Johns (*Poetical Works,* p. 15), and Pinto (*Poems,* p. 14). Attributed to Rochester by Thorpe (*Rochester's Poems,* p. 179).

TO THIS MOMENT A REBEL I
THROW DOWN MY ARMS

AUTHOR: Probably Rochester.

TEXTS:

Yale MS., p. 144: "Song"; no ascription. (In section of poems by or concerning Rochester.)

Victoria and Albert Museum MS. Dyce 43, p. 109: "Song"; no ascription.

Vienna MS. 14090, fol. 60^v: "Song"; no ascription.

A-1680-HU, p. 67: "Song"; ascribed to Rochester. Reprinted with ascription to Rochester in the other A-1680 editions and in A-1685, p. 57; A-1701, p. 51; A-1713, p. 59; A-1731, p. 53.

The Triumph of Wit, 1688 (not in Case), p. 133: "The Victory, or Beauties Conquest: A Song"; no ascription. Reprinted without ascription in the 2d ed., 1692 (not in Case), p. 139, and the 5th ed., 1707 (Case 244-e), p. 140. According to Thorpe (*Rochester's Poems*, p. 179), the poem also appears without ascription in the 4th ed., 1702 (not in Case). (The 1688 text was probably printed from A-1685.)

B-1691, p. 46: "A Song"; ascribed to Rochester. Reprinted with ascription to Rochester in B-1696, p. 43; B-1705, p. 43; B-1714, p. 24; B-1732, p. 24; B-1710-P, p. 18; B-1718-P, p. 80. (The 1691 text derives from one of the A-1680 editions.)

The Hive, 1724 (Case 331-1-a), p. 151: no title; no ascription. Reprinted without ascription in 1726 (Case 331-1-c), p. 124, and 1732 (Case 331-1-d), p. 127. (The 1724 version probably derives from an earlier printed text.)

A Complete Collection of Old and New English and Scotch Songs, 1735 (Case 400-2), p. 47: "Song LXVI. To this Moment, &c."; no ascription. (Probably derived from earlier printed text.)

ADDITIONAL NOTE: According to Pinto, a text of this poem, headed "The Submission," appears on p. 57 of the "Portland Miscellany" (*Poems,* p. 169).

PREVIOUS SCHOLARSHIP: Printed as Rochester's by Hayward (*Collected Works,* p. 19), Johns (*Poetical Works,* p. 31), and Pinto (*Poems,* p. 26). Attributed to Rochester by Thorpe (*Rochester's Poems,* p. 179).

HOW HAPPY CLORIS (WERE THEY FREE)

AUTHOR: Rochester (see Chapter 7).

TEXTS:

Yale MS., p. 146: "Song"; no ascription. (In section of poems by or concerning Rochester.)

Harvard MS. Eng. 636F, p. 8: "To A Lady, in A Letter"; signed "Rochester."

Portland MS., fol. 1ʳ: no title. This text, in Rochester's handwriting, is in process of revision.

B. M. Harl. MS. 7316, fol. 21ᵛ: no title; no ascription. (Copied from the Portland MS.)

A New Collection of the Choicest Songs, 1676 (Case 161), sig. A4ʳ: "Against jealousie"; no ascription.

The Last and Best Edition of New Songs, 1677 (Case 163), sig. D3ʳ: "Against Jealousie"; no ascription. (Derived from *A New Collection,* 1676 and probably also the manuscript from which the 1676 text was printed.)

A-1680-HU, p. 68: "Song"; ascribed to Rochester. Reprinted with ascription to Rochester in the other A-1680 editions and in A-1685, p. 58; A-1701, p. 52; A-1713, p. 60; A-1731, p. 54.

The Triumph of Wit, 1688 (not in Case), p. 132: "The Parley: A Song"; no ascription. Reprinted without ascription in the

2d ed., 1692 (not in Case), p. 138. (The 1688 text derives from A-1685.)

B-1691, p. 36: "To a Lady: in a Letter"; ascribed to Rochester. Reprinted with ascription to Rochester in B-1696, p. 33; B-1705, p. 33; B-1714, p. 19; B-1732, p. 19; B-1710-P, p. 15; B-1718-P, p. 73. (The 1691 text derives from a manuscript source.)

The Hive, 1724 (Case 331-2-a), p. 176: no title; no ascription. (Derived from some edition of *The Triumph of Wit*.)

PREVIOUS SCHOLARSHIP: Rochester's authorship doubted by Prinz (*Rochester*, p. 151). One version printed by Hayward as Rochester's (*Collected Works*, p. 15) but another printed as spurious (p. 313). Printed as Rochester's by Johns (*Poetical Works*, p. 25) and Pinto (*Rochester*, pp. 39–41; *Poems*, pp. 22, 167). Attributed to Rochester by Thorpe (*Rochester's Poems*, p. 179).

ALL MY PAST LIFE IS MINE NO MORE

AUTHOR: Rochester.

TEXTS:

Yale MS., p. 148: "Love & Life—a Song"; no ascription. (In section of poems by or concerning Rochester.)

Osborn MS. Box XXII, Number 3, p. 29: "To Phillis"; no ascription.

Harvard MS. Eng. 636F, p. 246: "Song"; signed "Rochester."

Folger MS. 4108, poem number 141: no title; no ascription. (Possibly copied from printed text.)

B. M. Add. MS. 27408, fol. 11ᵛ: "An Other"; no ascription. (Possibly copied from printed text.)

Bodl. MS. Rawl. Poet. 90, fol. 132^v: "(Joyes Past:)"; no ascription. Lacks the last stanza.

Bodl. MS. Add. B. 106, fol. 45^v: "Love & Life, a Song." To left
of title: "Roch:." (Probably copied from one of the A-1680
editions.)

Edinburgh MS. DC.1.3, p. 52: "Song"; no ascription.

Songs for i 2 & 3 Voyces, [1677] (Day and Murrie 44), p. 9:
no title; no ascription. Includes music by Henry Bowman.
Reissued without ascription in 1678 (Day and Murrie 47),
p. 9, and 1679 (Day and Murrie 50), p. 9.

In the British Museum copy of the 1677 edition, a contemporary hand has written in ink at the top of the page: "y^e.
words by y^e. Lord Rochester."

A-1680-HU, p. 69: "Love and Life, a Song"; ascribed to Rochester. Reprinted with ascription to Rochester in the other
A-1680 editions and in A-1685, p. 59; A-1701, p. 53; A-1713,
p. 61; A-1731, p. 55.

Songs set by Signior Pietro Reggio, [1680] (Day and Murrie
52), p. 36: "Verses by my Lord Rochester." Includes music
by Reggio. (Though this text is almost identical with that in
A-1680-HU, it seems to be independently descended. As Day
and Murrie indicate [p. 53], Reggio's volume was advertised
in the *London Gazette* for 6–9 December 1680. It had, however, been advertised as ready for subscribers in the issue for
22–26 July 1680, before the publication of A-1680-HU. Subscribers were solicited several months earlier in an advertisement in the issue for 8–11 March 1679/80.)

Female Poems On Several Occasions. Written by Ephelia, 2d
ed., 1682, p. 165: "Love and Life"; ascribed to Ephelia.
(Probably printed from one of the A-1680 editions.)

*Poems by Several Hands, and on Several Occasions Collected
by N. Tate*, 1685 (Case 181), p. 10: "Love and Life, a Song

by the same Author" (Rochester). (Probably printed from one of the A-1680 editions.)

The Theater of Music, 1685 (Day and Murrie 78), p. 58: no title; no ascription. Includes music ascribed to "Dr. John Blow." Reissued without ascription in *The New Treasury of Musick,* 1695 (Day and Murrie 134), p. ¹58. (The 1685 text may derive from one of the A-1680 editions.)

The Triumph of Wit, 1688 (not in Case), p. 136: "The Fickle Lover: A Song"; no ascription. (Probably printed from A-1685.)

B-1691, p. 41: "Love and Life. A Song"; ascribed to Rochester. Reprinted with ascription to Rochester in B-1696, p. 38; B-1705, p. 38; B-1714, p. 22; B-1732, p. 22; B-1710-P, p. 16; B-1718-P, p. 77. (The 1691 text is conflated from one of the A-1680 editions and a manuscript source.)

The Gentleman's Journal, August 1693 (Day and Murrie 119), p. 269: "To Phyllis"; ". . . said to be by the late Earl of Rochester." Includes a Latin translation, headed "Ad Phyllida" and beginning "Poscis ut omne meum soli tibi serviat aevum," which is reprinted in C-1714-1, p. 179. (The 1693 text of Rochester's song was printed from a manuscript.)

Wit and Mirth, 1700 (Day and Murrie 188), p. 261: "A Song. E. of Rochester." Includes John Blow's musical setting, here given without ascription. Reprinted without ascription in 1707 (Day and Murrie 214), p. 261; 1712 (Day and Murrie 222), p. 261; 1719 (Day and Murrie 234), p. 306; 1719 (Day and Murrie 239), p. 306. (The 1700 version may derive from an earlier printed text.)

The Hive, 1724 (Case 331-1-a), p. 131: no title; no ascription. Reprinted without ascription in 1726 (Case 331-1-c), p. 128, and 1732 (Case 331-1-d), p. 131. (The 1724 text was printed from an edition in the B series.)

ADDITIONAL NOTE: Pinto reports a text of this poem in the "Portland Miscellany" (*Poems*, p. 168).

PREVIOUS SCHOLARSHIP: Printed as Rochester's by Hayward (*Collected Works*, pp. xxviii, xlviii, 17), Norman Ault (*Seventeenth Century Lyrics*, 2d ed., New York, William Sloane Associates, 1950, p. 407), and Johns (*Poetical Works*, p. 28). Attributed to Rochester by Prinz (*Rochester*, p. 114), Pinto (*Rochester*, pp. 75–76; *Poems*, pp. xxvii, 24), Wilson (*Court Wits*, p. 97), and Thorpe (*Rochester's Poems*, pp. 179–80).

HOW BLEST WAS THE CREATED STATE

AUTHOR: Probably Rochester.

TEXTS:

Yale MS., p. 149: "The Fall a Song"; no ascription. (In section of poems by or concerning Rochester.)

Harvard MS. Eng. 636F, p. 66: "The Fall"; signed "Roch."

B. M. Add. MS. 27408, fol. 11^r: "The ffall of Man"; no ascription. (Possibly copied from printed text.)

A-1680-HU, p. 70: "The Fall, a Song"; ascribed to Rochester. Reprinted with ascription to Rochester in the other A-1680 editions and in A-1685, p. 60; A-1701, p. 54; A-1713, p. 62; A-1731, p. 55.

Female Poems On Several Occasions. Written by Ephelia, 2d ed., 1682, p. 164: "The Fall"; ascribed to Ephelia. (Probably printed from one of the A-1680 editions.)

The Triumph of Wit, 1688 (not in Case), p. 142: "The Comparison: A Song"; no ascription. Reprinted without ascription in the 2d ed., 1692 (not in Case), p. 145, and the 5th ed., 1707 (Case 244-e), p. 144. According to Thorpe (*Rochester's*

Poems, p. 180), the poem also appears without ascription in the 4th ed., 1702 (not in Case). (The 1688 text was probably printed from A-1685.)

B-1691, p. 39: "The Fall. A Song"; ascribed to Rochester. Reprinted with ascription to Rochester in B-1696, p. 36; B-1705, p. 36; B-1714, p. 21; B-1732, p. 21; B-1710-P, p. 16; B-1718-P, p. 75. (The 1691 text probably derives from one of the A-1680 editions.)

ADDITIONAL NOTE: Pinto reports a text of this poem in the "Portland Miscellany" (*Poems*, p. 168).

PREVIOUS SCHOLARSHIP: Printed as Rochester's by Hayward (*Collected Works*, p. 17) and Johns (*Poetical Works*, p. 27). Attributed to Rochester by Pinto (*Rochester*, pp. 41–42; *Poems*, p. 23) and Thorpe (*Rochester's Poems*, p. 180).

WHILE ON THOSE LOVELY LOOKS I GAZE

AUTHOR: Rochester.

TEXTS:

Yale MS., p. 151: "Song"; no ascription. (In section of poems by or concerning Rochester.)

Harvard MS. Eng. 636F, p. 67: "Song"; signed "Roch:."

B. M. Add. MS. 27408, fol. 11^r: "A Songe of MLR." (Possibly copied from printed text.)

A New Collection of the Choicest Songs, 1676 (Case 161), sig. A8^r: "Song"; no ascription. Includes, as an additional stanza, Rochester's eight-line song beginning "At last you'l force me to confess." For the authorship and other early texts of these additional lines, see Chapter 7 and my article, "Two Rochester Songs," *Notes and Queries*, *201* (1956), 338–39.

The Last and Best Edition of New Songs, 1677 (Case 163), sig.
D2^r: "Song"; no ascription. Includes 8 additional lines be-
ginning "At last you'l force me to confess." (Derived from
A New Collection, 1676.)

A-1680-HU, p. 71: "Song"; ascribed to Rochester. Reprinted
with ascription to Rochester in the other A-1680 editions and
in A-1685, p. 61; A-1701, p. 54; A-1713, p. 63; A-1731, p. 56.

The New Help to Discourse, 1684 (Case 141-c), p. 241: "A
Song"; no ascription. Includes 8 additional lines beginning
"At last you'l force me to confess." (Derived from *A New
Collection,* 1676.)

The Triumph of Wit, 1688 (not in Case), p. 144: "The Indifferent Lover: A Song"; no ascription. Reprinted without ascription in the 2d ed., 1692 (not in Case), p. 147, and the 5th ed.,
1707 (Case 244-e), p. 145. (The 1688 text probably derives
from A-1685.)

B-1691, p. 43: "A Song"; ascribed to Rochester. Reprinted with
ascription to Rochester in B-1696, p. 40; B-1705, p. 40;
B-1714, p. 23; B-1732, p. 23; B-1710-P, p. 17; B-1718-P,
p. 78. (The 1691 text probably derives from one of the A-1680
editions.)

The Hive, 1724 (Case 331-2-a), p. 122: no title; no ascription.
Reprinted without ascription in 1727 (Case 331-2-c), p. 122,
and 1733 (Case 331-2-d), p. 123. (The 1724 version probably derives from an earlier printed text.)

The Choice, 1733 (Case 353-3), p. 260: "Song ccxx"; no ascription. (Probably derived from earlier printed text.)

The Vocal Miscellany, 1738 (Case 388-2-b), p. 228: "Song
cclvi. Chloe, you may boast a Feature"; no ascription. (Probably derived from earlier printed text.)

The Syren, 2d ed., 1738 (not in Case), p. 171: "Song cxc";
no ascription. Reprinted without ascription in 1739 (Case

423-c), p. 171. (The 1738 version probably derives from an earlier printed text.)

The Merry Companion, 1739 (Case 424), p. 153: "Song CXXXVII. Chloe, you, &c."; no ascription. (Probably derived from earlier printed text.)

ADDITIONAL NOTE: Pinto reports a text of this poem in the "Portland Miscellany" (*Poems,* p. 169).

PREVIOUS SCHOLARSHIP: Printed as Rochester's by Hayward (*Collected Works,* p. 18), Norman Ault (*Seventeenth Century Lyrics,* 2d ed., New York, William Sloane Associates, 1950, p. 405), Johns (*Poetical Works,* p. 29), and Pinto (*Rochester,* p. 69; *Poems,* p. 25). Attributed to Rochester by Prinz (*Rochester,* p. 114), Wilson (*Court Wits,* p. 101), and Thorpe (*Rochester's Poems,* p. 180).

BY ALL LOVES SOFT, YET MIGHTY POW'RS

AUTHOR: Probably Rochester.

TEXTS:

[Yale MS.] This poem was probably among those removed by the fifth gap, pp. 153–58. (In section of poems by or concerning Rochester.)

Harvard MS. Eng. 636F, p. 69: "Song"; signed "Roch."

A-1680-HU, p. 72: "Song"; ascribed to Rochester. Reprinted with ascription to Rochester in the other A-1680 editions but omitted from A-1685, A-1701, A-1713, and A-1731.

PREVIOUS SCHOLARSHIP: Omitted from their editions of Rochester by Hayward (*Collected Works*), Johns (*Poetical Works*), and Pinto (*Poems*). Attributed to Rochester by Thorpe (*Rochester's Poems,* p. 180).

ROOM, ROOM, FOR A BLADE OF THE TOWN

AUTHOR: Thomas D'Urfey (see Chapter 6).

TEXTS:

[Yale MS.] This poem was probably among those removed by the fifth gap, pp. 153–58. (In section of poems by or concerning Rochester.)

Osborn MS. Chest 11, Number 39, p. 12: "Song. 23. The Towne Shift"; no ascription. (Probably copied from *The Last and Best Edition of New Songs,* 1677.)

Bodl. MS. Rawl. Poet. 173, fol. 132ᵛ: "The Bully, a Song. by the Same" (Rochester). (Probably copied from one of the A-1680 editions.)

The Last and Best Edition of New Songs, 1677 (Case 163), sig. A2ᵛ: "Another"; no ascription. The preceding poem is headed "In the Fool turn'd Critick."

A-1680-HU, p. 72: "Song"; ascribed to Rochester. Reprinted with ascription to Rochester in the other A-1680 editions and in A-1685, p. 61; A-1701, p. 55; A-1713, p. 64; A-1731, p. 57. (The text in A-1685, which is reprinted in A-1701, A-1713, and A-1731, is conflated from A-1680-HA and D'Urfey's *A New Collection,* 1683.)

Female Poems On Several Occasions. Written by Ephelia, 2d ed., 1682, p. 162: "The Town Blade"; ascribed to Ephelia. (Conflated from one of the A-1680 editions and some other source, possibly *The Last and Best Edition,* 1677.)

A New Collection of Songs and Poems. By Thomas D'urfey, Gent., 1683 (Day and Murrie 64), p. 3: "The Bully, a Song in the Fool turned Critick, set by Mr. Lock" (Matthew Locke); ascribed to D'Urfey. Music not included. (This text is an authoritative revision of D'Urfey's lyric.)

The Triumph of Wit, 1688 (not in Case), p. 144: "The Bully:

A Song"; no ascription. (Conflated from A-1685 and some other source, possibly D'Urfey's *A New Collection,* 1683.)

Wits Cabinet, 1703 (Case 173-k), p. 143: "The Bully"; no ascription. (Probably derived from D'Urfey's *A New Collection,* 1683.)

C-1707-a, p. ^{1}11: "Song"; ascribed to Rochester. Reissued in C-1707-b, p. ^{2}11, and reprinted with ascription to Rochester in C-1709, p. ^{2}73; C-1709-P, p. ^{3}5; C-1714-1, p. 106; and later editions in this series. (The text in C-1707-a was probably printed from one of the A-1680 editions.)

ADDITIONAL NOTE: Though D'Urfey evidently used this satirical song in his comedy *The Fool Turn'd Critick* (acted 18 Nov. 1676), it does not appear in the printed text of the play (1678).

PREVIOUS SCHOLARSHIP: Printed as Rochester's by Hayward (*Collected Works,* p. 108) and Johns (*Poetical Works,* p. 163). Rochester's authorship doubted by Prinz (*Rochester,* pp. 148–49). Attributed to Rochester or D'Urfey by Norman Ault (*Seventeenth Century Lyrics,* 2d ed., New York, William Sloane Associates, 1950, pp. 408, 514). Classified by Thorpe as "probably" by D'Urfey (*Rochester's Poems,* pp. 180–81). Omitted from his edition of Rochester by Pinto (*Poems*).

AGAINST THE CHARMES OUR BALLOCKS HAVE

AUTHOR: Probably Rochester.

TEXTS:

Yale MS., p. 152: "Song"; no ascription. All but the title and first 4 lines have been removed by the fifth gap, pp. 153–58. (In section of poems by or concerning Rochester.)

Harvard MS. Eng. 636F, p. 68: "Song"; signed "Roch."

A-1680-HU, p. 73: "Song"; ascribed to Rochester. Reprinted
with ascription to Rochester in the other A-1680 editions and
in A-1685, p. 62; A-1701, p. 56; A-1713, p. 65; A-1731, p. 57.

D-1718, p. 69: "On Mrs. W–llis"; ascribed to Rochester.
(Probably printed from a manuscript.)

PREVIOUS SCHOLARSHIP: Rochester's authorship doubted by
Prinz (*Rochester*, p. 151). Printed as Rochester's by Hayward
(*Collected Works*, p. 65) and Johns (*Poetical Works*, p. 214).
Attributed to Rochester by Wilson (*Court Wits*, p. 104) and
Thorpe (*Rochester's Poems*, p. 181). Omitted from his edi-
tion by Pinto (*Poems*).

I CANNOT CHANGE AS OTHERS DO

AUTHOR: Probably Sir Carr Scroope (see Chapter 8).

TEXTS:

Yale MS., p. 159: "Song By Sʳ Carr Scr:."

Osborn MS. Chest 11, Number 39, p. 46: "Song. 96. The Dying
Shepheard"; no ascription.

Osborn MS. Box 111, Number 27: no title; no ascription. Includes
last 8 lines only. At top of reverse side (verso) of same leaf,
apparently referring to this poem: "A song on Mrs Phraziar."

B. M. Add. MS. 27408, fol. 11ᵛ: "To Madam P ff G"; no ascription. (Possibly copied from printed text.)

Choice Ayres & Songs, 1679 (Day and Murrie 48), p. 8: no
title; no ascription. Includes music ascribed to "Mr. William
Turner."

A-1680-HU, p. 74: "Song"; ascribed to Rochester. Reprinted
with ascription to Rochester in the other A-1680 editions and
in A-1685, p. 63; A-1701, p. 56; A-1713, p. 66; A-1731, p. 58.

Female Poems On Several Occasions. Written by Ephelia, 2d ed., 1682, p. 163: "Song"; ascribed to Ephelia. (Probably printed from one of the A-1680 editions.)

The Triumph of Wit, 1688 (not in Case), p. 146: "The Constant Lover's Complaint: A Song"; no ascription. Reprinted without ascription in the 2d ed., 1692 (not in Case), p. 148. (The 1688 text was probably printed from A-1685.)

The Triumph of Wit, 1688 (not in Case), p. 159: "The Lover's Complaint to his Scornfull Mistriss: A new Song"; no ascription. Reprinted without ascription in the 2d ed., 1692 (not in Case), p. 158, and the 5th ed., 1707 (Case 244-e), p. 153. This version is preceded by 16 additional lines beginning "Ah, Cloris, pity or I dye." (The 1688 text probably derives from A-1685.)

B-1691, p. 62: "Constancy. A Song"; ascribed to Rochester. Reprinted with ascription to Rochester in B-1696, p. 59; B-1705, p. 59; B-1714, p. 34; B-1732, p. 34; B-1710-P, p. 25; B-1718-P, p. 94. (The 1691 text probably derives from one of the A-1680 editions.)

The Hive, 1724 (Case 331-1-a), p. 27: no title; no ascription. Reprinted without ascription under the title "Constancy" in 1726 (Case 331-1-c), p. 25, and 1732 (Case 331-1-d), p. 25. (The 1724 version probably derives from an earlier printed text.)

The Cupid, 1736 (Case 404), p. 93: "Song IX"; no ascription. Reprinted without ascription under the title "Song IX. As Amoret and Phyllis sat" in 1739 (Case 404-b), p. 103. According to Thorpe (*Rochester's Poems,* p. 182), the poem is reprinted without ascription in Dublin 1737 (not in Case). (The 1736 version probably derives from an earlier printed text.)

The Vocal Miscellany, 1738 (Case 388-2-b), p. 259: "Song

ccxciii. Greenwood Tree"; no ascription. (Probably derived from earlier printed text.)

ADDITIONAL NOTE: According to Pinto, a text of this poem, headed "Lett^r" and beginning with the word "Madam," appears in the "Portland Miscellany," p. 38 (*Poems*, p. 173).

PREVIOUS SCHOLARSHIP: Printed as Rochester's by Hayward (*Collected Works*, p. 25), Norman Ault (*Seventeenth Century Lyrics*, 2d ed., New York, William Sloane Associates, 1950, p. 415), Johns (*Poetical Works*, p. 43), and Pinto (*Poems*, p. 34). Attributed to Rochester by Prinz (*Rochester*, p. 114), Wilson (*Court Wits*, p. 93), and Thorpe (*Rochester's Poems*, pp. 181–82).

I SWIVE AS WELL AS OTHERS DO

AUTHOR: Probably Rochester (see Chapter 8).

TEXTS:

Yale MS., p. 160: "The Mock Song To I cannot Change &c"; no ascription. All but the title and first 4 lines have been removed by the sixth gap, pp. 161–84. (Probably in section of poems by or concerning Rochester.)

A-1680-HU, p. 75: "The Mock Song"; ascribed to Rochester. Reprinted with ascription to Rochester in the other A-1680 editions and in A-1685, p. 64; A-1701, p. 57; A-1713, p. 66; A-1731, p. 59.

The Triumph of Wit, 1688 (not in Case), p. 157: "The Misse's Confession: A Song"; no ascription. (Printed from A-1685.)

C-1714-1, p. 178: "The Mock Song"; ascribed to Rochester. Reprinted without ascription in the second volume of most later editions in this series, though it is ascribed to Dorset (Buckhurst) in C-1735, p. 144. (The 1714 text probably derives from one of the A-1680 editions. The 1735 text was printed from an earlier edition in the C series.)

ADDITIONAL NOTE: Pinto apparently reports a text of this poem, headed "Answer," in the "Portland Miscellany" (*Poems*, p. 173).

PREVIOUS SCHOLARSHIP: Printed as Rochester's by Hayward (*Collected Works*, p. 66) and Johns (*Poetical Works*, p. 213). Attributed to Rochester by Wilson (*Court Wits*, p. 104). Rochester's authorship doubted by Prinz (*Rochester*, p. 151) and Thorpe (*Rochester's Poems*, p. 182). Omitted from his edition by Pinto (*Poems*).

FOR STANDING TARSES WE KIND NATURE THANK

AUTHOR: Probably Buckhurst.

TEXTS:

[Yale MS.] This poem was almost certainly among those removed by the sixth gap, pp. 161–84.

Bodl. MS. Add. B. 106, fol. 44ᵛ: "Actus primus Scena prima. Enter Ubstboefs & Txkwfbouif. The Scene, a Bed-chamber"; ascribed to Rochester. (This text, which includes only the first 7 lines of the poem, was probably copied from one of the A-1680 editions. Obscene words are given in a simple cipher constructed by replacing each letter with the letter immediately following it in the alphabet; thus "Tarsander" and "Swiveanthe" become "Ubstboefs" and "Txkwfbouif.")

All Souls College, Oxford, MS. Codrington 174: "Tarsander, in imitation of the Lᵈ: Orreryes Poetry"; signed "Buckhurst."

A-1680-HU, p. 76: "Actus Primus Scena Prima. Enter Tarsander

and Swiveanthe. The Scene. A Bed-Chamber"; ascribed to
Rochester. Reprinted with ascription to Rochester in the other
A-1680 editions and in A-1685, p. 65. Omitted from A-1701,
A-1713, and A-1731.

C-1714-1, p. 155: "An Interlude. Actus Primus, Scena Prima.
Enter Tarsander and Swiveanthe. The Scene, A Bed-Chamber"; ascribed to Rochester. Reprinted without ascription in
later editions of this collection, usually in the second volume.
(The 1714 text was printed from one of the A-1680 editions.)

PREVIOUS SCHOLARSHIP: Printed as Rochester's by Hayward
(*Collected Works*, p. 73) and Johns (*Poetical Works*, p. 200),
but omitted by Pinto (*Poems*). Rochester's authorship doubted
by Prinz (*Rochester*, pp. 151, 175) and Thorpe (*Rochester's
Poems*, p. 182).

DREAMING LAST NIGHT ON MRS FARLEY

AUTHOR: Buckhurst (see Chapter 9).

TEXTS:

[Yale MS.] This poem was almost certainly among those removed by the sixth gap, pp. 161–84.

Harvard MS. Eng. 636F, p. 99: "A Letter from the Lord Buckhurst to Mr George Etheridge"; signed "Buckhurst."

Edinburgh MS. DC.1.3, p. 72: "Letter from ye Lord Dorsett,
to S^r. Geo: Etheridge."

A-1680-HU, p. 77: "The First Letter from B. to Mr. E.";
ascribed to Rochester. Reprinted with ascription to Rochester
in the other A-1680 editions and in A-1685, p. 68; A-1701,
p. 59; A-1713, p. 70; A-1731, p. 61.

C-1714-1, p. 157: "Epistles From B. to Mr. E."; ascribed to

Rochester. Reprinted with ascription to Rochester in later editions of this collection. (The 1714 text is reprinted from one of the A-1680 editions.)

PREVIOUS SCHOLARSHIP: Omitted by Hayward (*Collected Works*), Johns (*Poetical Works*), and Pinto (*Poems*). Rochester's or Buckhurst's authorship doubted by Prinz (*Rochester*, pp. 55–56, 146–47) and Harris (*Dorset*, pp. 103–05, 238). Attributed to Buckhurst by Wilson (*Court Wits*, pp. 20, 73) and Thorpe (*Rochester's Poems*, pp. 182–83).

AS CRAFTY HARLOTS, USE TO SHRINK

AUTHOR: George Etherege (see Chapter 9).

TEXTS:

[Yale MS.] This poem was almost certainly among those removed by the sixth gap, pp. 161–84.

Harvard MS. Eng. 636F, p. 103: "The Answer"; signed "Etheredge."

Edinburgh MS. DC.1.3, p. 73: "The Answer by S^r: Geo: Etheridge"; signed "Etheridge."

A-1680-HU, p. 80: "Mr. E——s Answer"; ascribed to Rochester. Reprinted with ascription to Rochester in the other A-1680 editions and in A-1685, p. 70; A-1701, p. 62; A-1713, p. 72; A-1731, p. 64.

C-1714-1, p. 160: "Mr. E——'s Answer"; ascribed to Rochester. Reprinted with ascription to Rochester in later editions of this collection. (The 1714 text is reprinted from one of the A-1680 editions.)

PREVIOUS SCHOLARSHIP: Omitted by Hayward (*Collected Works*), Johns (*Poetical Works*), Pinto (*Poems*), and Verity

(*Works of Etheredge*). Rochester's or Etheredge's authorship doubted by Prinz (*Rochester*, pp. 55–56, 146–47). Rochester's, Etherege's, or Buckhurst's authorship doubted by Harris (*Dorset*, pp. 103–05, 238). Attributed to Etherege by Wilson (*Court Wits*, pp. 20, 73) and Thorpe (*Rochester's Poems*, pp. 182–83).

IF I CAN GUESS THE DEVIL CHOAK ME

AUTHOR: Buckhurst (see Chapter 9).

TEXTS:

[Yale MS.] This poem was almost certainly among those removed by the sixth gap, pp. 161–84.

Harvard MS. Eng. 636F, p. 106: "Another Letter by the Lord Buckhurst, to Mʳ Etheredge."

Edinburgh MS. DC.1.3, p. 73: "Second Letter from the Lord Dorsett."

National Library of Scotland MS. Advocate 19.3.4: "Lo. Buckhurst to mʳ. Etheridge."

A-1680-HU, p. 82: "The Second Lettor from B—— to Mr. E——"; ascribed to Rochester. Reprinted with ascription to Rochester in the other A-1680 editions and in A-1685, p. 72; A-1701, p. 64; A-1713, p. 74; A-1731, p. 66.

C-1714-1, p. 163: "The second Epistle from B. to Mr. E.";ascribed to Rochester. Reprinted with ascription to Rochester in later editions of this collection. (The 1714 text is reprinted from one of the A-1680 editions.)

PREVIOUS SCHOLARSHIP: Omitted by Hayward (*Collected Works*), Johns (*Poetical Works*), and Pinto (*Poems*). Rochester's or Buckhurst's authorship doubted by Prinz (*Rochester*, pp. 55–56, 146–47) and Harris (*Dorset*, pp. 103–05, 238). Attributed to Buckhurst by Wilson (*Court Wits*, pp. 20, 73) and Thorpe (*Rochester's Poems*, pp. 182–83).

SO SOFT, AND AM'ROUSLY YOU WRITE

AUTHOR: Etherege (see Chapter 9).

TEXTS:

Yale MS., p. 185. The last 6 lines of the poem appear on this page. The rest has been removed by the sixth gap, pp. 161–84.

Harvard MS. Eng. 636F, p. 110: no title; signed "Etheredge."

Edinburgh MS. DC.1.3, p. 74: "Answer to ye 2^d. Letter by Sr Geo: Etthridge"; signed "Etheridge."

A-1680-HU, p. 85: "Mr. E——s. Answer"; ascribed to Rochester. Reprinted with ascription to Rochester in the other A-1680 editions and in A-1685, p. 75; A-1701, p. 67; A-1713, p. 78; A-1731, p. 68.

C-1714-1, p. 167: "Mr E——'s Answer"; ascribed to Rochester. Reprinted with ascription to Rochester in later editions of this collection. (The 1714 text is reprinted from one of the A-1680 editions.)

PREVIOUS SCHOLARSHIP: Omitted by Hayward (*Collected Works*), Johns (*Poetical Works*), Pinto (*Poems*), and Verity (*Works of Etheredge*). Rochester's or Etherege's authorship doubted by Prinz (*Rochester*, pp. 55–56, 146–47). Rochester's, Etherege's, or Buckhurst's authorship doubted by Harris (*Dorset*, pp. 103–05, 238). Attributed to Etherege by Wilson (*Court Wits*, pp. 20, 73) and Thorpe (*Rochester's Poems*, pp. 182–83).

COME ON YE CRITTICKS! FIND ONE FAULT WHO DARE

Author: Buckhurst (see Chapter 10).

Texts:

Yale MS., p. 186: "On Mr Edw: Howard upon his Brittish Princesse By ye L^d B:."

Harvard MS. Eng. 624: "L. B. on Mr Howards poem."

Harvard MS. Eng. 636F, p. 255: "Verses on the Same Subject"; no ascription.

B. M. Sloane MS. 4455, fol. 42^v: "A Prologue to Edw: Howards Eutopia made by Mr Bulkherst."

B. M. Add. MS. 18220, fol. 31^r: "A Satyr upon Ed: Howard's Poem, made by L^d. Buckhurst." Written at end: "Cõmunicat à D^{re} Sim: Patrick Sept. 6°. 1669."

Bodl. MS. Rawl. D. 260, fol. 30^v: "A Satyr upon Ed: Howard's poem made by Ld Buckhurst."

Bodl. MS. Eng. Poet. e. 4, p. 190: "To Mr Edward Howard on his British Princes"; signed "Charles B. Buckhurst, now E. Dorsett."

Bodl. MS. Don. b. 8, p. 284: "On Mr Edward Howards poeme, the L^d. Buckhurst ye supposed Authour."

Bodl. MS. Douce 357, fol. 142^v: "Upon M^r. Howards Brittish Princes"; signed "B."

Edinburgh MS. DC.1.3, p. 26: no title; signed "By the Ld Dorsett." Fragment including only the last 16 lines of the poem.

A-1680-HU, p. 88: "On Mr. E—— H—— upon his B—— P——"; ascribed to Rochester. Reprinted with ascription to Rochester in the other A-1680 editions and in A-1685, p. 78; A-1701, p. 69; A-1713, p. 81; A-1731, p. 71.

The Annual Miscellany: For The Year 1694, 1694 (Case 172-4-a), p. 298: "To A Person of Honour: Upon His Incomprehensible Poems. By——"; no ascription. Reprinted without ascription in 1708 (Case 172-4-b), p. 282. (The 1694 text was evidently printed from a manuscript.)

Poetical Miscellanies: The Fifth Part, 1704 (Case 172-5-a), p. 269: "To the Honourable Mr. E. H. on His Poems. By my Lord Buckhurst." (This version poses a problem. It seems to have been printed from *The Annual Miscellany: For The Year 1694* or from the manuscript which served as source for the 1694 text. Significant alterations have been made, however, including the correction of several readings from another source, probably one of the Rochester editions in the A series. The 1704 text is the earliest printed version to ascribe the poem to Buckhurst. The miscellanies of 1694 and 1704 were both published by Jacob Tonson.)

C-1714-1, p. 170: "To a Person of Honour, upon his Incomprehensible Poems"; ascribed to Rochester. Reprinted in later editions of this collection, usually in the second volume, with ascription to Dorset (Buckhurst). (The 1714 text was evidently printed from one of the A-1680 editions with alterations introduced from *The Annual Miscellany: For The Year 1694.* The ascription and the readings of individual lines are taken from the Rochester edition, but the title and the arrangement of the lines are those of the 1694 text. The ascription to Buckhurst in editions after 1714 probably derives from *The Third Part of Miscellany Poems,* 1716.)

The Third Part of Miscellany Poems, 1716 (Case 172-3-d), p. 69: "Upon the same. By the Lord Buckhurst." Reprinted with ascription to Buckhurst in 1727 (Case 172-3-e), p. 68. (The 1716 text is reprinted from *The Annual Miscellany: For The Year 1694;* the ascription may derive from *Poetical Miscellanies: The Fifth Part.* All three collections were published by Jacob Tonson.)

The Agreeable Variety, 1717 (Case 293), p. 148: "From the Lord Rochester." Reissued with ascription to Rochester in 1724 (Case 293-b), p. 148, and 1742 (Case 293-c), p. 148. Fragment of 4 lines. (The 1717 text was probably printed from one of the Rochester editions.)

A Collection of Epigrams, 1737 (Case 341-2), sig. C3ᵛ: "To the Honourable Mr. Edward Howard, on his Poem intitled, The British Princes"; no ascription. Fragment of 8 lines. (Probably printed from *The Annual Miscellany: For The Year 1694* or *The Third Part of Miscellany Poems.*)

The Works of the most celebrated Minor Poets, 1749 (Case 467-1-a), p. 125: "To Mr. Edward Howard, On his incompararable incomprehensible Poem, Called The British Princes"; ascribed to Dorset (Buckhurst). (Printed from some edition in the C series.)

ADDITIONAL NOTES: In his dedication of *Examen Poeticum,* 1693 (Case 172-3-a), Dryden remarks: "Ill Writers are usually the sharpest Censors: For they (as the best Poet, and the best Patron said), when in the full perfection of decay, turn Vinegar, and come again in Play" (sig. A4ʳ). The two lines of verse are quoted (inaccurately) from the poem under consideration, and "the best Poet, and the best Patron" is recognizable as Buckhurst. Dryden's statement antedates by eleven years the first printed text to include an ascription to Buckhurst (1704).

Gerard Langbaine, attributing the poem to Rochester, cites one of the A-1680 editions as his source (*An Account of the English Dramatick Poets,* 1691, p. 275). The ascription to Dorset (Buckhurst) by Giles Jacob evidently derives from a Rochester edition in the C series (*Poetical Register,* 2, 175). The similar ascription by Theophilus Cibber (who prints a complete text) evidently derives from *The Works of the most celebrated Minor Poets (Lives of the Poets, 3,* 15, 121). For other contemporary references to Buckhurst's poem, see Harris, *Dorset,* pp. 45–46, 199–200, 232–34.

PREVIOUS SCHOLARSHIP: Omitted by Hayward (*Collected Works*), Johns (*Poetical Works*), and Pinto (*Poems*). Rochester's authorship doubted by Prinz (*Rochester,* pp. 149–50). Attributed to Buckhurst by Helen A. Bagley ("A Checklist of the Poems of Charles Sackville," *Modern Language Notes,* 47 [1932], 454–61), Harris (*Dorset,* pp. 44–46, 199–200, 232–34), Wilson (*Court Wits,* pp. 178–79, 240), and Thorpe (*Rochester's Poems,* pp. 183–84).

AS WHEN A BULLY, DRAWS HIS SWORD

AUTHOR: Edmund Ashton (see Chapter 10).

TEXTS:

Yale MS., p. 192: "On the same Author upon his Brittish Princesse. By Major Aston."

Bodl. MS. Eng. Poet. e. 4, p. 197: "On the British Princes"; signed "E. A."

Edinburgh MS. DC.1.3, p. 63: "To M^r. Ed: Howard on his British Princess"; no ascription.

A-1680-HU, p. 89: "On the same Author upon his B—— P——"; ascribed to Rochester. Reprinted with ascription to Rochester in the other A-1680 editions and in A-1685, p. 79; A-1701, p. 70; A-1713, p. 82; A-1731, p. 72.

The Annual Miscellany: For The Year 1694, 1694 (Case 172-4-a), p. 304: "Upon the same"; no ascription. Reprinted without ascription in 1708 (Case 172-4-b), p. 285. (The 1694 text was evidently printed from a manuscript.)

C-1714-1, p. 172: "On the same Author"; ascribed to Rochester.

Omitted from later editions of this collection. (Printed from one of the A-1680 editions.)

The Third Part of Miscellany Poems, 1716 (Case 172-3-d), p. 71: "Upon the same"; no ascription. Reprinted without ascription in 1727 (Case 172-3-e), p. 70. (The 1716 text is reprinted from *The Annual Miscellany: For The Year 1694.* Both collections were published by Jacob Tonson.)

PREVIOUS SCHOLARSHIP: Omitted by Hayward (*Collected Works*), Johns (*Poetical Works*), and Pinto (*Poems*). Rochester's authorship doubted by Prinz (*Rochester,* p. 150). Attributed to Rochester by A. J. Bull ("Thomas Shadwell's Satire on Edward Howard," *Review of English Studies,* 6 [1930], 312–15), Harris (*Dorset,* p. 45), and Wilson (*Court Wits,* p. 178). Assigned to Rochester by Thorpe, though there is only "slender evidence on which to base an attribution" (*Rochester's Poems,* p. 184).

THOU DAMN'D ANTIPODES TO COMMON SENSE

AUTHOR: Uncertain; possibly Buckhurst, Wycherley, or Henry Savile (see Chapter 10).

TEXTS:

Yale MS., p. 189: "On Mr Edw: Howard upon his New Utopia. By Mr Hen: Savill."

Harvard MS. Eng. 636F, p. 253: "Upon Mr Edward Howards Playes"; signed "Witherley."

Bodl. MS. Rawl. Poet. 173, fol. 136v: "A Satyr on Mr Edward Howard. by the E. of Dorset." (Copied from Buckingham's *Works.*)

Bodl. MS. Eng. Poet. e. 4, p. 188: "On Mr Edward Howards New Utopia"; signed "Charles L. Buckhurst."

Edinburgh MS. DC.1.3, p. 26: "On M^r. Edward Howard"; no ascription.

A-1680-HU, p. 90: "On the same Author upon his new Ut——"; ascribed to Rochester. Reprinted with ascription to Rochester in the other A-1680 editions and in A-1685, p. 80; A-1701, p. 71; A-1713, p. 83; A-1731, p. 73.

The Annual Miscellany: For The Year 1694, 1694 (Case 172-4-a), p. 301: "Upon the same"; no ascription. Reprinted without ascription in 1708 (Case 172-4-b), p. 284. (The 1694 text was evidently printed from a manuscript.)

Miscellaneous Works, Written by His Grace, George, Late Duke of Buckingham, 1704 (Case 232-1-a), p. ^{1}74: "On Mr. Edward Howard. By the Earl of Dorset." Reprinted with ascription to Dorset (Buckhurst) in 1707 (Case 232-1-b), p. ^{1}74. (The 1704 text was evidently printed from a manuscript.)

C-1714-1, p. 173: "On the same Author, upon his Plays"; ascribed to Rochester. Omitted from later editions of this collection. (The 1714 text is reprinted from one of the A-1680 editions, but a few readings have been corrected from another source, probably *The Annual Miscellany: For The Year 1694*.)

The Third Part of Miscellany Poems, 1716 (Case 172-3-d), p. 70: "Upon the same"; no ascription. Reprinted without ascription in 1727 (Case 172-3-e), p. 69. (The 1716 text is reprinted from *The Annual Miscellany: For The Year 1694*. Both collections were published by Jacob Tonson.)

The Works of the most celebrated Minor Poets, 1749 (Case 467-1-a), p. 126: "To the same on his Plays"; ascribed to Dorset (Buckhurst). (Printed from *The Annual Miscellany: For The Year 1694* or *The Third Part of Miscellany Poems*. The ascription may derive from Buckingham's *Works*.)

ADDITIONAL NOTE: Gerard Langbaine, attributing this poem to Rochester, cites one of the A-1680 editions as his source (*An Account of the English Dramatick Poets*, 1691, p. 274).

PREVIOUS SCHOLARSHIP: Omitted by Hayward (*Collected Works*), Johns (*Poetical Works*), and Pinto (*Poems*). Rochester's authorship doubted by Prinz (*Rochester*, p. 150) and Thorpe (*Rochester's Poems*, pp. 184–85). Attributed to Buckhurst by Helen A. Bagley ("A Checklist of the Poems of Charles Sackville," *Modern Language Notes*, 47 [1932], 454–61), Harris (*Dorset*, pp. 44, 232–33), and Wilson (*Court Wits*, p. 179).

ONE DAY THE AM'ROUS LISANDER

AUTHOR: Aphra Behn.

TEXTS:

Yale MS., p. 213. The last 10 lines of the poem appear on this page. The rest has been removed by the seventh gap, pp. 195–212.

Harvard MS. Eng. 636F, p. 117: "An Imperfect Enjoyment, By M:ris. A: Behn."

Bodl. MS. Add. B. 106, fol. 40r: "The Disappointment"; ascribed to Rochester. (Copied from one of the A-1680 editions.)

A-1680-HU, p. 92: "The Disappointment"; ascribed to Rochester. Reprinted with ascription to Rochester in the other A-1680 editions and in A-1685, p. 82; A-1701, p. 73; A-1713, p. 85; A-1731, p. 75.

Poems upon Several Occasions . . . By Mrs. A. Behn, 1684, p. 70: "The Disappointment"; ascribed to Aphra Behn. (This edition was authorized by Aphra Behn herself.)

The Triumph of Wit, 1688 (not in Case), p. 60: "Loves Misfortune: Or, The Unhappy Disappointment. A Poem"; no ascription. Reprinted without ascription in the 2d ed., 1692 (not in Case), p. 57; 1707 (Case 244-e), p. 54; 1735 (Case 244-i), p. 41. According to Thorpe (*Rochester's Poems*, p. 185), the poem appears without ascription in the 4th ed., 1702 (not in Case). (The 1688 text was printed from A-1685.)

C-1714-1, p. 117: "The Insensible"; ascribed to Rochester. Reprinted with ascription to Rochester in later editions of this collection. (The 1714 text was printed from one of the A-1680 editions.)

Familiar Letters of Love, Gallantry, And several Occasions, 1718 (Case 305), p. 39: "An Imperfect Enjoyment"; ascribed to Aphra Behn. Reprinted with ascription to Aphra Behn in 1724 (Case 305-f), p. 39. This version is given as a postscript to a letter from Aphra Behn to her friend John Hoyle, in which she says, "I have herewith enclos'd to you my short Essay upon *Imperfect Enjoyment*: Read it over with your wonted Candour, and send me your impartial Sentiments." (The 1718 text was apparently printed from a manuscript.)

D-1718, p. 3: "The Imperfect Enjoyment"; ascribed to Rochester. Reprinted with ascription to Rochester in D-1761, p. 210 (misnumbered 110). (The 1718 text was apparently printed from a manuscript.)

ADDITIONAL NOTE: According to Thorpe (*Rochester's Poems*, p. 185), this poem appears without ascription in *Beau's Miscellany*, Part II, c. 173? (not in Case).

PREVIOUS SCHOLARSHIP: Printed as Rochester's by Hayward (*Collected Works*, p. 67) and Johns (*Poetical Works*, p. 169). Attributed to Rochester by Prinz (*Rochester*, pp. 107, 144). Attributed to Aphra Behn by Montague Summers (*The Works of Aphra Behn*, London, W. Heinemann, 1915, 6, 178, 425),

Wilson ("Two Poems Ascribed to Rochester," *Modern Language Notes*, 54 [1939], 458–60), and Thorpe (*Rochester's Poems*, p. 185). Omitted from his edition by Pinto (*Poems*).

WHILST HAPPY I TRIUMPHANT STOOD

AUTHOR: Aphra Behn.

TEXTS:

Yale MS., p. 214: "On a Giniper Tree now cut downe to make Busks. By Mrs Behn."

A-1680-HU, p. 97: "On a Giniper Tree now cut down to make Busks"; ascribed to Rochester. Reprinted with ascription to Rochester in the other A-1680 editions and in A-1685, p. 88; A-1701, p. 77; A-1713, p. 90; A-1731, p. 80.

Poems upon Several Occasions . . . By Mrs. A. Behn, 1684, p. 19: "On a Juniper-Tree, cut down to make Busks"; ascribed to Aphra Behn. (This edition was authorized by Aphra Behn herself.)

C-1714-1, p. 123: "On a Juniper-Tree, cut down to make Busks"; ascribed to Rochester. Reprinted with ascription to Rochester in later editions of this collection. (The 1714 text was printed from one of the A-1680 editions.)

ADDITIONAL NOTE: According to Thorpe (*Rochester's Poems*, p. 185), this poem appears without ascription in *Beau's Miscellany*, Part II, c. 173? (not in Case).

PREVIOUS SCHOLARSHIP: Printed as Rochester's by Hayward (*Collected Works*, p. 74) and Johns (*Poetical Works*, p. 175). Attributed by Prinz to Rochester in his text (*Rochester*, pp. 107, 141) but to Aphra Behn under "Corrigenda and Addenda" (p. 459). Attributed to Aphra Behn by Montague Summers (*The Works of Aphra Behn*, London, W. Heine-

mann, 1915, 6, 148, 422), Wilson ("Two Poems Ascribed to
Rochester," *Modern Language Notes, 54* [1939], 458–60),
and Thorpe (*Rochester's Poems*, p. 185). Omitted from his
edition by Pinto (*Poems*).

WHAT DOLEFUL CRYES ARE THESE
THAT FRIGHT MY SENSE

AUTHOR: Aphra Behn.

TEXTS:

Yale MS., p. 221: "On ye Death of that most Excellent Painter,
Mr Greenhill. By M^{rs}. Behn."

A-1680-HU, p. 101: "On the Death of Mr. Greenhill The Famous Painter"; ascribed to Rochester. Reprinted with ascription to Rochester in the other A-1680 editions and in A-1685,
p. 91; A-1713, p. 132; A-1731, p. 120. Omitted from A-1701.

Poems upon Several Occasions . . . By Mrs. A. Behn, 1684, p.
24: "On the Death of Mr. Grinhil, the Famous Painter";
ascribed to Aphra Behn. (This edition was authorized by
Aphra Behn herself.)

C-1714-1, p. 127: "On the Death of Mr. Greenhill, the famous
Painter"; ascribed to Rochester. Omitted from later editions
of this collection. (Printed from one of the A-1680 editions.)

ADDITIONAL NOTE: The poem is ascribed to Rochester by Giles
Jacob, whose information rather obviously derives from
an earlier printed text (*Poetical Register, 2,* 233).

PREVIOUS SCHOLARSHIP: Printed as Rochester's by Hayward
(*Collected Works*, p. 60) and Johns (*Poetical Works*, p. 218).
Attributed to Aphra Behn by Montague Summers (*The Works
of Aphra Behn*, London, W. Heinemann, 1915, 6, 151, 423),
Prinz (*Rochester*, p. 459), Wilson ("Two Poems Ascribed to

Rochester," *Modern Language Notes, 54* [1939], 458–60),
and Thorpe (*Rochester's Poems*, p. 185). Omitted from his
edition by Pinto (*Poems*).

HAVE YOU SEEN THE RAGING STORMY MAIN

AUTHOR: Uncertain; probably not Rochester.

TEXTS:

Yale MS., p. 249: "To all curious Critticks & Admirers of
   Meeter"; no ascription.

A-1680-HU, p. 104: "To all curious Criticks and Admirers of
   Meeter"; ascribed to Rochester. Reprinted with ascription to
   Rochester in A-1685, p. 94; A-1701, p. 81; A-1713, p. 94;
   A-1731, p. 83.

C-1707-a, p. ^{1}84: "To all Curious Criticks, And Admirers of
   Meetre"; ascribed to Rochester. Reissued in C-1707-b, p. ^{2}84,
   and reprinted with ascription to Rochester in C-1709, p. ^{2}128;
   C-1709-P, p. ^{4}1; C-1714-1, p. 33; and later editions of this
   collection. (The 1707 text was printed from one of the A-1680
   editions.)

The Agreeable Companion, 1745 (Case 447), p. 377: "To the
   Curious Criticks and Admirers of Metre"; no ascription.
   (Printed from one of the later editions in the C series.)

PREVIOUS SCHOLARSHIP: Printed as Rochester's by Hayward
   (*Collected Works,* p. 58) and Johns (*Poetical Works,* p. 113).
   Attributed to Rochester by Prinz (*Rochester,* p. 109) and
   Thorpe (*Rochester's Poems,* p. 185). Omitted from his edi-
   tion by Pinto (*Poems*).

WHAT TIMON DOES OLD AGE BEGIN
T' APPROACH

Author: Probably Rochester (see Chapter 11).

Texts:

Yale MS., p. 227: "Satyr. By Sr Char: Sidley."

Harvard MS. Eng. 623F, p. 52: "Satyr upon a Diner"; signed "Rochester."

Harvard MS. Eng. 636F, p. 228: "Satyr By Sr Charles Sidley."

Edinburgh MS. DC.1.3, p. 56: "A satyre"; no ascription.

A-1680-HU, p. 105: "Satyr"; ascribed to Rochester. Reprinted with ascription to Rochester in the other A-1680 editions and in A-1685, p. 95; A-1701, p. 81; A-1713, p. 95; A-1731, p. 84.

Miscellaneous Works, Written by His Grace, George, Late Duke of Buckingham, 1704 (Case 232-1-a), p. ^{1}53: "Timon, a Satyr, In Imitation of Monsieur Boileau, upon several Passages in some new Plays then Acted upon the Stage. By the Duke of Buckingham." Reprinted with ascription to Buckingham in 1707 (Case 232-1-b), p. ^{1}53. Reprinted with ascription to "the Duke of Buckingham, and the Earl of Rochester" in *The Works Of His Grace, George Villiers, Late Duke of Buckingham,* 1715, *1,* 159. Reprinted in later editions of this collection with ascriptions to Buckingham and Rochester or to Buckingham alone. (The 1704 text was printed from one of the A-1680 editions.)

C-1714-1, p. 131: "The Rehearsal. A Satire"; ascribed to Rochester. Reprinted with ascription to Rochester in later editions of this collection. (The 1714 text was printed from one of the A-1680 editions.)

ADDITIONAL NOTES: Pinto reports that a text of this poem, headed
"Satyr," appears without ascription in the "Portland Miscellany" (*Poems*, pp. 196–97).

Gerard Langbaine, attributing "Timon" to Rochester, cites
one of the A-1680 editions as his source (*An Account of the
English Dramatick Poets*, 1691, pp. 92–93). Giles Jacob
ascribes the poem to Rochester (*Poetical Register*, 2, 232) or
to Buckingham assisted by Rochester (2, 218); as Jacob's titles show, the former ascription derives from a Rochester edition in the C series, while the latter derives from Buckingham's
Works of 1715. Horace Walpole, assigning "Timon" to Buckingham and Rochester, cites Buckingham's 1715 *Works* as
his source (*Catalogue of Royal and Noble Authors*, 2, 79).
The similar ascription by Theophilus Cibber derives from
Buckingham's 1715 *Works* or from Jacob (*Lives of the Poets*,
2, 323). Also probably derived from a printed source is the
ascription to Rochester by Dean Lockier (Joseph Spence,
Anecdotes, ed. Samuel Weller Singer, London, 1820, p. 66).

PREVIOUS SCHOLARSHIP: Attributed to Buckingham and Rochester by Hayward (*Collected Works*, pp. 76, 331). Attributed
to Rochester alone by Johns (*Poetical Works*, p. 179), Prinz
(*Rochester*, pp. 96, 99–100), and Pinto in his biography
(*Rochester*, pp. 144–49). Attributed by Wilson to Rochester,
"perhaps in collaboration with Buckingham" (*Court Wits*, pp.
19, 130–31, 145, 182, 185, 224). Classified by Thorpe as a
doubtful poem, "probably at least in large part Rochester's
composition" (*Rochester's Poems*, pp. 186–87). Printed in his
edition by Pinto as probably "written by Rochester in collaboration with one or more of his friends" (*Poems*, pp. 99, 197).

SINCE THE SONS OF THE MUSES, GREW NUM'ROUS, AND LOUD

AUTHOR: Uncertain; possibly Elkanah Settle (see Chapter 12).

TEXTS:

Yale MS., p. 238: "A Session of ye Poets. Suppos'd to be written by Elk: Settle."

Osborn MS. Chest 11, Number 14, p. 1038: "The sessions off poetts: 1676/7"; no ascription. Incomplete copy ending with the line "And little Tom Essences Author was their."

Harvard MS. Eng. 623F, p. 43: "The Session of the Poets"; no ascription.

Harvard MS. Eng. 636F, p. 143: "The Session of Poets"; no ascription.

B. M. Lansdowne MS. 1039, fol. 5^r: "A Session of ye Poets"; no ascription. (Copied from one of the A-1680 editions.)

Bodl. MS. Rawl. Poet. 159, fol. 196^r: "A Session of Poets. 1676"; no ascription.

Bodl. MS. Rawl. Poet. 173, fol. 133^v: "A Tryall of the Poets for the Bays. In imitation of a Satyr in Boileau. By the D. of Buckingham." (Copied from Buckingham's *Works*, 1704 or 1707.)

Bodl. MS. Don. b. 8, p. 586: "A Sessions of Poetts"; no ascription.

Edinburgh MS. DC.1.3, p. 69: "The second session of Poet's"; no ascription.

A-1680-HU, p. 111: "A Session of the Poets"; ascribed to Rochester. Reprinted with ascription to Rochester in the other A-1680 editions and in A-1685, p. 101; A-1701, p. 87; A-1713, p. 101; A-1731, p. 90.

Miscellaneous Works, Written by His Grace, George, Late Duke of Buckingham, 1704 (Case 232-1-a), p. ^141: "A Tryal of the

Poets for the Bays, in Imitation of a Satyr in Boileau. By the Duke of Buckingham." Reprinted with ascription to Buckingham in 1707 (Case 232-1-b), p. ¹41. Reprinted with ascription to "the Duke of Buckingham, and the Earl of Rochester" in *The Works Of His Grace, George Villiers, Late Duke of Buckingham,* 1715, *1,* 151. Reprinted in later editions of this collection with ascriptions to Buckingham and Rochester or to Buckingham alone. (The 1704 text is reprinted from one of the A-1680 editions.)

C-1714-1, p. 138: "A Session of the Poets"; ascribed to Rochester. Reprinted with ascription to Rochester in later editions of this collection. (The 1714 text is reprinted from one of the A-1680 editions.)

The Second Part of Miscellany Poems, 1716 (Case 172-2-e), p. 96: "A Session of the Poets"; no ascription. Reprinted without ascription in 1727 (Case 172-2-f), p. 94. (The 1716 text is reprinted from C-1714-1.)

A Collection of Merry Poems, 1736 (Case 403-b), p. 27: "A Session of the Poets"; no ascription. (Derived from some edition in the C series.)

ADDITIONAL NOTES: Gerard Langbaine appears to question Rochester's authorship of "A Session," which he quotes from one of the A-1680 editions (*An Account of the English Dramatick Poets,* 1691, pp. 322–23). The poem is assigned to Rochester in Anthony Wood's *Athenae Oxonienses* (*4,* 169, 527, 685, 688), but the information is credited to one of the A-1680 editions and therefore does not seem to represent independent testimony. Similarly, the ascriptions to Rochester by Giles Jacob (*Poetical Register,* 2, 232) and Theophilus Cibber (*Lives of the Poets,* 2, 229, 326) appear to derive from earlier printed texts. Horace Walpole, attributing the poem to Buckingham and Rochester, cites Buckingham's 1715 *Works* as his source (*Catalogue of Royal and Noble Authors*, 2, 79).

Wilson ("Rochester's 'A Session of the Poets,' " p. 115) errs in saying that "A Session" is attributed to Rochester by John Crowne in "The Epistle to the Reader" prefixed to his *Caligula*, 1698. Crowne's actual words are: ". . . his Lordship [Rochester] in his poem, call'd the Sessions of Poets charges me not with theft, but my scenes with dulness and want of wit, and poetry . . ." (*The Dramatic Works of John Crowne*, ed. James Maidment and W. H. Logan, Edinburgh, W. Paterson, 1873–74, 4, 353–54). This statement, which does not correspond to any part of the passage on Crowne in "A Session," clearly echoes the following sarcastic couplet in Rochester's "An Allusion to Horace":

> For by that *Rule*, I might aswel admit,
> *Crowns*, tedious *Scenes*, for *Poetry*, and *Wit*.
>
> (A-1680-HU, p. 41)

Crowne's phrase "the Sessions of Poets" is evidently used in a generic sense.

Hayward (*Collected Works*, p. 333), Ham ("Dryden Versus Settle," p. 412), and Greene ("Otway and Mrs. Barry," p. 307) state incorrectly that "A Session" appears in *Poems on Affairs of State*, 1697 (Case 211-1-a). The verses printed there (p. [1]217) are "The Session of the Poets, to the Tune of Cook Lawrel" ("Apollo concern'd to see the Transgressions"), an entirely separate work.

PREVIOUS SCHOLARSHIP: Printed as Rochester's by Hayward (*Collected Works*, p. 131) and Johns (*Poetical Works*, p. 187). Rochester's authorship accepted by Pinto in his biography (*Rochester*, pp. 153–54, 188) but doubted by Prinz

(*Rochester*, pp. 70, 73, 75, 84, 85, 100–04). Attributed to Settle by Roswell G. Ham ("Otway's Duels with Churchill and Settle," *Modern Language Notes, 41* [1926], 73–80; "Dryden Versus Settle," *Modern Philology, 25* [1928], 409–16; *Otway and Lee*, New Haven, Yale Univ. Press, 1931, pp. 108–12; "The Authorship of 'A Session of the Poets' [1677]," *Review of English Studies, 9* [1933], 319–22). Attributed to Buckingham by Graham Greene ("Otway and Mrs. Barry," *London Times Literary Supplement*, 16 April 1931, p. 307), but assigned to Rochester by D. M. Walmsley ("A Trial of the Poets," *London Times Literary Supplement*, 28 May 1931, p. 427) and J. C. Ghosh (*The Works of Thomas Otway*, Oxford, Clarendon Press, 1932, *1*, 18–22). Settle's authorship doubted by Hugh Macdonald (*A Journal from Parnassus*, London, P. J. Dobell, 1937, p. ix; *Dryden Bibliography*, p. 221). Attributed by Wilson to Rochester, or Rochester in collaboration with other Court Wits ("Rochester's 'A Session of the Poets,' " *Review of English Studies, 22* [1946], 109–16; *Court Wits*, pp. 19, 147, 174, 180–85). Wilson's conclusions accepted by Thorpe (*Rochester's Poems*, pp. 186–87) and by Pinto in his edition (*Poems*, pp. 104, 202–03).

NOW CURSES ON YE ALL, YE VIRTUOUS FOOLS

AUTHOR: John Oldham.

TEXTS:

Yale MS., p. 264: "Satyr. By Mʳ Oldham. Aude aliquid brevibus Gyaris aut carcere dignum Sivis esse aliquis—Indem Sat. Suppos'd to be Spoken by a Court Hector. Pindarique." In margin beside title: "Written July/77."

Osborn MS. Chest 11, Number 14, p. 985: "Aude aliquid brevibus gyaris aut carcere dignum sivis esse Aliquis—Juven: sat: Supposed to be spoken by a court Hector Pindaricque"; ascribed to Oldham. The ascription consists of an introductory anecdote, headed "1677," which claims to relate how Oldham's poetry was first brought to the attention of Buckingham and other Court Wits, and how Oldham came to write this satire. For the full text of the anecdote and a discussion of its significance, see my article, "John Oldham, the Wits, and *A Satyr against Vertue*," *Philological Quarterly*, *33* (1953), 90–93.

Harvard MS. Eng. 623F, p. 58: "A Pindarick Ode in Praise of vice"; no ascription. Incomplete copy ending with the line "Envyed Mankind the hon^{re}. of thy Wikedness."

Harvard MS. Eng. 636F, p. 202: "Aude Aliquid Brevibus gyaris aut Carcere dignum, Sivis esse Aliquid &^{c}. Supposed to be spoken by a Court Hector"; no ascription.

Princeton MS. AM 14401, p. 109: "Audi aliquid brevibus Gyari aut carcere dignum Sivis esse aliquis Inden Sac. Supposed to be Spoken by a Court Hector. Pindarique"; no ascription.

B. M. Add. MS. 14047, fol. 116^v: "Supposed to be spoken by ye Court-Hector who demolised ye sund-Diall:—A Satyr against Virtue—Mr Oldham." At end of text, scored out: "Ld Roch^r:—."

Bodl. MS. Rawl. Poet. 123, p. 3: "Aude aliquid brevibus Gyaris & carcere dignum Si vis esse aliquis.—Juven. Sat. Pindarique." In margin beside title: "July 1676 at Croydon." Facing title on opposite page: "Suppos'd to be spoken by a Court-Hector at Breaking of ye Dial in Privy-Garden." This text is in the handwriting of John Oldham.

Bodl. MS. Add. B. 106, fol. 34^r: "Satyr. Aude aliq^d brevibus &c: Suppos'd to be spoken by a Court Hector. Pindarique." In margin beside title: "Roch:." At end of text: "This Satyr is in Oldhams Poems & the subsequent Apology." (Copied from one of the A-1680 editions.)

Bodl. MS. Rawl. D. 1480, fol. 201ʳ: "A Satyr against Vertue ibm
Aude aliquid brevibus Gyaris et carcere dignum, Si vis esse
aliquis—Juvenl Sat. Pindarique Ode. Book yᵉ 1ˢᵗ page 93."
"Ibm" in the title refers back to fol. 199ʳ, where another poem
is said to be "taken out of Oldham works." (Copied from Oldham's *Satyrs upon the Jesuits*, several editions of which begin
the poem on p. 93.)

A Satyr against Vertue, 1679, p. 3: "A Poem: Supposed to be
spoken by a Town-Hector. Pindarique, In Imitation of Mr.
Cowley"; no ascription.

A-1680-HU, p. 115: "Satyr. Aude aliquid brevibus Gyaris aut
carcere dignum Sivis esse aliquis—Indem sat. Suppos'd to be
spoken by a Court Hector Pindarique"; ascribed to Rochester.
Reprinted with ascription to Rochester in the other A-1680
editions and in A-1713, p. 135, and A-1731, p. 123. Omitted
from A-1685 and A-1701.

  Beside the title of this poem in A-1680-S-S (Sterling copy),
a contemporary hand has added "said to be Oldham's."

Satyrs upon the Jesuits, 1681, p. 97: "A Poem: Supposed to be
spoken by a Town-Hector. Pindarique, In imitation of Mr.
Cowley." Reprinted in later editions of Oldham's poems, such
as *The Works of Mr. John Oldham, Together with his Remains*, 1684; for detailed descriptions of these editions, see
Brooks, "Oldham Bibliography." (Though the 1681 edition
was authorized by Oldham himself, the text of the poem was
printed from the unauthorized *A Satyr against Vertue*, 1679.)

ADDITIONAL NOTES: Brooks reports that this poem, together with
others by Oldham which "were evidently transcribed from
MSS. in circulation," appears (p. 12) in a manuscript owned by
H. M. Margoliouth. It carries no ascription and is headed
"Aude aliquid brevibus Gyaris et Carcere dignum Sivis esse

aliquid . . . Supposed to be spoken by a Court Hector Pindarique" ("Oldham Bibliography," pp. 16–17).

The poem is assigned to Oldham in Anthony Wood's *Athenae Oxonienses* (4, 120, 121). Giles Jacob's ascription to Oldham seems to derive from some edition of Oldham's works (*Poetical Register*, 2, 121).

PREVIOUS SCHOLARSHIP: Omitted by Hayward (*Collected Works*) and Johns (*Poetical Works*). Attributed to Oldham by Prinz (*Rochester*, p. 146), Brooks ("Oldham Bibliography"), Wilson (*Court Wits*, p. 20), Thorpe (*Rochester's Poems*, pp. 187–88), and Pinto (*Poems*, p. xlviii).

MY PART IS DONE, AND YOU'LL I HOPE EXCUSE

AUTHOR: John Oldham.

TEXTS:

Yale MS., p. 284: "An Apology to the foregoeing Satyr by way of Epilogue. By ye same Author [i.e. Oldham]."

Osborn MS. Chest II, Number 14, p. 1008: "An Apologie for the preceeding poem by way of Epilogue to be annexd att the end: p: 994: 1677: poem: pind:"; no ascription.

Harvard MS. Eng. 636F, p. 216: "Apology For the Former Verses, by way of Epilogue"; no ascription.

Princeton MS. AM 14401, p. 271: "An Apologie. by way of Epilogue to ye pindaricks"; no ascription.

B. M. Add. MS. 27408, fol. 60^v: no title; no ascription. Fols. 60^v–61^r contain scattered passages from the poem.

Bodl. MS. Rawl. Poet. 123, p. 16: "Apology for ye foregoing Verses by way of Epilogue." In the handwriting of John Oldham.

Bodl. MS. Add. B. 106, fol. 38^r: "An Apology to the foregoing

Satyr, by way of Epilogue"; ascribed to Rochester. Above the
title, at the end of the preceding poem, is written: "This Satyr
is in Oldhams Poems & the subsequent Apology." (Copied
from one of the A-1680 editions.)

A Satyr against Vertue, 1679, p. 13: "An Apologie for the preceeding Poem, by way of Epilogue, to be annexed"; no ascription.

A-1680-HU, p. 127: "An Apology to the fore-going Satyr by way
of Epilogue"; ascribed to Rochester. Reprinted with ascription
to Rochester in the other A-1680 editions but omitted from
A-1685, A-1701, A-1713, and A-1731.

Satyrs upon the Jesuits, 1681, p. 115: "An Apology for the preceding Poem, by way of Epilogue, to be annexed." Reprinted
in later editions of Oldham's poems, such as *The Works of
Mr. John Oldham, Together with his Remains,* 1684; for detailed descriptions of these editions, see Brooks, "Oldham
Bibliography." (Though the 1681 edition was authorized
by Oldham himself, the text of the poem was printed from
the unauthorized *A Satyr against Vertue,* 1679.)

ADDITIONAL NOTES: Brooks reports that this poem, together with
others by Oldham which "were evidently transcribed from
MSS. in circulation," appears (p. 18) in a manuscript owned
by H. M. Margoliouth. It is headed "The Apology for the
former verses" and signed "By a Country Parson" ("Oldham
Bibliography," pp. 16–17). According to Pinto, another text,
headed "An Apology to yᵉ foregoing Satyr by way of Epilogue," appears in the "Portland Miscellany" (*Poems,* p.
xlviii).

PREVIOUS SCHOLARSHIP: Omitted by Hayward (*Collected
Works*) and Johns (*Poetical Works*). Attributed to Oldham

by Brooks ("Oldham Bibliography"), Wilson (*Court Wits*, p. 20), Thorpe (*Rochester's Poems*, pp. 187–88), and Pinto (*Poems*, p. xlviii).

TELL ME ABANDON'D MISCREANT, PRITHEE TELL

AUTHOR: John Oldham.

TEXTS:

Yale MS., p. 299: "Upon the Author of the Play call'd Sodom. By ye same Author [i.e. Oldham]." In margin beside title: "Jan ye 20th 1677/8."

Bodl. MS. Rawl. Poet. 123, p. 84: "Upon ye Author of ye Play call'd Sodom." Parts of the poem appear on pp. 82–86, 90–92, and 98. This text, in the handwriting of John Oldham, exhibits the poem in various stages of composition and revision.

Bodl. MS. Add. B. 106, fol. 44^r: "Upon the Author of a Play call'd Sodom"; ascribed to Rochester. (Copied from one of the A-1680 editions.)

A-1680-HU, p. 129: "Upon the Author of a Play call'd Sodom"; ascribed to Rochester. Reprinted with ascription to Rochester in the other A-1680 editions and in A-1685, p. 105; A-1701, p. 90; A-1713, p. 105; A-1731, p. 94.

C-1707-a, p. ^{1}77: "On the Author of a Play call'd Sodom"; ascribed to Rochester. Reissued in C-1707-b, p. ^{2}77, and reprinted with ascription to Rochester in C-1709, p. ^{2}126; C-1709-P, p. ^{3}16; C-1714-1, p. 98; and later editions of this collection. (The 1707 text, which omits 21 of the more obscene lines of the poem, was printed from one of the A-1680 editions. The 1714 text, which restores the missing lines, is conflated from C-1709 and one of the A-1680 editions.)

PREVIOUS SCHOLARSHIP: Printed as Rochester's by Hayward (*Collected Works*, pp. xvii, 95) and Johns (*Poetical Works*, p. 154). Attributed to Rochester by Prinz (*Rochester*, pp. 172, 175–76). Attributed to Oldham by Percy L. Babington ("Dryden not the Author of 'MacFlecknoe,' " *Modern Language Review, 13* [1918], 25–34), Brooks ("Attributions to Rochester," *London Times Literary Supplement*, 9 May 1935, p. 301; "Oldham Bibliography"), Wilson (*Court Wits*, p. 20), and Thorpe (*Rochester's Poems*, pp. 187–89). Omitted from his edition by Pinto (*Poems*).

RAT TOO, RAT TOO, RAT TOO, RAT TAT TOO, RAT TAT TOO

AUTHOR: Alexander Radcliffe.

TEXTS:

Yale MS., p. 303: "A Call to ye Guard by a Drum"; no ascription.

Edinburgh MS. DC.1.3, p. 24: "A Call to the Guard"; no ascription.

A-1680-HU, p. 131: "A Call to the Guard by a Drum"; ascribed to Rochester. Reprinted with ascription to Rochester in the other A-1680 editions but omitted from A-1685, A-1701, A-1713, and A-1731.

 Beneath the title of this poem in A-1680-S-S (Sterling copy), a contemporary hand has added "By Ratcliff."

Wit and Drollery, 1682 (Case 114-c), p. 130: "A call to the Guard"; no ascription. (Textual evidence, though inconclusive, suggests that this version was conflated from one of the A-1680 editions and a manuscript source.)

The Ramble: an Anti-Heroick Poem. Together with Some Terrestrial Hymns and Carnal Ejaculations. By Alexander Radcliffe . . . Printed for the Author . . . , 1682 (Macdonald

217), p. 63: "A Call to the Guard by a Drum." Reissued in *The Works of Capt. Alex. Radcliffe*, "third edition," 1696, p. ²63. (Though *The Ramble*, 1682 was authorized by Radcliffe himself, the text of this poem was printed from one of the A-1680 editions, as is shown by the inclusion of corrupt readings peculiar to A-1680-PRa.)

The Second Part of Miscellany Poems, 1716 (Case 172-2-e), p. 103: "A Call to the Guard by a Drum. By Captain Alexander Radcliffe." Reprinted with ascription to Radcliffe in 1727 (Case 172-2-f), p. 101. (The 1716 text derives from *The Ramble*, 1682.)

ADDITIONAL NOTE: The poem is assigned to Radcliffe by Giles Jacob, whose information evidently derives from *The Second Part of Miscellany Poems*, 1716 (*Poetical Register*, 2, 170).

PREVIOUS SCHOLARSHIP: Omitted by Hayward (*Collected Works*), Johns (*Poetical Works*), and Pinto (*Poems*). Attributed to Radcliffe by Prinz (*Rochester*, p. 146), Wilson (*Court Wits*, p. 20), and Thorpe (*Rochester's Poems*, p. 189).

HOW FAR ARE THEY DECEIV'D WHO HOPE IN VAIN

AUTHOR: Probably Etherege (see Chapter 13).

TEXTS:

Yale MS., p. 340: "Ephelia to Bajazet"; no ascription.

Osborn MS. Chest II, Number 14, p. 1180: "Ephelia to Bajazet"; no ascription.

Harvard MS. Eng. 602F: "Ephelia to Bajacet"; no ascription. (Copied from one of the A-1680 editions.)

Huntington MS. Ellesmere 8736: "Ephelia to Bajazett"; no ascription.

B.M. Add. MS. 28253, fol. 158ʳ: no title; no ascription. (Probably copied from one of the A-1680 editions.)

B. M. Egerton MS. 2623, fol. 78ʳ: "Ephelia to Bajazett"; no ascription.

Bodl. MS. Rawl. Poet. 173, fol. 66ᵛ: "Epelia (a Deserted Lover) to Bajaset. which may serve as a Caveat to Women. By Lᵈ. Ro:." (Probably copied from an edition in the A series.)

Edinburgh MS. DC.1.3, p. 22: "Ephelia to Bajazett"; no ascription.

Female Poems On several Occasions. Written by Ephelia, 1679, p. 104: "In the Person of a Lady to Bajazet, Her unconstant Gallant"; ascribed to Ephelia. Reissued with ascription to Ephelia in the "second edition," 1682, p. 104.

A-1680-HU, p. 138: "Ephelia to Bajazet"; ascribed to Rochester. Reprinted with ascription to Rochester in the other A-1680 editions and in A-1685, p. 107; A-1701, p. 92; A-1713, p. 107; A-1731, p. 96.

The Triumph of Wit, 1688 (not in Case), p. 39: "Memphia to Menacles: or, The forsaken Ladys Epistle to her Wanderer, &c. A Poem"; no ascription. Reprinted without ascription in the 2d ed., 1692 (not in Case), p. 37, and the 5th ed., 1707 (Case 244-e), p. 35. (This version, beginning "What is the thing call'd Love, we so much prise," probably derives from A-1685.)

C-1707-a, p. ¹72: "To the Right Honourable, the Earl of Rochester"; no ascription. At foot of p. ¹71: "Having before inserted his Lordship's [Rochester's] Answer to the following Letter, several Gentlemen desir'd us to add the Letter it self." Reissued without ascription in C-1707-b, p. ²72. (Though this version clumsily addresses the male recipient in the second person rather than the third, it probably derives from one of the A-1680 editions.)

C-1709, p. [2]116: "A Letter From the Lady K. S—— To the Right Honourable the Earl of Rochester. Which occasion'd that Preceding." Reprinted with ascription to "the Lady K. S——" in C-1709-P, p. [3]14. (The text in C-1709 is reprinted from C-1707-b.)

C-1714-1, p. 149: "An Epistle from Ephelia to Bajazet"; ascribed to Rochester. Reprinted with ascription to Rochester in later editions in this series. (The 1714 text is probably conflated from C-1709 and one of the A-1680 editions.)

ADDITIONAL NOTES: Pinto reports a text of this poem in the "Portland Miscellany" (*Poems*, p. 178).

The poem is probably referred to in the following couplet in "A Familiar Epistle to M[r] Julian Secretary of the Muses" ("Thou Comon Shore of this Poetique Towne"), written during spring or summer of 1677:

Poor George, grows old, his Muse worne out of fashion
Hoarsly she sung Ephelias Lamentation.

(Yale MS., p. 353)

In Taylor MS. 2, a marginal gloss identifies "Poor George" as "S[r] George Etheridge" (p. 23).

PREVIOUS SCHOLARSHIP: Attributed to Rochester by Prinz (*Rochester*, p. 147). Printed as Etherege's by J. Woodfall Ebsworth (*Roxburghe Ballads*, 4 [Hertford, Ballad Society, 1883], 573–74), Verity (*Works of Etheredge*, p. 401), and Hayward (*Collected Works*, pp. 303, 350). Omitted by Johns (*Poetical Works*). Attributed tentatively to Etherege by Wilson (*Court Wits*, p. 234) and Thorpe (*Rochester's Poems*, pp. 189–90). Described by Pinto as "almost certainly" by Etherege (*Poems*, p. 178).

IF YOUR DECEIV'D, IT IS NOT BY MY CHEAT

AUTHOR: Probably Rochester (see Chapter 13).

TEXTS:

Yale MS., p. 344: "A very Heroicall Epistle in Answer to
Ephelia"; no ascription.

Osborn MS. Chest 11, Number 14, p. 1181: "A very Heroicall
Epistle in answer to Ephelia"; no ascription.

Harvard MS. Eng. 602F: "Answere"; no ascription. (Copied
from one of the A-1680 editions.)

Huntington MS. Ellesmere 8736: "A very Heroicall Epistle in
Answer to Ephelia"; no ascription.

B. M. Egerton MS. 2623, fol. 79ʳ: "A very Heroicall Epistle in
Answer to Ephelia"; no ascription.

Bodl. MS. Rawl. Poet. 173, fol. 67ᵛ: "His answer"; no ascription. (Probably copied from an edition in the A series.)

Bodl. MS. Don. b. 8, p. 602: "An Heroicall Epistle in answer to
Ephelia by Rochester." Catchword on p. 601: "Rochesters."

Edinburgh MS. DC.1.3, p. 23: "The answer by Sʳ. Charles
Scroope."

*A Very Heroical Epistle from My Lord All-Pride to Dol-Com-
mon,* 1679: "The Argument. Dol-Common being forsaken by
my Lord All-pride, and having written him a most lamentable
Letter, his Lordship sends her the following answer"; no
ascription. Narcissus Luttrell's note on his copy of this broadside: "Agᵗ yᵉ Lᵈ Mulgrave" (C. H. Wilkinson, "Lord Rochester," *London Times Literary Supplement,* 11 July 1935, p.
448).

A-1680-HU, p. 140: "A very Heroical Epistle in Answer to
Ephelia"; ascribed to Rochester. Reprinted with ascription to
Rochester in the other A-1680 editions and in A-1685, p. 109;
A-1701, p. 94; A-1713, p. 109; A-1731, p. 98.

Female Poems On Several Occasions. Written by Ephelia, 2d
ed., 1682, p. 156: "An Answer to Ephelia's Letter to Bajazet";
no ascription. (Probably printed from one of the A-1680 editions.)

The Triumph of Wit, 1688 (not in Case), p. 41: "Menacles to
Memphia: Or, A Poem In Answer to the foregoing, &c."; no
ascription. Reprinted without ascription in the 2d ed., 1692
(not in Case), p. 39, and the 5th ed., 1707 (Case 244-e), p. 37.
(This version, beginning "Madam, What makes you of your
Fate complain," probably derives from A-1685.)

C-1707-a, p. ¹46: "To a Lady who Accus'd him of Inconstancy";
ascribed to Rochester. Reissued in C-1707-b, p. ²46, and reprinted with ascription to Rochester in C-1709, p. ²112, and
C-1709-P, p. ³13. (The text in C-1707-a was probably printed
from one of the A-1680 editions.)

C-1714-1, p. 152: "A very Heroical Epistle in Answer to Ephelia"; ascribed to Rochester. Reprinted with ascription to Rochester in later editions in this series. (The 1714 version is probably conflated from C-1709 and one of the A-1680 editions,
though these two sources exhibit few textual differences.)

ADDITIONAL NOTE: Pinto reports a text of this poem in the "Portland Miscellany" (*Poems,* p. 178).

PREVIOUS SCHOLARSHIP: Attributed to Sir Carr Scroope by J.
Woodfall Ebsworth (*Roxburghe Ballads,* 4 [Hertford, Ballad
Society, 1883], 568, 575–76). Rochester's authorship accepted
by Prinz on some pages (*Rochester,* pp. 147, 212) but denied
on another (p. 148). Printed as Rochester's by Hayward (*Collected Works,* p. 107) and Johns (*Poetical Works,* p. 195).
Attributed to Rochester by Pinto (*Rochester,* pp. 170–71;
Poems, p. 43), Wilson (*Court Wits,* pp. 117–18), and Thorpe,
though "it is lack of evidence to contradict Rochester's author-

ship rather than positive proof . . . which allows [this poem]
to be attributed to Rochester" (*Rochester's Poems*, pp. 189–
90).

CRUSHT BY THAT JUST CONTEMPT HIS FOLLYS BRING

Author: Probably Rochester (see Chapter 13).

Texts:

Yale MS., p. 348: "On Poet Ninny"; no ascription.

Osborn MS. Chest 11, Number 14, p. 1182: "On poett Ninney";
no ascription.

Huntington MS. Ellesmere 8737: "On Poet Ninny"; no ascription.

B. M. Egerton MS. 2623, fol. 80ʳ: "On Poet Ninny"; no ascription.

Edinburgh MS. DC.1.3, p. 24: "on S. C. S. [Sir Carr Scroope]
For Answering Ephelia to Bajazett"; possibly ascribed to
Mulgrave.

A-1680-HU, p. 143: "On Poet Ninny"; ascribed to Rochester.
Reprinted with ascription to Rochester in the other A-1680
editions and in A-1685, p. 111; A-1701, p. 96; A-1713, p. 112;
A-1731, p. 100.

C-1714-1, p. 175: "On Poet Ninny"; ascribed to Rochester. Footnote to title: "Sir C. Scroop." Omitted from later editions in
this series. (Probably printed from one of the A-1680 editions.)

Additional Notes: Pinto reports a text of this poem in the
"Portland Miscellany" (*Poems*, p. 211).

   This poem may be the one referred to in a letter from John
Verney to Sir Ralph Verney dated 25 April 1678: "Lord
Rochester has been very ill and very penitent, but is now

bettering.—Here enclosed are his verses on Sir Car. Scroope at large" (HMC, *Seventh Report*, p. 470).

PREVIOUS SCHOLARSHIP: Printed as Rochester's by Hayward (*Collected Works*, p. 63), Johns (*Poetical Works*, p. 210), and Pinto (*Poems*, p. 114). Attributed to Rochester by Wilson (*Court Wits*, pp. 179–80) and Thorpe, though "it is lack of evidence to contradict Rochester's authorship rather than positive proof . . . which allows [this poem] to be attributed to Rochester" (*Rochester's Poems*, pp. 189–90).

BURSTING WITH PRIDE, THE LOATH'D IMPOSTUME SWELLS

AUTHOR: Probably Rochester (see Chapter 13).

TEXTS:

Yale MS., p. 350: "My Lord All-Pride"; no ascription.

Osborn MS. Chest II, Number 14, p. 1183: "My Lord All-pride"; no ascription.

Huntington MS. Ellesmere 8738: "My Lord Allpride"; no ascription.

B. M. Egerton MS. 2623, fol. 80^v: "My Lord Allpride"; no ascription.

Edinburgh MS. DC.1.3, p. 24: "Ansuerd againe by S^r. CR: Scroope on y^e. l^d. Alpride."

A Very Heroical Epistle from My Lord All-Pride to Dol-Common, 1679: "Epigram upon my Lord All-pride"; no ascription. Narcissus Luttrell's note on his copy of this broadside: "Ag^t ye Ld Mulgrave" (C. H. Wilkinson, "Lord Rochester," *London Times Literary Supplement*, 11 July 1935, p. 448).

A-1680-HU, p. 144: "My Lord All-Pride"; ascribed to Rochester. Reprinted with ascription to Rochester in the other A-1680 editions and in A-1685, p. 112, but omitted from A-1701, A-1713, and A-1731.

Beneath the title of this poem in A-1680-S-S (Sterling copy), a contemporary hand has added "now D. of Bucks."

C-1714-1, p. 177: "My Lord All-Pride"; ascribed to Rochester. Omitted from later editions in this series. (Printed from one of the A-1680 editions.)

ADDITIONAL NOTES: Pinto reports a text of this poem in the "Portland Miscellany" (*Poems*, p. 212).

The phrase "looby *Meene*" in this poem is echoed in the following couplet in "Rochester's Ghost" ("From the deep-vaulted Den of endless Night"), written about 1682:

> I'll speak not of his slouching Looby Mien,
> Altho it is the worst that e'er was seen.
> (*Poems on Affairs of State*, 1703 [Case 211-2-a],
> p. 131)

Since this couplet occurs in a passage which represents Rochester's ghost speaking about Mulgrave, the implication is apparently that Rochester wrote "My Lord All-Pride" and that Mulgrave is its subject.

PREVIOUS SCHOLARSHIP: Rochester's authorship considered "not quite certain" by Prinz (*Rochester*, p. 189). Printed as Rochester's by Hayward (*Collected Works*, p. 64), Johns (*Poetical Works*, p. 208), and Pinto (*Poems*, p. 115). Attributed to Rochester by Wilson (*Court Wits*, pp. 118–19) and Thorpe, though "it is lack of evidence to contradict Rochester's authorship rather than positive proof . . . which allows [this poem] to be attributed to Rochester" (*Rochester's Poems*, pp. 189–90).

WHILST DUNS WERE KNOCKING AT MY DOOR

AUTHOR: Alexander Radcliffe.

TEXTS:

Yale MS., p. 359: "Captaine Radcliffs Ramble."

Osborn MS. Chest 11, Number 14, p. 1234: "The Ramble, writt in 1668"; no ascription.

Harvard MS. Eng. 636F, p. 152: "Cap:tt Radcliffes Ramble."

Edinburgh MS. DC.1.3, p. 8: "Captaine Radcliffs Debauch."

A-1680-HU, p. 146: "Captain Ramble"; ascribed to Rochester. Reprinted with ascription to Rochester in the other A-1680 editions and in A-1685, p. 122; A-1701, p. 105; A-1713, p. 122; A-1731, p. 110. (The text in A-1701, which is reprinted in A-1713 and A-1731, is conflated from A-1685 and *The Ramble*, 1682.)

  Beneath the title of this poem in A-1680-S-S (Sterling copy), a contemporary hand has added "by Ratcliff of Greys-Inn."

Wit and Drollery, 1682 (Case 114-c), p. 123: "The Ramble"; no ascription. (Apparently printed from one of the A-1680 editions with a few readings corrected from another source.)

The Ramble: an Anti-Heroick Poem. Together with Some Terrestrial Hymns and Carnal Ejaculations. By Alexander Radcliffe . . . Printed for the Author . . . , 1682 (Macdonald 217), p. 85: "The Ramble." Reissued in *The Works of Capt. Alex. Radcliffe*, "third edition," 1696, p. ²85. In *The Ramble*, 1682, "The Booksellers Preface to his Customers" states:

> But there having been some part of *The Ramble* formerly printed, under the notion of a Natural Presumptive to my Lord *Rochester*, for Justice to that Noble Lord, as also for defending of Liberty and Property to my Author, whose Right as well as my own is invaded; I resolved to bring an *Habeas Corpus*, and remove *The Ramble*

home again, which was so falsly, maliciously, imperfectly, and feloniously made publick.

I am likewise to tell you, that the aforesaid Poem called *The Ramble,* is here enlarged above two thirds more than heretofore you have seen it. (Sigs. A6ʳ–A6ᵛ)

(There is no evidence that the authorized text in *The Ramble,* 1682 was influenced by earlier printed versions.)

The Second Part of Miscellany Poems, 1716 (Case 172-2-e), p. 108: "The Ramble. By Captain Alexander Radcliffe." Reprinted with ascription to Radcliffe in 1727 (Case 172-2-f), p. 106. (The 1716 text derives from *The Ramble,* 1682.)

ADDITIONAL NOTES: Anthony Wood confuses this poem with Rochester's "A Ramble in St. James's Park"; his remarks provide no additional evidence of its authorship (*Athenae Oxonienses, 3,* 1230). The poem is attributed to Radcliffe by Giles Jacob, whose information evidently derives from *The Second Part of Miscellany Poems,* 1716 (*Poetical Register, 2,* 170).

PREVIOUS SCHOLARSHIP: Omitted by Hayward (*Collected Works*), Johns (*Poetical Works*), and Pinto (*Poems*). Attributed to Radcliffe by Prinz (*Rochester,* p. 146), Wilson (*Court Wits,* p. 20), and Thorpe (*Rochester's Poems,* p. 191).

IF ROME CAN PARDON SINS, AS ROMANS HOLD

AUTHOR: Possibly Rochester (see Chapter 14).

TEXTS:

Osborn MS. Chest 11, Number 4, p. 25: "On yᵉ Popes Indulgencies by yᵉ Earle of Rochester Lᵈ: Willmote."

Osborn MS. Box III, Number 27: "by yᵉ E of Ro——r." At top of reverse side (recto) of same leaf: "On yᵉ Church of Rome by yᵉ E of Ro:."

Osborn MS. Box LVIII, Number 4: "Rome's Pardon—a Tale"; signed "Rochester." This copy includes the first 3 lines only, followed by the signature, followed by a longer narrative poem elaborating the theme of "On Rome's Pardons." (Possibly derived from printed text.)

Harvard MS. Eng. 586, p. 188: "I remember to have seen a Copy of Verses written by the Earl of Rochester (who had read and seen all the Fopperies and Idolatries of the Church of Rome, as they are practis'd abroad) to which our poor deluded English Papists are utter Strangers; I thinke they are very pathetick, as follows." (Possibly derived from printed text.)

Harvard MS. Eng. 606, p. 8: "The Earl of Rochester on Romes pardons." (Possibly derived from printed text.)

Folger MS. M. a. 187, fol. 165ʳ: "E: Rotchester on Romes pardons." (Possibly derived from printed text.)

B. M. Sloane MS. 1731A, fol. 171ʳ: "To the Romanist"; no ascription. Appears on a single sheet exhibiting fold-marks.

Bodl. MS. Rawl. Poet. 152, fol. 115ᵛ: "On ROOMs Pardon"; no ascription. (Possibly derived from printed text.)

Bodl. MS. Rawl. Poet. 173, fol. 123ᵛ: "On Rome's Pardon"; no ascription. (Probably copied from an edition in the A series.)

Bodl. MS. Add. B. 106, fol. 33ᵛ: "On Romes Pardons." In margin beside title: "Roch:." (Probably copied from an edition in the A series.)

Bodl. MS. Don. e. 23, fol. 29ᵛ: no title; no ascription. (Possibly derived from printed text.)

Bodl. MS. Smith 27, p. 7: no title; no ascription. On outside of formerly folded sheet: "Verses about Roman pardons and indulgences."

Bodl. MS. Sancroft 53, p. 69: "On Rome's pardons"; signed "E. of Rochr." (Possibly derived from printed text.)

A-1680-HU, p. 151: "On Rome's Pardons"; ascribed to Rochester. Reprinted with ascription to Rochester in the other A-1680 editions and in A-1685, p. 127; A-1701, p. 111; A-1713, p. 128; A-1731, p. 116.

Rome Rhym'd to Death, 1683 (Case 170), p. 21: "On Rome's Pardons, By the E. of R." (Probably derived from one of the A-1680 editions.)

A Second Collection of The Newest and Most Ingenious Poems, Satyrs, Songs, &c. against Popery and Tyranny, 1689 (Case 189–2), p. 18: "On Romes Pardons, by the E. of R." (Probably derived directly or ultimately from the A-1680 editions.)

C-1707-a, p. ^{1}97: "On Rome's Pardons"; ascribed to Rochester. Reissued in C-1707-b, p. ^{2}97, and reprinted with ascription to Rochester in C-1709, p. ^{2}145; C-1709-P, p. ^{4}7; C-1714-1, p. 102; and later editions in this series. (The 1707 text probably derives directly or ultimately from the A-1680 editions.)

A Collection of Merry Poems, 1736 (Case 403-b), p. 26: "On Rome's Pardons"; no ascription. (Probably derived from an earlier printed text.)

ADDITIONAL NOTE: Hayward evidently errs in his statement that "On Rome's Pardons" was published as a broadside in 1685 (*Collected Works*, p. 361). The sole authority he cites is J. Woodfall Ebsworth, who reproduces the poem, not from a broadside, but from A-1685. The colophon-like phrase beneath Ebsworth's text ("Printed for *A. Thorncome*, and are to be sold by most Booksellers, 1685") is the imprint of A-1685, and his title includes a corruption ("Pardon" for "Pardons") which originated in A-1680-F and was transmitted to A-1685 through A-1680-HA. In effect, Ebsworth identifies his source as A-1685 by indicating in a footnote that he has emended one of its corrupt readings (*Roxburghe Ballads, 4* [Hertford, Ballad Society, 1883], 187). Hayward's error is followed by Thorpe (*Rochester's Poems*, p. 191).

PREVIOUS SCHOLARSHIP: Printed as Rochester's by Hayward (*Collected Works*, p. 62), Johns (*Poetical Works*, p. 159), and Pinto (*Poems*, p. 124). Attributed to Rochester by Prinz (*Rochester*, pp. 107, 133–34) and Thorpe (*Rochester's Poems*, p. 191).

Appendices

Appendix A:

Additional Poems in the Yale Manuscript

1. Poems in the First Hand

WERE I TO CHOOSE WHAT SORT OF SHAPE I'D WEARE

AUTHOR: Griffith or Pococke.

TEXTS:
Yale MS., p. 22: "The Answer"; no ascription. (In section of poems by or concerning Rochester.)
For further information on this poem, see Chapter 6.

SINCE NOW MY SILVIA, IS AS KIND AS FAIRE

AUTHOR: John Sheffield, Earl of Mulgrave, later Marquis of Normanby and Duke of Buckinghamshire.

TEXTS:
Yale MS., p. 194: "On the Enjoyment of his M^{rs} By ye Ld Mulgrave." All but the title and first 12 lines have been removed by the seventh gap, pp. 195–212.

The poem appears without ascription in Taylor MS. 3, p. 7; Victoria and Albert Museum MS. Dyce 43, p. 128; Vienna MS. 14090, fol. 70^v; and the dated and undated issues of *The Enjoyment*, 1679. In a copy of the undated issue at the University of Texas, a contemporary hand has written "By John Wilmot Earl of Rochester" above the title and "J Dryden" after the text.

The poem is ascribed to Rochester in Bodl. MS. Eng. Poet. d. 152, fol. 67^r. It was printed as Rochester's from a manuscript source in *Poems on Affairs of State*, 1697 (Case 211-1-a), p. ^{2}1, and reprinted with the same ascription in 1697 (Case 211-1-b), p. ^{2}10; 1697 (Case 211-1-c), p. ^{1}255; 1699 (Case 211-1-d), p. ^{1}255; 1702 (Case 211-1-e), p. ^{1}255; and 1703 (Case 211-1-f), p. ^{1}255. It was again printed as Rochester's in C-1707-a, p. ^{1}63, where the ascription probably derives from *Poems on Affairs of State* even though the text was printed from the folio leaflet of 1679. The text in C-1707-a was reissued in C-1707-b, p. ^{2}63, and reprinted with ascription to Rochester in C-1709, p. ^{2}78; C-1709-P, p. ^{3}1; and C-1714-1, p. 34. A single couplet of the poem attributed to Rochester in *The Agreeable Variety*, 1717 (Case 293), p. 148, may derive from one of the earlier printed texts which assign the poem to him; this couplet was reissued in 1724 (Case 293-b), p. 148 and 1742 (Case 293-c), p. 148.

The poem is ascribed to Mulgrave in Harvard MS. Eng. 636F, p. 124. In National Library of Scotland MS. Advocate 19.1.12, fol. 62^r, it is "Said to be writt by MLM upon Mrs K." (Mall Kirke?). In *Chorus Poetarum*, 1694 (Case 202), p. 93, where the poem was printed from a manuscript source, it is attributed to "the Marquess of M."; this text was reissued with the same ascription in 1696 (Case 202-b), p. 93, and 1698 (Case 202-c), p. 93.

From the folio leaflet of 1679, the poem was printed as Mulgrave's in *Poems on Several Occasions*, 1717 (Case 260-2-a), p. 20, which was edited by his friend Alexander Pope; Pope's adoption of the text of 1679 may argue that it is authoritative. Pope's text was reprinted by Edmund Curll in the unauthorized *Works of The Most Noble John Sheffield, Late Duke of Buckingham,* 1721, p. 70. In Rochester editions in the C series after 1714, the poem appears under Rochester's name but its text is reprinted from Pope's miscellany and it is accompanied by a footnote explaining that "The Duke of *Buckingham* has lately been pleas'd to own this Poem" (C-1718-1, p. 34). One of these Rochester editions is the source of the text in Bodl. MS. Rawl. Poet. 152, fol. 130ᵛ, which reproduces the double ascription to Rochester and Mulgrave. Also descended from Pope's miscellany are the text and ascription to Mulgrave printed in *The Muse in Good Humour,* Part II, 1744 (not in Case), p. [25], and reprinted in 1745 (Case 450-2-b), p. 19.

According to Charles Gildon, the poem was "said to be written by a nobleman of the first magnitude" who was still alive at the time (*The Laws of Poetry,* 1721, p. 92); Mulgrave died early in 1721, whereas Rochester had died in 1680. Giles Jacob's ascription to Rochester evidently derives from an edition in the C series; his ascription to Mulgrave comes directly or indirectly from Pope's miscellany (*Poetical Register,* 2, 182, 233).

The poem was omitted from their editions of Rochester by Hayward (*Collected Works,* p. xiii), Johns (*Poetical Works*), and Pinto (*Poems*). Similarly, Prinz classified it as spurious (*Rochester,* p. 148). It was attributed to Mulgrave by Norman Ault (*Pope's Own Miscellany,* London, Nonesuch Press, 1935, p. xciii) and Wilson (*Court Wits,* p. 100).

UNDER THIS STONE DOTH LYE

AUTHOR: George Villiers, 2d Duke of Buckingham.

TEXTS:
Yale MS., p. 245: "An Epitaph"; no ascription.
Appears without ascription in Harvard MS. Eng. 636F, p. 140; Bodl. MS. Douce 357, fol. 117ʳ; and National Library of Scotland MS. Advocate 19.1.12, fol. 174ᵛ. Printed in an un-

dated folio half-sheet as *An Epitaph upon Thomas Late Lord Fairfax. Written by a Person of Honour.*

Ascribed to Buckingham in Osborn MS. Chest II, Number 14, p. 1060; B. M. Add. MS. 18220, fol. 119ʳ; and Bodl. MS. Don. b. 8, p. xxxi. Printed as Buckingham's from a manuscript source in *A Third Collection of The Newest and Most Ingenious Poems, Satyrs, Songs, &c. against Popery and Tyranny,* 1689 (Case 189-3), p. 27. Apparently the 1689 volume is the source of the following texts, all ascribing the poem to Buckingham: in *The Muses Farewel to Popery & Slavery,* 1690 (Case 191-1-b), p. 155, reissued in 1697 (Case 191-d), p. 155; in *Poems on Affairs of State,* 1697 (Case 211-1-a), p. 132, reprinted in 1697 (Case 211-1-b), p. 132, 1697 (Case 211-1-c), p. ¹123, 1699 (Case 211-1-d), p. ¹123, 1702 (Case 211-1-e), p. ¹123, 1703 (Case 211-1-f), p. ¹123, 1710 (Case 211-1-g), p. ¹123, and 1716 (Case 211-1-h), p. ¹123; and in *The First Part of Miscellany Poems,* 1716 (Case 172-1-e), p. 226, reprinted in 1727 (Case 172-1-f), p. 218.

Printed as Buckingham's, probably from a manuscript source, in *Miscellany Poems upon Several Occasions,* 1692 (Case 197), p. 109. Printed as Buckingham's, possibly from a manuscript source, in *Miscellaneous Works, Written by His Grace, George, Late Duke of Buckingham,* 1704 (Case 232-1-a), p. ¹1; reprinted with the same ascription in 1707 (Case 232-1-b), p. ¹1, and in *The Works Of His Grace, George Villiers, Late Duke of Buckingham,* 1715, *1, 135.*

Assigned to Buckingham in Anthony Wood's *Athenae Oxonienses (4,* 209). Giles Jacob's ascription to Buckingham evidently derives from an edition of the Duke's *Works (Poetical Register, 2,* 217). Theophilus Cibber's similar ascription probably derives from a printed source (*Lives of the Poets, 2,* 323). Horace Walpole, attributing the poem to Buckingham, cites the Duke's *Works* of 1715 as his source (*Catalogue of Royal and Noble Authors, 2,* 78).

Attributed to Buckingham by Winifred, Lady Burghclere (*George Villiers, Second Duke of Buckingham,* London, J. Murray, 1903, p. 80) and John Harold Wilson (*A Rake and His Times,* New York, Farrar, Straus and Young, 1954, p. 198).

AT FIVE THIS MORNE, WHEN PHOEBUS RAISD HIS HEAD

Author: Rochester.

Texts:

Yale MS., p. 251: "Tunbridge Wells A Satyr"; no ascription. For further information on this poem, see Chapter 11.

NOE; SHE SHALL NE'RE ESCAPE, IF GODS THERE BE

Author: John Oldham.

Texts:

Yale MS., p. 289: "Upon a certaine Woman who by her falshood & scorne was yᵉ Death of my Friend By yᵉ same Author" (i.e. Oldham).

A few lines of this poem appear without ascription in B. M. Add. MS. 27408, fols. 60ᵛ–61ʳ. The poem appears in Oldham's own handwriting in his poetical notebook, Bodl. MS. Rawl. Poet. 123, p. 54. It was printed in his authorized *Satyrs upon the Jesuits,* 1681, p. 143, and reprinted in later editions of his poems such as *The Works of Mr. John Oldham, Together with his Remains,* 1684; for detailed descriptions of these editions, see Brooks, "Oldham Bibliography." Giles Jacob's ascription to Oldham evidently derives from some edition of Oldham's works (*Poetical Register, 2,* 121, 122).

ALL HUMAN THINGS ARE SUBJECT TO DECAY

Author: Dryden.

Texts:

Yale MS., p. 314: "Mac Flecknoe A Satyr. By Mʳ Dryden."
Appears without ascription in Harvard MS. Eng. 636F, p. 161; Folger MS. 7040; B. M. Harl. MS. 6913, fol. 5ʳ; Lambeth

Codices Manuscripti Tenisoniani 711, item 8; Bodl. MS. Rawl.
Poet. 123, pp. 232–35, 214; Cambridge MS. Add. 6339, fol.
1ʳ; and Edinburgh MS. DC.1.3, p. 57. Ascribed to Dryden in
an uncatalogued MS. at the University of Illinois. Printed as
Mac Flecknoe . . . By the Author of Absalom & Achitophel,
1682 (Macdonald 14a).

The authorized version was printed in *Miscellany Poems*,
1684 (Case 172-1-a), p. ¹1, and reprinted in 1692 (Case
172-1-b), p. 1; 1692 (Case 172-1-c), p. 1; 1702 (Case 172-1-d),
p. 1; 1716 (Case 172-1-e), p. 1; and 1727 (Case 172-1-f),
p. 1. For other early reprintings of this authorized text, see
Macdonald, *Dryden Bibliography.* Two manuscript versions
evidently descend from the printed text of 1684: one is found
in Osborn MS. Box xii, Number 14, the other in an uncatalogued manuscript at the University of Illinois.
For discussions of the text of this poem, see G. Blakemore Evans,
    "The Text of Dryden's *Mac Flecknoe*," *Harvard Library
    Bulletin,* 7 (1953), 32–54, and Vinton A. Dearing, "Dryden's
    Mac Flecknoe: The Case for Authorial Revision," *Studies in
    Bibliography,* 7 (1955), 85–102.

A SAD MISCHANCE I SING ALAS

AUTHOR: Unknown.

TEXTS:
Yale MS., p. 328: "Upon a late fall'n Poet. Suppos'd to be
    Written by Mʳ Shadwell."
Apparently this lampoon on Dryden is otherwise unrecorded.

THOU COMON SHORE OF THIS POETIQUE TOWNE

AUTHOR: Possibly George Villiers, 2d Duke of Buckingham.

TEXTS:
Yale MS., p. 352: "A Familiar Epistle to Mʳ Julian Secretary
    of the Muses"; no ascription.
For further information on this poem, see Chapter 13.

I SING THE PRAISE OF A WORTHY WIGHT

AUTHOR: Unknown.

TEXTS:

Yale MS., p. 369: "A New Ballad to an Old Tune Call'd Sage Leafe"; no ascription.

Appears without ascription in Taylor MS. 1, p. 62; B. M. Add. MS. 23722, fol. 3ʳ; B. M. Harl. MS. 7315, fol. 46ᵛ; Victoria and Albert Museum MS. Dyce 43, p. 171; and Vienna MS. 14090, fol. 93ʳ. Printed without ascription as *A Ballad*, [1679] (Macdonald 189). Printed from a manuscript source in *Poems on Affairs of State*, 1698 (Case 215), p. 33, where it carries no ascription.

　　Ascribed to Dryden in Harvard MS. Eng. 636F, p. 240. Printed from a manuscript source in *Poems on Affairs of State*, 1703 (Case 211-2-a), p. 216, where it is ascribed to "Mr. D——n"; reprinted with this ascription in 1703 (Case 211-2-b), p. 216, and reissued in 1716 (Case 211-2-c), p. 216. Dryden's authorship doubted by Macdonald (*Dryden Bibliography*, p. 213).

FROM A PROUD SENSUALL, ATHEISTICALL LIFE

AUTHOR: Unknown.

TEXTS:

Yale MS., p. 377: "The D: of B: Letany"; no ascription.

Appears without ascription in Osborn MS. Chest 11, Number 14, p. 983; Taylor MS. 1, p. 66; Taylor MS. 3, p. 159; Harvard MS. Eng. 636F, p. 257; B. M. Add. MS. 23722, fol. 62ᵛ; B. M. Harl. MS. 6914, fol. 4ʳ; B. M. Harl. MS. 7315, fol. 49ᵛ; Victoria and Albert Museum MS. Dyce 43, p. 28; and Vienna MS. 14090, fol. 21ʳ. Printed without ascription as *The Litany. Of The D. of B.*, [1679]. Also printed without ascription from a manuscript source in *Poems on Affairs of State*, 1704 (Case 211-3-a), p. 91, and reprinted without

ascription in 1716 (Case 211-3-b), p. 82, and in *A New Collection of Poems Relating to State Affairs*, 1705 (Case 237),
p. 406.

AS COLON DROVE HIS SHEEPE ALONG

AUTHOR: Probably Dorset (Buckhurst).

TEXTS:

Yale MS., p. 382: "Satyr"; no ascription.

Appears without ascription in Osborn MS. Chest II, Number 14,
p. 1143; Osborn MS. Chest II, Number 52; Osborn MS.
Box LXXXIX, Number 7; Taylor MS. 3, p. 14; Harvard MS.
Eng. 636F, p. 286; B. M. Sloane MS. 3516, fol. 169^r; B. M.
Add. MS. 23722, fol. 23^v; B. M. Add. MS. 27407, fol. 22^r;
B. M. Harl. MS. 7317, fol. 54^v; Bodl. MS. Eng. Poet. d. 152,
fol. 52^r; Bodl. MS. Don. b. 8, p. 598; Bodl. MS. Douce 357,
fol. 66^v; and Edinburgh MS. DC.1.3, p. 53. Printed without
ascription in *Poems on Affairs of State*, 1697 (Case 211-1-a),
p. 141; 1697 (Case 211-1-b), p. 141; 1697 (Case 211-1-c),
p. ^{1}132; 1699 (Case 211-1-d), p. ^{1}132; 1702 (Case 211-1-e),
p. ^{1}132; 1703 (Case 211-1-f), p. ^{1}132; 1710 (Case 211-1-g),
p. ^{1}132; 1716 (Case 211-1-h), p. ^{1}132.

Ascribed to Dorset in B. M. Harl. MS. 6913, fol. 40^r; Victoria and Albert Museum MS. Dyce 43, p. 297; National
Library of Scotland MS. Advocate 19.1.12, fol. 98^r; and
Vienna MS. 14090, fol. 158^r. Printed from a manuscript
source in D-1718, p. 59, where it is ascribed to Rochester;
reprinted with this ascription in D-1761, p. 240.

According to the standard biography of Dorset, this poem "has
been ascribed" to him (Harris, *Dorset*, p. 82).

2. Poems in the Second Hand

THE PARSONS ALL KEEPE WHORES

AUTHOR: Uncertain.

TEXTS:

Yale MS., p. 392: "A new Ballad. To ye Tune of Chivey Chace"; no ascription.

Appears without ascription in Harvard MS. Eng. 636F, p. 285; Bodl. MS. Don. b. 8, p. 513; and All Souls College, Oxford, MS. Codrington 116, fol. 42^v. Ascribed to Rochester in B. M. Harl. MS. 6914, fol. 1^r; Victoria and Albert Museum MS. Dyce 43, p. 23; and Vienna MS. 14090, fol. 18^v.

FUCKSTERS, YOU THAT WILL BE HAPPY

AUTHOR: Uncertain.

TEXTS:

Yale MS., p. 394: "Advice to a C——t Monger"; no ascription.

Appears without ascription in Osborn MS. Chest 11, Number 1, and in Taylor MS. 3, p. 6. Ascribed to Rochester in Harvard MS. Eng. 636F, p. 245 (misnumbered 145).

WHEN TO THE KING I BID GOOD MORROW

AUTHOR: Probably Rochester.

TEXTS:

Yale MS., p. 396: "Dialogue"; no ascription.

Ascribed to Rochester in B. M. Harl. MS. 6914, fol. 2^v; Bodl. MS. Firth C. 15, p. 25; Victoria and Albert Museum MS. Dyce 43, p. 26; and Vienna MS. 14090, fol. 20^r. Appears without ascription in All Souls College, Oxford, MS. Codrington 116, fol. 22^r. In Osborn MS. Chest 11, Number 3, the table of contents lists "A Dialogue betweene Nell Gwin and Portsmouth and the King" as appearing on p. 111; the leaf containing the poem has, however, been cut out of the volume.

Attributed to Rochester by John Harold Wilson (*Nell Gwyn:*

Royal Mistress, New York, Pellegrini and Cudahy, 1952, p. 188).

O THAT I COULD BY SOME CHYMICK ART

AUTHOR: Uncertain; probably not Rochester.

TEXTS:

Yale MS., p. 397: "Votum"; no ascription.

Appears without ascription in Edinburgh MS. DC.1.3, p. 78. Printed without ascription in *The Second Part of Merry Drollery,* [1661] (Case 132-2-a), p. 31. Ascribed to Rochester in Taylor MS. 3, p. 254; Harvard MS. Eng. 636F, p. 75; and an uncatalogued manuscript at the University of Illinois. Printed as Rochester's from a manuscript source in C-1714-1, p. 112, and reprinted with the same ascription in later editions of this collection.

Printed as Rochester's by Hayward (*Collected Works,* p. 120) and Johns (*Poetical Works,* p. 131) but omitted by Pinto (*Poems*). Attributed to Rochester by Prinz (*Rochester,* p. 142). The case against Rochester's authorship is presented by James Thorpe ("Authenticity of 'The Wish' as a Rochester Poem," *Modern Language Notes, 62* [1947], 267–68).

ONE WHORE IS DEAD

AUTHOR: Unknown.

TEXTS:

Yale MS., p. 397: "A Song"; no ascription.

Appears without ascription in Osborn MS. Chest II, Number 3, p. 161, and in Bodl. MS. Don. b. 8, p. 626. Printed without ascription in *Poems on Affairs of State,* 1704 (Case 211-3-a), p. 190, and reprinted without ascription in 1716 (Case 211-3-b), p. 169.

YOUNG JEMMY WAS A LAD

AUTHOR: Aphra Behn.

TEXTS:

Yale MS., p. 398: "Upon y^e. Duke of M———th. supposed to be written by My Lady B. Felton."

Printed in *Female Poems On Several Occasions. Written by Ephelia*, 2d ed., 1682, p. 131, with ascription to Ephelia. Printed as Aphra Behn's in her authorized *Poems upon Several Occasions . . . By Mrs. A. Behn*, 1684, p. 123.

Printed as Aphra Behn's by Montague Summers (*The Works of Aphra Behn*, London, W. Heinemann, 1915, 4, 210).

AFTER THE SWEETEST PANGS OF HOT DESIRE

AUTHOR: Richard Duke.

TEXTS:

Yale MS., p. 400: "Song: supposed to be written by My L^d M———^{ve}."

Printed without ascription in *The Newest Collection of the Choicest Songs*, 1683 (Day and Murrie 65), p. 69. Printed without ascription in *Choice Ayres and Songs*, 1683 (Day and Murrie 59), p. 64, and reissued in *The New Treasury of Musick*, 1695 (Day and Murrie 134), p. ^{4}64. Printed without ascription in *Examen Poeticum*, 1693 (Case 172-3-a), p. 387; reissued in 1693 (Case 172-3-b), p. 387, and reprinted without ascription in 1706 (Case 172-3-c), p. 222. Printed with ascription to Richard Duke in *Poems by the Earl of Roscomon*, 1717 (Case 301), p. 414. Printed without ascription in *Wits Cabinet*, 1731 (Case 173-0), p. 132, and in *The Choice*, 1733 (Case 353-2), p. 85.

CLOSE BY A STREAM, WHOSE FLOWRY BANCK MIGHT GIVE

AUTHOR: Sir Carr Scroope.

TEXTS:

Yale MS., p. 401: "The Parting betweene Sireno & Diana"; no ascription.

Appears without ascription in B. M. Harl. MS. 6913, fol. 65ʳ. Printed with ascription to Scroope in *Miscellany Poems,* 1684 (Case 172-1-a), p. 173; 1692 (Case 172-1-b), p. 108; 1692 (Case 172-1-c), p. 108; 1702 (Case 172-1-d), p. 77; 1716 (Case 172-1-e), p. 49; and 1727 (Case 172-1-f), p. 46.

Appendix B:

Checklists

Besides identifying precisely many of the manuscripts and printed books cited in the present study, the following checklists offer other information, such as the locations of some rare items, which is not given earlier. For printed books, I have generally noted only the copies I have used; other copies will usually be listed in the standard bibliographies of Prinz, Case, Day and Murrie, Macdonald, and Brooks, as well as in the Wing short-title catalogue. In the second section, most of Narcissus Luttrell's dates are taken from C. H. Wilkinson, "Lord Rochester," *London Times Literary Supplement*, 11 July 1935, p. 448.

1. Manuscripts

a. In the Yale University Library
   Yale MS. Described in Chapter 3.

b. In the Collection of Mr. James M. Osborn, 77 Edgehill Road, New Haven, Connecticut. (Some of these manuscripts are in process of donation to the Yale University Library.)

MS. Chest ii, Number 1	MS. Chest ii, Number 39
MS. Chest ii, Number 3	MS. Chest ii, Number 52
MS. Chest ii, Number 4	MS. Box iii, Number 27
MS. Chest ii, Number 9	MS. Box xii, Number 14
MS. Chest ii, Number 13	MS. Box xxii, Number 3
MS. Chest ii, Number 14	MS. Box xxii, Number 8
MS. Chest ii, Number 28	MS. Box lviii, Number 4
MS. Chest ii, Number 32	MS. Box lxxxix, Number 7

c. In the Collection of Mr. Robert H. Taylor, 511 Lake Drive, Princeton, New Jersey

MS. 1. Folio manuscript volume, almost certainly in the same hand as the Yale MS. Partially described in Chapter 3.

MS. 2. Folio manuscript volume, almost certainly in the same hand as Bodl. MS. Firth C. 15 and the Ohio MS. Partially described in Chapter 1.

MS. 3. Quarto manuscript volume beginning with "A Prologue" ("Gentle reproofs have long bin try'd in vain").

d. In the Houghton Library, Harvard University

MS. Eng. 584	MS. Eng. 623F
MS. Eng. 585	MS. Eng. 624
MS. Eng. 586	MS. Eng. 636F
MS. Eng. 602F	MS. Eng. 652F
MS. Eng. 606	

e. In the Princeton University Library

MS. AM 14401. Described by James Thorpe, "New Manuscripts of Sodom," *Princeton University Library Chronicle, 13* (1951–52), 40–41.

f. In the Folger Shakespeare Library

MS. 789.4	MS. M. a. 187
MS. 4108	MS. M. b. 12
MS. 7040	

g. In the Library of Ohio State University

Ohio MS. Partially described in Chapter 1.

h. In the Library of the University of Illinois

MS. 20 D 43 Ellis	MS. 30 Je 45 Stonehill

Uncatalogued manuscript containing texts of *Mac Flecknoe* and other poems of the Restoration period.

Uncatalogued manuscript containing a fragment of *Mac Flecknoe*. Described by G. Blakemore Evans, "The Text of Dryden's *Mac Flecknoe*," *Harvard Library Bulletin*, 7 (1953), 32–54.

i. In the Henry E. Huntington Library
MSS. Ellesmere 8736–38   MS. HA 12525
MS. Ellesmere 8793   MS. HA 13404

j. Owned by the Rosenbach Company, Philadelphia
Phillipps MS. 9500. The present location of this manuscript is unknown to me. I was allowed to consult it in January 1951 through the kindness of Mr. Edwin Wolf II.

k. In the British Museum
Sloane MS. 655   Add. MS. 28253
Sloane MS. 1009   Add. MS. 29497
Sloane MS. 1458   Add. MS. 30162
Sloane MS. 1504   Add. MS. 34362
Sloane MS. 1731A   Harl. MS. 6057
Sloane MS. 2332   Harl. MS. 6207
Sloane MS. 3516   Harl. MS. 6913
Sloane MS. 4455   Harl. MS. 6914
Add. MS. 4456   Harl. MS. 6947
Add. MS. 4457   Harl. MS. 7003
Add. MS. 6269   Harl. MS. 7315
Add. MS. 14047   Harl. MS. 7316
Add. MS. 18220   Harl. MS. 7317
Add. MS. 21094   Harl. MS. 7319
Add. MS. 23722   Burney MS. 390
Add. MS. 27407   Egerton MS. 2623
Add. MS. 27408   Lansdowne MS. 1039

l. In the Bodleian Library
MS. Rawl. Poet. 81   MS. Firth C. 15
MS. Rawl. Poet. 90   MS. Don. b. 8
MS. Rawl. Poet. 123   MS. Don. e. 23

MS. Rawl. Poet. 152   MS. Eng. Poet. d. 152
MS. Rawl. Poet. 159   MS. Eng. Poet. e. 4
MS. Rawl. Poet. 172   MS. Tanner 306
MS. Rawl. Poet. 173   MS. North b. 24
MS. Rawl. A. 341   MS. Ballard 50
MS. Rawl. D. 260   MS. Sancroft 53
MS. Rawl. D. 1171   MS. Douce 357
MS. Rawl. D. 1480   MS. Smith 27
MS. Add. B. 106

m. In the Library of All Souls College, Oxford
MS. Codrington 116   MS. Codrington 174

n. In the Cambridge University Library
MS. Add. 29   MS. Add. 6339
MS. Add. 42

o. In the Victoria and Albert Museum
MS. Dyce 43

p. In the Lambeth Palace Library
Codices Manuscripti Gibsoniani 941
Codices Manuscripti Tenisoniani 711

q. In the Library of the University of Nottingham
Portland MS. Described in Chapter 7.

r. In the Library of the University of Edinburgh
MS. DC.1.3

s. In the National Library of Scotland
MS. Advocate 19.1.12   MS. Advocate 19.3.4

t. In the Nationalbibliothek, Vienna
MS. 14090. Described in detail by Rudolf Brotanek in
Festschrift der Nationalbibliothek in Wien (Vienna, Öster-
reichische Staatsdruckerei, 1926), pp. 145–62.

2. Broadsides and Pamphlets of Poems

Corydon and Cloris or, The Wanton Sheepherdess.
> Possibly assigned to 1677 by J. Woodfall Ebsworth, though he may refer to another broadside (*Roxburghe Ballads*, 6 [Hertford, Ballad Society, 1889], 135).
> Copy used: British Museum.

A Satyr against Mankind. Written by a Person of Honour.
> Prinz 1.
> Dated June 1679 by Anthony Wood (*Athenae Oxonienses*, 3, 1229). Dated 1679 by Narcissus Luttrell, who paid 1*d.* for his copy (Wilkinson).
> Copies used: Yale; University of Kansas; University of Texas; Huntington.

An Answer to the Satyr against Mankind.
> Dated July 1679 by Wood (*Athenae Oxonienses*, 3, 1229). Dated 1679 by Luttrell, who paid 1*d.* for his copy (Wilkinson).
> Copy used: Yale.

A Letter From Artemiza in the Town, to Chloë in the Country. By a Person of Honour.
> Prinz v.
> Dated 1679 by Luttrell, who paid 2*d.* for his copy (Wilkinson).
> Copies used: University of Texas; Bodleian.

Artemisa to Cloe. A Letter from a Lady in the Town, to a Lady in the Country; Concerning The Loves of the Town: By a Person of Quality. London, Printed for William Leach, at the Sign of the Crown in Cornhil: M. DC. LXXIX.
> Described in "A Rochester Poem," *Bodleian Library Record*, 4 (1952–53), 183–84.
> Copy used: Bodleian.

Upon Nothing. A Poem. By a Person of Honour.
> Copies used: Yale; Harvard; University of Texas.

Upon Nothing A Poem. By a Person of Honour.
> Prinz iv, 1.
> This broadside and the one preceding represent two separate editions. One of the two was dated 1679 by Luttrell, who paid 1*d.* for his copy (Wilkinson).
> Copy used: University of Texas.

*Upon Nothing. A Poem. By the Right Honourable, John late Earl of Rochester. Now First Correctly Printed. London: Printed for E. Curll, at the Dial and Bible in Fleetstreet. 1711. Price 2*d. *Where may be had, The Correctest Edition of his Lordship's Works hitherto Extant. Price 5*s.
> Prinz iv, 2.
> Copies used: Yale; British Museum.

A Very Heroical Epistle from My Lord All-Pride to Dol-Common. . . . Printed in the Year, 1679.
> Dated 1679 by Luttrell, who paid 1*d.* for his copy. He also noted that the contents were directed "Ag^t ye Ld Mulgrave" (Wilkinson).
> Copy used: British Museum.

The Enjoyment. . . . To be Sold at the Judges Head in Chancery-Lane, near Fleetstreet.
> Dated 1679 by Luttrell, who paid 1*d.* for his copy (Wilkinson).
> Copy used: University of Texas.

The Enjoyment. . . . London, Printed in the Year, 1679.
> Prinz ii.
> This folio leaflet and the one preceding are variant issues, with all but the colophon printed from the same setting of type.
> Copies used: Harvard; University of Texas.

An Epitaph upon Thomas Late Lord Fairfax. Written by a Person of Honour.
> Copy used: Yale.

An Exclamation Against Julian, Secretary to the Muses; With the Character of a Libeller. By a Person of Quality.

> Macdonald 191.
> Dated 1679 by Luttrell, who paid 1*d*. for his copy (Macdonald, *Dryden Bibliography*, p. 215).
> Copies used: Harvard; British Museum.

A Ballad.

> Macdonald 189.
> Dated 1679 by Luttrell (Macdonald, *Dryden Bibliography*, p. 213). This is probably the broadside "ballad" mentioned by Wood as having come out against Buckingham in 1679 (*Athenae Oxonienses, 4,* 211).
> Copy used: British Museum.

The Litany. Of the D. of B.

> Dated 1679 by Wood (*Athenae Oxonienses, 4,* 211).
> Copy used: Yale.

A Satyr against Vertue. Aude aliquid brevibus Gyaris aut carcere dignum Si vis esse aliquis——Juven. Sat. London: Printed in the Year, 1679.

> Brooks 3.
> Copy used: Yale.

Mac Flecknoe, or a Satyr upon the True-Blew-Protestant Poet, T. S. By the Author of Absalom & Achitophel London, Printed for D. Green, 1682.

> Macdonald 14a.
> Copy used: Yale.

Corinna; or, Humane Frailty. A Poem. With an Answer to the E. of R——'s Satyr against Man. . . . London, Printed by J. W. and Sold by J. Nutt, 1699.

> Copy used: Harvard.

3. Early Editions of Rochester's Works

a. A Series

A-1680-HU

Poems on Several Occasions By the Right Honourable, the E. of R — — —. Printed at Antwerp, 1680.

> Copies used: Huntington; Pepysian Library, Magdalene College, Cambridge.
> For bibliographical descriptions of the other A-1680 editions, see Thorpe, *Rochester's Poems*, pp. 153–59.

A-1685

Poems on Several Occasions. Written by a late Person of Honour. London, Printed for A. Thorncome, and are to be Sold by most Booksellers. 1685.

> Prinz xii.
> Copies used: William Andrews Clark Library; British Museum.

A-1701

Poems on Several Occasions. By the R. H. the E. of R. London, Printed for A. T. and are to be Sold by most Booksellers. 1701.

> Prinz xv.
> Copy used: Bodleian.

A-1713

Poems On Several Occasions. By the R. H. the E. of R. London: Printed for A. B. and are to be Sold by most Booksellers, 1713.

> Prinz xxiv.
> Copy used: Victoria and Albert Museum.

A-1731

Poems On Several Occasions. By the R. H. the E. of R. London: Printed for A. B. and are to be Sold by most Booksellers, 1731.

> Copy used: Folger.

b. B Series

B-1691
Poems, &c. on Several Occasions: with Valentinian, a Tragedy. Written by the Right Honourable John Late Earl of Rochester. London, Printed for Jacob Tonson at the Judge's-Head in Chancery-Lane near Fleet-Street, 1691.

> Prinz XIII.
>
> Copies used: Yale; Harvard (includes paste-on cancels); Huntington (two copies, one of which preserves leaves D3 and D7 in the uncanceled state).

B-1696
Poems, (&c.) On Several Occasions: with Valentinian; a Tragedy. Written By the Right Honourable John Late Earl of Rochester. London: Printed for Jacob Tonson, at the Judge's Head, near the Inner-Temple-Gate in Fleetstreet, 1696.

> Prinz XIV.
>
> Copies used: Yale; D. M. Vieth.

B-1705
Poems On Several Occasions: with Valentinian; a Tragedy. Written by the Right Honourable John, late Earl of Rochester. London, Printed for Jacob Tonson, within Grays-Inn Gate next Grays-Inn Lane. 1705.

> Prinz XVII.
>
> Copy used: Princeton.

B-1710-P
Poems on Several Occasions: with Valentinian; a Tragedy. To which is added, Advice to a Painter. Written by the Right Honourable John, late Earl of Rochester. London: Printed by H. Hills, and Sold by the Booksellers of London and Westminster, 1710.

> Prinz XXII.
>
> Copy used: Yale.

B-1714
The Works of John Earl of Rochester. Containing Poems, On

*Several Occasions: His Lordship's Letters To Mr. Savil and Mrs.
* * with Valentinian, a Tragedy. Never before Publish'd together. London: Printed for Jacob Tonson, at Shakespear's Head
over-against Katherine-street in the Strand. M DCC XIV.*

 Prinz xxvi.
 Copies used: Yale; Huntington.

B-1718-P
*The Works of the Right Honourable John Earl of Rochester.
Consisting of Satires, Songs, Translations, and Other Occasional
Poems. London: Printed for the Booksellers of London and
Westminster. 1718. Price 1s.*

 Prinz xxviii.
 Copy used: Bodleian.

B-1732
*The Works of John. Earl of Rochester: Containing Poems On
Several Occasions: His Lordship's Letters To Mr. Savil and Mrs.
*** with Valentinian, a Tragedy. Never before Published to-
gether. The Fourth Edition. London: Printed for J. Tonson at
Shakespear's Head over-against Katherine-street in the Strand.
M DCC XXXII.*

 Prinz xxxiii.
 Copies used: Princeton; Huntington.

c. C Series

C-1707-a
*The Miscellaneous Works of the Right Honourable the Late
Earls of Rochester And Roscommon. With The Memoirs of
the Life and Character of the late Earl of Rochester, in a Letter
to the Dutchess of Mazarine. By Mons. S^t. Evremont. To which
is added, A curious Collection of Original Poems and Translations by The Earl of Dorset, The Lord S——rs, The Lord
H——x, The Lord G——lle, Sir Roger L'Estrange, Mr. Otway,
Mr. Prior, Mr. Walsh, Mr. Smith. Mr. Rowe, &c. London*

Printed: And sold by B. Bragge, at the Raven in Pater-Noster-Row, against Ivy-Lane. 1707.

Prinz xviii; Case 242.

Copies used: Princeton; University of Texas.

C-1707-b

The Works of the Right Honourable the Late Earls of Rochester and Roscommon. With A Collection of Original Poems, Translations, Imitations, &c. by the most Eminent Hands. To which is prefix'd, Memoirs of the Earl of Rochester's Life, by Monsieur St. Evremont. In a Letter to the Dutchess of Mazerine. The Second Edition. London: Printed for Edmund Curll, at the Peacock without Temple-Bar. 1707.

Copies used: Princeton; Huntington.

C-1709

The Works of the Right Honourable The Earls of Rochester, and Roscommon. With Some Memoirs of the Earl of Rochester's Life, by Monsieur St. Evremont: In a Letter to the Dutchess of Mazarine. The Third Edition. To which is added, A Collection of Miscellany Poems. By the most Eminent Hands. London: Printed for E. Curll, at the Peacock without Temple-Bar, 1709.

Prinz xix; Case 242-c.

Copies used: Harvard; University of Kansas; British Museum.

C-1709-P

The Works of the Right Honourable The Earls of Rochester, and Roscommon. With Some Memoirs of the Earl of Rochester's Life, by Monsieur St. Evremont: In a Letter to the Dutchess of Mazarine. The Third Edition. Part I. To which is added, A Collection of Micellany Poems. By the most Eminent Hands. London, Printed: and Sold by the Booksellers of London and Westminster, 1709.

Prinz xx.

Copies used: University of Texas; Huntington; Kongelige Bibliothek, Copenhagen.

C-1711-P
*The Works Of the Right Honourable the Earls of Rochester
and Roscommon with Some Memoirs of the Earl of Rochester's
Life by Monsieur St. Evremont: In a Letter to the Dutchess of
Mazarine. Part I. To which is Added, A Collection of Micellany
Poems. By the most Eminent Hands. London, Printed by J.
Bradford, in Fetter-Lane, 1711.*
    Prinz XXIII.
    Copy used: British Museum.

C-1714-1
*The Works Of the Earls of Rochester, Roscommon, Dorset,
&c. In Two Volumes. Adorn'd with Cuts. The Fourth Edition.
London: Printed for E. Curll, at the Dial and Bible against St.
Dunstan's Church in Fleet-street. M.DCC.XIV. Price 5s.*
    Prinz XXV.
    Copies used: Princeton; University of Kansas.

C-1714-2
*Poems on Several Occasions. By the Earls of Roscommon, and
Dorset, &c. London: Printed for E. Curll, MDCCXIV.*
    Prinz XXV.
    Copies used: University of Kansas; Westdeutsche Biblio-
    thek, Marburg.

C-1718-1
*The Works Of the Earls of Rochester, Roscomon, Dorset, &c.
In Two Volumes. Adorn'd with Cuts. London: Printed in the
Year M.DCC.XVIII. Price 5s.*
    Prinz XXVII.
    Copy used: British Museum.

C-1718-2
*Poems on Several Occasions, By the Earl of Roscomon, &c.
With Some Memoirs of his Life. Volume II. London: Printed
in the Year M.DCC.XVIII.*
    Prinz XXVII.
    Copy used: British Museum.

C-1721-a-1
The Works Of the Earls of Rochester, Roscommon, Dorset,
The Duke of Devonshire, &c. In Two Volumes. Adorn'd with
Cuts. London, Printed in the Year M DCC XXI.
> Prinz xxx.
> Copies used: Ohio State University; D. M. Vieth.

C-1721-a-2
Poems on Several Occasions, By the Earls of Roscommon, and
Dorset, and The Dukes of Devonshire, Buckinghamshire, &c.
Volume II. London: Printed in the Year M DCC XX.
> Prinz xxx.
> Copy used: Ohio State University.

C-1721-b-1
The Works Of the Earls of Rochester, Roscommon, Dorset,
The Duke of Devonshire, &c. In Two Volumes. Adorn'd with
Cuts. London, Printed in the Year M DCC XXI.
> Prinz xxx; Case 323-1-a.
> Copy used: Bodleian.

C-1721-b-2
Poems on Several Occasions, By the Earls of Roscommon, and
Dorset, And the Dukes of Devonshire, Buckinghamshire, &c.
Volume II. London, Printed in the Year M DCC XXI.
> Prinz xxx; Case 323-2-a.
> Copy used: Bodleian.

C-1731-1
The Works Of the Earls of Rochester, Roscomon, and Dorset;
The Dukes of Devonshire, Buckinghamshire, &c. With Mem-
oirs of their Lives. In Two Volumes. Adorned with Cuts. Lon-
don: Printed in the Year M.DCC.XXXI. Price 5s.
> Prinz xxxi; Case 323-1-b.
> Copies used: Folger; Bodleian.

C-1731-2
Poems By the Earls of Roscomon and Dorset; The Dukes of

Devonshire, Buckingham, &c. Vol. II. London: Printed in the Year M.DCC.XXXI.
 Prinz xxxi; Case 323-2-b.
 Copies used: Folger; Bodleian.

C-1735
The Works Of the Earls of Rochester, Roscomon, and Dorset: Also those of the Dukes of Devonshire, and Buckinghamshire; To which is added, the Cabinet of Love, And several other Poems On diverse Subjects, never before printed. Adorned with Cuts. London: Printed by T. Goodourl, 1735. [Price bound 2s. 6d.]
 Prinz xxxiv.
 Copies used: British Museum; Bayrische Staatsbibliothek, Munich.

d. D Series

D-1718
Remains of the Right Honourable John, Earl of Rochester. Being Satyrs, Songs, and Poems; Never before Published. From a Manuscript found in a Gentleman's Library that was Cotemporary with him. London: Printed for Tho. Dryar; and sold by T. Harbin in the New-Exchange in the Strand; W. Chetwood at Cato's Head in Russel-Court, near the Play-House; and by the Booksellers of London and Westminster. 1718. Price 1s. 6d.
 Prinz xxix.
 Copy used: Bodleian.

D-1761
The Poetical Works Of that Witty Lord John Earl of Rochester: Left in Ranger's Lodge in Woodstock Park, where his Lordship died, and never before Printed; with Some Account of the Life of that ingenious Nobleman. Extracted From Bishop Burnet, and other Eminent Writers. London: Printed in the Year M DCC LXI.
 Prinz xliii.
 Copy used: Harvard.

4. Miscellanies, Song-Books, and Other Printed Volumes

In citing libraries, the following symbols are used:

Bodl.	Bodleian Library, Oxford
B. M.	British Museum, London
B. P. L.	Boston Public Library
Folger	Folger Shakespeare Library, Washington
Harv.	Harvard University Library, Cambridge, Massachusetts
L. of C.	Library of Congress, Washington
Peabody Libr.	Peabody Library, Baltimore
Pepysian Libr.	Pepysian Library, Magdalene College, Cambridge
Princeton	Princeton University Library
R. C. of M.	Royal College of Music, London
U. of C.	University of Chicago Library
W. A. Clark	William Andrews Clark Library, Los Angeles
Yale	Sterling Library, Yale University, New Haven

The Second Part of Merry Drollery, [1661] (Case 132-2-a)	Bodl.
A True Relation of the Engagement of His Majesties Fleet . . . In a Letter from H. S. Esquire, 1672	Harv.
A Collection of Poems, Written upon several Occasions, By several Persons, 1672 (Case 151)	Yale
————, 1673 (Case 151-b)	Yale
A Collection of Poems By Several Hands, 1693 (Case 151-c)	Yale
The Temple of Death, a Poem, 1695 (Case 151-d)	Yale

*A Collection of Poems: Viz. The Temple of
Death,* 1701 (Case 151-e)   Yale

————, 1702 (Case 151-f)   Yale

————, 1716 (Case 151-g)   Yale

*An Explication of the Diall Sett up in the Kings
Garden at London, an. 1669 . . . By the Reverend Father Francis Hall, otherwise Line,* Liége,
1673   W. A. Clark

A New Collection of the Choicest Songs,
1676 (Case 161)   Yale

The Last and Best Edition of New Songs, 1677
(Case 163)   Bodl.

The Wits Academy: or, The Muses Delight, 1677   Bodl.

*Songs for i 2 & 3 Voyces Composed by Henry
Bowman,* [1677] (Day and Murrie 44)   B. M.

————, 1678 (Day and Murrie 47)   Bodl.

————, 1679 (Day and Murrie 50)   R. C. of M.

New Ayres and Dialogues, 1678 (Day and
Murrie 46)   B. P. L.

Choice Ayres & Songs, 1679 (Day and Murrie 48)   Harv.

*Female Poems On several Occasions. Written by
Ephelia,* 1679   Harv.

————, *The Second Edition,* 1682   B. M.

*Lucida Intervalla: Containing divers Miscella-
neous Poems, Written at Finsbury and Bethlem
by the Doctors Patient Extraordinary* [James
Carkesse], 1679   Yale

Songs set by Signior Pietro Reggio, [1680] (Day
and Murrie 52)   Yale

Satyrs upon the Jesuits [by John Oldham], 1681
(Brooks 6)   Yale

*Poems, and Translations. By the Author of The
Satyrs upon the Jesuits,* 1683 (Brooks 10)   D. M. Vieth

Wit and Drollery, 1682 (Case 114-c)   Harv.

*The Ramble: an Anti-Heroick Poem. Together
with Some Terrestrial Hymns and Carnal
Ejaculations. By Alexander Radcliffe, of Greys
Inn, Esq.,* 1682   Yale

    *The Works of Capt. Alex. Radcliffe In
    one Volume. . . . The Third Edition
    Augmented,* 1696   Peabody Libr.

Rome Rhym'd to Death, 1683 (Case 170)   Yale

*A New Collection of Songs and Poems. By
Thomas D'urfey, Gent.,* 1683 (Day and
Murrie 64)   Harv.; B. M.

The Newest Collection of the Choicest Songs,
1683 (Day and Murrie 65)   B. M.

Choice Ayres and Songs, 1683 (Day and Murrie
59)   B. M.

The Theater of Music, . . . The First Book,
1685 (Day and Murrie 78)   B. M.

The Theater of Music, . . . The Second Book,
1685 (Day and Murrie 79)   B. M.

The New Treasury of Musick, 1695 (Day and
Murrie 134)   B. M.

The New Help to Discourse, 1684 (Case 141-c)   B. M.

*Poems upon Several Occasions: with a Voyage
to the Island of Love. By Mrs. A. Behn,* 1684   Yale

Pastoralle, [1684] (Day and Murrie 71)   Pepysian Libr.

Miscellany Poems, 1684 (Case 172-1-a)   Yale

————, 1692 (Case 172-1-b)   Yale

————, 1692 (Case 172-1-c)   Harv.

————, 1702 (Case 172-1-d)   Yale; D.M. Vieth

The First Part of Miscellany Poems,
1716 (Case 172-1-e)   Yale

————, 1727 (Case 172-1-f)   Yale

*Sylvae: or, The Second Part of Poetical
Miscellanies*, 1702 (Case 172-2-d)   Yale

The Second Part of Miscellany Poems,
1716 (Case 172-2-e)   Yale

————, 1727 (Case 172-2-f)   Yale

*Examen Poeticum: Being the Third Part
of Miscellany Poems*, 1693 (Case 172-3-a)   Yale

————, 1693 (Case 172-3-b)   Harv.; D. M. Vieth

————, 1706 (Case 172-3-c)   Yale

The Third Part of Miscellany Poems,
1716 (Case 172-3-d)   Yale

————, 1727 (Case 172-3-e)   Yale

*The Annual Miscellany: For The Year
1694*, 1694 (Case 172-4-a)   Yale; D. M. Vieth

————, 1708 (Case 172-4-b)   Yale

Poetical Miscellanies: The Fifth Part,
1704 (Case 172-5-a)   Yale; D. M. Vieth

The Sixth Part of Miscellany Poems,
1716 (Case 172-6-b)   Yale

————, 1727 (Case 172-6-c)   Yale

*Valentinian: a Tragedy. As 'tis Alter'd by the
late Earl of Rochester*, 1685 (Prinz LIX)   Yale

Miscellany, Being A Collection of Poems By several Hands, 1685 (Case 177)   Yale

Poems by Several Hands, and on Several Occasions Collected by N. Tate, 1685 (Case 181)   Yale

The Lives Of the most Famous English Poets,
. . . Written by William Winstanley, 1687   Yale

Poetical Recreations, 1688 (Case 186)   Yale

The Triumph of Wit, 1688 (not in Case)   C. H. Wilkinson

————, 2d ed., 1692 (not in Case)   L. of C.

————, 5th ed., 1707 (Case 244-e)   B. M.

————, 9th ed., 1735 (Case 244-i)   Yale

A Second Collection of The Newest and Most Ingenious Poems, Satyrs, Songs, &c. against Popery and Tyranny, 1689 (Case 189-2)   Yale

A Third Collection of The Newest and Most Ingenious Poems, Satyrs, Songs, &c. against Popery and Tyranny, 1689 (Case 189-3)   Yale

The Fourth (and Last) Collection of Poems, Satyrs, Songs, &c., 1689 (Case 189-4)   Yale

The Muses Farewel to Popery and Slavery, 1689 (Case 191-1-a)   Yale

————, 1690 (Case 191-1-b)   Yale

Poems on Affairs of State, The Second Part, 1697 (Case 191-d)   Yale

Miscellany Poems upon Several Occasions, 1692 (Case 197)   Yale

The Gentleman's Journal, 1693 (Day and Murrie 119)   Yale

De Re Poetica: or, Remarks upon Poetry. . . . By Sir Thomas Pope Blount, 1694   Yale

Chorus Poetarum, 1694 (Case 202)   Harv.

    Poems, on Several Occasions, 1696
    (Case 202-b)   Harv.

    The Poetical Remains of the Duke of
    Buckingham, 1698 (Case 202-c)   B. M.

Poems on Affairs of State: From The Time of
Oliver Cromwell, to the Abdication of K. James
the Second, 1697 (Case 211-1-a)   Yale

    ————, 1697 (Case 211-1-b)   Yale

    ————, 1697 (Case 211-1-c)   Yale

    ————, 1699 (Case 211-1-d)   Yale; D. M. Vieth

    ————, 1702 (Case 211-1-e)   Yale

    ————, 1703 (Case 211-1-f)   Yale

    ————, 1710 (Case 211-1-g)   B. M.

    ————, 1716 (Case 211-1-h)   Yale

Poems on Affairs of State, from The Reign
of K. James the First, To this Present Year
1703. . . . Vol. II, 1703 (Case 211-2-a)   Yale; D. M. Vieth

    ————, 1703 (Case 211-2-b)   Yale

    ————, 1716 (Case 211-2-c)   Yale

Poems on Affairs of State, From 1640. to
this present Year 1704. . . . Vol. III, 1704
(Case 211-3-a)   Yale; D. M. Vieth

    ————, 1716 (Case 211-3-b)   Yale

Poems on Affairs of State: From Oliver
Cromwell, To this present time. . . . Part
III, 1698 (Case 215)   Yale

A New Collection of Poems Relating to
State Affairs, 1705 (Case 237)   Yale; D. M. Vieth

Wit and Mirth: or, Pills to Purge Melancholy . . . The Second Part, 1700 (Day and Murrie 188) — B. M.

———, 1707 (Day and Murrie 214) — B. M.

———, 1712 (Day and Murrie 222) — Harv.; B. M.

Songs Compleat, . . . Vol. IV, 1719 (Day and Murrie 234) — B. P. L.

Wit and Mirth: . . . Vol. IV, 1719 (Day and Murrie 239) — Harv.

Wits Cabinet, 1703 (Case 173-k) — Bodl.

———, 1731 (Case 173-o) — Yale

Miscellaneous Works, Written by His Grace, George, Late Duke of Buckingham, 1704 (Case 232-1-a) — Yale; D. M. Vieth

———, 1707 (Case 232-1-b) — Harv.

The Second Volume of Miscellaneous Works, Written by George, Late Duke of Buckingham, 1705 (Case 232-2) — Harv.; Princeton

The Works Of His Grace, George Villiers, Late Duke of Buckingham, 1715 — Yale; D. M. Vieth

Deliciae Poeticae, 1706 (Case 240) — Harv.

Mirth Diverts all Care, 1708 (not in Case) — Folger

———, 1709 (not in Case) — Folger

The Works of Anacreon, and Sappho, 1713 (Case 271) — Yale

The Odes and Satires of Horace, 1715 (Case 286) — Yale

———, 1715 (Case 287) — Yale

———, 1717 (Case 287-b)	Yale
———, 1721 (Case 287-c)	Yale
———, 1730 (Case 287-d)	Yale
———, Dublin 1730 (not in Case)	Yale
Poems on Several Occasions, 1717 (Case 260-2-a)	Yale
Poems by the Earl of Roscommon, 1717 (Case 301)	Yale; D. M. Vieth
The Agreeable Variety, 1717 (Case 293)	Yale
———, 1724 (Case 293-b)	B. P. L.
———, 1742 (Case 293-c)	B. M.
Familiar Letters of Love, Gallantry, And several Occasions, 1718 (Case 305)	B. P. L.
———, 1724 (Case 305-f)	Harv.
The Works of the Most Noble John Sheffield, Late Duke of Buckingham. Printed for E. Curll, 1721	Yale
The Works Of the Honourable Sir Charles Sedley Bar^t., 1722	Yale
The Hive, 1724 (Case 331-1-a)	Yale
———, 1726 (Case 331-1-c)	Yale
———, 1732 (Case 331-1-d)	Harv.
The Hive. . . . Volume the Second, 1724 (Case 331-2-a)	Yale
———, 1727 (Case 331-2-c)	Yale
———, 1733 (Case 331-2-d)	Harv.
Ovid's Epistles: with His Amours, 1725 (Case 165-k)	B. M.

————, 1727 (Case 165-l)	Yale
————, 1729 (Case 165-m)	B. M.
————, 1736 (not in Case)	Yale
————, 1748 (Case 165-n)	Bodl.
The Triumphs of Bacchus, 1729 (Case 357)	B. M.
A Collection of Bacchanalian Songs, 1729 (Case 357-b)	Yale
The Choice, 1729 (Case 353-1-a)	B. M.
————, 1732 (Case 353-1-b)	B. M.
————, 1737 (Case 353-1-c)	Harv.
The Choice: . . . Volume II, 1733 (Case 353-2)	B. M.
The Choice: . . . Volume III, 1733 (Case 353-3)	B. M.
The Windsor Medley, 1731 (Case 371)	Yale
The Vocal Miscellany, 1734 (Case 388-1-b)	Yale
————, 1738 (Case 388-1-c)	Yale
————, 1738 (Case 388-1-d)	Yale
The Vocal Miscellany. . . . Volume the Second, 1738 (Case 388-2-b)	Yale
A Complete Collection of Old and New English and Scotch Songs, . . . Volume I, 1735 (Case 400-1)	Harv.
A Complete Collection of Old and New English and Scotch Songs, . . . Number I. of Volume II, 1735 (Case 400-2)	Harv.
A Complete Collection of Old and New English and Scotch Songs, . . . Number II. of Volume IV, 1736 (Case 400-7)	Harv.
A Collection of Merry Poems, 1736 (Case 403-b)	Harv.

The Cupid, 1736 (Case 404)   Yale

————, 1739 (Case 404-b)   Harv.

A Collection of Epigrams, 1737 (Case 341-2)   Yale

The Syren. . . . The Second Edition, 1738
(not in Case)   B. P. L.

————, 1739 (Case 423-c)   Yale

The Merry Companion, 1739 (Case 424)   U. of C.

————, 1742 (Case 424-b)   B. M.

Philomel, 1744 (Case 444)   B. M.

The Muse in Good Humour: . . . Part I,
1745 (Case 450-1-d)   Yale

*The Muse in Good Humour: . . . Part
Second,* 1744 (not in Case)   Yale

————, 1745 (Case 450-2-b)   Yale

The Agreeable Companion, 1745 (Case 447)   Yale

*The Works of the most celebrated Minor
Poets,* 1749 (Case 467-1-a)   Yale

Index

For most of the poems discussed in this study, the main entry is under first line rather than title or author. Works appearing under an author's name are listed in order of publication. Italicized page references indicate the principal discussion of the work.

Yale Studies in English

This volume is the one hundred and fifty-third of the Yale Studies in English, founded by Albert Stanburrough Cook in 1898 and edited by him until his death in 1927. Tucker Brooke succeeded him as editor, and served until 1941, when Benjamin C. Nangle succeeded him.

The following volumes are still in print. Orders should be addressed to Yale University Press, New Haven, Connecticut.

DATE DUE